SEVEN AGAINST THE NIGHT

BOOKS BY PAUL ELDRIDGE

My First Two Thousand Years
Salome
The Invincible Adam
Prince Pax
If After Every Tempest
Madonna with the Cat
Two Lessons in Love
And Thou Shalt Teach Them
One Man Show
Men and Women
The Intruder
The Bed Remains
Cobwebs and Cosmos
I Bring a Sword
Horns of Glass
Maxims Are Gadflies
Crown of Empire
Tales of the Fortunate Isles
The Second Life of John Stevens

Seven Against
the Night

by
PAUL ELDRIDGE

New York • THOMAS YOSELOFF • London

To
SYLVETTE
My Lighted Lamp

CONTENTS

SEVEN AGAINST THE NIGHT

OF MEN AND OWLS

"If you introduce a ray of light into a nest of owls, you will injure their eyes and excite their cries," thus Denis Diderot, annoyed by the clerics and hounded by the police, explained the way of man with man.

The light which Diderot introduced was the *Encyclopédie*—the first great modern work offering mankind the sum total of knowledge and wisdom culled from the centuries by the bravest, the wisest, the most learned.

The owls had their nests not only in France, but everywhere in the Western world in which the men discussed in this book breathed and functioned. (It is rumored that even in this our most illumined age, the owls still pullulate—East and West, North and South—and still hoot ominously when the rays of light are introduced into their nests.)

Denis Diderot was preceded by three men, who were his spiritual forefathers, for already more than two millennia ago, Epicurus, noblest of Greeks, proclaimed his profound and irrefutable dictum: "Nothing is created out of nothing."

There was Desiderius Erasmus, nameless bastard, who invented his two names from the Latin and the Greek, each signifying the "Desired One"—the Twice-Desired, he who barely escaped suffocation by his nurse, who found him too ugly and too unpropitious for life.

Erasmus scattered knowledge with the largesse of a sun and spread the gospel of good will among all men of all nations where the countless editions of his books were read by every literate person. He became the High Priest of the new movement—Humanism—which preached the classic philosophy that man is the measure of all things—*homo mensura*. His inextinguishable passion was peace. It seemed so simple to him that with a bit of reason (which, after all was the sole mark of

11

man's divinity) war and strife could forever be banished from
the face of the earth.

Alas, despite his titanic efforts of pen and tongue, at court, in
the hall of learning, in the market-place, the madness of hate
grew wilder, and he escaped the flames of the stake only by vulpine strategies.

Forsaken and forgotten—he who had been the most famous
and the most sought-after of Europeans—his works buried in
"The Index," he died poisoned by the malignancy of man, the
ever brimming goblet of hemlock.

Three or four years Erasmus' junior, Niccolò Machiavelli
achieved meager glory during his life-time, but soon after his
death, by the publication of a fragment of a manuscript, entitled
The Prince, he became, and has still remained, one of the most
famous—or rather infamous—figures in the Republic of Letters. His name, turned into both adjective and abstract noun—
Machiavellian—Machiavellianism—has been synonymous with
duplicity, cunning, dishonesty, infidelity, intrigue.

Poor Niccolò! He must pay for all the sins of man! Should
a physician be scourged for recognizing disease and describing
the disagreeable symptoms? Should a thinker be an unconscionable Procrustes, mutilating truth to suit the sickly eyes of owls?

Every human society is based upon the eternal and incontrovertible axiom—might makes right. And he who seeks might
must be both lion and fox, must have claws of steel and words
of craft. This is what Niccolò Machiavelli saw in the glamorous
days of the Renaissance. He saw it in Florence; he saw it in
Rome; he saw it in Paris. He saw it in the annals of heroic antiquity. He foresaw it in the endless tunnel of the days to come.
For, it is as sound to divide history into compartments of time—
past, present, future—as to carve the sea with a pen-knife and
plant straws to indicate boundaries. He saw and recounted in
crystalline words. And the owls—the predatory owls—have
never ceased hooting.

Three years before the death of Erasmus in 1535, a son was
born unto a Jewish mother (turned Huguenot, then Catholic,

then Huguenot again) and a father of Spanish ancestry, and he was destined to become "the wisest of Frenchmen."

Michel de Montaigne belonged to that branch of Humanism which extended into the Garden of Epicurus. There the Tree of Knowledge bore fruit which did not hide the seed of sin, but the honey of tolerance.

And Montaigne, in words fresh and succulent, offered delicious pabulum to all who sought solace and reason in a troubled and irrational world. The owls hooted that Montaigne dismissed the gods, who ignoring the existence of men, did not punish them in life, and did not molest them in death. There was in his philosophy only the Earth—neither Heaven nor Hell. On what, pray, should the owls feed, then?

There lived in Paris a little watchmaker, who became a great dramatist, an inventor, a millionaire, a confidant of royalty— and the harbinger of a great Revolution. Pierre-Augustin Caron de Beaumarchais outlived Denis Diderot by fifteen years, long enough to witness the fall of Bastille. For his considerable services to his *patrie,* he evaded the loss of his head by a mere fluke. And for his vast aid to America and the American Revolution, he has been rewarded by the New World with contemptuous neglect.

The hooting of the owls never ceased during his life. The common people from whom he sprang never forgave him for becoming a lord; the lords never suffered him because of his vulgar origin. The professionals—the writers, the financiers, the statesmen, the musicians—all decried him, for he surpassed them all. And like his immortal character—Figaro—he laughed that he might not weep.

Arthur Schopenhauer and Anatole France, separated in time by a half-century and in space by a river, which has kept two great nations apart and in perpetual warfare, held the fundamental idea that human life was a tragedy, a cosmic error. The Teuton expounded it with mathematical lucidity; the Gaul with iridescent playfulness. The Teuton scowled; the Gaul laughed. The owls hooted.

The Seven Against the Night differed from one another in temperament and in manner, and their careers were diverse. Some were illustrious and rich; others poor and ignored. All of them, however, suffered in one way or another for their ideas, and while not one mounted the scaffold or was bound to a stake, each felt the ugly breath of bigots and sadists, and three rotted in dungeons for various periods of time.

And all of them have become classics—that is, their names are often invoked, but their works rarely read.

DESIDERIUS ERASMUS

The Old Man Goes Home

The old man yearned to return home. He was mortally wounded by Time and Disillusion and he yearned for home. He had been the spirit of Europe, the mind which illumined it, but now he reverted to the elemental physical fear of dying in a strange place, and he yearned to go home.

Shrunken to a mass of bones kept intact by a skin as yellow as parchment, his pointed nose riding far out of his face, his sad eyes caught in a web of wrinkles, he barely managed to enter the postchaise, and started for home. He started from Freiburg near the border of the Black Forest and had as his destination Rotterdam, Holland, or as it was called at the time, Brabant.

It was late autumn. The roads were sticky with mud and it was cold. The old man had always felt cold. There had never been enough heat on earth to warm him up. He was always bundled up in cloths and furs. Icy drafts kept running up and down his spine and only one special kind of burgundy coursing into his stomach could counter them.

But now, added to terrestrial chill was the chill in his soul— a chill for which no wine, however ancient and however rare its vintage, could prevail. For the old man went home to die, but not alone. He carried in his shivering arms the world—his world—dying as himself. For so many years, he had tended it with paternal tenderness; he had soothed it with his wisdom; he had enlightened it with his wit; he had cleansed it from bigotry; he had chased its prejudices, as a faithful shepherd chases the ravenous foxes and wolves from the fold.

But now it was dying as himself. His world had been colossal —the aristocrats, the scholars, the educated, the cultured, and even those of the commonality, who had an innate sense of humanity—all were his children, his pupils. His voice resounded athwart all the lands of Europe and his name—*Desiderius Erasmus*—was a clarion call to reason and to peace.

17

Now, however, he realized it had all been illusion, or a dream. His world was only as big as himself, and he was a shivering, little old man on the brink of death. He and his world were about to be swept off the face of the earth. Even his tongue, that exquisite Latin, which he cleansed and rubbed and shined until it dazzled as in its pristine glory—it, too, was on the brink of death, stampeded by the new, barbarous dialects without grammar, without rhetoric.

Europe which had seemed to him on the road to become a suitable habitation for a civilized man, was quickly becoming a jungle that even wild beasts would find too ferocious. From every corner had come tidings tearing at his entrails. There was Berquin, his translator, roasted to death in Paris. There were his friends, almost his brothers, John Fisher, Chancellor of Cambridge University, and Thomas More, the incomparable author of *Utopia,* both beheaded in London. Zwingli slain at Kappel. Thomas Munzer tortured to death. Baptists and Anabaptists tearing one another's tongues out. Flames consuming towns; flames consuming books and manuscripts; flames consuming men for their ideas, even for their silent thoughts. "Noisy, crazy epoch. . . . May God gather me soon unto Himself so that I quit this mad world," he muttered, as the postchaise shook and made him sick.

Ten years previously when Erasmus came to Freiburg im Breisgau, a city in Austria, to be able to pursue his work unmolested by the ferocious bigotry of Evangelism or Papism, which had already broken out in most parts of Europe, he was met in solemn procession by the town's officials, the solid burghers and the scholars. Wherever Erasmus deigned to set foot, that spot became Europe's center of culture. He was as a precious jewel studded into the heart of a locality. Not to mention that it was excellent business as well. Hotels, inns, postchaises, bookshops, all began to flourish. Dignitaries would come from all corners of the civilized world in the hope of gaining an hour's audience with the "Doctor Universalis," "The Prince of Scientific Learning," "The Father of Study," "The Light of the World."

"Everyone who does not wish to remain a stranger in the realm of the Muses admires him, glorifies him, sings his praises. He who is capable of extracting a letter from Erasmus has already achieved fame and can celebrate a veritable triumph. But he who is allowed converse with Erasmus may count himself among the blessed that walk this earth." So said Camerarius, himself a famous Humanist, who, under ordinary conditions, would have suffered from professional jealousy and maligned his colleague. Candles may vie with one another's light, but however tall and luminous one might be, it could only evoke universal ridicule should it have the audacity to compare itself with the sun.

Not merely the scholars, the authors, the poets, starved for the manna of recognition, waited at the famous man's gate, but the great and the powerful of the earth vied with one another for recognition. Charles V offered him a place on the Council of the Empire. Henry VIII urged him to become an Englishman and join his court. If he would only come to Vienna, Ferdinand would grant him a regal pension. Francis I begged him to become a citizen of Paris. Universities implored him to teach in them. A cardinal's hat could have been obtained as readily as a skull cap in a neighboring shop.

Yet, now at his departure from Freiburg, there were hardly a dozen hands to shake. Ten years, and he had become an old man; the world had become an abattoir, and heart-sick and lonely, he implored divinity to send him the Angel of Death. But had the King of Terrors actually made his appearance, Erasmus would have addressed him in the choicest Latin, asking him to be good enough to straighten out his lap robe and return whence he came—alone.

The Doctor Universalis had been in fear of death all the days of his years. Whisper "epidemic" and he would rush away; say "riot" or "rebellion," and he would barricade his home. In an age when bathing was considered almost immoral, he was metic-

ulous about his hygiene, and his linen was always clean. He
viewed with horror any vermin creeping upon his skin, when
the beards even of princes were not immune from their visitation, while candidates for sainthood boasted of their variety
and multitude, and counted upon them to form a rope to climb
to Heaven.

In truth, he had no reason to cling so passionately to a body
which gave him perennial discomfort and pain. He had "the
stone"; his stomach was ulcerated; he was racked by intermittent fevers. His letters are full of moans and groans. But to
compensate for these torments, he had a nervous system which
could withstand endless labors and a brain, which, like a cupola,
rotated about the world, registered its knowledge, then scattered it as light wherever human eyes looked.

The days were getting shorter; the cold sharper; the postchaise more rickety; the postilion's whip reverberated as a gun
and shattered the old man's ears. He could not pursue his itin-
erary. He would stop at Basle, and in the spring, when the ice
broke, he would voyage home down the Rhine. Besides, he
wished to visit Basle once more, Basle, the city of his first glory,
the city where so many of his books saw the light of day, the
city where thought and opinion were unfettered. But that was
dead here, too. His world was dead in Basle, too. The Evange-
lists who took over also burned at the stake those whom they
considered heretics. They clamored for freedom of worship—
their worship—and no one else's.

How lovely Basle used to be—a neat little city, streets clean,
citizens dignified and courteous, paying allegiance neither to
war-mongering princes nor to war-mongering monks. Here was
a great university; here were subtle scholars; here was the
artist Holbein, who did such magnificent portraits of Erasmus
and illuminated his books; here was Frobenius, the incomparable printer, the master craftsman, the loyal friend.

How wonderful had been the eight years of his residence in
this Swiss city! He could not expect to repeat that experience,
for during the decade that he had been away from the place, it

had become infected with that universal virus of intolerance, and he himself had become old and wounded all over by the arrows of malignity hurled by both the Catholics and the Protestants. Old and forsaken.

Was it possible—could one be so forsaken who once was so sought after? People buried the living as well as the dead. He should have known—had he not read all the histories of all the nations?—that applause was but empty noise and the palms which created it so often curved into murderous fists. There was this consolation, if consolation it was, that in the distance mockery and applause sounded alike.

At any rate, he would stop at Basle—and then—home. Home? Was not all the Earth his home? Had he not been the citizen of all Europe—the First Citizen? Had he not worked himself to the bone to erase the frontiers between one nation and another? How often had he said, for all to hear: "The entire world is one common fatherland!" How often had he thundered—no, not thundered, for his voice was too softened by culture—affirmed, that the quarrels among nations were senseless, that the hatred among them was sheer madness and due largely to names and name-calling! "Why do such foolish names still keep us sundered?" Had he not urged at all courts a general union—The United States of Europe?

And now he was going home. Why, he had not been there for near a half century, and had invariably spoken ill of the country and its inhabitants. The people were coarse and mannerless. They built atrocious homes. Their food was detestable. Their conversation lacked luster. And what sort of a nation was this, below the surface of the sea, which had to be locked on the perennial threat of universal drowning?

Well, he may have been unreasonable in his criticism. It may have been *aus lauter Liebe*—"out of pure love." It may have been a matter of courtesy to belittle what he possessed in order to obviate envy and to give the listener a sense of superiority. Only boors waved their country's flag on foreign soil. His pat-

tern had become too intricate for unilinear explanations. He
was old. He was going to die. He yearned to go home. One
should end where one started.

The Start

On October 28, 1465, 1466, or 1467, a male child was born
unto a woman in the city of Amsterdam, Holland. The woman
was either a servant or a member of the bourgeoisie, lower or
upper, and was unmarried. The baby was rather homely and
was certainly not robust. He had beautiful eyes, a long sharp
nose, and a small head. The midwife had doubts that he would
survive, what with the winter so near at hand and the lack of
attention paid to bastards. And if he should grow up, he would
certainly not astound the town with his smartness. So little a
head had no room for the exercise intelligence required to keep
vigorous and alert. So prone is mankind to confound greatness
with size, eminence with pedestal, sanctity with robe.

There was no jubilation in the family. If anything, there was
a great deal of muttering. One more bastard! Who is going to
support them? That fool of a woman thinks that gulden grow
on trees. No shame, no dignity, no modesty. The first time you
could, perhaps, excuse—a virgin, inexperienced with men, didn't
know how babies came about, let herself be seduced or maybe
even it was a forced seduction, seeing the brazen ways of the
present young generation. But now—again! Again! Two bastards! And was this the end of the "romance" or would it continue indefinitely, every couple of years another bastard?

And who does she say the father is—Gerard Gerardszoon?
She is surely pulling our legs. Why, half of Brabant's population
is "Gerard" and the sons of "Gerard!" And if you were to look
for him, your chances would be as bright as finding a needle in
a haystack.

But, who, indeed, sired the man who was to become the most

famous personality Europe had known, not considering, of course, those monstrous beings whose fame is rooted in the infamy of vast murder and measureless destruction? Europe pullulated with men of God of all varieties—monks, priests, bishops, church officials, theologians. The monks alone were of endless kinds—Cordoliers, Cletes, Minors, Minims, Benedictines, Augustinians, Williamsists, Jacobines. And most of them, once invited to the table, stayed for the bed. And Europe became a world of bastards.

But in the days when the men of God were busy creating worshipers (and it was surely more civilized than by the sword), bastardism was rather mildly condemned, and many on the highest seats of State and Church were recruited from its ranks. Moreover, the Church made it easy for those who had been bound in the flesh, but not in the law, to regularize their affair and legitimize their offspring, if and when they so desired or circumstances allowed. The bride would appear before the priest performing the ceremony in her cloak of chastity, a wide cape underneath which the children, whatever their number and age, would be hidden. The words which sanctified the union between the man and woman also sanctified the premature fruits of their love. The concealed progeny would emerge, heads high, rights assured.

Was the father of young Gerardszoon a man of God awaiting the favorable moment to cast his robes and become a normal citizen capable of marriage and entitled to raise a family? Was he an irresponsible philanderer who took his pleasures wherever the prey offered neither danger nor responsibility? Was he a scholar, a man of latent gifts, from whom the boy inherited his genius? History has no answer and legend no merit.

Whoever the father may have been and whatever his intentions, he died when the children were still very young. The mother must have had some assured income, for she sent the boys to the best school of the times, at Deventer to the east of Rotterdam. The school was run by the Brethren of the Common Life—a sort of communistic order, that made the burghers uncomfortable, for then, as now, Christians viewed with panic a mode of life which was Christian.

The Brethren were kindly and pleasant-mannered, but as teachers they considered it their solemn duty to be rigid in their discipline and pedantic in their method, for how otherwise train the soul to properly meet face to face the Head Master in Heaven, who sits at a golden desk and knows his Latin backward? So, poor Gerardszoon junior, frail and critical (for his nose was more than an exaggerated ornament, it was a vital organ for "smelling rats") at school, and later on in the world at large suffered keenly. He had heard about the New Learning circulating in the great capitals of Europe, and would have liked very much to take a look at it, but even as the word "common" made the burghers see red, so the word "new" made the Brethren see scarlet. There was virtue only in the old, since these men, though carnally normal, envisaged the world as eunuchs, considering everything "new" as "young" and therefore potentially lecherous.

As for the old learning, the youngster so outclassed all the other students, that his teachers already saw him as some day the most learned man of Europe, and in that they were right. But if he was to be a celebrity, how could he be distinguished from the others, since every second man in Holland was a Gerard or a Gerardszoon? He needed a name worthy of his talents —*nom de guerre,* "a war name," as the French call a pen name, and properly so.

The Germanic dialect which was to become Dutch was still in a state of flux, and the young scholar discovered, perhaps fallaciously, but conveniently, that the word "Gerard" came from the word *begeren,* "to desire," and that made him, in a Latinized form—*Desiderius.* But that was not enough. He needed two names, for it had become customary to have a patrimonial as well. Well, he would get a "father's" name, too. *Begeren,* he discovered, had some connection with the Greek *eraomai,* which also meant "to desire." He Latinized the Greek, and that was *Erasmus. Desiderius Erasmus!* "The twice desired one"—he who was entirely undesired!

Did he laugh ironically over the joke he would perpetrate upon the world? Did he weep at his loneliness? Had he chosen the names as a sort of witch's incantation to overcome the "undesired" condition and bring on the "desired?" Or is the choice of these names only a literary conjecture concocted centuries later, and had the young man come to them in a totally different fashion? Desiderius Erasmus had never been explicit. Perhaps he wished to give the impression that his name had never varied. At any rate, he was destined, indeed, to become the "twice desired" one, but years had to pass and much misery endured.

At about this time, his mother died, and he and his brother, Peter, were in a very precarious condition. Some uncles assumed the responsibility of caring for the orphans upon whom the stigma of illegitimacy would henceforth remain permanent. Conditions in the Lowlands were not too bad; excellent, if compared to Middle Europe. The country had not been badly devastated by wars or the plague, and many a burgher was becoming prosperous. As yet, Holland was not the empire which would compete with England for the supremacy of the seas; nor, as yet, had the Spanish and Portuguese Jews and Maranos sought refuge there, bringing with them precious stones, which they could most conveniently hide as they took the perilous journey. Bringing with them, as well, commercial genius and knowledge of peoples and languages, which would be of so great a service in foreign trade. Indeed, even America had not yet been discovered, and few were the colonies which could be mulcted.

But if money could be made, it required money to start with, and the uncles were not ready to risk guldens on two nephews, who were nice boys, to be sure, but who would have been better unborn, and better if disposed of without too much trouble. And so—the Church. No Foreign Legion ever had volunteers with such strange backgrounds, or who joined for such a multitude of reasons.

The boys did not wish to become monks. There was doubtless

much argument, but the uncles held all the trump cards. They
were constantly reminded of their status, social and financial.
And besides, where could they have such security coupled with
such little risk? They were sure of their board and as for the
beds—well, the young men were old enough to understand that
with a tiny bit of savoir-faire there were few which were not at
their disposal. Moreover, their very labors were sheer profit,
investments in the Lord, for which they would obtain an interest
which no usurious money-lender would dare contemplate in dealing with his Christian masters—a century of heaven for an hour
of prayer.

And the boys nodded acceptance.

The Monk Unfrocks Himself

Before entering the monastery, Desiderius did his preparatory studies in a school at Bois le Duc. At Deventer, while he
was bored with the Brethren of Common Life, he had, at least,
the privilege of coming in contact with some of the best teachers
of his generation. In this place, however, he met men of hollow
formalism, dreary didactics, and scowling countenances. The
crucifixes dangling from their necks and confronting them whenever they raised their eyes on walls and columns, had a pernicious influence upon them. They were certain that only through
torture could man achieve redemption and only by inflicting
physical pain and mental anguish upon the young in their care
would their souls eventually be suitable for the pastures of the
Lord.

Desiderius was already a far better Latinist than any of his
instructors and since he could prate about the infinitely preposterous theological notions fragmented into infinitesimal problems, was considered worthy of entering an Augustinian monastery. In 1487, therefore, he became an inmate of the cloister of

Steyn, a settlement near the city of Gouda, where he had spent a portion of his childhood.

Bois le Duc was purgatory and Steyn was hell. The stinking boiled fish served twice a week ruined the novitiate's stomach for the rest of his life, and the perennial absurd doings would have ruined his mind, had he not from the first planned his escape. It was not easy to break the shackles, though. The love and goodness forced upon these clerics generated such monstrous hate and cruelty in them that neither history nor legend records vengeance so merciless as that in which they indulged.

Erasmus knew himself. He knew he was no lion for courage and no bull for frontal attack. He was related to the fox and the chameleon. And often in his career would he pretend death and often would he alter his color. Worse (or better still), he glowed with all the colors at once, and in truth, possessed none. He foreshadowed the Jesuits, who were organized about the time of his death. But only in their subterranean means, for his aim was peace and tolerance toward all and kindness and mercy for transgressors.

He did not throw off his cloak angrily or challenge his superiors. He pretended modesty and submission, and even composed conventional religious exercises, but the writing was chiefly to prove the elegancies of his Latin style, which, in time, would become the model and the despair of his competitors. Meanwhile, he succeeded in persuading the Bishop of Cambrai to appoint him as his Latin secretary for the journey the prelate was contemplating.

This gave him the excuse of leaving the monastery, temporarily as his superiors believed—for good, as he proposed. Many would be the times, in after years, that Erasmus would receive supplications to return; the supplications would change to warnings; the warnings would stiffen into threats. To no avail. The fox would never again put his paw into the trap. Moreover, he managed to get papal dispensations from wearing the priestly garb and from the observance of prescribed fasts.

But the fox never quite relinquished his priesthood (he was

ordained priest in 1492 by the Bishop of Utrecht) and died in the odor of sanctity. Foxes never relinquish anything entirely, for they say to themselves—who knows but that which is disdained today may not be desired tomorrow? And he who underestimates his enemies has victories at home and defeats on the battlefield.

In the generation in which he lived, it was one thing to put away your cassock neatly with the papal note of permission pinned to it and another to have it torn off your back. Quite often, the skin would go along with it. Thus, whenever it suited his purposes, Erasmus was a priest in good standing, member of that mighty freemasonry whose headquarters were in the City to which all roads led and where countless caravans of gold unloaded.

The Bishop of Cambrai had engaged Erasmus as his Latin secretary because he planned to go to Rome for a visit to the Vatican. Many letters would have to be written and speeches read, and what one said mattered much less than how one said it. Pedantry was on the throne, since truth was in exile. A bishop's document should be not only in elegant Latin, but studded with quotations as thickly as a child's dream of a good bread studded with raisins. The quotations would remove whatever truth the document might still possess, and honesty would be stifled in the honey of rhetoric. There was hardly another one in Europe who could do the job better than Erasmus—at least no one who was as miserably off as Erasmus and who could be procured for so little.

But the Bishop changed his mind, and Erasmus who had so much desired to see the Fountainhead, whence the New Learning flowed, was in imminent danger of becoming a begging friar, the type he roasted later on the spit of satire. "These monks are so detested that it is considered bad luck if one crosses your path. Most of them capitalize on their dirt and poverty by whining for food from door to door. They push into inns, ships, and public conveyances, to the great disadvantage of the regular beggars. These smooth fellows simply explain that by their very filth, ignorance, boorishness, and insolence, they enact the lives of the apostles for us."

But as it would often happen to Erasmus, a *deus ex machina* appeared in the shape of a stipend granted by the Bishop of Cambrai to enable him to pursue his studies in Paris, and particularly Greek, a language which had become the rage, but which few knew. The stipend was so paltry, however, that Erasmus bitterly called his avaricious patron, "Antimaecenas," since Maecenas had been so generous to the men of letters of his day, and even Vergil and Horace were indebted to him for favors.

Oh, had the Bishop of Cambrai but known how celebrated this humble monk would become, and that his own name would be immortal merely because it was associated with his, his largesse would certainly have had no peer! To think that forever he must be known as a miser, when a few purses filled with gold from the sale of indulgences would have made the name of Bishop of Cambrai the synonym of generosity!

Erasmus, now thirty years old, enrolled in Collège Montagu, a celebrated institution of futile and dreary knowledge, situated in the Latin Quarter of Paris on Mt. St. Michel, which four centuries later was the Boulevard St. Michel, or "Boul. Mich." as the students and artists call it, and where the cafés are full, cocottes aggressive, debates noisy, and real talent scarce.

Compared to Montagu, Steyn was paradisiacal. Its head was the leader of the "New Devotion," a movement to reform the sinks of iniquity, which were the monasteries, into cloisters fit for the service of God and the preparation of eternal life. Once upon a time, man had imagined his gods gay and happy and was ready to imitate them with his own limited means. There was Bacchus and Priapus and Venus and foolish little Cupidon—and there was wine and love and laughter. What curse had darkened the mind of man that for fifteen centuries he had the illusion that God demanded misery and cruelty and

pain, and accepted only the ignorant and the gelded as his everlasting companions?

Collège Montagu was a model farm for the raising of sheep
which the leaders thought would be delectable for the Great
Shepherd. The students lived like pigs. The dormitories were
icy cold and near the open latrines. The food was foul, the eggs
stank, the meat was rotten, the wine was sour, the water was
disease-laden. Only four hours were allowed for sleep, but the
vermin devoured the bodies. "Do you come from Montagu,"
one of the characters in Erasmus' *Colloquia* asks, "then undoubtedly you were crowned with laurels?"

"No, with fleas," is the reply.

And there was corporal punishment. Once it was said: *Mens
sana in corpore sano*—"a healthy mind in a healthy body"—
but these men of God considered swollen rumps and a ripped
back the suitable habitation of a holy mind. And there were
those who submitted to the whip humbly, for they had less pride
than the donkey who kicks with his hind legs his vicious and
stupid master. And at a later time, the founder of the Jesuit
Order welcomed the scourge of Montagu upon himself for
two decades "for the good of my soul." How evil must his soul
have been to require such a purification! And how black the
bile stored in the hearts of those men who were ready to torment fellow-men and set fire to cities and nations! In the name
of the God on the Cross they nailed the cross on the back of
Man.

Erasmus, however, felt no need of the scourge for his soul's
purification. His soul was not ill. He could not endure the stench
of decay of scholasticism, and the hair-splitting method of education sickened the man destined to become the great teacher of
men. "None can disentangle the mysteries of their science. . . .
All that you have learned about *bonae litterae,* you must forget.
. . . I try not to say a single word of Latin, a single word that
pleases or that may pass as witty, and I am making such progress in this endeavor, that maybe on one day to come they may
recognize me as one of themselves."

But that day did not come. He fell dangerously ill and left to recuperate—never to return to the "Collège Vinaigre," insulting that sister of wine, so good for salads and for the washing of ladies' hair.

Of God, Man, and the Devil

A civilization may be judged by the size of the ransom man must pay for the exorcism of the Devil. In the period in which Desiderius Erasmus lived the ransom nearly wrecked him. He had to submit his mind to be darkened; he had to have his ears deafened to reason; he had to bow before lies and crush truth underfoot; he had to welcome poverty, disease, and dirt as the ineffable gifts of the Lord of Life, inalterable and eternal.

Man's vision is short and narrow. He cannot grasp his history in its entirety and so divides it into bits, places labels upon them, and grades them as teachers grade their pupils, for effort, achievement, and conduct.

The epoch during which Erasmus functioned, it is related, was either the Middle Ages or the Renaissance—or half and half. In truth, it was a mixture of the Dark Ages and the Middle Ages and the Renaissance and Ancient and Modern Days, for it was a moment of human history, and every moment of history contains the whole of time. Else would it be possible, half a millennium after the birth of Erasmus, to find that the same superstitions flourish and the same lies stalk the land? Between the immutable banks of falsehood the waters of the myriad truths flow on forever.

At the time Columbus discovered what later proved to be the outer islands to a new and immense world, Western Europe was totally Catholic. Feudalism was still in vogue, and princes, secular and ecclesiastical, tore at one another's throats. The estates of the nations were rigidly graded into classes—guildsmen, soldiers, officials, handicraftsmen, peasants, beggars—all severely apart, fearful of contaminating one another with the disease of humanity.

Nevertheless, despite the sharp talons of Church and State, men began to wriggle themselves out, bleeding and maimed, to be sure, into freedom. There were minds that asked questions; there were minds that ferreted out strange and exciting information about other peoples and other ways of living. And there were those who felt the pressure of God too heavy, and they gazed at man and said: "The business of man is man," for they had read what the pagan poet had said centuries before: *Homo sum: humani nihil a me alienum puto*—"I am a man: nothing human is foreign to me."

And they read more of those pagan poets and philosophers, and they began to revere them, and imitate them, and think like them—and in whispers, speak like them. And they began calling themselves Humanists.

Desiderius Erasmus *Rotterdamus* (for now he feared that there might be another Erasmus around, and he wished to make sure there was no mistaking his identity) was definitely out of monasteries and scholastic institutions, and instinctively found his way among the students of "humanities," himself destined to become the greatest and most illustrious of them all.

But before becoming the greatest Humanist he became the most expert of schnorrers. The belly is inescapable. One must fill it, and all the arts and philosophies cannot assuage its clawing or silence its clamors. And the belly of Desiderius Erasmus Rotterdamus had been much abused by the stuff he had fed it. There were ulcers and spasmodic nerves, and he needed an expensive burgundy to silence and soothe them, and he needed the best the kitchen of the day offered. And so, he began writing letters in a Latin that even Vergil would have praised, asking for money from those who had so much they did not know what to do with it. They did know, however, what they did *not* wish to do—to help a monk who ought to go back to his cell and mind his orisons. One, here and there, doubtless, allowed him to eat in the kitchen or filled his palm with coppers. He managed to would not give him peace until he decided to cast the die. Baron Mountjoy was worthy of his name. He took his teacher in hand, and began to rub off the rust of monasteries and the dust of tomes which had buried the witty, charming, delightful companion. Erasmus learned to ride and follow the hounds; learned to consort with women of refinement and aristocrats of the Church and the Land; his tongue unfroze, his eyes glittered with cunning, his lips acquired the smile which combined gentleness with irony—the outward manifestations of his nature. For irony is the measure of truth and gentleness the measure of wisdom.

He was *persona grata* everywhere. Thomas More and John Fisher, two of the most brilliant men of the period, became his intimate friends until evil days came for free minds, and they were both beheaded. John Colet, dean of St. Paul's, Bishop Warham, and Bishop Cranmer, Archbishop of Canterbury, who later was burned at Oxford, were his patrons. Even the Prince who was to become King Henry VIII, and who, next to loving women, loved letters, asked that the little priest should be introduced to him. Oh, had the King but loved a little more his books and a little less his flesh! Alas, that the senses should be the foes of sense!

Whether Erasmus had warmed his shivering body not only with wine, but also by women, is nowhere recorded. Some charming lady, now forever dust, could have achieved immortality by making the tongues of the courtiers wag about her romance with the little Dutchman. Or, was the romance stifled for fear of a husband's sharp sword? Was it consummated in the flesh and relegated to oblivion? How beautiful is sin when poets sing of it! How pointless is virtue in the silence of the tomb!

Never had Erasmus been so cheerful, so aware of the sweetness of life, for he was essentially a social creature, deriving spiritual inspiration and physical well-being from contact with people. Nor did he accept these gifts without returning greater ones himself. He soon became famous as one of the most brilliant of the younger set. It was not a vacuous brilliance, but one

live while his mind concocted things which would r
immortal.

Many, who themselves had never battled with hu
cized his lack of pride. But what was an artist or scho
The day when he could prostitute himself to the publ
had not yet arrived, and he was forced to prostitute
one or several patrons.

But this lack of pride in Erasmus was one of his ch
colorations. The more he had to exhibit it the stiffer l
personality (which would never succumb to bribery
honors, not even to that of bishop or cardinal), th
would write against the evils of flattery and chastise t
in power, accept it. He calls flatterers "this malicious t
Let no one think that the evil of flatterers should be pa
The most flourishing empires of the greatest kings
overthrown by the tongues of flatterers. . . . When
was asked what animal was the most dangerous of al
'If you mean among the wild beasts, I will say the
among the tame ones, the flatterer.' "

Erasmus, however, did not depend entirely on th
of the frivolous and the ostentatious, whom he licke
tongue and lashed with his pen. He taught privately
mate in a scholar's search for a living, placing him at
of vain and unwilling pupils and the hawk-like scru
dulgent and foolish parents—a little more significan
dog, a little less than the servant, and as secure as cap

Fortune, however, which had been so negligent o
defrocked monk, whether on purpose to teach him ho
lot of man can be without her, or by sheer unconcern
began to smile upon him. She gave him William Blour
lishman, as his pupil. William Blount, who afterwar
Baron Mountjoy, invited his teacher to pay him
England.

The thought of the choppy waters of the Channel
mount to eating the stinking fish at Steyn, and his st
belled against the venture. But Fortune, now interest

realities, including science, made its appearance. Once again, however, its leaders were professors or ministers of the gospel, and once again they tried by psychological sinuosities to bind Heaven to Earth; but despite their ingenious maneuvers the knots were undone and they were left, like storks before the rain, one leg in the air.

Another branch of the movement relinquished the God who was the Father of Jesus and embraced the *Unknown God,* a pantheistic notion with reverential overtones. And what happened to it only the *Unknown God* knows.

Many have been the gods that man has created; some day, perhaps he will learn to create Man.

"Money Doesn't Stink"

Pecunia non olet, says the Latin proverb—"money doesn't stink." And Erasmus, though his nose was keen and sharp, found nothing objectionable in money which was cooked in pot-boilers. But they were pot-boilers that had wit and charm and luminosity, for his mind was what a teacher's mind should be— a shedder of light and maker of order. His fingers were phosphorescent and whatever they touched, though it was night all around, shone and guided. Indeed, as the second portion of his life continued, it became evident to all that he had no equal either within the walls of schools or without.

He became the teacher of teachers for generations after his chilled body had stopped trembling in the ice of death, and his soul wandered about in the shape of words. His pupils were greater than he and achieved more permanent renown and that, too, was the sign of a successful teacher. His pupils were the men of the Enlightenment, the Encyclopedists, Swift, Voltaire, and Rabelais, who while Erasmus moaned in his last sickness, sent him a message: "Everything that I do, all that I am, I owe to you; and were I to fail in acknowledging my debt, I should prove the most ungrateful man alive. Greeting and yet again greeting, dearest father and honor of the land which gave you birth, champion of the arts, invincible for truth."

The first of the pot-boilers was *Adagia,* maxims and proverbs and pithy sayings of the ancient sages, which he had jotted down and collected for many years, all enlivened with his own comments often more brilliant and more telling than the original ones. And this, too, was to become his forte—adaption and commentary. Except in his masterpiece, *The Praise of Folly,* he was not an originator of ideas, nor an innovator of style or manner of presentation. He was a collector, an expositor, an excavator, but one who made his labels and his footnotes as exciting as his texts, and often more so. His style enlivened the ponderous materials. It was conversational, easy, pungent, and the facility with which he wrote made him one of the most prolific writers of his day, of any day. His pen, dipped in the juices of his mind, moved on swiftly, noiselessly, eighteen hours a day —at his desk, in the printer's shop, on postchaises—while the sun was up, by a flickering candle.

"As I read you," Zwingli, the Swiss reformer, wrote to him, "it seemed to me that I could hear you speaking, and could see your small and dapper figure moving about before me in the pleasantest manner."

Adagia came on time, as indeed any work must if it is to achieve success, for "when" is more important than "what" in the Market of Letters. It is this fine balance between "when" and "what" which makes many a genius starve and many a man of limited talent prosperous and famed. Nor is it certain (even if that were adequate compensation) that a future generation will undo the wrong perpetrated by a previous one. For even as one comes too early for one's contemporaries, one may come too late for their descendants.

Adagia appeared in Paris in 1500, when the snobs, princes, princelings, hangers-on, wished to appear intellectual. To *be* intellectual—that entailed too much labor, too much strain on eye and rump. The eye should remain clear to please the inamorata and the rump should be hardened in the saddle dashing after the fox and the deer. But after the sword and the plume and the lance, there was still a bit of room for the mind as an ornament. It was so smart to be able to quote a Latin poet's line in the midst of broken Latin or the new languages, and it was quite elegant to pepper one's letters with wise sayings from a resurrected philosopher.

And here was manna—food to please all tastes and all conditions. One could be learned by merely opening the book by that man Erasmus Rotterdamus. Everything was there. "Have you seen *Adagia?* Have you read *Adagia?* Do you own *Adagia?*" From mouth to mouth the news spread of a book without which a man *comme il faut* was simply lost. And *Adagia* became a best-seller. Edition after edition appeared in quick succession, but the shrewd Dutchman saw to it that each edition had new material, so that the pirates of books could not circulate spurious copies. The book, indeed, grew to double its size, and more people found it a *sine qua non.* Every country of Europe buzzed with the name of Erasmus, the author of *Adagia.* And the author suddenly was no longer a beggar, a writer of letters which remained unanswered and even unread. Now a letter from the famous author was something to show proudly to your friends, perhaps start a conversation with a lady at the dinner table which might end in the boudoir. Each step toward a goal is itself a goal.

Encouraged by his success, Erasmus became a veritable cataract. He wrote on morals, on education, on literary etiquette, on devotional exercises which became exercises in common sense rather than theological abracadabra. His *De Ratione Studii* was introduced at St. Paul's and became "the fundamental philosophy of the grammar school in England." It is chiefly concerned, as Erasmus explains, "with the knowledge of words, rather than with the knowledge of truths, for if the latter is first in importance, the former is acquired first in the order of time."

The student was to be thoroughly grounded in Latin and Greek grammar, in the technique of reading for content and

style, and in composition and declamation. The student could
have at the tip of his "tongue a *summa* of rhetoric; that is, propositions, the 'places' of proofs, exornations, amplifications,
formulas of transitions." To further aid the unfortunate student, Erasmus wrote two textbooks—*Copia* and *Parabolae,*
which showed how to develop a theme by logical analysis, examples, figures of speech, and exornation or the "gorgious
beautifying of the tongue with borrowed wordes, and change of
sentence of speech with much varietie." At the climax of the
course came the formal declamation, which the student studied
"from exordium to narration, from narration to division, from
division to reasoning, from proposition to proposition, from
reason to reason, from the argument to the epilogue or peroration." The student developed facility by treating the same
subject in a variety of ways, by essaying "suasory, dissuasory,
hortatory, dehortatory, narrative, gratulatory, expostulatory,
commendatory, consolatory."

And *this* was to be Ariadne's thread to take man out of the
malignant maze of hollow words through which his futile
thoughts reverberated! The pedagogues of the day screamed as
if stabbed in their most sensitive parts, for this man of Rotterdam was spoiling the youth of the lands, coddling them, making
learning easy, when it should be full of travail and misery, and
they said to their pupils, as Yahweh to Eve: "I will greatly
multiply thy sorrow and thy conception; in sorrow thou shalt
bring forth knowledge."

Nevertheless, Erasmus' "joyous" system continued for centuries in the great schools of England, and those who mastered
the abracadabra became *gentlemen.* This gave them the right
to treat with contempt the poor, to take high seats in Parliament and Court, to press taxes out of the landless, until they
dried them as stones and nothing more would flow. And it gave
them the right (aided by sword and gun) to subject peoples of
other colors and other cultures to slavery and misery, to illiteracy and ignorance. It gave them the right to cause dissension
among populations, to bring about civil wars and fratricide, so

that they would never in all time regain their freedom and independence. For, if they remembered nothing of their classics, they never forgot the maxim of the Roman Senate—*divide et impera*—"divide and rule."

In the days of Erasmus of Rotterdam, and in the days which followed him, as well as in the days which preceded him, man constructed colossal halls of words for tiny thoughts to wander in, while his tongue, like a serpent's stung with the venom of bigotry, hate, and lie. Words serve the civilized man's mind as clothes serve his body—to hide defects, to emphasize qualities, to shield and protect and deceive. It is as anti-social to appear naked mentally as physically. Language is the translation of man's original weapons—fist, rock, club—and is still his most formidable arsenal. All our evil ancestors live on our tongues.

As an accompaniment to his other text-books, Erasmus published *Colloquia,* a series of dialogues in polite Latin to be used in facilitating the mastery of that fashionable language. It achieved even greater fame than his previous volumes, and it, too, became the standard text for generations.

The function of the Humanist was not to be an artist in his own language, but to spread the light of the classics, and to a great degree that was also Erasmus' intentions. But his genius drowned his intentions, and the classics became not the aim, but the means, of exposing his own ideas. They were fairly simple, and they seemed to him so easily realizable. If only man would listen to a little common sense! If he would only listen to his heart—would he accept war, would he accept persecution of his fellow-man, would he allow injustice, would he separate himself from his fellow-beings, just because they lived across the river, or over the mountain, or merely over a line artificially drawn in the middle of a road? Why, "animals destitute of reason, live with their own kind in a state of social amity. Elephants herd together; sheep and swine feed in flocks; cranes and crows take their flight in troops; storks have their public meetings to consult previously to their emigration and feed their parents when unable to feed themselves; dolphins defend each other by mutual assistance; and everybody knows that both ants and bees have respectively established, by general agreement, a little friendly community."

Yet man, and only man, despite his reason, despite all the teachings of philosophers and poets and saints, is the most discordant of animals. Man and "the Horse, that comes so near to man in understanding, is also partaker of his misery. . . . In the Battel, while he contends for Victory, he's cut down himself, and together with his Rider, 'lies biting the earth'; not to mention those Bits, sharp Spurs, close Stables, Arms, Blows, Rider, and briefly, all that slavery he willingly submits to, while, imitating those men of Valor. . . ." Man, therefore, poisons the sweet nature of all creatures that come in contact with him and submit to his follies.

Slowly, in book after book, Erasmus' ideas became clearer to himself, and book after book, he subordinated the ostensible purpose of writing it to the subtler morals he wished to preach. Incapable of prejudice and free of superstition, Erasmus became the great pacifier of his age. Skeptic, he could not accept any idea as possessing the absolute truth, nor could he accept the immutability of any truth. No truth was a monument. At most it might become a stepping stone to another truth. And in time divine truths became schoolboys' legends.

Therefore, he argued, why could not people compromise, and relinquishing a portion, acquire the whole—and the whole was peace and good will. Every man had the right to his opinions, even theological, but men had no right to needlessly expand the area of their disagreement and thereby introduce the danger of conflict. We cannot load guns without making enemies. Even sheep suspect the glitter of knives.

Before long the educated people of Europe began speaking of "Erasmism"—a supranational and pan-human ideal. Those who believed with him—and they were found in all classes, men and women, nobles and priests, kings and merchants—hoped that the day was at hand when mankind could be humanized via reason and peaceful persuasion. For a brief day, Erasmus rode triumphantly at the head of the finest spirits of the Western World, under the banner of "Humanity." When the day would be over, a madness, monstrous and collective, would grip mankind, and seas of blood would flow, as if to erase every word ever uttered for peace and reason. Although reason is but a candle in the general darkness, its light smarts so many eyes that there is a constant and ubiquitous blowing of breaths.

When a woman complained to Erasmus of her husband's religious indifference, he wrote a book to console her, but the book became the catechism of the new evangelical form of piety and devotion, breaking the net of tradition and injecting the freer spirit to the extent possible under the circumstances.

How he hated the arguments, which often terminated in murderous schism, about problems as preposterous as the one which asked: "Could Jesus have appeared in the form of a gourd? If so, how could he have preached, performed miracles, and been crucified?" How he despised the theological slumber! "There are many," he wrote to his friend, Thomas Grey, in England, "that in their sleep, not only write, but slander and get drunk, and commit other indiscretions, the pseudo-theologians of our time, whose brains are rotten, their language barbarous, their intellects dull, their learning a bed of thorns, their manners rough, their life hypocritical, their talk full of venom, and their hearts as black as ink." How he abominated the greedy members of the priestcraft! "The roads to Heaven are so crowded with toll collectors that no one is rich enough to reach the destination." With what contempt he regarded the over-zealous! "We must be as sandpaper rubbing the face of bigotry."

His restless hand wrote on. He would gather the light of ages into himself and then scatter it in countless rays athwart the earth. He was not the typical scholar, hunchbacked beneath the load of useless details. He was not a hod carrier of knowledge carrying on the rickety ladder his measure of cement to glue, brick to brick, the endless, meaningless tower of Babel, in a confusion of tongues. His work was done in white heat, under the passion of his ideas. His thoughts were crackling fire scattering sparks in all directions. He read, he wrote, *"tumultuarie, praecipitanter, uno impetu."*

He had to be impetuous, he had to work in storm, for there was so much to do and man's days were short, made shorter still by a night which was settling over the earth, and whose chill shadows he felt all about him. Perhaps, if he brought his light to the market place for all to see, he could set other torches afire, and the night would not be so dense or so long.

What Men Live By

All things come to those who wait, and who while waiting, labor. Erasmus of Rotterdam labored and waited, and now at the age of forty, the possibility of going to Rome, his desire for two decades, was realizable. It was the year 1505 and he was visiting his friend Lord Mountjoy. Erasmus had already acquired the habit of wandering from city to city and staying with friends, but not for long. He would have his friends welcome him with open arms, and then lead him to the gate, begging him to make sure to call again. He seemed to know precisely the fine line which divides pleasure from duty, and when the mouth opens for speech or for yawning. He knew that human relationships hang by a thread, and he would not strain the thread.

But now Baptista Boerio, the King's private physician, asked Erasmus to go to Italy as the tutor of his two young sons, whose education would not otherwise be complete—even as later on, it became a necessity to go to Paris. The two young men left no record of their trip and we shall never know how much they profited by the company of the witty scholar, but, certainly, greater privilege no youths ever had. Yet, after all, the plane only removes the splinters; it cannot alter the quality of the wood.

Erasmus stopped at Turin, where he received his doctorate. From Turin they went to Bologna, where the three spent a year at the university, founded in the fifth century. Through its halls reverberated all the truths and all the lies of the generations, now so woven together in the vast pattern that the hand which dared to separate the threads would wither from irreverence.

When the young men had had enough of education and perhaps also of the Man of Rotterdam, who probably overwhelmed them with his knowledge, his industry, and the keenness of his mind, they returned home. Freed from the burden, and doubtless the boredom of catering to ignorance, Erasmus proceeded to Venice where Aldus, the most distinguished printer of his day, published a new and beautiful edition of *Adagia*—now nearly four times as thick as when it originally made its appearance. For a time, Erasmus also served in the capacity of general adviser to the Aldus presses, then switched to the house of Frobenius in Basle which, thanks to his work and presence, became the most illustrious in Europe.

He pursued his journey on to Padua where he met another of his pupils, Alexander Stewart, a bastard like himself, whose father was James IV of Scotland. Together the illegitimates arrived in Rome, where illegitimates were pullulating in all the chambers of the palace of the Monarch of Christendom. Now Erasmus was glad that all those years had passed, for by now his fame had penetrated the Vatican and he was received with great honors.

The Reformation had not yet its mighty Leader, but there were already skirmishes on the outskirts of the realms of the Church which foreshadowed the mighty war, not merely for the possession of territory, but for the survival of the Empire of the Cross. The Vatican, always sensitive to its detractors, always conscious of its many shortcomings, but always unwilling to repair more than the façade, was sharpening all its swords to strike down not only its enemies, but even its half-friends.

For the moment, however, a sharp pen was a more propitious weapon, and the goose quill of the Man of Rotterdam had no

equal throughout Europe. It was, when he so wished it, a steel
rapier, but it was also a tender feather capable of tickling the
vanity and changing enmity into friendship.

Serpents could not hiss more ominously nor doves coo more
sweetly than the Men of the Vatican, nor could hands fleece
more closely nor soothe more tenderly than their hands. They
cooed into the ears of Erasmus and caressed him and promised
him the goods of the Earth and special sweets in Heaven. As
for Heaven, Erasmus was never much concerned. He seems to
leave that entirely to the Owners of the Upper Hostelry, and
he is not a bit worried as to what sort of baggage he will take
along when the painful journey must be undertaken. Once in a
while he warns princes, lay and clerical, of evil consequences to
themselves at the Judgment Seat if they do not act according to
reason and in the spirit of magnanimity. The poor he never
threatens with post-terrestrial tribulations, since evidently they
had enough of them in their short journey through time and
space and could take anything in their stride. They would quite
probably find their new tormentors amateurs and laugh at
their exhibitions. "You ought to see what our blessed Mother
Church has in store for *her* delinquents!"

The earthly goods, however, that the Vatican promised
Erasmus were not easily dismissed. There were enviable honors.
He would become the Pope's private secretary with a high rank
—a cardinal eventually. He would have the luxury he needed
to remain well—the best wines, the choicest food, crackling
fireplaces, finest linens, and a beautiful library with specially
bound volumes and rare first editions, for he was not only a
reader and a writer, but also a collector. And he could wield
power second only to the Holy Father himself.

It was probably precisely this idea more than any other, that
finally after much struggling, as with Jacob and the angel, made
him reject the proposition, and go his way. For power would
have meant oppression of those in opposition, would have meant
accepting the evils of the Church, nay, proclaiming them as
divinely ordained, would have meant the death of "Erasmism,"

a delicate flower which could thrive only in freedom and tolerance, in anti-fanaticism, in the precedence of intellect over
authority.

"Erasmism," moreover, was an organism for progress. It
had as its chief aim education, since it considered the passion
for destruction and bestiality rooted in illiteracy. Education,
therefore, should percolate from higher levels to lower until
all mankind was freed from the incubus of ignorance. This was
diametrically opposed to the scheme of the Church, which believed in an unvarying hierarchy and considered the masses
safely in the fold only as they remained ignorant and obedient
to the bellwether. Even the passion for destruction in the masses
was, according to the Church, a good, as necessary to the body
politic as blood-letting was to the physical well-being. Indeed,
without this periodic madness man might sink into a religious
coma from which it could never awaken. A religion which could
not stir its adherents to a holy war or to a crusade was a dying
religion. And those who asked the Church to become the champion of permanent peace asked her to commit suicide. Without
the aid of the sword, the cross would long ago have joined the
caravan of gods whose worshipers turned their cheeks and
could not or would not wield the sword. "I bring a sword,"
must ever be the motto emblazoned on the flag of the conqueror.

However, the Humanism of the days of Erasmus could not
properly be considered in complete opposition to the Church.
Although the Church was a totalitarian regime more utterly
inclusive than any past or future, for it embraced both life upon
earth and life beyond it, Humanism itself was not a democratic
movement, except indirectly. Humanism was a new order of
knights, wielding goose quills instead of swords, their chests
protected by armor fashioned of parchment inscribed with
Latin and Greek cabalistic symbols, and therefore impervious
to lance or fire. But like every other knighthood it was doomed
to extinction by the ease with which it could be caricatured not
only by great novelists, but by simple onlookers and even by its
own followers.

The aristocratic thinking for which Erasmus is often blamed, nevertheless touches democracy at many points, and the "cowardice" so frequently attributed to him, if viewed in perspective, has many features of heroism. He lived at the crossroads of history when the Past pulled at one's tail and the Future at one's arms. To move at a tangent, the Present, was a feat he was determined to achieve, for the Present was exceedingly precarious and if ignored, Time's dimensions might have no more meaning for mankind. Yet, how shall man understand the present if he does not know the future—the present which forever flows into the past—the future which forever eludes him?

Erasmus left the Vatican without the burden of the golden chain to do battle for peace and concord among all people in Christendom, for what a disgrace it was for Christians to be fighting among themselves. "Every Angle hates the Gaul and every Gaul the Angle for no other reason than that he is an Angle. The Irishman, just because he is an Irishman, hates the Briton; the Italian hates the German . . . and so on through the list. District hates district; city hates city. . . ."

Now Erasmus traveled like a gentleman. He could afford three horses, one for himself, one for his servant, and one for his writing materials; the latter perhaps, too, for the good wine which had become so essential to his well-being. Certainly it was far safer than the water everywhere—except as it tumbled from the mouth of the mountain into the mouth of the man. It was a perilous journey northward through steep mountains filled with hobgoblins, devils, and witches, not to mention robbers. The horses, wiser than the men, were given full freedom to meander over the intricate pathways, on the rim of the abysses, as dark and as deep as the cellars of hell.

One's buttocks were peeled and studded with blisters and one's legs had lost the art of upholding the body, but the brain could work, could compose, and make ready for the hand, armed with the quill of the stupidest of birds, to transcribe in hooks and lines the strange images called thoughts—thoughts, which to have validity, should have wings. Thoughts are wild steeds and they who wish to ride them must have much skill and courage and be ready to dash through uncharted roads to unforeseen destinations.

On and on the tiny caravan pursued its road, and clearer and clearer the thoughts of Erasmus became, and now and then he would laugh. It was difficult for the servant to interpret the little explosions, to know whether they were caused by sheer well-being or by something that only such wise and learned eyes as those of his master could discern.

"Folly, good Folly, thou makest all things live and prosper," Erasmus muttered to himself. But what he did not then know, nor would ever find out, was that Folly made him immortal.

Folly Saveth the Skin

When evil men rule it is prudent for those who wish to denounce evil to don the jester's garb—the motley coat, the tight breeches, the pointed cap and bells, the staff with the inflated bladder. Make the evil men laugh—that is the price wisdom has to pay. It is not an easy feat, for the evil men are shrewd and they see through the masquerade, but they are, fortunately, also vain, and wish to pose as even cleverer than the mockers, and that is their Achilles' heel. They laugh and the world laughs, but the echoes of the laughter are the truth and the echoes wander endlessly and they become mighty winds which carry off the men and their evil and smash them.

That is what Erasmus meditated on as he was riding across the mountains followed by his servant, and he laughed, for he had already donned mentally the jester's garb and saw the dénouement. He was too sanguine, as any artist is when his mind is excited by an idea. Evil is not so easily dismissed, nor so easily recognized. Let us drive out evil with circumspection since once it was the good, heralded and worshipped; and as the new good enters with pomp and flourish, let us be wary, for in time we may discover that it is evil again, shrewdly disguised.

The Man of Rotterdam was not an innovator of either ideas or literary forms. He was an improver. He turned ponderous, leaden-footed pronouncements into light, winged sentences. He poured gold on iron and blew upon embers and inflamed them. He might never have discovered the manner in which he penned his masterpiece, however, had not others first experimented with it.

In 1494, two years after Erasmus had been ordained priest, Sebastian Brant, an innkeeper's son from Strasburg, completed a manuscript. He had received the law degree at the University of Basle, but preferred to spend most of his time pushing the quill and publishing books. The recently improved printing from movable type had attracted many bright young men. They realized that there was a great future for that machine, although more than eighty percent of the Christians were illiterate, and the countries where the churches, whether Roman or Greek, dominated the lives of men were to keep the vast masses of their citizens in the purblindness of illiteracy for centuries to come. Knowledge was the Devil's way of insinuating himself into the souls of the people. Poor Devil—God's scapegoat! How often had he been sacrificed in order to prove that an all-powerful, all-loving divinity should not be blamed for the monstrous miseries that befell the children of Adam and Eve, first betrayed by the Devil's hissing ambassador!

The manuscript which Brant published was entitled *Narrenschiff*, the ship of fools, or as the English title had it, *Grete Shyppe of Fooles*. One hundred and fourteen species of fools were gathered on this new Ark, bound for Fool's Paradise. Whether it would have reached its destination, we shall never know, for the author having enumerated all the traits of his characters, was out of wind, and could not push the ship from the harbor. Or, perhaps, he became aware of the fact that being a fool meant inhabiting paradise, wherever one might be, and that would disturb the smart ones who consigned the fools to hell.

The book was an instantaneous hit. It was translated into French, English, and Latin, and created a vogue of "fool" books. Basius Ascenius, a Belgian writer who afterwards became one of the most famous printers in Paris, wrote a sequel to Brant's book, entitled *Stultiferae Naves* or *Shiploads of Foolish Women*. There would thus be no discrimination, with attendant jealousy, between the two branches of *Homo sapiens,* and a loving understanding would be established between them so that the creation of fools could go on forever.

The Ship of Fools was less a satire than a collection of aphorisms pictorially illustrated, teaching conservative and conventional morals. A fool, it said, is one who does not conform to the accepted behavior; a fool is one who is not industrious; a fool is one who is not prudent; a fool is one who does not lead a sensible life on earth, because he would lose heaven as well. All in all, a sincere, pedestrian, static comprehension of feudal and Catholic teaching. It may be that there were those who read negations between the lines, who, knowing the weaknesses of certain leaders, recognized possible caricatures and could laugh at their discomfiture. But the key has been lost, and the value of the book is purely for the academy and because it fired the mind of Desiderius Erasmus Rotterdamus in his voyage back from Rome.

The voyage was long but otherwise uneventful, by way of Constance, Strasburg, and Antwerp. Erasmus finally reached London safely, in the late autumn of 1509. From there he went to Bucklersbury, the residence of his dear friend, Thomas More. The trip had been hard on his back and he was forced to take to bed with an attack of lumbago. And the miracle happened, for the creation of a work is a miracle always, impossible before it makes its appearance, stranger even to its author than to its reader. Is this the incarnation of the agony, the travail, the exultation? Is this what he had really wished to say? Perhaps;

perhaps not. Now it is no longer possible to know. Now all those strange images in the brain, those pangs in the guts, those gallopings in the blood, have vanished, and there is only this mass of words, hardened into this shape, which stares at him. "I am thy book!"

Some years later, Erasmus tells in a letter how it all happened: "I was staying with More after my return from Italy and I was kept several days in the house by an attack of lumbago. My books had not yet arrived and even if they had, my illness forbade exertion in more serious studies. So, in order to have something to do, I began to amuse myself with *The Praise of Folly,* not with the intention of publishing the result but to relieve the discomfort of sickness by this sort of distraction. . . . I spent some seven days on the work, an expenditure of time which I thought out of proportion to the importance of the subject. . . . Afterwards my friends contrived to have the book taken to France and have it printed, but from a copy not only faulty, but also incomplete. . . . The book was reprinted seven times in a few months and that in different places. I wondered myself what people found to like in it."

This was his official recantation and the casting of the book to the flames, if the authorities so desired. A foolish book about foolishness, faulty, incomplete, published by anonymous friends without his knowledge. A shrewd jester Erasmus Rotterdamus —and a coward.

He did not whisper the aside, like Galileo Galilei—"*eppur si muove!*" But let not those who scream when the matches blister their fingers as they light their cigarettes sit in judgment of a man who might have roasted slowly, or had his flesh torn with red-hot pincers, by proclaiming that he wrote his book in great anger against the iniquities of princes, secular and religious, and that his jovial manner was only a trap to make them hearken to his words!

The truth is, however, that the manuscript as printed, was complete and corrected, and that he himself had taken it to

Paris to the printer in April, 1511, and that he knew it was the best work he had done so far—creative, artistic, ripe. He might even have suspected that it was the appropriate coin to pay the Ferryman to cross the River of Mortality to the Land of Eternal Life.

Having had its importance and almost its parentage disclaimed, so that it was a bastard even as its sire, *The Praise of Folly* entertained the very people it meant to scorch—the Pope, bishops, noblemen, scholars. Let them laugh! Their laughter would be hurled against their heads and rip them off their necks—in time. If not they, their descendants. There were those, however, who were more perspicacious. They knew that this book was no more a toy than "saltpeter," also called gunpowder, which was highly recommended by soldiers who laughed at civilians and played tricks on them with the loud detonations. One of them even said as much: "Erasmus in the guise of a jester is destroying the whole Church with his quips and jokes."

Erasmus saw more than forty editions of the book, and translations into French, German, Dutch, and Flemish. Later on, when the masses were allowed to listen to the wisdom of Dame Folly, there followed translations into every language of Europe, and then further, beyond her boundaries.

The Praise of Folly was dedicated to Thomas More, and its original title, *Moriae Encomium,* was intended as a playful pun on More's name—since *moriae* means "folly." It was meant to show once more that the whole matter was a game of no consequence. Still fearful, however, he ended the dedication shrewdly. Having explained his purposes more or less tangentially, he says: "But why do I run over these things to you, a person so excellent an Advocate that no man better defends his Client, though the cause many times be none of the best? Farewell, my best disputant More, and stoutly defend your Moriae." *Your* Moriae!

More had no need to defend his friend's book, but when the

time came, to defend himself, years later, he was unsuccessful
and he lost his head, one of the finest of the century. How
Erasmus escaped the nets thrown in his direction by all the
factions, and achieved man's *desideratum*—to die in bed—was
a masterpiece of slipperiness, never equaled by eels.

It is Folly herself who comes before the Assembly of Man in
her own defense, or rather, being Folly, in her own praise. Men
are most ungrateful—obtaining so many benefits, yes, including
life itself, from her—yet they malign her, or at best pretend not
to know her personally. "From me," she says, "you shall hear
an extemporaneous and unlabored speech. . . . And what is
the point of drawing a shadowy picture of myself when you see
me clearly in person? I am exactly what you see, the giver of
all good things, in Latin called *Stultitia* and in Greek, *Moria.*"

If it were not for her, there would be no life on Earth or on
Olympus. Even Jove, when he wishes to beget children, must
put aside his three-pronged thunderer and do what all the rest
do. And as for the Stoic, who considers himself godlike, he, too,
must shed his gravity, stop frowning, abandon his principles,
and be a silly fool. "I ask whether the head, the face, the breast,
the hand or the ear—each an honorable part—creates gods and
men? I think not, but instead the job is done by that foolish, even
ridiculous part which cannot be mentioned without laughter.
That is the sacred fountain from which all things rise. Hence
from my ridiculous and crazy game are produced supercilious
philosophers, their present day successors, vulgarly called
monks, kings in purple robes, pious priests, thrice-holy
popes. . . ."

In the same incontrovertible manner, Folly points out all the
good things she procures for man. "If people would avoid contact with wisdom and dwell continuously with me, there would
be no old age, but only the joy of perpetual youth. . . . My
morons are fat, blooming, and sleek . . ." As for human relations—take marriage for instance: "What divorces or worse,
would not occur if married life were not upheld and strength-

ened by blarney, joking, compromise, infatuation, duplicity—
all aspects of me?... In short, without me no society or mortal
union can be pleasant or lasting."

So far, Folly has hardly stepped on anyone's toes, but she
begins before long to particularize, to denounce, to condemn.
Having disposed of the gods, she takes up the monarchs. "Kings
cannot eat or travel or spend an hour without fools, in whom
they take the greatest delight. . . . Counsellors, confident in
their wisdom and forced to speak the unpleasant truth, bring
only problems to princes, but fools bring what rulers are looking for—jokes and laughter."

As for the noblemen—"They swear that the sound of the
horn and the baying of the hounds fill them with indescribable
joy. I understand that even the dung of the dogs smells like
cinnamon to them. And what is so delightful as an animal being
butchered? . . . They think they are living royally, whereas
they are really gaining nothing from this butchery and eating of
animals, except to degenerate into animals themselves."

There are other fools, such as gamblers, and those who enjoy
telling and hearing monstrous lies. "They are most pleased by
stories that are farthest from the truth. Such wonders are very
profitable, especially for priests and pardoners." Closely related
are those who have reached the foolish but comforting belief
that if they gaze on the picture of Polyphemus-Christopher,
they will not die that day; or that whoever speaks the right
words to an image of Barbara will return unharmed from battle; or that a novena to Erasmus, with proper prayers and
candles will shortly make one rich. . . . Then, what shall I say
of those who happily delude themselves with forged pardons
for their sins? They calculate the time to be spent in Purgatory
down to the year, month, day, and hour. . . . There are also
those who propose everything they desire by relying on magical
charms and prayers devised by some pious imposter for the
sake of his soul, or for profit. They will have wealth, honor,
pleasure . . . and at last a place next to Christ in Heaven.

However, they don't want that seat of honor until the last minute; celestial pleasures may come only when worldly pleasures, hung on to with tooth and nail, finally depart. . . . I picture a businessman, a soldier, a judge, taking from all this loot one small coin as proper expiation for the infinite evil of his life. He thinks it possible to buy up, like notes, so many perjuries, rapes, debauches, fights, murders, frauds, lies, and treacheries. . . . The same thing on a large scale occurs when sections of the country set up regional saints and assign peculiar rites and powers to them. One gives relief from toothache, another aids women in labor . . . the list is too long to finish. Some are helpful in a number of difficulties, especially the Virgin Mother, whom the common people honor more than they do the Son. . . . Why should I go farther on this sea of superstitions? The life of Christians everywhere runs over with such nonsense. Superstitions are allowed and even promoted by the priests; they do not regret anything so profitable. . . . Anyway, man's mind is much more taken up with appearances than with reality. This can be easily and surely tested by going to church. When anything serious is being said, the congregation dozes or squirms. But if the ranter—I mean the reverend—begins some old wives' tale, as often happens, everyone wakes up and strains to hear."

Folly picks out other groups—authors, scholars, lawyers, each with its follies and prejudices and injustices. "Perhaps," she says, "it would be wise to pass over the theologians in silence. That short-tempered and supercilious crew is as unpleasant to deal with as Lake Camarina"—a stinking swamp in Sicily. "They may attack me with six hundred syllogisms; and if I do not recant, they will proclaim me a heretic. . . . They explain (to suit themselves) the most difficult mysteries: how the world was created and set in order; through what channels original sin has passed to successive generations; by what means, in what form, and for how long the perfect Christ was in the womb of the Virgin; and how accidents subsist in the Eucharist without their subject." And is it reasonable "to worship a charcoal picture on the wall as if it were Christ Himself—that is, if it has two fingers extended, the hair unshorn, and three rays in the halo behind the head?"

Now Folly has forgotten that she is to stimulate laughter in her audience and that those fools whom she describes are her own sons and daughters, cherishing her and cherished by her, and she whips them and prongs them and rips their masks off skin and all. And to this extent, *The Praise of Folly* is an imperfect book. But Folly is no longer Folly now, except from time to time, when fearful that the world would catch on, she re-introduces herself. Folly has become Desiderius Erasmus Rotterdamus, who, too full with anger against the countless injustices of his day, has cast off his jester's garb and has become the prophet who chastises the wicked, and in particular the wicked who call themselves the men of God.

"At the same time," Erasmus goes on enumerating the wiles and wrongs of the monks, whom he hates especially, "and even though they are not a part of the state, no one quite dares to attack these people. . . . The mendicants are particularly safe because they get hold of everybody's secrets through what they call confessions. Of course, they consider it a sin to divulge anything, except when they are drunk and want to entertain themselves by telling some good stories."

And now the hierarchy, and here Erasmus had better be careful. Here he deals with those who burn and hang and quarter their critics, and their toes are extremely sensitive. Still Folly-Erasmus cannot stop. "The bishops never give a thought to the meaning of the word bishop—labor, vigilance, and solicitude—except when money is to be made, and then they are bishops indeed, overlooking nothing. . . . The cardinals, likewise, might reflect that they are the successors of the apostles. . . . Why all this money, anyway, for the successors of the poor apostles? Finally, if the Supreme Pontiffs, who are the vicars of Christ, tried to imitate his life, his poverty, labors, teaching, who would purchase that office at the cost of every effort? Why would he retain it by the sword, by poison, and by every other means? If wisdom should come to the popes, it would deprive them of all wealth, honor, and possessions; all the triumphant progresses, offices, dispensations, tributes, and indulgences. . . . In their place, wisdom would bring vigils, fasts, tears, prayers, and a thousand similar trials. And think of the hardships on all those copyists and notaries, all those advocates, promoters, bankers, pimps—I was about to add a softer, but perhaps, a naughtier name. In short, all those who bring shame—I mean fame—to the Roman See would have to beg for their bread. This would be terribly inhuman, and even worse, for those very princes of the Church and true lights of the world would be reduced to a staff and a wallet."

And what is the chief occupation of the popes? "Our popes neglect everything to devote themselves to war, although war is so monstrous a thing that it befits beasts and not men. . . . They can show how a man may draw his sword and run it through his brother's guts, and at the same time live in that perfect charity which Christ tells us a Christian owes his neighbor."

Now Erasmus had really better stop. Now he'd better don the jester's cap once again. Now he'd better play ventriloquist to Goddess Folly. "However, it is not my intention to write biographies of popes and priests. That might result in satire rather than in eulogy. Nor should it be thought that good princes are criticized when I praise bad ones. . . . But indeed I have long since forgotten who I am and have run out of bounds. If anything I have said seems sharp and gossipy, remember that it is Folly and a woman who has spoken. . . . I see that you are expecting a peroration, but you are certainly foolish if you think that I can remember any part of such hodgepodge of words as I have poured out. There is an old saying—'I hate a drinking companion with a memory.' Here is a new one—'I hate an audience that remembers anything.'

Wherefore farewell, clap your hands, live and drink lustick, my most excellent Disciples of Folly!"

And so the wise fox dashed away, his fur unsinged, his tail intact.

The World Splits

While *The Praise of Folly* pursued its merry career and its author became the most famous man in Europe, the Man of Rotterdam wrote on and on. He translated the New Testament from the Greek into the Latin, making many revisions, generally putting more sense into the puerilities the ignorant translators had presented as the words of God. He wrote articles and rewrote and enlarged previous books. His *Querela Pacis,* the *Plaint of Peace,* was issued in every language and circulated among the masses—"peace, rejected by all the nations and peoples of Europe, and driven forth and slain." He had already written an essay in *Adagia,* which bore the title: *"Dulce bellum inexpertis"*—"only to those who have never experienced it is war beautiful."

He had, indeed, become the first man of letters in modern times to advocate pacifist ideals, and already discovered how grateful man is toward his benefactor. "It comes to this, that if one ventures to open his mouth against war, he is looked upon as not much better than a brute beast, as a fool, and as being un-Christianly." Nevertheless, he never ceased inveighing against this calamity without compare among the multitudinous misfortunes which befall man—a calamity which need not be his, if only he would employ reason and a bit of charity. It was a simplistic philosophy, that did not take into account the collective madness which possesses towns and countries and whole continents periodically—a madness which does not spend itself until the earth is torn and burnt and blood bespatters all, as if ejected by myriad geysers.

Is reason a sufficient force to overcome this madness? Is appeal to brotherly love a deterrent? Reason is a persuasive *for* the cause of war, and civil wars between brother and brother are the most violent of all. Is there a bellicose impulsion in man, which overcomes his fears and his loves? A hundred wars have been fought since the days of Erasmus and yet we still speak of reason, charity, brotherly feelings as the antidotes to the massacres. Is there nothing more effective? Cannot the laboratories which manufacture weapons discover the drug that would make man refuse to use them? Must every advance in civilization be paralleled by an advance in lethal weapons of war, so that man may predict one by the other and forever gauge man's wisdom by his folly, and his goodness by his cruelty?

Because Erasmus was the friend of monarchs, he dared to write them letters and articles which afterward were printed and circulated in vast quantities, always urging them to desist from war or threats of war. "All monarchs are cut from the same cloth. Some are busied with collecting sinews of war; some, with leaders and machines; but hardly any are planning for the betterment of human life, which is the source of everything else and pertains with equal importance to all."

There were those who said that there were wars and wars, and some were desirable, particularly wars for God. But Erasmus believed in peace at any price. "There are occasions when, if peace can be had in no other way, it must be purchased. It can scarcely be purchased too dearly, if you take into account how much treasure you must inevitably expend in war, and what is of infinitely greater consequence than treasure, how many of the people's lives you save by peace."

In March 1514, he urged an end to war through international arbitration. "But you will say, that the rights of sovereigns must be maintained. I only know this, that *summum jus*, extreme right, is often *summa injuria*, extreme wrong. . . . But suppose there is a real dispute, to which some sovereignty belongs, where is there need of bloodshed?" And even if the arbiters were corrupt, the evil suffered by a biased decision would be far less than if there had been "recourse to arms, to the irrational and doubtful decision of war." As for himself, whatever the epithets hurled at his head, "I cannot help execrating strife. I cannot help loving peace and concord."

In the year 1515 Erasmus was asked to join the court of Prince Charles, who was to become Charles V, king of Spain in 1516, and emperor of Germany in 1519, master of immense domains, of Spain and her colonies, of part of Italy, Flanders, and Austria—who used to boast that the sun never set on his empire. He planned to become lord of the whole earth, for which he had to fight Francis I in four wars, Soliman II, sultan of the Ottomans, and the Protestants of Germany. And finally, unable to achieve his dream, he retired to a monastery to die at the age of fifty-eight.

Erasmus accepted, because, being a good teacher, he knew how much easier it is to teach than to unteach, and Charles was only fifteen or sixteen, not yet hardened in his ideas and ways. Immediately, Erasmus set to work and wrote the *Institutio principis Christiani*—"The Education of a Christian Prince." The book was dedicated to Charles and it appeared on June 17, 1516, the same year as More's *Utopia* and sixteen years before *Il Principe*—"The Prince," by Machiavelli.

There were many editions of the book and several translations, both during the author's life and long after his death, and it became a sort of textbook for princes for generations. But like all textbooks, they were put away as soon as the class was over, and forgotten.

Erasmus believed that monarchy was the best form of government, but "monarchies are royal insofar as the monarch rules according to law over willing subjects." Moreover, "I declare that the citizens ought every one actually be given a share in the government." Nor must a prince forget that "the state should be governed for the benefit of the common people, not the ruler." The prince must also realize that "all governments last longest if they serve the masses; it is better to rule as wisely as possible than to try to extend the kingdom." He must know that "the king rejoices in the freedom of his people; the tyrant strives to be feared, the king to be loved. . . . The king does everything and allows everything that will bring peace to his country, for he realizes that war is the source of all misfortunes to the state."

Long before Rousseau's *Contrat Social,* Erasmus says: "A large part of the ruling authority is in the consent of the people, which is a factor that first created kings." As for religion, the prince should deserve the name of "Christian," but so far, "century after century there has been no harmony between Christian princes; no treaties have secured peace; there has been no end to bloodshed, and there has been less disorder among the heathens. . . . The priests are the very firebrands of war. The bishops are not ashamed to go about in the camp. . . . What is more ridiculous, Christ is in both camps, as if he were fighting against himself."

As for the nobles, who are the indolent gamesters, "effeminate through sensual pleasures, with no knowledge of any useful vocation. Why, I ask you, why should this class of persons be placed on a higher level than the shoemaker or the farmer?" As for laws, "they should see in the main that no wrong is done to any man, be he poor or rich, noble or commoner, servant or slave, official or private citizen. But they should lean more in the direction of leniency toward the weaker." And the Prince must not overlook that fact that "nature created all men equal." The prince must not be greedy, and taxes must be raised so that "as little as possible of the hardships will fall on the poor. It is perhaps desirable to bring the wealthy to a simple life."

Erasmus continues to expound his idea of an educated prince —his culture, his understanding, his magnanimity, his imperviousness to baseness, to vanity, his courage to die like a man. "Death is not to be feared, nor should we wail when it comes to others, unless it was a foul death. The happiest man is not the one who has lived longest, but the one who has made the most of his life."

The *speculum principis*—a "mirror for princes"—is an ancient genre of letters, and in the Western World it preceded *The Education of a Christian Prince* by a thousand years. Princes have ever been a dangerous breed, and philosophers, theologians, pedagogues would "polish mirrors" for them, that they might see themselves as they *should* be—prudent, magnanimous, continent, and just. Generally speaking, however, the image reflected was that of a cruel, vain, lewd, besotted, illiterate popinjay, reeking with scent and blood. And the Prince Erasmus would civilize became one of the bloodiest of rulers. A Holy Roman Emperor, he sacked Rome, and died, as was natural, in the stench of sanctity in the monastery of St. Justus in Estramadura.

The *"speculum"* of Erasmus, while not an innovation, excelled all others, as was the case with every work he touched—this Midas of Culture. Besides, he developed and enlarged the concept until it became a general study of government and morals. He blazed paths in all directions, so that for centuries, even into the twentieth and beyond, people would find their way more easily out of the maze of ignorance and injustice.

Although Humanism was a "gentleman's" philosophy and its followers walked on stilts lest their feet might touch the mud of the earth, and Erasmus himself kept his long, sarcastic nose high in the air, the very luminosity of his mind and his essentially good heart made him a defender of the poor and the illiterate, those of "under age," as he spoke of them contemptuously—and piteously.

Now Erasmus was fifty, master of intellectual Europe, master of princes, revered and quoted with bated breath. His rooms were cluttered with gifts from all countries—golden goblets, silver table-services, rare and precious books, masterpieces of painting, casks of old wines. No wonder he wrote to a friend: "At the present moment I could almost wish to be young again, for no other reason but this, that I anticipate the near approach of a golden age."

The applause jammed the tumult of the furious upheaval, which would, before long, reach him and surround him and never lift the siege until he relinquished his body to the vermin he so detested. What is wisdom if it cannot foretell your destiny; and if wisdom could foretell, would it be wisdom to foretell? It is best, perhaps, not to ask for Wisdom, for if our wish be granted, it may be folly greeting us. It is the consequences which determine whether our deeds have been rooted in wisdom or folly, and the consequences are mockers of deeds.

On October 31, 1517, while Erasmus was writing at his accustomed furious pace, a stout, thickset, hard-boned, full-blooded monk, angered by a friar's peddling of indulgences which did not conform with his idea of the forgiveness of sin, nailed a sheet of paper with "theses," inviting academic discussions, on the gate of the University of Wittenberg. That little hammering of the nails was to grow into the most violent thundering which Europe had ever witnessed and would end with the breaking of the chains of the Vatican, in country after country.

Erasmus heard nothing save the noises of the presses of Frobenius which were doubtless printing some new edition of one of his books with beautiful title pages drawn by Hans Holbein. He heard nothing save the fresh praises he had received that day, fresh flowers brought to him by some prince of church or state. Ah, if life could go on this way and one could remain—well—at least middle-aged!

No, Desiderius Erasmus Rotterdamus, life will not go on this way, and Dame Fortune having been so kind to you for so long now, will demand a heavy tribute. Here, it has begun already! Read this letter! It is dated March 28, 1519, and it is by that same monk, so full of animal energy, who swaggers and roars like an organ with all stops out, who boasts that he gorges himself like a Bohemian and gulps down his liquor like a German. Read it! It is crowded with fulsome flattery. It says: "What man alive has not his mind full of thoughts concerning

Erasmus? Whom has he not taught, whom does he not govern?
. . . I would beseech you, therefore, most benevolent of men,
that you deign to notice this poor little brother in Christ, who
can claim no right to live under the same heaven and the same
sun as you . . . Martin Luther."

Why do you pale and tremble, Erasmus? You are sensitive
and you have a premonition of evil, while your nose, which in
centuries to come will be your trait most remembered, smells a
rat. And what a rat! It will grow to the proportions of a bull,
ferocious and maddened, and will gore your world and stamp
on it and tear it to shreds. You feel that. You don't *know* it, but
you *feel* it.

Martin Luther, Doctor of Theology, believes that you ought
to join him to cleanse the stable which has become the Roman
Church—you, who so often have written against its monstrous
iniquities. Remember *The Praise of Folly?* But you refuse, not
out and out—as yet. You speak of reason and peace and moderation. But Luther doesn't know the meaning of these words.
He is not a little elderly man whose spine is always chilly and
who needs furs and delicate wines and blazing fires. He does
not joust fairly, cleverly, with weapons steeled in the classics.
Luther is the symbol of the *furor teutonicus.* "As soon as I arrive in the arena," he says, "I deal blows with my cudgel." He
feels light-hearted only after he has fought madly, cruelly, and
has stamped on the head of the fallen adversary. There is no
chivalry in him. "If you want to better humanity and reform
the Church, you cannot afford to fight shy of a good, thumping
lie."

Erasmus began to build a redoubt, which would give him the
possibility of surveying the field of battle, and yet protect him
from the arrows that he was certain now would come from all
sides. "I wish to keep neutral," he said, imploring everyone to
let him be, "in order to continue to do my share in promoting the
renascent sciences; and I believe that a shrewdly manipulated
reticence will achieve more than impetuous interference."

Later, prodded by Luther and the Vatican, he hardened. "*Nulli concedo,*" he wrote, "to neither shall I belong." *Homo per se,* "man as man," would he remain, without label.

But the times were out of joint, and the spirit of Erasmism was soon to be snuffed out. The Reformation succeeded, and the Protestant movement promptly cracked into many factions, all murdering one another, and together warring against the Roman Church.

The two men, Luther and Erasmus, were paired together for a time, but each knew that the other had become superfluous. From flattery, the words of Luther changed to mere politeness and finally to gutter language. "He who crushes Erasmus cracks a bug which stinks even worse when dead than when alive. . . . I take you all as witnesses for what I am about to declare. In my testament I mean to declare plainly that I hold Erasmus to be the greatest enemy of Christ, such an enemy as does not appear more than once in a thousand years. . . . When I pray 'Blessed be Thy holy name,' I curse Erasmus and his heretical congeners who revile and profane God. . . ."

Now Erasmus must be more than usually careful, for the arm of the Protestant had stretched greatly and might reach him, and the arm of the Vatican had also begun to move in his direction. Now he must use his technique of evasion at its maximum efficiency. Now he must become the wiliest of contortionists.

He did indeed succeed, but at the cost of his name and his fame. He was hated, then despised, then forgotten. No one needed him. No one asked his opinion. He was not even worth the trouble of lighting a fire around a stake. Martin Luther won—Martin Luther the vulgarian, the fighter, the hater. Desiderius Erasmus lost—Desiderius Erasmus, the aristocrat, the compromiser, the Humanist.

And to make certain that his work and name would be turned forever into ashes, less than a quarter of a century after his death, the Vatican ordered his books to be placed on "The Index"—*first category*—that is, the works of heretical authors, whose *entire* output is forbidden under threat of excommunication for all those who read or possess any portion of it.

The Old Man Arrives Home

The son of his late friend, Frobenius, helped him out of the postchaise and showed him to his room. "Only until the ice breaks, my son," Erasmus moaned, "and then I shall go home."

"As long as you desire, Master. You are always our welcome guest."

Now the old man could barely get off the bed, but even so he pushed with trembling hand one of the goose quills which lay in a heap on the table near him. There was no need of strewing dust over the pages to dry the ink. Dust was already gathering on all his work, and little of it would ever succeed in crawling out from under the stifling hill. But he wrote on and on—this industrious and incomparable Ant of Letters. . . .

The ice had broken and spring came, and the boats on the Rhine were like giant sea gulls carrying on their wings all those who would go home. But they did not carry Desiderius Erasmus home. He could not move. Only his hand moved on and on. Then his hand, too, stopped. His friends gathered about him. "Job's comforters," he called them. Like that other great Teacher of Athens, he spoke to them on the meaning of life and death. He spoke of freedom and reason; of the horror of war and the beauty of peace; of the need for all men to work together for justice and mutual help.

Now the old man no longer feared death. It was only a trip—on the waters of eternity—going home—home whence one came—whither one should go—home. . . .

Bon voyage!

And Desiderius Erasmus Rotterdamus arrived home on July 12, 1536.

NICCOLÒ MACHIAVELLI

Geneology—Genesis—
Geopolitics—Guicciardini

Messer Bernardo Machiavelli dreamed of patrician splendor, for was he not descended from the Marquessi of Tuscany who held sway in Val di Greve and Val di Pesa, and were lords of Montespertoli since the ninth century? And was he not entitled to use his ancestral coat of arms—a cross azure, field argent, with four nails, likewise azure at the four corners of the cross—*mali clavelli*—"evil nails"—for those who offended them, and from which was derived the appellation of Machiavelli? And had not his forefathers been elected Gonfalonieri of Justice thirteen times, and had not another fifty-three members been elected priors, officials of the highest rank?

Bernardo had his dream, but the dream bore little resemblance to reality. He was the tail end of the dynasty and his patrimony had been dwindling steadily. Poverty is a giant moth devouring the robe of glory, leaving the wearer in pathetic nudity. In an age in which many a Florentine became wealthy in business or banking, Bernardo stood helpless, having talent neither for figures nor for trade.

Nor was his wife any shrewder, and her dowry, without which no marriage was conceivable to a Florentine of whatever station in life, was negligible. Madonna Bartolomea, daughter of Stefano Nelli, was equally well descended. Her family derived from the ancient counts of Borgonuovo and of Fucecchio who flourished in the tenth century, but like the Machiavellis now possessed only the rags of memory. Widow of Niccolo Benizzi, Bartolomea was a virtuous woman—*rara avis* in a generation in which chastity was a sort of perversion. Cultured and not without poetic talent, she composed verses and hymns, mostly to the Holy Virgin—who, according to the impious, is totally unconcerned with quality and is critical only of logic.

71

Fearing bankruptcy, Bernardo, holder of a law degree, obtained a job in the government as treasury official and consulting tax attorney. It was a position in which he discovered the duplicities and the craftiness of the House of Medici, Europe's vastest network of banks, but defeated and belittled, he learned to "know his place" and keep his mouth shut.

The Medici, rulers of Florence in all but name, would never have tolerated whispers of criticism, and adverse political opinions by one of their employees would have been fraught with the gravest peril. But why bother? Who in Florence was interested in honesty in private and rectitude in public? As for ideals—what were they but helpless lambs, devoured by the foxes of ruthless events? And idealists—who were they but ridiculous seekers of pearls in empty oyster shells?

Nevertheless, there was an imperishable tradition of liberty in Florence, such as no other city in all Italy quite possessed. Tyrants knew that the daggers of the Florentines were ever sharp and ever ready for use. Bernardo's own forebears preferring the rank of citizens to the luster of title, joined the *populani* —the bourgeosie—who often welcomed rebellions to break the stranglehold of those who abused power.

"It is natural for the Florentines to dislike every form of government and to find every occasion proper to create division among themselves . . . We know not how to endure servitude. . . . We can never rest content with any government, for we have never been able to agree upon how to live freely and we cannot submit to be slaves. . . . Florence is a city too greatly given to talk and one judges things here by their success, not by their merits. . . . And always the city is ungrateful toward her benefactors . . ." Thus will say later Bernardo's son Niccolò, one of her benefactors.

There would be more than one rebellion and chains would be soldered and broken again and again, but Bernardo was now interested in his growing family—two sons and two daughters. The second son made his entrance into the world on May 5, 1469. He had been preceded by his brother, Toto, six years earlier. Toto proved his worthlessness soon and died young, without issue. The two girls, by the very nature of femininity in the age of Christian chivalry, were rocks upon the neck of their disillusioned father and the perpetual consternation of their harassed mother.

The second boy, Niccolò, was born in the small three-story house which Bernardo had inherited from his ancestors. It was situated not far from the Ponte Vecchio in a narrow street later named Via Guicciardini—after him who in life had been a faithful friend of Niccolò and had a far more distinguished career than he—in life.

Francesco Guicciardini (1483–1540) was born in Florence of an illustrious and noble family. He graduated from the universities of Ferrara and Padua and his ambition was to enter the Church as a cardinal—an easy matter had his father allowed it. But his father would allow none of his five sons to become "members of so corrupt an institution."

Not that Francesco was religious. He was a man of the Italian Renaissance, whose fundamental philosophy was anti-Christian and scornful of all matters dealing with supra-terrestrial affairs. "The philosophers and theologians who write about supernatural and invisible things make a thousand senseless statements; because, in fact, men are in the dark in these matters and such inquiries serve rather as mental exercises than to discover the truth. . . . Speculation on supernatural matters, or anything which cannot be seen, is sheer idiocy."

To Guicciardini all the gold mines of Heaven were not worth a handful of Earth's dust. Life had mysteries, but he rejected preposterous fables explaining them, and faith was but the exchange of one ignorance for another.

Despite his philosophy and cynicism toward all things clerical, Guicciardini was the favorite of three popes, for his cold intellect and his ability to meet fraud with treachery and unravel plots and counterplots, suited their purposes. They offered him their highest offices—that of lieutenant-general of the papal army and the governorship of Romagna, Bologna, and other dominions. He was, in truth, the virtual ruler of the Papal States.

However, the twenty years that he served the Ecclesiastical Empire only aggravated his hatred for the Church, to whose temporal ambitions, he, like Machiavelli, attributed all the woes of Italy. "Where God's men thrive, the rest are bankrupt."

By his contemporaries, Guicciardini was considered cruel, venal, grasping, seeker after power and emoluments, and avaricious, for he said: "We must hold our money tightly, because a ducat in our purse brings us more honor than ten spent." But contemporaries are devoured by jealousy and envy and mold truth to soothe vanity.

At any rate, Guicciardini treated Machiavelli with cordiality and respect, and it is said that only in his company did he doff his armor of vigilance and gravity, and laughed. He welcomed Machiavelli's correspondence and in his latter years often invited him to his home.

Guicciardini's mind was subtler and better trained than that of Machiavelli. He did not entertain, for instance, the preposterous notion of signs and portents. "How happy are the astrologers who are believed if they tell one truth to a hundred lies, while other people lose all credit if they tell one lie to a hundred truths." He was more logical and more consistent. The world being what it is, he considered it a waste of time to try to reform it, "asking it to have a horse's legs when it has only those of an ass."

His relationships were the essence of diplomacy—then and always. "We must be frank so that when we resort to simulation people will be more likely to believe us, and as bad men are more numerous than good, it is well to believe little and trust less."

Not only the popes, but princes and kings considered Guicciardini the oracle of Europe. Charles V said: "In one moment I can create a hundred Spanish grandees, but in a hundred years not one single Guicciardini."

He weathered the tempests which raged over Italy for so

many years since he was willing and able "to roll stones" and do other unclean work required by his masters. He who does not bend cannot rise and he who wishes to rise very high must learn the crawling art of the worm.

His luck held out until three years before his death when, stripped of his powers and in disgrace, he retired to his villa. There he wrote his *Storia d'Italia,* a detailed account of Italy's plight from 1494 to 1534. For sheer intellectual power, the book is one of the most important works conceived by an Italian mind. With the objectivity of a physician performing an autopsy, he removes the diseased organs, examines, and records. He has neither likes nor dislikes, no indignation, no moral judgment, no prognosis for the fate of his country. He recognizes neither principles nor truths which are absolute and history, he concludes, is ever determined by self-interest. Peoples and armies are but the puppets for the real actors of the drama, who by violence, astuteness, deceit, and good fortune move them and use them for their own proper ends. From which it follows that they who fail are invariably in the wrong, and the stronger are also the virtuous, for they fix the scales of justice and propound the standards of morality.

Storia d'Italia is in twenty volumes, and had fate willed it, it might have had as tremendous an effect on men's minds as Machiavelli's work. But for three centuries the ten books which showed the true genius of Guicciardini lay buried in the family archives. When released, they could only be of interest to historians and to philosophers who know that if fortune only favored the most worthy, men would lose their chief source of consolation.

Florence is situated on the Arno River and whenever Pisa was part of its territory (for Pisa had a habit of rebelling and seeking independence) it had an excellent outlet to the sea and to the centers of the world. Four states surrounded it—Naples at the far south, the Papal States in the center, Milan to the northwest and Venice to the northeast. Of the four, the Papal

States, headed by vicars of the Church, were the worst misruled and the most miserable, while Venice was the richest and the strongest and unfortunately, the most aggressive.

"There are various opinions concerning the word Florentia, the original name of Florence," Machiavelli wrote. "Some suppose it to come from Florinus, one of the principal persons of the colony; others think it was preceded by the name of Fluentia, and suppose the word derived from *fluente,* or flowing of the Arno. . . . However derived, I think the name was always Florentia, and whatever the origin, it occurred under the Roman Empire, and began to be noticed in the times of the first emperor."

A later version of the name was Fiorenze, followed by the present one of Firenze, and to its modern inhabitants it means *La Città di Fiori*—"the city of flowers"—a name it richly deserves.

During the time of the Roman emperors merchants sailed on the River Arno and did business with the people of the valley. When, however, the Empire began to disintegrate, Florence was destroyed by Totila, king of the Ostrogoths. Two and a half centuries elapsed before it was rebuilt by Charlemagne, in the early part of the ninth century.

Time destroys gently, almost painlessly—leaves a pillar, a wall, a picture, paints a soft patina over a cracked roof. Man destroys maniacally, tears and burns and uproots and leaves no traces save those of savagery and torment.

From the reconstruction by Charlemagne until the year 1215, Florence participated in the fortunes and misfortunes of the descendants of Charles, then of the Berengarii, and lastly of the German emperors.

When the pontiffs acquired greater influence and the power of the German emperors was on the wane, the Florentines began to take sides—the Guelphs were for the pope and the Ghibellines for the emperor. For years the disastrous civil wars went on, bringing now one party to power, now the other, spreading misery among the deluded people, who are ever ready

to die when they have Caesars to hail. Yet, the ridden reach the
same destination as the riders, and it is often difficult to determine for whom the trip was undertaken—the riders or the
ridden.

At last the two factions laid aside—temporarily—their jealousies and the united Florentines began to formulate laws for
a free government. The method of governing was calculated to
remove the possibility of dictatorship and yet afford the ambitious a chance to wield some power and parade in lordly gait.
As order could not be preserved without force, the *Anziani*—
the "elders"—as the governors were called (equivalent to
"senators," whose meaning is also "elders," since age had not
yet become the object of vulgar contempt and puerile jest)
fashioned an army of citizens. The attitude toward the old was
still as Vergil wrote:

> And when they saw a man of grave aspect
> And full of virtue and of years,
> At once they all were hushed,
> And, listening, stood with eager ears.

"To give solemnity to this enterprise," Machiavelli wrote,
"they had a bell called Martinella, which was rung during a
whole month before the forces left the city, in order that the
enemy might have time for his defence; so great was the virtue
then existing among men, and with so much generosity of mind
were they governed, that as it is now considered a brave and
prudent act to assail an unprovided enemy, in those days it
would have been thought disgraceful, and productive of only a
fallacious advantage."

Yet, in another place, Machiavelli says: "Men ever praise
the olden time and find fault with the present, though often
without reason. They are such partisans of the past that they
extol not only the times which they know only by the accounts
left of them by historians, but having grown old themselves,
they also laud all they remember to have seen in their youth.
Their opinion is generally erroneous."

Thus, the Florentines established their freedom. "Nor is it possible to imagine the power and authority Florence in so short a time acquired. She became not only the head of Tuscany, but was enumerated amongst the first cities of Italy, and would have attained greatness of the most exalted kind, had she not been afflicted with the continual divisions of her citizens."

The tragi-comedy of one lordling grabbing power by chicanery and assassination only to be repaid in coin by another in a few months or a few years, pursued its vicious circle. The lower classes, discontented, rebelled—now successfully, now disastrously, always trying to keep some semblance of their liberty. Upon one occasion, one of the most daring of their leaders, in a harangue unique in the annals of demagoguery, urged them to take up arms and avenge themselves. "Be not deceived about that antiquity of blood by which they exalt themselves above us; for all men having one common origin, are equally ancient, and nature has made us all after one fashion. Strip us naked and we shall all be found alike. Dress us in their clothing, and they in ours, *we* shall appear noble, *they* ignoble, for poverty and riches make all the difference. . . . Neither shame nor conscience ought to have any influence with you. . . . Conquerors, by what means soever, are never considered aught but glorious . . . If you but notice human proceedings, you may observe that all who attain great power and riches make use of either fraud or force. Those who either from imprudence or want of sagacity avoid doing so, are always overwhelmed with servitude and poverty; for faithful servants are always servants, and honest men are always poor; nor do any escape from servitude but the bold and the faithless, or from poverty, but the rapacious and the fraudulent. . . . Men feed upon each other, and those who cannot defend themselves are devoured. . . . How often have I heard you complain of the avarice of your superiors and the injustice of your magistrates. Now is the time, not only to liberate yourselves from them, but to become so much superior that they will have more causes of grief and fear from you than you from them . . ."

Upon the tongue of the demagogue Utopia blossoms; in his purse it withers, and they rule best who are not in power.

This rebellion, by one of those fortuitous or even absurd incidents determining success or failure which Machiavelli so often found in human history, succeeded. Soon after, however, the people discovered that those whom they lifted upon their shoulders remained to ride upon their necks, and the new masters had to solve the problem of how many injustices make justice and how many lies make truth.

"Republican governments, more especially those imperfectly organized, frequently change their rulers and the form of their institutions; not by influence of liberty or subjection, but by that of slavery and license. . . . When, however, a good, wise, and powerful citizen appears (which is but seldom), who establishes ordinances capable of appeasing or restraining these contending dispositions . . . then the government may be called free and its institutions firm and secure; for having good laws for its basis and good regulations for carrying them into effect, it needs not, like others, the virtue of one man for its maintenance. . . . Tyranny cannot please the good; license is offensive to the wise. . . ."

Such a "good, wise, and powerful" citizen was Giovanni di Bicci de' Medici, who was instrumental in pacifying the factions by preaching (and practicing) moderation. "With regard to state affairs," he said to his son Cosimo on his deathbed, "if you would live in security, take just such a share as the laws and your countrymen think proper to bestow, thus you will escape both danger and envy; for it is not what is given to any individual, but what he has determined to possess, that occasions odium. . . ."

Giovanni died, regretted by everyone. And Machiavelli writes his eulogy: "He was compassionate. . . . He loved all; praised the good and pitied the infirmities of the wicked. . . . He loved peace and shunned war. . . . He never applied the public money to his own use, but contributed to the public wealth. . . . He died exceedingly rich in money, but still more in good fame and the best wishes of mankind. . . . And the wealth he left behind was not only preserved but increased by his son, Cosimo."

Cosimo—Piero—Lorenzo the Magnificent

Cosimo was a faithful son. His father's teachings took deep root in his soul and he achieved the optimum of education by making virtue more delectable than vice and knowledge more palatable than ignorance. And as a tribute to his teacher, he surpassed him.

Cosimo de' Medici was born in 1389 when the Western World was still partially feudal, kings and noblemen fighting one another for supremacy. Humanism was a vague dream in the minds of the learned and the Renaissance—the *Rinascimento*—was only a seed. But by the time Cosimo was fifty and the virtual ruler of Florence, the delicate hues of the new era were already visible on the horizon. And he was one of the men responsible for its advent.

Past master of the circuitous ways of business and banking, he became the richest man of his day and one of the most powerful. He possessed two and a half tons of fine gold and held in pawn castles of noblemen and of princes of the Church in England, Scotland, and Bohemia, while the Don of Castile pledged the jewels of his crown and the King of France guaranteed his loan with the incomes of provinces. "Cosimo de' Medici, Figli e Nepoti"—"Cosimo de' Medici, Sons and Nephews"—was the culmination of a mercantile and banking dynasty two centuries old, feared and honored in all the markets of the world, with branches in London, Paris, Tunis, Morocco, Greece, and Asia Minor.

Fluid money replaced most barter transactions and the far-flung banking centers with their public and long-term credits made possible the crystallization of the nations, particularly France and England. Italy, alas, was barely a name, and neither the genius of Cosimo, nor that of his descendants, nor that of the popes, nor that of Machiavelli, could make it a reality. It was, perhaps, poetic justice that Rome which had conquered and destroyed so many nations, should herself be conquered and destroyed, and that her fragments should be put together only when all the rest had been healed.

Under Cosimo's rule, Florence enjoyed a prosperity without equal. In the Piazza of the Mercato Nuovo—the New Market —there were a hundred bankbooths, although bankers like the Cosimos had their offices in great buildings in the city. But a century-old tradition required bankers to have seats and do their money changing in the Market. Here gold florins were weighed and locked in bags and the Florentine seal stamped upon them was an unquestioned guarantee of purity and honesty.

Cosimo encouraged builders and architects, and villas and palaces rose as if by magic in the city and the suburbs. The old wooden structures were torn down and edifices of stone and marble took their place. The rich became richer, and as a counterpoise, the poor became poorer, since prices for land and commodities galloped, while wages crawled. But the *miserabili,* bewildered by the splendors of the city, accepted their own wretchedness, for vanity is the manna upon which men feed and forget.

Florence became a world center for trade and industry, chief of which was the manufacturing of textiles. Her fame for beautiful and artistic creations spread to the four corners of the Earth. From Greece, Sardinia, Cyprus came wool for spinning. From the Middle East and China silks for embroidering. From England materials for dyeing and refining.

Between the Mercato Vecchio—the Old Market—and the Arno, bazaars were weighted with goods to tempt the most fastidious of "madonnas" and the most exacting of "messers," local and foreign. They flocked to Florence as centuries later they would flock to Paris, to buy the choicest of materials to be manufactured in the latest styles, for Florence dictated the sartorial fashions of Christendom.

While the textile industry was the most prominent—out of a population of one hundred thousand, two hundred manufacturers employed thirty thousand—other marvels were produced as well in brass and bronze, in gold and silver, and glassblowers competed with the rainbow in color and with the dew in fragility. Only when the mark upon the object indicated that its origin was in Via di Callimala, Florence, was it worthy of admiration—and of snobbism—in any part of the world.

The workers were organized in Guilds or *Arti* (Arts), since they considered themselves not merely laborers, but creators, and their long apprenticeship and family tradition gave them full rights to the title. The Guilds were divided into the *Greater Arts* and the *Lesser Arts*. The former were seven in number— lawyers, doctors, bankers, wood merchants, cloth merchants, silk merchants, and skinners and furriers. The latter—fourteen —butchers, blacksmiths, shoemakers, stone masons, woodcarvers, wine merchants, inn-keepers, tanners, saddlers, oil sellers, locksmiths, carpenters, and armorers. The Guilds demanded besides the necessary knowledge of the techniques of the trades and professions, entrance fees, and certificates of respectability and solvency.

Cosimo was a dictator, but being wise, he allowed the outward form of the Republic to continue, while from the counting-room of his bank, he pulled the strings that made the government function. And being generous, he aided businessmen in distress, noblemen who had lost their wealth in gambling or foolish investments, professionals on the verge of ruin because of usurious rates of interest, and he only regretted, he said, that God was not his debtor, too. Nor did he forget the poor maidens, who because of lack of dowry were in danger of spinsterhood. He established the *Monte delle Fanciulle*—Insurance for Girls—in which parents could pay premiums according to their financial capacity and be relieved of the perpetual nightmare of marriageable daughters moping around the house or finding their way to the nunnery or the brothel.

With an uncanny political sense, Cosimo, unlike most dictators, ancient and modern, did not persecute his foes, murder or imprison them. On the contrary, he salved their vanity by offering them posts, which although nominal in function, brought honors and remuneration. He felt instinctively what Niccolò Machiavelli would expound in his aphoristic logic: "Rulers should remember never to esteem a man so lightly that having heaped injuries and insults upon him, he will not seek to revenge himself, even at the risk of his own life. . . . You must bind men to you by benefits. . . . Never reduce them to the alternative of having either to destroy you or perish themselves."

Cosimo knew that no society could subsist without jealousy, envy, hate. Only their unbalanced proportion to other emotions made them evil and dangerous. Aristocrat by blood and instinct, Cosimo found it unnecessary to strut or dazzle with robes golden-laced and studded with jewels. His very simplicity of manner and speech made his nobility more evident. Whenever possible, he avoided pompous sessions in the Palace of the Signoria, the seat of government. He neither boasted nor asked for praise and applause for his successes.

Aware that no hammer is mighty enough to break the gossamer webs of tradition and custom in which men are enmeshed, Cosimo respected, or pretended to respect (for he believed in the power and magic of appearances) the vanities, the credulities and the absurd habits of his people. "It is not essential that a Prince should have all the good qualities," Machiavelli will say, "but it is essential that he should *seem* to have them. . . . I will even venture to affirm that if he has and invariably practices the good qualities, they are hurtful, whereas the *appearance* of having them is useful."

Thus without scepter or miter, Cosimo ruled a community of unruly men, and without violence won over both the simple and the subtle and removed the fear of death and exile, the usual solution to the political problems of the Republic prior to his coming to power.

For generations the patricians of Florence combined their genius for business with their passion for culture—a passion which percolated to the bourgeoisie, and made an impression upon the common illiterate folk.

They were aware of the fact that riches fit fools as crowns fit asses. They did not seek knowledge for the sake of knowledge, but knowledge for the sake of living. Knowledge, culture, science, poetry—these intensified joy, both of the spirit and of the flesh. "We love unmixed colors, lights, voices, the gleam of gold, the whiteness of silver, learning, and the soul," wrote Marsilio Ficino, famous Platonist.

In the year 1453 a great tragedy befell the Christian world— the Ottoman Turks captured the mighty city of Constantinople and Mohammedans henceforth were to share the lands of Europe destined only, by divine decree, to be owned and raped by the worshipers of the God who died upon the cross that men might have peace. For centuries thereafter the Christian nations tried to wrench the Metropolis out of the bloody claws of the Camel Driver's descendants, but to no avail, until at last the city lost both power and prestige and was even demoted from its rank of the capital of the nation.

But there is no disaster in human affairs. Every disaster is someone's long awaited opportunity. The Greek scholars from Byzantium grabbed whatever books and manuscripts they could save from the holocaust and wended their way by water and by land, on horse, donkey or *per pedes apostolorum* to the cities of the West. Never had refugees been laden with more precious possessions or been received with greater honor and joy. One did not have to be a scholar of distinction to become the revered guest of palace or court or hall of learning. Merely to know how to read and write the tongue of Aristotle and Plutarch was an international passport and visa.

Cosimo rebuilt the crumbling monastery of San Marco to install there the finest library of the Western World. He paid for Roman and Greek manuscripts their weight in gold. And now began a most ferocious and unprecedented warfare among the wealthy families of Florence for the possession of books hidden in the coffers of ruined churches and buried in the debris of forlorn cities. Our urge to acquire things is due less to the passion to possess them than to the vanity of feeling superior to those who envy our possession of them. And what we have not poisons what we have.

So angered was Cosimo de' Medici at Strozzi, a member of as ancient and at times almost as influential a family as his own, for outfitting an expedition to Constantinople in order to bring the first copy of Aristotle's *Politics,* that violating his own principles, he banished him from the Republic.

Humanism had now taken firm root in Florence and San Marco became the center for the meeting of scholars from all parts of the world. Here they found a congenial atmosphere, and relieved of worries, could pursue their studies and promulgate the philosophy of the classic masters—a philosophy of moderation and resigned stoicism to a city which was a cauldron of emotions, unrestrained and violent, and prone to accept only a distorted Epicureanism.

From Florence swiftly radiated to all Europe the magnificent culture that had been hibernating for so many centuries and mingled with it her own fresh and resplendent achievements in all the arts and sciences. And it was the *Rinascimento*—the Renaissance—the Rebirth. Always man hopes that the past was but a rehearsal for the new great drama in which he would play his grand role. Now all values were in the balance, and neither sanctity nor privilege would save from perdition the false and the futile. No more asceticism, no more self-abnegation, no more fear of hell, no more languishing for heaven. *Mors acerba, fama perpetua*—"Death is bitter, but fame is everlasting." That became the motto of the day. Transfer all

the goods to Earth. Man was Adam again—a new Adam—
spurning Eden with its thundering overlord and its hissing rep-
tile—Man hailing the Earth—the Earth upon which he would
walk, unfettered, fearless, proud—molder of his own destiny.

And all the nations—France, Germany, England, Holland—
acknowledged that the small Tuscan city was the resurrected
Athens of her days of glory, mistress without peer of the new
civilization.

No matter what road we take, or how circuitous; no matter
how we hasten our step, or how we slacken it, we reach our
grave at the scheduled hour. We need neither guide nor passport, and everyone pronounces "shibboleth" correctly and
passes the sentinel. And the scheduled time for Cosimo de'
Medici came in the year 1464, when he was seventy-five, an age
comparable to that of the Biblical patriarchs, when one considers the vicissitudes and the perils of his career and the slender
life expectancy of his contemporaries.

Life, the gracious Hostess of Mortals, knowing that her favorite guest, Cosimo, had to leave before long, made his final
years so miserable that he would not regret his departure too
grievously. His son, Giovanni, the apple of his eye, died. He
himself became an invalid, tormented by a variety of pains.
Forced to look on helplessly at the inevitable decay of his fortune and the destruction of his beloved city—the former due to
his descendants and his agents; the latter to her citizens, vain
and greedy—he shut his eyes even before the fingers of Death
drew their lids, and refused to open them again upon the iniquitous world.

In his latter years, Cosimo, unafraid, had often spoken of
death. At San Marco, where he used to take refuge from the
burdens of state and bank, he would listen to Marsilio Ficino
and Argiropulo, one of the most erudite men of the time whom
he had brought from Greece to instruct the youth in Hellenic
literature, speak of Socrates and his final, glorious hours. In a

sense, he too had drunk hemlock, for was not every man condemned to death? To think only of life and not of death is an
infantile burying of the head in the pillow, fearful of the
shadows at the window. It would destroy all our past, consign to
oblivion every beautiful relationship that once was ours, remove
all measurements of value and explain a fugitive world in terms
of a congealed lump, without history, without a future.

"He died at the zenith of his glory," Machiavelli wrote, "and
in the enjoyment of the highest renown. The city and all the
Christian princes, condoled with his son, Piero, for his loss. His
funeral was conducted with the utmost pomp and solemnity, the
whole city following his corpse to the tomb in the Church of
Saint Lorenzo, on which by public decree, he was inscribed
PATER PATRIAE—father of his country.

"If, in speaking of Cosimo," Machiavelli continues, "I have
rather imitated the biographies of princes than general history,
it need not occasion wonder; for of so extraordinary an individual I was compelled to speak with unusual praise."

The four years during which Piero, son of Cosimo, ruled
Florence were replete with treachery, tumult, and anxiety. Foes
of the Medici who had been unable to cope with the father, were
now conspiring to take revenge by ruining his son, both as politician and as banker, and more than once they almost succeeded
in assassinating him.

Piero was an honorable man, but neither his virtue nor his
goodness were appreciated by his countrymen, who had too long
been kept in restraint, and needed to spill blood and destroy
property. He fought back bravely, though paralyzed and barely
capable of moving any part of his body except his head.

We could bear the cruelties of nature with equanimity if to
them were not added the cruelties of man. And Piero, finally,
weary of the perpetual struggle, expired at the age of fifty-three.
Placated by his death, the Florentines buried him with all the
pomp and solemnity due his exalted station and their own sting-

ing conscience, near his father, in the Church of Saint Lorenzo.

Our death brings hope to our competitors, comfort to our enemies, gifts to our inheritors, profit to the undertaker. Thus the passing of a man, like that of all good animals, is not without its utility, and should offer comfort to the dead and be as a last sacrament with humanity.

The ambitious noblemen began once again to plot, and to achieve their aggrandizement, they were ready to destroy that which they wished to possess. But the world exists because people thwart one another's intentions.

In a most remarkable chapter, Machiavelli analyzes the varieties of conspiracies. "Subjects," he says, "cannot undertake more foolhardy and more perilous enterprises than conspiracies, which are in every respect most difficult, and dangerous; and thence it is that, though so often attempted, they so rarely attain the desired object. . . . There is danger in the plotting and the execution of the plot, and even after it has been carried out. . . . Such are the majesty and reverence that ordinarily surround the person of a prince, that it may easily mitigate the fury of the murderer, or fill him with fear. . . . A man who has a guilty conscience readily thinks that everybody speaks of him. . . ."

And thus it happened that the plot to kill Giuliano and Lorenzo, the two sons of Piero, and drive the Medici out of Florence, failed, except for the death of Giuliano. How Guiliano would have ruled the city had he lived, it is impossible to say, nor can one surmise whether the two brothers would have been content each with half of the patrimony and the powers, or following the example of the first two brothers, Cain and Abel, one would have exterminated the other.

By his firmness, intelligence, and eloquence, Lorenzo extirpated his foes and won the populace to his side. He became the sole ruler of Florence and his reign was the most glamorous of its annals, comparable to that of the oriental despot, Solomon, King of the Jews, and the occidental autocrat, Louis XIV, King of the French.

Lorenzo—quite properly nicknamed *Il Magnifico*—"the Magnificent"—inherited one of the largest fortunes ever to fall into the hands of a descendant. One generation garners and the next squanders, and Lorenzo, no longer the banker but the prince, despised every manifestation of business and set himself to scatter the gold as if his coffers were the sun and the florins the rays eternally pouring upon the earth. Yet, during the decade and a half that he was master of the city, there was internal peace, and the gaiety, the brilliance, the magnificent works of art created by his generosity and encouragement, were never equaled.

His palace in Via Larga was open to all who showed even a modicum of talent in any of man's endeavors—poetry, philosophy, science, painting, sculpture, mathematics. There was not, as at the Court of Versailles two centuries later, the stiff etiquette, the perpetual obeisance, the fictitious awe. Free and easy, the guests argued and expounded their theories, read their poetry, presented plans for new edifices.

But desire was followed by extravagance with increasing intensity in Lorenzo's career. Everything—palaces, gardens, jewels, paintings, statues, books—rare and precious and coveted by others, had to become Medicean. Nothing was too expensive. Nothing must be inaccessible. And for the populace, carnivals such as dreams alone concoct. Always *panem et circenses*— bread and circuses. Make them shout "Long live Lorenzo!" and stifle the voices which warn of disaster and misery. All the Caesars, the good and the bad, in all ages, have known this trick of the trade.

"Now arose many of those evils which usually result from peace," said Machiavelli, "for the youth having become more dissolute than before, more extravagant in dress, feasting, and licentiousness, and being without employment, wasted their time and means on gaming and women; their principal study being how to appear splendid in apparel, and attain a crafty shrewdness in discourse. . . ."

There are periods in history in which the people imitate the follies of their leaders; there are periods in which the leaders imitate the follies of their people. But where is it recorded that leaders and people imitate the virtues of each other?

"He enjoyed much favor both from fortune and from the Almighty," Machiavelli carves Lorenzo's epitaph in the stone of history. "All his enterprises were brought to a prosperous termination. . . . His skill, prudence, and fortune were acknowledged with admiration not only by the princes of Italy, but by those of distant lands. . . . In council he was eloquent and acute, wise in determination, and prompt and resolute in execution. Nor can vices be alleged against him to sully so many virtues; though he was fond of women, pleased with the company of facetious and satirical men, and amused with the games of the nursery, more than seemed consistent with so great a character; for he was frequently seen playing with his children and partaking of their infantine sports; so that whoever considers this gravity and cheerfulness, will find united in him dispositions which seem almost incompatible with each other. In his later years, he was greatly afflicted; besides the gout, he was troubled with excruciating pains in the stomach, of which he died in April, 1492, in the forty-fourth year of his life; nor was there ever in Florence, or even in Italy, one so celebrated for wisdom, or for whose loss such universal regret was felt. As from his death the greatest devastation would shortly ensue, the heavens gave many evident tokens of its approach; among other signs, the highest pinnacle of the Church of Santa Reparata was struck with lightning and a great part of it thrown down, to the terror and amazement of every one. The citizens and all the princes of Italy mourned for him and sent their ambassadors to Florence to condole with the city on the occasion; and the justness of their grief was shortly after apparent. . . . Evil plans began to germinate, which in a little time ruined Italy and continue to keep her in desolation."

Thus ends the incomparable career of Lorenzo de' Medici;
also the incomparable *Istorie Fiorentine,* the last book from the
pen of Niccolò Machiavelli.

Niccolò Machiavelli

When Lorenzo died, Niccolò Machiavelli was twenty-three
years old—almost middle-aged considering the life expectancy
of his time. Although he was to write so flatteringly of the
Magnificent One many years later, he had never belonged to
the inner circle of the illuminati and may never have even passed
through the gates of the palace. It was not because of his youth,
for there were among the habitués men of tenderer age, as for
instance, Pico della Mirandola, who died at thirty-one—"illustrious in poetry, philosophy, architecture, music, eloquent in
several languages, eminent in all the qualities of the intellect, as
lovable in character as handsome in person."

Niccolò had to reach double his present age before he would
show glimpses of the genius he possessed, and which would
never have matured and been consummated save by the largess
of Fortune in the guise of tragedy and disgrace, and by Life's
irrevocable command that wisdom must be gathered from
thorns.

Il Machia, as his boon companions called him affectionately
(for despite the malicious reputation, Niccolò was well liked by
men and women—the simple and the disinherited), was at this
time a middle-sized man with a rather small head and aquiline
nose, dark-haired, lean, and pale. Two things might have indicated (if there is a relationship between appearance and spirit)
the inner genius—his eyes and his mouth—his eyes black and
penetrating, and his lips thin and tight. Eventually, he would
delve into the soul of man and would utter the bitter and vile
things he discovered there. He would utter them using a pen
dipped into indelible and phosphorescent ink, which would so

scare the pious of the Land across the Channel that they nicknamed the Devil "Old Nick." But while their abracadabra
could exorcise Beelzebub of Hades, their logic was no match
for Niccolò of Florence, and he remained in the body politic of
that nation for all time.

What had Niccolò Machiavelli done with his twenty-three
years? He lived like other young men of his day, worked and
frolicked—worked as little as possible and frolicked as much
as the purse allowed. He was not distinguished in any way. So,
at least, it seems, for no contemporary found him interesting
enough to mention him in a book or even in correspondence. And
those who survived him remembered him only as he had been in
maturity. He himself, in the solitude of exile, never reminisced
about his youth.

> Nessun maggior dolore
> Che recordarsi del tempo felice
> Nella miseria.

There is "no greater pain than recalling the time of happiness
in misfortune," ruminated Dante.

The time of happiness, or at least of serenity and resignation,
for Machiavelli was not his early manhood. It was the middle
period when he was active in the affairs of state and labored
for a strong and independent Florence.

He started his education in the narrow, muddy streets near
Ponte Vecchio, where he first saw the light of day. His play-
mates were tough and wild, as he, too, had to be. They witnessed
cruel and ugly deeds—murders, robberies, rapes. And some of
them became members of the *sbirri,* gangs of organized criminals, terrorizing communities and hiring themselves to blot out
individuals. The streets, unpoliced, unlit, were shattered by the
shrieks of victims and the laughter of thugs, and the Arno
River, when its waters were high, carried off many a corpse,
with or sans head. Simple murder, while profitable, procured
little pleasure.

The extraordinary vitality of the Florentines demanded relief in vast creations, in tumultuous dissipation, in revolutions futile and absurd, in the swift plunging of daggers, in the meticulous torture of foes.

The boys, without the calming perspective of years and events, were more cruel, more vicious, more relentless than their elders. They begged and stole and mocked those who dared chase them or admonish them. Yet, strangely, but inevitably, out of this morass blossomed men of talent and integrity, patriots, scholars, and "gentlemen," according to the definition of Baldassare Castiglione (1478–1529), author of *Il Cortegiano* —"The Courtier."

Castiglione, himself a *cortegiano* and writer at the Court of Pope Leo X, set forth the requirements of a true "gentleman" —nobility of ideas, physical prowess, spiritual courage—which generations of men in all the Western World accepted as their standard of conduct, though often violated and misinterpreted. Still, it is better to have a target to aim at even if men rarely hit the bull's-eye, than to shoot into empty air.

The tortuous, narrow streets, the cruel and nasty episodes, the language of the gutter—all the symbols of implacable reality—entered into Niccolò's eyes, his nose, his mouth, his soul, and never forsook him wherever he traveled, at whatever age of his career. We always carry with us our roots, the mud of our passions, and the fertilizer of our prejudices, and although we move about, we are essentially as fixed as the world of plants. Yet, the roots of our being rest far deeper than we imagine and are fed by streams whose waters we never hear.

What Niccolò's formal education was, whether he was a dull, listless pupil, or a brilliant one, what his early ambitions were, we shall never know. He did learn Latin and was deeply interested in Roman history. Greek he probably never learned, for he was already a grown man when it became fashionable to know the language, and he never became a true Humanist. He did not study music, architecture or painting, and when he met Michelangelo and Raphael, they seemed shadows of an undiscovered world. He was, as Aristotle spoke of man in general, a political animal. Not in the sense of desiring power, but of understanding power and its vast ramifications—social structure, war, peace, justice, wealth, poverty—unadorned and unlacquered.

"Machiavelli," wrote the contemporary historian, Varchi, "is not a *letterato*—"a man of letters"—but rather a man without literary culture." Perhaps so. Yet Machiavelli was to write the best history of Florence, the best Italian comedy of the century, the profoundest political tracts for many centuries, and no one, save Boccaccio, exercised upon the Italian language as great and as good an influence.

His parents, as it often happens, were of two minds as to what their son's role in life should be. Madonna Bartolomea subtly tried to inculcate religion and persuade him to become a priest. Ah, how wonderful it would be to offer as sacrifice her son to the Great Madonna to whom she had composed so many hymns of adoration! Among the benefits she would derive, including that of entrance to Heaven, would be the salvation of her husband from the eternal fires of Hell, because of his anticlerical vituperations and his mockery of Christianity.

Alas, poor mater, Niccolò was his father's son, and in the streets of Florence youngsters heard only maledictions against the black-robed, who often found it hazardous to walk unarmed. As Niccolò would write: "Whilst the popes caused all the West to tremble with their censures, the people of Italy were in open rebellion against them; nor had they or the popes any other purpose, but deprive each other of reputation and authority. . . . Nor can there be greater proof of the decadence of religion than to witness the fact that the nearer people are to the Church of Rome, the less religious they are. . . . The evil example of the Court of Rome has destroyed all piety and religion in Italy. . . ."

Pope Alexander VI, for instance, a Spaniard of the rare fair type, a magnificent physical specimen, "one who loves life and has a joyous nature," forsook the Christians, became a "Greek" and claimed the title of *Il Formoso*—"the handsome one," the well-rounded man—the man without benefit of God or His Only Begotten Son.

Or Pope Leo X, who laughed: "What profit has not the fable of Christ brought us!" Yet, in his *Bull Honestis,* February 15, 1521, he ordered the excommunication of any official and the suspension of all religious services in any locality refusing to execute without examination the sentences of the Inquisitors, or turn over to the Church the property of the condemned—"which was the chief objective."

Messer Bernardo, Niccolò's father, wished him to become a lawyer. A man, he believed should have a profession—even a trade—something to fall back upon in days of need, something tangible, something that had a definite and recognizable appellation. I am a doctor or a blacksmith or a saddler or a lawyer— I am a member of the Guild—of the "Greater Arts" or the "Lesser Arts." He did not approve of those, who because they had written a poem or painted a picture or translated a sonnet from the Greek, found bed and board and a purse of florins in Lorenzo's palace, considered themselves, therefore, set for life and candidates for immortality. They were deluded fools. A favorite's splendor had no greater solidity than a drop of dew upon which the morning sun shines for an hour and one mistakes it for a precious gem that neither hammer nor time can crumble.

But of all the professions law was the most honorable, he said. If a jurist was faithful to the hierarchy of the government (as any prudent man should be), he had the opportunity of climbing the ladder from one office in the State to another, higher and higher. And there were also occasions to gain something on the side—people always getting into trouble and the law offering convenient loopholes. And one must never forget that among dishonest men honesty is not a weapon of defence, and who, pray, was honest in Florence? When counterfeit is honored on the Exchange, it is dangerous to present legal tender.

Niccolò wished to be neither priest nor lawyer, and it is not recorded that he had ever submitted a poem to the Magnifico or that he ever petitioned that he be permitted to flourish in his luminous shadow. He did write poetry, however, at various times in his career—*Capitoli,* for example, moralistic pieces on "Opportunity," "Ambition," "Ingratitude," and in the manner of the day, *Stanze* and *Canzoni*—sonnets and carnival songs. They were sometimes lascivious or bantering, at other times allegorical, but generally speaking, rather arid.

Machiavelli lacked the imagination, the sensitivity, the spontaneity, required of a veritable poet. Logician and critic, he was the man of mind, rather than of heart, and he needed the freedom and fluidity of prose to express his ideas. He became Italy's greatest *prosateur* of the Renaissance, unconscious of form, therefore the master of form.

Whether there were noisy scenes between father, mother, and son, or recriminations between husband and wife, we do not know, since Niccolò never wrote about his family. This might be interpreted in various ways: that he was too indignant and disgusted, or too ashamed and abased, or that the family life of the Machiavellis was the normal type—worthy neither of excessive anger nor of special eulogy—the two passions which prompt men to unburden their souls in print.

Whatever the answers or arguments Niccolò offered his *genitori,* it must be assumed that they were those of a spirited youth who would not be swayed in his determination. And maybe Messer Bernardo, himself so long humbled by adverse circumstances, felt a secret joy at this manifestation of pride— noble blood reasserting itself in the veins of his descendant. As for Madonna Bartolomea, accustomed to male perversity, sought—and no doubt found—surcease in secret tears and the composition of more poems to the Virgin Mother, who herself may have had difficulties on Earth with her Joseph, husband and putative father.

The death of Lorenzo opened Pandora's box of misfortunes for Florence. Never again would she know peace, and the glory

and prosperity which made her—a tiny principality—the ornament of Italy and the guiding star of the nations beyond the
Alps, would rapidly dwindle and wither and leave her lusterless
and bankrupt.

Whether another Lorenzo, or another Cosimo, could have
prevented the catastrophes that befell the Republic, is merely
a problem in academics. Does the leader determine the course
of history, or is he but a symbol, the recording tablet of the
events, fateful and without remedy? Is a man—or a nation—
under the total sway of Fortune or Fate? "Fortune is the mistress of but half of our actions, leaving the control of the other
half, or a little less, to ourselves. Men may aid Fortune, but
not withstand her; they may weave her webs, but not break
them. . . . I would compare her to an impetuous river that,
when turbulent, inundates the plains, casts down trees and
buildings, removes earth from one side, and places it on the
other; everyone flees before it, and everything yields to its
fury without being able to oppose it; and yet though it is of
such a kind, still when it is quiet, men can make provision against
it by banks and dykes, so that when it rises it will either go into
a canal or its rush will not be so wild and dangerous. . . . The
power that governs us ordains that nothing under the sun is
stable, or ever will be. . . . Thus it is, and was, and shall be in
all eternity, ordained that evil succeed good and good succeed
evil, and that one be always the cause of the other. . . . But
men should never despair on that account; for not knowing the
aims of Fortune, which she pursues by dark and devious ways,
men should always be hopeful, and never yield to despair, whatever troubles may befall them, or in whatever straits they may
be."

On the philosophic seesaw, Niccolò Machiavelli propounds
now free will, now determinism, now predestination, and offers
at last only the pitiable gift of hope—deceiver and betrayer of
man. Christian theology, Renaissance sophistry, classic stoicism,
and vulgar common sense, all become entangled in his tapestry

of morality. And still, unable to decide, he pursues his weaving.

"Fortune's greatest power arises from man's incapacity to modify his own nature." He says it also in verse:

> E non potendo tu cangiar persona,
> nè lasciar l'ordin de che il ciel ti dota,
> nel mezzo del cammin la t'abbandona.

"And being unable to change thy nature, or to give up the disposition that heaven has given thee, in the middle of thy road she [Fortune] will abandon thee."

One more design—the most important, the most prominent of all, determining the quality and the validity of the entire web. This, however, is reserved for men aflame with virtue— virtue as the Romans understood it—not humility or gentleness or peace, but virility, manliness, courage, vigor, vision, ambition, and even unscrupulousness.

"I hold this to be the truth, that it is better to be impetuous than cautious, because Fortune is a woman, and to keep her in submission it is necessary to beat her and ill-use her. . . . And always like a woman, she favors the young, because they are less scrupulous, and fiercer, and master her with greater audacity."

But where was there such a young man in Florence—one so imbued with *virtù,* that he could reverse the course of Fate for the Republic—overcoming the evil which inevitably follows the good, and mastering the woman—the whore—Fortune? A man capable of *agere et pati fortia*—doing and suffering greatly?

Pietro, Lorenzo's son and heir, was as little interested in statesmanship as his father had been in banking. Thus one generation is traduced by the next and every generation is the broken hope of the preceding one.

Befogged by wine and dizzied with the pleasures of Eros, Pietro was unaware of the vertiginous pace at which things were changing all about him. He felt the perfumed zephyr of the courtiers' flattery, but did not hear the angry winds blown by his foes. He wished neither glories of art nor glories of war.

Sufficient unto the day to him were both the evil and the magnificence thereof. He meant to disturb no one; why should anyone wish to disturb him? What did he ask of life save tranquility, the asylum of his palace, and the cheer of his little harem?

Alas, poor Pietro, he did not know that "when Princes devote themselves to pleasure rather than to arms, they lose their dominions." Nor did he realize that the sword is faithful only to the hand that wields it, and his hand had dropped it. Yet, he was not alone in Florence in discarding the sword. Those who had been under his father's influence—artists, thinkers, aristocrats of the mind, Humanists—the glittering archipelago of intellect—despised violence and considered war vulgar murder without honor and without profit. They derided the barbarian nations—Spain, France, England, and the Turkish canaille—madmen driven by atavistic passions, doomed to self-destruction.

"I do not hold it my duty to die for a citizen of my city, not even for two or three. Least of all do I consider it my duty to suffer death for the sum of all the citizens whom I do not know and who mean nothing to me." So said Valla, the historian of the day and his words were gist and essence of the philosophy of his circle. And if the barbarians knocked at the gates of the city, give them gold and send them off. Gold blinds the fool and the wicked.

There was in this renunciation of force an unconscious regression to the Christian teaching which they had discarded, since the lords of the Church, in truth, discarded it also and were acting like the barbarians whom they despised. They considered mankind the only God and every man its prophet. But by the immutable circularity of all things, the most sophisticated men of any generation, past or future, had reached the same conclusion as the ingenuous carpenter of Nazareth.

Niccolò Machiavelli belonged to no clique and seemed totally uninterested in the political scene. But he was an oak and needed

much sun and much rain and many tumultuous storms before
reaching his predestined height and girt. He himself was surely
unaware of his arboreal condition, and would have laughed uproariously had a resurrected Pollarus, guardian of the sacred
fowls of the Roman Republic which he was to glorify, read in
the feeding of the chickens his extraordinary career.

In later years, however, he would not have laughed, not because he would be more convinced about his own immortality,
but because he was of the opinion that the system of auguries
was the cause of the prosperity of the Roman Republic. "It
pleases them to deride these religious practices," Machiavelli
quotes Livy, whom he considered the wisest and greatest of
historians, "for they care not whether the fowls eat or whether
they come out slowly out of their cages. . . . These are trifles
to them, but such small matters are not to be contemned, for it
is by their strict observance that our ancestors made this republic great." And as a commentary, Machiavelli pursues: "In
truth there never was any remarkable lawgiver amongst any
people who did not resort to divine authority. . . . The wise
politician will always respect religion, even if he have no belief
in it, since there have been frequent proofs that through incul-
cating it, even by craft, much valor has been aroused. . . . The
Romans, either by good faith or by calculation, always enforced
respect for religion, and found their profit therein. . . . And
as Seneca, the Philosopher, has said, 'Religion is regarded by
the common people as true; by the wise as false; by the rulers as
useful.' "

Indeed, the ruler who is a disbeliever is apt to carry greater
conviction. The believer may have doubts and scruples and the
people quickly detect the undertones and waver; the disbeliever,
however, knows all the arguments, does not waver in orthodoxy
and is solidly entrenched in his fortress of hypocrisy against
which no cannon prevails. Naturalness is affectation's most cunning disguise, and the shrewd one molds his face to fit his mask.

"The Church by not knowing how to be *properly* hypocritical, destroyed religion. . . . St. Francis and St. Dominic by restoring the principles of the Gospel, brought about evil, in declaring it wrong to speak ill of others and right to obey even wicked prelates, leaving it to God to chastise them, thus assisting them to do the worst they can. . . . Our religion has promised blessedness rather to the humble than to active men. It has made the highest good contempt for earthly things, demanding strength in suffering and not in mighty deeds. . . . This manner of life has weakened the world and made it a prey to evildoers."

And the misfortune and the disunity of Italy, Machiavelli will attribute to the popes. "It will be seen how the popes, first with censures and afterwards with these and arms, mingled with indulgences, became both terrible and venerable; and how, from having abused both, they ceased to possess any influence, and were wholly dependent on the will of others for assistance in their wars." And the others came as friends and stayed as foes, and Italy became the dumping grounds of Europe.

Niccolò had not yet articulated these matters, but in the coffers of his memory he stored up countless incidents that he had witnessed proving that success came by dissemblance, mendacity, guile, perversion, and perfidy, while truth, honesty, sincerity, fidelity were stumbling blocks, which often, as in his own case, brought disaster and secular infamy.

At this juncture of his career, however, Niccolò felt surfeited with Bohemianism (although his taste for pleasure remained always and he would bring zest and practiced skill to "the band," making him indispensable) and he sought to establish himself as a serious citizen of the Republic.

Luckily, his former teacher, Marcello di Virgilio de'Adriani, recently appointed one of the chief officers of the Florentine Court of Chancery, was in need of a secretary and offered him the job. Niccoló showed himself punctilious in the fulfillment of his duties and his steadfastness was rewarded five years later, when his employer recommended him to the Chancery of the Second Court. Within one month, he was promoted as Second

Chancellor and Secretary of the "Ten of Liberty and Peace." For fourteen years he held the post, and much water and much blood flowed under the bridges of Florence during that time.

Exit the Medici—Enter Savonarola— City of God Turns to Ashes

With political astuteness Lorenzo allied himself to Naples and Milan. Thus safe on the north and the south, he could keep at bay Venice and the Pope, both jealous of the fame of Florence and greedy for her wealth. Particularly jealous was the Borgian, Alexander VI, who yearned to become master of all Italy and who hated the Medicis, their arrogance, and their achievements.

However, new enemies, far more powerful and far more dangerous were about to stalk across the land, bury fangs and claws into it and suck its marrow, never letting loose, century after century, until it was but a carcass, awaiting the miracle of resurrection.

It is the inexorable logic of history that the weak will succumb to the strong. Italy was fragmented, while France, England, Spain, and the Hapsburg Empire were becoming solidified, and power seeks more power and will tolerate no equal. One World —that has been the ambition of every Caesar—not for the sentimental reason of brotherhood, but for security and permanence. For there is neither security nor permanence when a rival exists or conditions are such that he may burgeon forth. Therefore, suppress—exterminate—ravage—annihilate whatever is dangerous or may become dangerous. Invent enemies and crush them, that friends may take warning.

Futile malignity. No empire, however vast shall ever achieve this dominance; no Caesar, however mighty, shall have arms wide enough to embrace and crush the globe. All things that live in time and space shall never know permanence or security,

and immortality exists only for things unconsummated and unborn—seeds forever asleep.

Extraordinary events were taking place in all parts of the
world, but the reins of Florence were still in the flaccid hands of
Pietro and the citizens were still dozing in the retreating sun of
the late Lorenzo. *Carpe diem*—rejoice today, for tomorrow
you may die. But if tomorrow you still live? Does not God take
care of the little sparrow? Perhaps. But of man? Hearken to
the words of Niccolò Machiavelli:

> Creder che senza te per te contraste
> Dio, stanoti ozioso e ginocchioni,
> Ha molti regeri e molti stati guasti.

"The belief that by kneeling idly thou canst leave all to God
has brought many kingdoms and states to ruin."
And further:

> Ma non sia di si poco cervello
> Che creda se la sua casa reveria,
> Che Dio da salvi senz' altro puntello.

"Let no man be so senseless as to think that if his house fall,
he can leave it to God to save him."

Oh, thou drab little sparrow, how much trouble thou hast
brought to man! Go to, devour his fields, but cease thy pious
teaching!

There was, for instance, that Quixotic voyage to prove that
the earth being round, one could reach the fabulous land of
India more safely and more swiftly by sailing westward than by
trudging overland eastward. Undertaken by a valorous Italian
forced to seek the subsidy of Spain, the adventure brought neither glory nor wealth nor a vast empire to his fatherland but
rather to the foe of his fatherland, to His Most Christian Majesty, Ferdinand of Aragon. To that king, whom Machiavelli
later chose, among the legion of evil rulers, to prove that power
is won by violence and rascality, and whom he offered as model
to a weak and inexperienced prince for the purpose of uniting
Italy.

"Ferdinand," Machiavelli says, "king of a torn land, mounted a shaky throne and with the money of the Church and of the people, always under the cloak of religion, with a shamelessness which was unparalleled, first drove the Jews from his kingdom, created an army with their money, and devoted himself with pious cruelty to making war on Africa, invading Italy and finally attacking France, thereby keeping the minds of his subjects in suspense and admiration. . . . And he always preached peace and good faith. . . . My fellow citizens want a preacher who will show them the way to paradise. I want to find one that will show them the way to the Devil. I want to find a base liar and hypocrite, for to find the true path to paradise one must know the way to hell, and then avoid it."

The new roads no longer led to Rome, but to the great cities which but recently were uncharted villages, while famed old towns were snubbed and by-passed and allowed to tumble into ruin and flounder in misery.

And presently the thunderous oratory of a truculent monk by the name of Martin Luther, would shake the foundations of the mighty Church of the West that called herself Catholic or Universal, despite the challenge of the Church of the East, and would cleave her and bring about changes in human attitudes as radical as the discovery of paper and the printing press.

Another of those who would swallow the Earth was the twenty-four year old hunchback King of France, Charles VIII. Because he bore the same name as his ancestor, who seven centuries previously called himself Roman Emperor and who survived in history as Charlemagne or Charles the Great, he was certain that he, too, would achieve that eminence.

Charles was a romantic youth with a variety of ambitions—reforming and purifying the Church, converting the heathens to Christianity, driving the unspeakable Turk into the murky waters of the Black Sea. Upon his royal flags he had embroidered: "God's Will"—"Emissary of God."

When men invoke God there is often the Devil to pay, and triumphant Messiahs come riding on scapegoats.

To begin his career, Charles laid dynastic claim to Naples and prepared to invade it. In need of allies and money, for the French considered their monarch a crackbrained visionary and would offer him not a single gold coin, he sent emissaries to the more important cities of Italy to try to inveigle them into joining his venture.

Florence, because of geographic position and fabulous wealth, Charles tried to flatter into friendship. To reinforce his offer of amity, he made it known that he was on the march with twenty-five thousand archers, lancers, cross bowmen, and unlimited artillery, and that among his soldiers there were several thousand Swiss, the terror of Europe. Would he obtain an invitation or must he, regretfully, crash the gate?

Recalling his father's admonition, or perhaps unwilling to be molested in his dalliance, Pietro refused to become involved in the King's scheme and would allow him neither free passage nor offer him money. The *populani,* however, considered this the long-awaited opportunity to rid the city of the Medici and re-establish their free Republic. Moreover, Charles' army had already crossed the Alps, plundering as it marched, in the eternal manner of armies, Rapallo, Turin, Piacenza, and holding triumphant celebrations.

Now they were on Tuscan soil—in Pisa—a day's journey from Florence, if one stopped on the way to do a little robbing and raping. The Florentines were seized with terror. With enthusiasm, too. "In our hearts bloom the lilies," a poetaster expressed their affection for the great northern neighbor, whose intentions, if not honorable, were auspicious. Ancient is the Italian adage—*Se non è vero, è ben trovato.* "If it is not true, it is opportune." And had not someone long, long ago asked: "Truth, what is truth?" And Honor, what is honor? Man must live—why place obstacles in his path?

The Signoria, the ruling body of Florence, for such a long time a nominal institution, now asserted itself and disregarding

Pietro, was ready to ratify the alliance with Charles. But Pietro, even if a fool, did not lack a sense of self-preservation. Seeing how the wind was blowing, he dashed forward, as ruler and as host of the Republic to receive the King. He presented him with all the fortresses of Tuscany and opened every mountain pass, made impregnable by his father, including in the bargain all the future taxes of Florence.

In the illusion of security, Pietro returned to Florence on the 8th of November, 1494. He realized, however, that he was *persona non grata,* despite his efforts at reconciliation with his subjects. Presently convinced that his very life was in jeopardy, he sought refuge in Bologna.

Meanwhile, Charles and his soldiers were received enthusiastically by the Florentines, but when he demanded the restoration of Pietro, they were enraged and threatened to fight the soldiers to the death from every street and every house.

Bewildered by this *volte-face,* Charles might have taken it into his volatile head to suppress the Signoria and proclaim himself sole ruler of the Republic, but for the intervention of a monk who was to become a historic figure, absurd, illustrious, and tragic.

Girolamo Savonarola was born in Ferarra in 1452, son of a banker and grandson of a physician. Precocious, he knew the entire Bible by heart before he was out of his teens and was already writing satires denouncing the corruption of the Church. At twenty-two he became a Dominican monk and was transferred to San Marco, where he was elected prior in 1491. But long before that, he had become one of the most celebrated personalities of Florence and his sermons and invectives made people say, "A prophet is among us!"—a sentence which invariably means that there is trouble ahead, for he who appoints himself messenger of God brings bad news to men.

Savonarola considered Pietro and all the rest of the Medici only miserable puppets, contemptible targets. The chief foe of the city and of the Christian world was "that painted doll, the voluptuous, shameless whore, worse than a brute," who went by the name of Pope Alexander VI. All Christendom should rise against this trafficker in gold and vice. For money this wicked Lord of the World opened the gates of the temple, distributed offices, forgave sins, and plucked evil souls out of hell.

The complaint against the ways of the Vatican already had a long history. Did not Boccaccio, a century and a half previously, relate in one of his wonderful tales how a Jew having visited Rome was ready to turn Christian, seeing that God allowed so corrupt a religion to prosper?

Savonarola recognized the authority of the pope and would have regarded the splitting of the Church a tragedy of the greatest magnitude, since upon her universality and oneness life on earth and life beyond it, were premised. He questioned neither dogma nor tradition. He was not, as it might seem, the forerunner of Martin Luther. He was a Latin, an Italian, and he harbored no strange divinities in his unconscious self.

Luther, the Teuton, could hear in the recesses of his mind the mighty voices of the gods who once upon a time inhabited the great forests of the north—Odin, the All-Father; Frigga, his wife; Thor, the Thunderer; Tyr, the Lord of War; Bragi, Master of Poetry; Freya, Mistress of Love and Beauty; Locki, the Evil One, the Devil.

A schism, a rupture with Rome, did not appear so overwhelming to Luther. Perhaps, indeed unaware, in the fearful cavern of his volcanic soul, he desired it. Was he not a son of the barbarians who had more than once swooped upon Rome, sacked and burned her, thus mocking her claim to sanctity and eternity?

The problem for Savonarola, as for all reformers who were ready to risk the fires of the Inquisition, was, and has remained, insoluble—how reconcile a vast temporal empire with the unadulterated teachings of Jesus, whom it professes to worship and follow; how proclaim the glory of poverty and humility and yet display the necessary pomp and glory to hypnotize hundreds of millions; how preach peace and submission, and yet practice war and conquest; how exalt death and yet command fecundity that the faith continue to spread and never die?

Savonarola and his confrères confound legend with reality, and preferring legend, would destroy both legend and reality, and therefore must perish.

"I am like the hail, which striketh all who are uncovered," warned Savonarola. "O Florence, thou art nothing but flesh with eyes. The days of thy songs and dances are forever gone. Cleanse thy streets and thy places with streams of tears. Cursed be the useless books, cursed be vain beauty. Cursed be false science, cursed be the sinners in the fruit of their bodies and their fields, in the toils of their houses and their cities. Cursed be pleasure, cursed be all who live for pleasure and from pleasure."

The Florentines flocked to his sermons, and the poor, the simple, and even some of the aristocrats of intellect, hearkened to his bitter words and did indeed weep. Pico della Mirandola became the monk's disciple. He burned his books, gave his fortune to poor girls for dowry, renounced the heresy that even the greatest mortal sin, being finite, could not merit eternal punishment, and labored as hard to acquire ignorance as he had done to acquire knowledge. Fortunately, he died before tragedy overwhelmed his hero and the consummation of his own purification had taken place.

Even before Charles VIII made his triumphant entry into Florence, Savonarola hailed him as the man chosen by God to deliver the world from the "Beast of Rome." Now, in his quandary how to treat the Signoria for its refusal to recall Pietro, he conferred with the monk. Savonarola urged him to leave Florence, discard the Medicis, march on Rome and reform the Church, and "the sea and the earth, yea, even the heavenly regions" would ring with the name of Charles.

His eloquence stirred the King, but he could not have done his bidding without the gift of the Signoria of 120,000 gulden, for the army was clamoring for its wages and would have gladly sacked the city.

Charles was not entirely ungrateful, for he offered Florence a commercial treaty whereby the Florentines would enjoy equal privileges with the French in trading with his kingdom, and *mirabile dictu,* the two parties abided by the agreement. For the Florentines this remained the foundation of their prosperity, even of their survival, for presently new and cleverer competitors appeared who drove them out of the world market. France, however, always remained their assured zone of trade.

The Signoria bestowed upon Charles the title of "Restorer and Protector of Florentine Liberty" and Savonarola blessed his army marching off to Rome. His blessing, however, was of little avail, for before long Charles lost both the war and his life.

Savonarola, now at the height of his popularity, could have become dictator of Florence, had he had the Will which Lorenzo the Magnificent believed in, the Will that mastered all phenomena in nature—storm and thunder and snow, and all phenomena in man—love and hate and perfidy—the Will, which Schopenhauer three centuries later, expounded as the Force of Life. He did cry out: "O sword, sword, thou shalt restore order everywhere!" But he did not organize the men of the sword who would support him in his goal. "All armed prophets have been victorious and all unarmed prophets have been destroyed. . . . Savonarola does not know that time cannot be waited on, that fortune changes and that evil cannot be appeased by kindness." So said Machiavelli, who watched the monk sharply.

Perhaps Savonarola did know, and that very knowledge constricted him. Who better than Machiavelli should have understood this, he the past master of all the subtleties of power, yet powerless himself, precisely because he suffered from understanding? They who succeed act from incomprehensible instinct, deriving energy from a reservoir too deep within them to tempt them to look—and drown. And in the final analysis life is a school wherein man learns to no purpose, for the lesson follows the deed.

The monk, trained to invoke and invect, and steeped in the rhythmic language of the prophets of Judea, proclaimed: "Italy's wicked sovereigns have been sent us as punishment.

Their palaces and courts are refuges for criminals, houses of all
the monsters of the earth for their boundless concupiscence.
There they live unabashed, sucking out the blood of the people.
There fawning philosophers invent new glories and the poets
trump up genealogies for their masters. But what is worst, in
this Babylon, in this city of fools and godless men, priests are
seen in alliance with the Evil One."

In his naïveté, Savonarola placed his trust in those whom he
considered innocent, simple, and ignorant, the veritable children
of Jesus—the common folk. But the Florentines were weathercocks, and adverse winds were beginning to blow. The Pope,
Italy, all the independent powers of Europe were alarmed and
warned that they would join to destroy the city which harbored
the most dangerous of creatures—an honest man—unless the
city rid herself of the monstrosity.

"Open up, O Lord, the hearts of this people," Savonarola
implored, "that they may understand the things that live in me
and that thou hast revealed and commanded unto me!"

What were those things? Piety, purity, but more than all, the
blissfulness of dying. "We live in this world, my brethren, only
to learn how we are to die well."

The Florentines, in truth, died in great numbers from pestilence and hunger, for the world refused to buy their linen and
brocade, and the bankers and merchants of Europe ignored their
pleas for credit and raw materials.

But a far more perilous pestilence for Savonarola was the
prevalence of sin. He would stamp it out. His new constitution
required beating drunkards, putting gamblers to the torture,
piercing tongues which uttered blasphemies. And to crown it all,
he ordered the "Bonfire of Vanities."

"Suffer the children to come unto me," said Jesus. And Savonarola said: "Let the children seek out iniquity and extirpate it."
Divided into small companies, led by grownups, the youngsters
knocked at all doors and demanded everything that was "accursed," everything that could serve for pleasure of flesh or
mind. They collected mirrors, cosmetics, perfumes, portraits of

beautiful courtesans, books by Boccaccio and the secular poets, statues, silks, jewelry.

In hundreds of sacks they dragged the vanities of life which had lent charm and delight to life, to the Piazza and set fire to them. The flames were as tongues singing hallelujahs and the church bells rang their joyous accompaniment. It was the merry preview of the fires of hell awaiting those who persisted in sinning. Ah, if but the monk had had the power to mix sins and sinners. How the fattened smoke would have delighted the sensitive nostrils of the Lord!

Save us, O Lord, from Thy saviors!

This was the Festival of Faith supplanting Lorenzo's Festival of Flesh. This was Virtue conquering Vice. This was the purity of Death annihilating the Error of Life.

And on Palm Sunday, 1496, to bind in holy matrimony heaven and earth, Girolamo Savonarola proclaimed Jesus King of Florence—*Gesù Re di Fiorenza*. So staunch a republican and hater of overlords as the monk could not conceive of Jesus as Gonfaliere or President. Let earthly tyrannies perish, but long live the tyranny of heaven!

Savonarola had overreached himself. Jealous friars of other orders, envious lay priests and furious members of the upper classes loathed his arrogance and the excesses into which he had plunged the city. He defended himself valiantly. "We do not wish to change our faith; nor do we wish to change the law of the Gospel; nor the power of the Church; but we wish men to become better."

Men become better—The clamorous champions of men, trample upon man. To save the woods they fell the trees. They fashion keys to treasure-houses which do not exist. It is not wise to demand too much of man, for he becomes so conscious of his deficiencies and so panicky that he tramples upon what he has already achieved and reverts to a condition of beast in search of relief from responsibility.

Men become better—But men only seek relief from pain which they call happiness. They must not see things in their true proportions, for they would lose sight of themselves. The mole hills upon which men stand must always appear higher than the mountains in the distance.

Men become better—Poor Savonarola, he wove the rope with which they hanged him. The people of Florence no longer could bother about the condition of their souls, for the condition of their bodies was desperate. Become better—that had been the root of the grievous state in which they found themselves. Now they understood clearly. The better kills the good, and this man killed the good. All over Christendom, cities trembled lest they, too, hatch a monk who would bring misfortune for the days of their years in exchange for heavenly eternities. However certain they were of paradise, they were more certain still of the earth, and however sweet the heavenly manna, sweeter still was the terrestrial bread.

Pope Alexander VI considered Savonarola, if not a fool, at least a mediocrity. He was uninterested in his moralistic fulminations. Ever since the Church had supplanted the Empire, fanatical dogs barked and snapped. Every pontiff had to deal with them in one way or another, according to his temperament. As for himself, Humanist and "Greek," he was ready to treat this homely, trumpet-nosed friar (he hated ugliness in any form) with Christian moderation. He would consign him to some monastery, where he might compose hymns and pray and fast, so that his weightless body could the more easily fly to Heaven. Perhaps, too, if he should in his hallucinations contrive some miracle, such as the visitation of the Madonna, who seemed to be the traveling member of the Family, he might even be sanctified in centuries to come. (His Holiness was ever proud of his sense of humor!)

"Pope Alexander VI," says Machiavelli, "had no care or thought but how to deceive, and always found material to work on. No man ever had a more effective manner of asseverating, or ever made promises with more solemn protestations, or observed them less. And yet, because he understood this side of human nature, his frauds always succeeded."

Alexander had tried to placate, in his own way, the monk of San Marco, but unable, he was determined to stop that foolish sheep from bleating against him and trying to incite those wolves, the French, from invading his States. And so, in the year 1497, Alexander VI excommunicated Girolamo Savonarola.

The monk hurled back monstrous curses and continued to celebrate mass and preach. But his followers, even the most faithful, were perplexed and uncomfortable, for the bells of the churches rang against him and the tapers at the altars were extinguished as a sign of papal sorrow for the excommunicate. The Church was ever the merciful Mother and the tortures she was compelled to inflict were for the good of her erring children. What mattered it what happened to the body if thereby the soul was saved? That many intellectuals and Humanists misunderstood this holy purpose proved again and again that only the blind saw clearly and only the simple-minded knew the truth, and that ignorance and darkness were the Lord's special gifts to man.

Fearful of contagion of the fatal sin, only a handful of worshipers now still dared to assemble at San Marco to hear the monk curse his foe at Rome. Even they, however, shivered. "Is the Pope to you more than God?" he thundered.

Whatever the reply, the fact was that the Pope—any pope—was God's representative on earth—with plenipotentiary rights to reward and to punish, and no Christian possessed the prerogative to question the validity of these rights, much less to disdain or reject them.

As for lifting robes to see what they concealed—what under the sun would continue to exist? Honor, glory, beauty, virtue, morality, decency—all turned to nought! Deplume a peacock and what have you? A miserable barnyard fowl. Unrobe a man, and what have you? A miserable forest ape. The robe—the robe is all!

The pattern of a culture is not undone by pulling out threads here and there. The design remains inalterable for long periods of time. After a half-dozen years of the monk's rule, Florence, the city of gaiety, began to clamor for open taverns and wine shops, for carnivals, for beautiful women displaying their feminine treasures, for singing and carousing in the Piazza.

She was weary of sanctimonious graybeards and impudent youths parading fictitious angelic miens. She was weary of poverty and isolation. She wished to sell her wonderful brocades and her incomparable pieces of bronze and marble. And if the Pope planned no trouble for her, she would plan none for him. Peaceful co-existence—at least for a while.

The Signoria concocted a series of complaints against Savonarola, including treasonable alliances, and put him to the torture. Unable to endure the pain, he confessed that he had indeed issued false prophecies in order to be considered saintly, and that ambition, and not the Holy Spirit, had been the source of his inspiration. Words of agony. Nothing could, in truth, be proved against him, for he was guilty only of unworldliness and of a passion to alter the unalterable ways of man. He fought evil, but evil and good are so intertwined that cut into one and the other bleeds. Every good is flanked by two evils—the one from which it issued and the one into which it grows.

While in his prison cell, his hand maimed by the torture, Savonarola wrote his last book, *Miserere*. In his solitude he heard more keenly the cries of the poor, the oppressed, and the tortured, and he saw more sharply the wicked souls of tyrants, their mercilessness, and their brutality. "He whom it pleases not to murder his neighbor, he who does not sow rebellion and dissension, is no man to them."

Aware of his utter helplessness at the hands of his tormentors, he asked: "Can a man resist alone the superior might of the enemy? Can he be stronger than Evil which everywhere gushes forth from within?" The world neither heard nor answered.

Dulce et decorum est pro patria mori—"Sweet and glorious it is to die for one's country." What was Savonarola's country but the bosom of his Lord Jesus? And he prayed to the Lord. "Grant me the martyr's death and let me die for Thee as Thou hast died for me." And his prayer was answered. The Pope sent him absolution, but his compatriots would not forgive him the long, lean years of enforced virtue, and he was condemned to die.

The twenty-third day of the merry month of May of the year of our Lord 1498 was proclaimed a holiday in Florence for young and old. Food and wine were provided by the government for all who would come to the Piazza della Signoria. And all, save the bedridden and the crippled, came. Never since the glorious days of Lorenzo the Magnificent had the place witnessed such animation and joviality. It was spring in the world and spring in the hearts of men and women.

The gibbet was ready and the rope was dangling. Mischievous boys tried it around their necks and their elders roared with laughter. The Florentines were famous for their fondness for children and for spoiling them.

Now the joyous farce was about to be enacted. Girolamo Savonarola, shivering, dressed in tatters, was dragged to the gibbet by the executioner and his assistant, preceded by a priest. The latter muttered the required prayer, pressed the wooden cross to the livid lips of the victim and descended.

The reverent silence during the religious function over, the spectators broke into tumultuous shouts. Obscenities mingled with quotations from the Bible and laughter mingled with belching and other elemental noises. The executioner, without any further formalities, pushed the haggard, pinched head into the noose.

"Prophet! Prophet!" a thousand voices shouted. "Thy hour has come! Perform thy miracle! Prophet, speak! Answer, Prophet!"

The executioner pulled the rope vigorously, and presently a black, foaming tongue stuck out of the mouth disdainfully.

"Speak, Prophet! Speak!"

And the Prophet spoke: "Wicked fools! You have made me immortal!"

The boys, whose shirts bulged with stones, began pelting the cramped body swinging lightly in the breeze. It was a special privilege granted the members of the new generation, and he who struck the bull's-eye, the nose, was applauded and rewarded.

Meanwhile, the executioner and his assistant set fire to the faggots underneath the corpse, for in reality, Savonarola was condemned to be burned alive, but as an act of Christian clemency, the Signoria allowed hanging first.

This was the *pièce de résistance* of the *festa*. Men and women danced around the gibbet to the music of pipes and drums. At the tables of the taverns the "gilded" youths sang the latest *Canti Carnascialeschi*—bawdy parodies of sacred hymns—while the red wine gurgled out of their overbrimming throats, making bloody pools around the feet of the celebrants.

The monk's body was a mound of hot ashes, bits of fat and guts sizzling, and unconsumed bones sticking out in various spots. The executioner and his assistant, impatient to join the merrymakers, did not wait until the complete consummation, but shoveled it into a wheelbarrow and rushed to dump it into the Arno, thick and yellow with recent rains, waddling like some vast pregnant monster.

The ashes swam awhile upon the surface—the ashes of Girolamo Savonarola and the ashes of the City of God reigned over by *Gesù Re di Fiorenza*—and then, heavy with the waters of the river, sank and vanished.

Niccolò Machiavelli Discovers His Prince

Less than two months after the disappearance of Girolamo Savonarola, on the 15th of July, 1498, Niccolò Machiavelli took over his post as Second Chancellor and Secretary to the *Dieci di Libertà e Pace*—"Ten of Liberty and Peace."

The two events, as the perspective of time would show, had a peculiar relationship in the history of Power, although Girolamo was unaware of Niccolò's existence and Niccolò regarded Girolamo, as he did all other clerics, a vulture hovering over his cherished dove, his fatherland.

The monk considered Power the prerogative of God; the Secretary the prerogative of Man. To Girolamo the State was the handmaiden of religion; to Niccolò religion had no meaning save to frighten or persuade men into submission to the State. Yet for both, Power was all, and man's history the struggle to achieve it. Its infallible touchstone was the oppression and annihilation of the weak, whatever the trappings, the pretensions, the gloss.

Savonarola had power in his hand, but he was incapable of wielding it, and thus terminated for all time in Florence the prerogative of God. Machiavelli, himself unambitious, would teach princes how to wield it, but he, too, was unsuccessful, for the princes were unworthy of their counsellor. And Florence would never be either the free city of God or the free city of Man.

The "Ten of Liberty and Peace" was a subordinate branch of the Signoria. It exercised a separate control over the departments of war and interior, sent its own ambassadors—and spies —to foreign powers, transacted affairs of the cities of the Florentine domain, controlled the military establishment of the commonwealth, dealt with the unruly and unreliable *condottieri,* the hired soldiery, inspected fortresses, and examined the bills presented to the city—the latter a function of the most delicate nature, but mutual distrust is a solid foundation of confidence.

Less exalted than the Signoria, the "Ten of Liberty and Peace" had, in reality, more influence over the lives of the citizens, restraining the upper strata from their compulsion to tyrannize and the lower from their urge to steal.

Immediately upon entering the Chancery, Niccolò felt as one who having long been tossed in turbulent seas without compass and without guiding star, suddenly and unexpectedly finds himself in port.

The Council Hall where he went daily, except when sent on

ambassadorial trips, was a large dreary room, badly ventilated, badly furnished, and icy in the winter. The Florentines, persistently trying to delude travelers, succeeded in deluding themselves that their beloved city knew only spring and summer, and disdainfully refused to install stoves in their homes and in their offices. The ladies, however, would put hot pans (which with typical Florentine irreverence they called *preti*—priests) in their beds. To warm their frostbitten *culi*—so husbands grumbled; so lovers laughed.

No literary masterpieces of the day pleased Machiavelli half as much as the varied documents he handled, and everything that transpired in the office received his attention. "It is necessary to observe even the smallest matters," he wrote, "because great things arise out of small and because one can see the men behind things even in trivialities."

Here was not glazed fiction, but splintery reality, and for Machiavelli far more interesting. He was the seeker of truth, the scientist who accepts the conclusions of his research with equanimity. Here he observed man in the raw and found him vain, vengeful, scheming, cruel, foolish, dishonest, dishonorable, weary of peace, ready to quarrel with his neighbor, and to kill him. And nations, being aggregates of men, displayed the same characteristics, vastly exaggerated and therefore vastly more terrible.

Machiavelli was not unaware of the more amenable traits of man, but they were conditioned by fear, courtesy, long and wearisome training, and remained always superficial, cracking under the hammer of adverse circumstances. They were the products of reason, and reason was ever the unwelcome accountant in human affairs. Reason proposes; passion disposes. How many reasons man invents to stifle reason!

The root of life is evil. In evil all creatures live, for they are forced to trap and devour one another to subsist. Man, because of his intelligence and power and ambition, is the most evil of all. Not only does he destroy all other creatures, but also his fellow man, his brother, and in the end himself, for he is bored and discontented and even victory soon palls. Given jealousy and envy—the passion to hold what we have and the urge to obtain that which our neighbor possesses—and we can recreate the human soul in its entirety.

But having discovered what he considered the essence of the nature of man, Machiavelli was not ready to destroy him. He would send neither flood nor fire as his creator, Yahweh, had done, nor would he thunder the end of the world in the manner of enraged prophets, who prophesy as they hope.

There is no more pietistic attitude than that of seeing no evil, hearing no evil, speaking no evil in a world of monstrous evils. Although he was forced "to follow in the footsteps of many a one who wore a finer cloak," and he knew all the guises hypocrisy assumed, including that of beatific sincerity, Machiavelli was never hypocritical. He saw evil, he heard evil, and he spoke of evil. "There is a very great difference between the way men live and the way they ought to live, and he who clings to what should be instead of what is, works for his own destruction." What held true with the individuals, held also true with nations, and nations which did not understand the subtle workings of evil, were doomed. He was anxious to see Italy live and he would warn her by pointing out the perils in the nature of things and of man, and later, when his genius ripened, he would also offer remedies.

Niccolò found not only his work but also his subordinates to his liking. They were rough, obscene, lazy, and unreliable, but he understood them, sympathized with their poverty, their disillusions, their hopelessness, and their search for compensation in sexual bravado. In their company he relaxed and was relieved of obsessions too deep within his soul for recognition. He could tell taller tales of brothels and his language was more highly peppered than theirs.

The tongues of the male Florentines, said the amazing Pietro Aretino, were dipped in *"il mielo del culo della donna."* And Aretino should know, for no tongue or pen in the annals of letters was ever as licentious, nor ever received such aureate recompense for slander and gossip. Feared and lionized, he, a bastard of the slums of Arezzo (from which place he took his name), spent his life at the courts of princes and popes. So inflated did he become with praise and applause that he styled himself the "divine" and the "scourge of princes." And when he died in 1556, at the age of sixty-four, it was by falling from his chair in a fit of laughter brought on by hearing an obscene story about his sisters. *Se non è vero è ben trovato.*

A wit who hoped to replace Aretino at the papal court, composed his epitaph:

> Qui giace l'Arentin' poeta tosco,
> Chi disse mali d'ognun fuorche Dio,
> Scusandosi col dir—"Non lo conosco."

> Here lies the Tuscan poet Aretino,
> Who evil spoke of everyone but God,
> Giving as his excuse—"I do not know him."

Indefatigable and conscientious, Niccolò was often constrained not only to revise the work of his clerks (sloppiness being from time immemorial the hallmark of their profession everywhere), but also to do it *da capo*. Bored, they would throw their pens away and play cards or feigning sickness or claiming familial tragedies, would stay away for days. Knowing that spite is the weapon of the inferior, Machiavelli would never scold or intimidate, but mollify by laughter or ribaldry.

His superiors soon realized that they had not only an intelligent and educated servant—there were such in Florence—but a reliable and honest one—a unique phenomenon among the bureaucrats. And he did not pretend condescension toward his job, an attitude most common in a period of insecurity in which braggadocio and pretense gave the illusion of importance and authenticity.

Machiavelli had, if he so wished, claims to nobility, but he believed in democracy. "I say that the people are more prudent and stable, and have better judgment than a prince, and it is not without reason that it is said: '*Vox populi vox Dei*'—'The Voice

of the People is the voice of God, . . . Not individual prosperity, but the general good makes cities great; and certainly the
general good is regarded nowhere except in republics, because
whatever they do is for the general good. . . . Republican
governments have more resources in time of distress and flourish
longer because they can better accommodate themselves to the
necessities of different times. . . . Liberty is the Golden Age
in which everyone has his opinion and the right to defend it. . . .
By 'gentlemen' I mean such men as live in idleness and luxury on
the income of their possessions without ever troubling to cultivate them, or working in any other way for a living. Subjects like
these are pernicious in any province. But more pernicious still
are those who besides having money are also the owners of castles and have subjects who obey them. Men of that type are all
of them enemies of civilization. . . . The aim of the people is
more honorable than that of the nobles, the latter seeking to
oppress, the former not to be oppressed."

The French invasion of the Peninsula revealed the weakness
of its great cities which knew how to unite neither in time of
peace nor in time of aggression. Each called in foreign troops to
defend her against her sister republics, and each paid in gold
and precious goods, exciting the cupidity of the false champions.
"Money is not the sinews of war," Machiavelli cautioned again
and again. "Money alone, so far from being a means of defense
will only make the city more liable to be plundered. . . ." If
sheep but understood the world, they would shed their wool and
develop fangs.

As for the popes and their States, "sometimes in zeal for religion, at others moved by their own ambition, were continually
calling in new parties and exciting new disturbances. As soon as
they had made a prince powerful, they viewed him with jealousy
and sought his ruin; and never allowed another to rule the country, which from their own imbecility, they were themselves unable to govern."

To cope more efficiently with the machinations and treacheries of friends and foes perpetually scheming to destroy Flor-

ence's independence, the "Ten of Liberty and Peace" had wisdom enough to send as their ambassador to Italian and European courts their honest, reliable, and talented servitor, Niccolò Machiavelli. The honors and emoluments, however, as is the custom everywhere and always, went to those "who wore finer cloaks."

In the month of November, 1503, shortly before leaving for Imola on a mission to Cesare Borgia, the most momentous in his career, Niccolò married Marietta Ludovico Corsini, a simple woman with a modest dowry and much younger than himself. Though often tormented by the neglect of her husband, who, in his long bachelorhood had acquired a penchant for whores, Marietta seems to have remained faithful, and during his years of evil fortune and poverty, uncomplaining.

The couple was blessed, as the unwary saying goes, with five children, one of whom died at birth or soon after. Of the sons this may be said: Guido, the youngest, gentle and sweet of disposition, joined the Church but did not attain to any eminence; in the business of the two worlds success requires quite other qualities than sweetness and gentleness. But perhaps it was just as well, for our own success makes us arrogant; the success of our friends embitters us; success is man's heaviest yoke.

Bernardo, the oldest, was a violent youth, who, involved in brawls which terminated in fatalities, made his escape to Constantinople, where he died a few years after his father's death.

Ludovico was equally violent and he, too, became enmeshed in unsavory quarrels, but some months before his father's death, when Florence fought her last battle for freedom, he joined the militia and was killed defending the Republic. The bereaved father accepted his heroic finale as atonement for all the evil his son had caused him.

As is often the case, Baccia, the sole daughter, proved the faithful pillar of the family. She married Giovanni Ricci, and her own daughter, Hyppolita, entered the wealthy family of Serristori. To her progeny, Giuliano, we owe the greater portion of Niccolò's letters and the manuscripts of his minor works.

The Machiavelli family continued to exist, via one branch and another, until fairly recent times and still owned the small house and property at San Casciano, where, abandoned by the little men on the stools of power, but guided by the immortal Muses, Niccolò Machiavelli penned all his books.

Cesare Borgia, Duke Valentino, was the son of Pope Alexander VI. From him he inherited his physical beauty. He was tall, well-built, with golden hair and beard and a light complexion. "The Pope's son is most gallant to behold and amazingly beautiful to see." Alexander was pure Spanish, but although Cesare was half Italian, he was even more than his father the true Spaniard of the sixteenth century—cruel, fierce, ruthless, proud, and vengeful. Upon his sword he had inlaid his motto in the French of his day: *Fays ce que je dois, advien que pourra.* "Do what I should; come what may."

And what he should do was to achieve the conquest of Romagna, the Central Italy, which Alexander claimed as his State, but could not hold because of the ever warring lords of the cities of Urbino, Faenza, Imola, Forli, Perugia. Beyond that, Cesare would capture Florence and Venice, and perhaps the whole of the Peninsula.

Unlike his father who was a voluptuary, communicative and gay, Cesare would allow neither pleasure nor social glitter to distract him. A spider of magnificent cunning, he stretched his intricate, elusive webs in all directions. Into them tumbled princes and generals and adventurers who considered themselves the most astute of men—enemies, friends, allies—and none escaped.

Four years of warfare conducted by craft and skillfully conceived and executed battles, proved the efficacy of the strategy of this brilliant young man. No pope had ever been so secure on his throne as Alexander was now, nor had anyone owned as much territory. For centuries to come the papacy would remain mistress of her lands and her architecture and her arts would never be surpassed. Yet, the Borgias and the Medici who had planned and encouraged and won these treasures for the Church were considered anathema by the future occupants of the Vatican and by generation after generation of Christians who had only heard of their atrocities and their paganism. Ingratitude begins at home. Had holy men of the type of Savonarola occupied the throne at Rome, the Papal States would have been swallowed up by the Spaniards or the French, the artistic glories of the Vatican would never have been created, or if already created, would have been destroyed, and the Catholic Church would have been a village religion, rigid, primitive, without glamor and without influence, its bishoprics at odds with one another, without a central capital or an acknowledged supreme head. As for the crimes the Humanist popes committed, they were peccadillos compared to those perpetrated by their followers, including the monstrous atrocities of the Office of the Holy Inquisition.

Now the Pope's son, Cesare Borgia, was by God's grace Duke of Romagna, Valence, and Urbino, Prince of Andrea, Lord of Piombino, Gonfaliere and Captain-General of the Holy Roman Church. And the time had come to look northward to Florence and Venice, both protected by treaties with France. But no one knew better than Cesare that treaties are "scraps of paper." He did not need the advice which Machiavelli, long after they both had departed this world, offered in his maxims to generations of princes: "If all rulers were good, you ought to keep your word, but since they are all dishonest and do not keep faith with you, you in return need not keep faith with them."

Cesare was certain that the French were not ready for war and that they would disregard their alliance with the two Italian cities. But Venice, he believed, was strong enough to defy him, while the Florentines, who hated war and were perennially annoyed by Pisa and the followers of the Medici, watching for a chance to re-establish themselves as the lords of the Republic, would succumb even without a struggle.

In truth, Florence was shivering and the Signoria turned in futile circles of uncertainty. Should they surrender and accept Cesare as their master—Cesare whom they abominated for his treacheries and cruelties, or should they attempt to fight him and see their beloved city sacked and in flames? Should they hire mercenaries or attempt to organize a militia?

"In hypocrisy I have long since received baptism, confirmation, and communion. In lying, I even possess a doctor's degree. Life has taught me to temper falsehood with truth and truth with falsehood." So provisioned, Machiavelli considered himself well prepared to meet one of history's most subtle and most unscrupulous liars and hypocrites, to discuss the fate of Florence.

He could only discuss it, for the "Ten of Liberty and Peace" had not empowered him to make decisions. Cesare, however, was unaware of this, and he received the emissary with all the honors due an ambassador both *de facto* and *de jure*. Niccolò did not undeceive him, and in this first encounter, he seemed to win a point.

While the two men talked in the ancient and accredited manner of diplomacy—out of both sides of their mouths—there was soon created between them a sort of no man's land of honesty and truth, where they would now and then exchange views on peace and war, and the meaning of Power.

The Duke, whose black velvet waistcoat and heavy golden chain about his neck emphasized his beauty, did not dislike the little man with the cadaverous face out of which shone the most penetrating eyes. It was smart of the Florentines not to have sent an ambassador who might compete with him in elegance and manly beauty and excite his jealousy. His Spanish pride suffered no jolt. It could not have occurred to Cesare, of course, that he was in the presence of a genius whose celebrated book would be based upon the lessons drawn from his own spectacular career and who would thus keep his memory alive in the minds of men for century after century. What did it matter that he would be the symbol of cruelty and craft, as long as he would not be for-

gotten and would retain that spark of life called immortality?
One spark out of a conflagration, and yet who would not barter
the conflagration for the spark, for what merit has life if death
must so soon follow? Oh, the quarries emptied of their marble
to fashion slabs to inscribe names upon which for a handful of
years might still be read by "gentle passers-by!" Oh, the mighty
forests felled that tomes be penned of which one line to a thousand millions by kindly fortune remains, and tagged to it, perchance a name—one whiff from a hurricane! Oh, the heavens
men in their delusion create where sans guts, sans love, sans
laughter, sans play, dreary wraiths in empty space forever and
forever stare, that they might not die and turn to dust whence
they came! Not to die—not to die—to hold Time by one fragile
thread! But all the centuries have flown into eternity and eternity is not longer by one hour.

Nor, indeed, would the idea of his own immortality have occurred to Niccolò. On what basis, pray? Who was he, but the
secretary to ten men, who seemed never willing to equate duty
well performed with the appropriate title and appropriate
remuneration? As for writing books—that had not yet crossed
his mind. He was writing, though, extraordinary reports, replete with shrewd observations, with maxims not yet sharpened
to razor-edge, to be sure, but already capable of cutting deeply
into the sensitive flesh of craven bureaucracy. "I report nothing
but the truth." There is an inflexible pride in truth which alien-
ates our affections, while falsehood fawns and flatters and con-
quers our hearts.

The Duke invited Machiavelli to accompany him on his
campaign. He would show him how he entrapped his enemies
posing as his friends, and his friends who might become enemies.
Cesare was vain and the vain, uncertain of themselves, always
seek confirmation of their claims. Wily flatterers know this and
they bring on their undoing. Often it is the sole way tyrants
and tyrannies are disposed of.

What Machiavelli witnessed during the four months that he
spent with Cesare Borgia filled the ruling Florentines with

horror, disgust, terror. "The Bandit! The Bandit!" they shouted. "Borgia has within him an infinity of cruelty, more than has ever before been seen or heard of. . . . I know not whether I am capable of writing down the wickedness of Cesare, for I tremble from fear of God even to listening to tales of it. . . ." So the rulers wrote; so they wrung their hands.

Machiavelli was not a monster. He hated cruelty as much as the Signori to whom he sent the accurate descriptions of what transpired. But he saw better than they; he saw deeper; he cast his plumbline into the facts and struck the heart of Power. Cesare was Power—evil because it had to deal with evil. Cesare murdered, deceived, robbed, but he rid Romagna of the cruel, deceiving, murderous clerical lords.

"The lords who ruled in Romagna were examples of all living evil. On the slightest pretext they gave themselves to rapine and slaughter. They made unjust laws and reduced the population to misery. . . . Cesare was reputed cruel, yet his cruelty restored Romagna, united it, and brought it order and obedience, so that it will be seen that he was in reality merciful."

Cesare's violence destroyed violence once and for all. "Men act only upon compulsion. From the moment they have the option and liberty to commit wrong with impunity, they never fail to carry confusion and disorder everywhere. . . . Those cruelties are well employed, which are done once and for all under the necessity of self-preservation, and are not afterwards persisted in, but as far as possible modified to the advantage of the governed. Injuries, therefore, should be inflicted all at once, that their ill savor being less lasting may the less offend; whereas benefits should be conferred little by little, that they may be more relished. . . . And I will say, in conclusion, that it is necessary for a prince to possess the friendship of the people; otherwise he has no resource in time of adversity. . . . And one who by his own valor and measures animates the mass of the people, he will not find himself deceived by them, and he will find that he has laid his foundations well, which contradicts the old saw that he who builds on the people builds on mire."

The people, always the people, is the concern of Niccolò Machiavelli, maligned as the apologist of tyranny. "If I taught princes how to tyrannize, I also taught the people how to destroy them."

Machiavelli watched Cesare as a scientist watches a living specimen under the microscope, recording, interpreting. The Duke's technique, he saw, was not a haphazard affair, trusting to *combinazione* and auspicious signs and portents, pagan or Christian. It was based upon the logic of life, upon what his keen young mind had grasped as the permanent phases of human nature. He had had good teachers in the Borgia family, and in his father's mansion there were many rooms—all inhabited by treacherous occupants of endless varieties. Might is right—that was the quintessence he had extracted from his experiences. And that was the conclusion Niccolò himself had reached, gathered from equally good teachers—the streets of Florence in his boyhood, the rule of the Medici, the fiasco of Savonarola, the invasion of the French, the history of the Romans which he had been studying assiduously, and which was to become the centrality of his philosophy.

And was it not true as well among beasts and plants—all things that live and feed and die? In the shadow of the great oak the shivering sapling is doomed; no sheep, however eloquent its bleat, has proved its case against the wolf, who howled the ultimate truth: "Small teeth chew grass; big teeth chew sheep."

"I can find no fault with Cesare," Machiavelli wrote in his analysis of the man whom he respected most, despite the last tragic, dwarfing years of his career, brought about by the bite of a mosquito of the swamps of the Eternal City. That was the clownish trick of Fortune to warn all men that they are less than the least and thus quench the fires of their vanity. "Nay, it seems to me to be reasonable to put Cesare forward as a pattern for all. . . . There is no brighter example than in the actions of this Prince for whosoever deems it necessary to secure himself against enemies, to gain friends, to conquer by force or fraud, to make himself beloved and feared by the people, followed and reverenced by the soldiers, to destroy those who can and may injure him, introduce innovations into old customs, to be severe and kind, magnanimous and liberal, suppress the old militia, create a new one, maintain the friendship of kings and princes in such a way that they must see that it is for their interest to aid him and dangerous to offend."

Cesare Borgia, for the time being at least, was willing to spare Florence for the price of thirty-six thousand ducats. The sum was promptly given by the Signoria, and he returned to Rome.

Now "The Son of Fortune," as Cesare was called, was abandoned by his capricious Mother, Fortune, and afflictions came trooping upon him in long files like geese cackling malignities. His father, Alexander VI, died suddenly, and he himself racked with fever, was unable to leave his bed. Instantly, his enemies began taking advantage of the situation. They grabbed his fortresses and his territories and his caches of gold. The troops of the *condottieri* plundered the city and his own Castel Sant 'Angelo was surrounded. "I foresaw everything that could happen upon my father's death," he told Machiavelli, weeping from sheer weakness, "except that I would be lying motionless and at death's door myself."

Alexander was followed by Pope Pius III, senile and bewildered, who, after a reign of three weeks, cast off body and crown to seek entrance into Paradise by right of succession upon Earth to the Master of the Keys of Heaven.

From his sick bed, Cesare helped elect Cardinal Giuliano della Rovere to the throne of Christendom. Giuliano, who assumed the name of Pope Julius II, had been a typical prince of the Church in the days of the Renaissance—lover of luxury, women, and art, a doting father, a generous uncle, a man of war. He had fought with varying successes the Borgias, and in particular Alexander, whom he despised.

For Cesare's favor, Julius promised him the resumption of the post which he had held so valiantly during his late father's reign—Captain-General of the Holy Roman Church. Thus he would be given the chance once again to prove that the fox-lion was still the king of the forest—and woe to his foes!

How could Cesare, whose mouth was a furnace of lies, believe that the mouth of the Cardinal was a hive of honey? How could he, mocker of gratitude, expect a pope to remember what a cardinal promised? The spider was caught in his own web, while the fly buzzed triumphant and free.

Machiavelli says that "the only thing Cesare can be accused of is that in the creation of Julius II, he made a bad choice, for men commit injuries through fear and hate." And Julius had excellent reasons to harbor both emotions toward him. "And whoever thinks that in high personages, new benefits cause old offences to be forgotten, makes a great mistake."

Poor Cesare, he could not avail himself, as did princes of later generations, of the acid wisdom of Machiavelli's as yet unwritten momentous maxims, among which: "He who is the cause of another's greatness is himself undone, since he must work either by address or by force, each of which excites distrust in the person raised to power."

Politicians, cardinals, noblemen, kings, princes—all the hypocrites, the sycophants, the liars, the traitors, rubbed their hands in glee, each certain that the new Pontiff, sixty-two years old, worn by debauchery, fastidious and vain, would be the wooden handle to his boiling kettle of ambition.

How mistaken the master-craftsmen of ingenious traps and toils were! They had never thought of inventing one that could hinder Power from pouring molten steel into the veins, transmuting a tomcat into a tiger. And Julius became a tiger from the very hour of his accession to the throne. His vigor, his imagination, his resolution, so startled all that he was surnamed *Il Terribile*. He gained Bologna, put down the Venetians, drove the French from Italy, and Rome, ever brewing with plots and counter-plots, became a city of peace and security.

Among the first things that Pope Julius II did was to divest Cesare Borgia of all power, making him a virtual prisoner. Recalling the fate that awaited those in similar situations when *he* was master, Cesare made his escape to Naples. There, Ferdinand of Aragon, compared to whom the Duke was a country bumpkin in treachery and hypocrisy, had promised him safe-conduct, but arrested him immediately and sent him to Spain. A dungeon for the rest of his mortal days would have been the cheeriest prospect, but he made a dramatic escape and a mad ride brought him to Navarre—whose king was his brother-in-law.

Whatever intricate plans Cesare might have conceived, little of him was heard until four years later, when fighting for his brother-in-law, he was killed in a single-handed battle against a troop of Aragonese. His body, when found, was covered with wounds, proof of his princely mettle to the end. He was splendidly entombed in the Church of Santa Maria at Viana. Later, however, his tomb was desecrated and destroyed, and there is no trace of it or of his bones. He was thirty-two years old.

Mors ultima ratio—"Death—the final reason."

To Arms—La Festa del Grillo— Leonardo

"Forget Florence for a while," Machiavelli implored his fellow citizens, "and survey all Italy. You will see only hostile forces. You are dependent upon France and threatened by Venice and the Pope. You trust in your alliance with the French and refuse to arm yourselves. But if you wish France to keep her promises, you must not be a featherweight on the scales of Italy. You must be as strong as you can. Among private persons, laws provide for observance of deeds and contracts; among states only arms decide. We must regard as enemies all who are stronger than we are and all those who are capable of conquering us, even though we be temporarily in league with them. It is not yet three months since the existence of Florence hung by a thread as a consequence of Cesare's threats, his march through our territory, and the uprisings in the provinces. At that time, when you saw burning villages and plundered cities in Tuscany, you were willing to pay all that you had originally refused to pay. Sovereignty rests upon Power and forethought. You must forget neither the one nor the other. Despite all treaties we must not close our eyes for one moment. Do not forget that the course of events is almost always contrary to expectations. . . . The chief foundations of all states, whether new, old, or mixed, are good laws and good arms."

But neither mercenaries nor *condottieri,* the hired soldiers, nor auxiliaries, the armies of foreign nations invited to protect the country, are desirable; indeed, they are both useless and dangerous. "The *condottieri* have no love or other motive to keep them in the field beyond a trifling wage, which is not enough to make them die for you. . . . The soldiers are such poltroons and there reigns such disorder in the armies that a horse turning its head or shaking its nosebag, marks the difference between victory and defeat."

Who are these mercenaries but criminals, debtors in brothels and wine shops? Every company is a colony of malefactors, and their commanders blustering adventurers who believe it enough for them "to think of clever retorts in written negotiations, to contrive deceptions, to bedeck themselves with gold and gems, to live more splendidly than others, to revel in sensuality, and to make their own words as oracular utterances. . . . The *condottieri* eat like ogres, steal unscrupulously, plunder treasuries, and are incapable of defending territories entrusted to them."

As for the auxiliaries, "they may be good in themselves, but they are always dangerous for those who borrow them, for if they lose you are defeated, and if they conquer, you remain their prisoner. . . . In a word, the greatest danger with mercenaries lies in their cowardice and reluctance to fight, but with the auxiliaries the danger lies in their courage."

A society which has lost the inclination to kill in self-defence is doomed. Wealth, education, art, philosophy are circumventions which soon become apparent to neighbors—therefore enemies—who still possess the instinctive urge to murder their fellow men, both as sport and as a means of enriching themselves without the unpleasant necessity of toil.

"The world remains very much in the same condition, and the good in it always balances the evil; but the good and the evil change from one country to another."

How protect the good; how keep away the evil men who would destroy the good? By a powerful establishment—a militia composed of the citizens who would rather die fighting than witness their homes in flames, their women raped, their country enslaved. "We also see that troops cannot be good unless they are well trained and disciplined, and this cannot be done with any troops other than the natives of the country, for a state is not and cannot be always engaged in war, therefore troops must be trained and disciplined in time of peace, and this can only be done with the subjects of the state." And centuries would pass before the nations of Europe would fully adopt Machiavelli's plan and the *miserabili* would be ready to die for their fatherland.

"A militia—a militia—a militia—" Niccolò clamored, day in, day out. He was finally listened to by the new Gonfaloniere or President, Piero Soderini. Fearful of dictators, Florence chose her gonfalonieri for two months at a time, but this rendered the government weak, and often had the opposite effect of encouraging dictatorship. At last, however, the city found a man whom she could trust.

Piero Soderini (1450–1513) was the scion of a wealthy aristocratic family, of which one brother was a cardinal in Rome. He was a kindly, cheerful man, curiously unambitious. *Aurea Mediocritas*—"the Golden Mean"—was his guiding principle, that and an unvarying optimism in a city of cynicism and raillery. So strange a bird could be empowered with the reins of government, the Great Council decided, and he was made Gonfaloniere for life.

Delighted with the scrupulous manner in which Machiavelli

kept his official papers and secret documents—a highly unusual
condition in the chanceries of Florence, and a characteristic of
his own as well, Soderini adopted the younger man as his most
trusted assistant. The job lasted for eight years, until tragic
events drove both men into exile—one to write his masterpieces,
the other to die in obscurity and be remembered only for what
the younger had written about him, in particular a jocular
epitaph.

Not that the Gonfaloniere was always ready to accept
the plans or suggestions of this impetuous patriot, but often
Niccolò's luminous logic brightened the dark spaces of doubt
that he entertained and he would succumb, as in the case of or-
ganizing a militia.

The youth of Florence was not to be conscripted. They could
not be trusted. As always, peasants were considered simpler,
more honest, more reliable, and did they not love their soil with
arboreal tenacity? Nor would any superior be allowed a higher
rank than captain, and all commands must come from the civil-
ian authority. Always the fear of tyrants—the very fear which
inevitably brought on tyranny, for no man could be trusted to
defend the city in days of danger. "Republics which in a time of
urgent need do not take refuge in dictatorship (limited in
period), or some similar power will always be ruined when
difficulties mount."

As always, although Machiavelli worked with skill and energy
and achieved considerable success, he held neither the title nor
received the remuneration which he deserved. But he had become accustomed to this unjust subordination to men who
neither worked nor cared.

The affection that Soderini had for Machiavelli was only
partially reciprocated. Niccolò was fond of the man, but despised the Gonfaloniere. No philosophy was more abhorrent to
him than that entertained by his superior: *in media stat virtus*
—"virtue [or *virtù* as interpreted by the men of the Renais-
sance] is in the center"—in other words, avoiding extremes. To
Machiavelli the center was mediocrity, cowardice, and like neu-

trality, the origin of national disaster. "The neutral is hated by him who loses and not esteemed by him who wins; and it is preferable to act and regret than not to act and regret."

Soderini discarded violence; to Machiavelli violence was natural, "although an act of humanity and benevolence will have more influence over the minds of men than violence and ferocity." Soderini would rule by the letter of the law; Machiavelli believed in law, "but one should never allow an evil to run out of respect for the law, especially when the law itself might easily be destroyed by the evil." Soderini was ever ready to compromise; to Machiavelli compromise was often but a period of grace for the enemy to prepare for worse offences.

"A man who wished to make a profession of goodness in everything must necessarily come to grief among so many who are not good. . . . Therefore it is necessary to learn how not to be good and use this knowledge and not use it, according to the needs of the case."

When Soderini died in exile—the fate Machiavelli shared because of his master's weakness—Niccolò laughed—the laughter of the gallows—and its echo has persisted for centuries.

> La notte che morì Pier Soderini,
> l'alma n'andò dell' Inferno alla bocca,
> ma Pluto le gridò: "Anima sciocca,
> che Inferno? Va al Limbo dei bambini!"

> The night that Piero Soderini died,
> His soul descended to the depths of Hell.
> "Thou fool, no Hell for thee!" old Pluto cried,
> "Get thee to the Limbo where the infants dwell!"

And these verses became the ultimate judgment of the man who was honest and virtuous and who lost because honesty and virtue in this world—and the next—are childish folly, deserving not even of Hell!

In the Piazza wagons pulled by mules and oxen cluttered over the cobble stones. The wagons were bedecked with flowers and ribbons and filled with tiny cages made of wood or tin, each containing a grasshopper, silent and motionless, untempted by a leaf of cabbage or lettuce.

The merchants descended, tied their animals to iron posts and arranged their goods. Some, pushing carts or carrying on their arms and shoulders linen and brocades, took positions on both sides of the Arno River. Others meandered with baskets on their heads filled with spice bread, sweets, hazel nuts, confetti. A merry-go-round with grotesque little beasts turned by a rachitic donkey; games of chance, cards, dice; hoops to be thrown over iron spikes; wheels that stopped at lucky numbers; old women offering crosses, candles, amulets; beggars playing on flutes or singing current sentimental ditties or improvising to flatter young couples passing by, exciting their generosity.

Innkeepers removed the shutters of their shops and placed tables and benches in front of them, shouting to the ambulant merchants not to crowd too near, reminding them that they paid rent; the others retorted that they paid taxes and that Florence was a free city.

Now pedestrians began flowing in from all directions, laughing, shouting, imitating the music of grasshoppers, making no impression, however, on the authentic ones, congealed in mutism.

"Buy a grasshopper, *signore!*"

"Rare songsters here!"

"Caught on the leaf this morning—fresh as the dew!"

"Grasshoppers in golden cages!"

"Charity, *signori,* for *La Festa del Grillo!* It will bring you good luck!"

"Get your spice bread here—the tastiest in town!"

"Confetti for your sweethearts, *belle fanciulle!*"

"But he doesn't sing, *mascalzone.* You promised he would—"

"He's a modest fellow, *signore!* Wait till he gets home. He'll deafen you!"

"The grasshopper is a prisoner, *bambino,* and prisoners don't sing."

"Why, *babbo?*"

"I hope you will never know, *caro mio.*"

The Feast of the Grasshopper was the merriest and the most innocent of the city, dedicated to the children. No one, however poor, would go home without a cage and a grasshopper, which, if it lived and sang meant luck for the whole year.

Two middle-aged men sat at a table of one of the wine shops facing the Arno, sipping wine. One was tall with long blond hair and beard and dressed in a cloak of flowing red velvet; the other was clean-shaven, rather short, swarthy, dressed in a doublet of black velvet buttoned to the chin.

"The Florentines haven't enough religion to honor a Christian saint. They do homage to a grasshopper," one said ironically.

"It's the symbol of youth and joy," the other said.

"A rose or a bird might have been more appropriate."

"I disagree with you, Niccolò. The grasshopper is the most fortunate of creatures. The gods were in merry mood when they created him. He begins by being old, accumulates food for his descendants, eats, and digests—but what a magnificent final act to his drama! His last few weeks—corresponding to the whole period of youth in man—a carnival of love! No food, no cares, nothing but singing and mating! Alas for man—how mournful *his* last act!"

"You are right, Leonardo," Niccolò sighed. "It is an ancient Roman holiday, and our ancestors had an uncanny intuition into the nature of things. How superior paganism is to Christianity!"

"By the way, Niccolò, I translated a poem which seems appropriate to the occasion. Marco Polo, the Venetian, brought it from Kublai Khan of Cathay. It was in Lorenzo's library. I came across it recently. Would you care to hear it?"

"By all means, Leonardo. You know I'm something of a poet myself."

"Of course I know, Niccolò."

"Ariosto seems not to know it, however," Niccolò laughed bitterly. "In his *Orlando Furioso* he has mentioned every writer in Italy, but myself. When you go to Rome, if you meet him, Leonardo, give him my regards and tell him that he forgot only me—like a dog among so many poets. But please read the poem."

Leonardo produced a roll out of the inner pocket of his cloak and stretched it open on the table.

"Wonderful calligraphy, Leonardo," Niccolò complimented.

"Not half as beautiful as the original. The Chinese are incomparable artists. Some day the world will know what a great civilization is hidden behind colossal walls to the east of us. They say that the new sea route discovered by our compatriot will make it possible to reach that country without all the terrible hazards encountered by the brave Marco Polo. But here is the poem—a poor translation, for no language can imitate the marvelous drawings the Chinese call poetry. The poem is entitled 'To-Fo—Passé'—evidently the poet's own description:

> To-Fo twirls slowly
> His long mustaches,
> Sharp and thin as two pins,
> And muses:
> Today the flower girl looked at you
> Serenely,
> And her breast was still.
> Therefore, To-Fo, your youth is dead!
> Bury it!
> Do not carry it about
> Roguishly,
> Like a blue butterfly,
> Perched,
> Wings folded
> Upon a mandarin's sword.
> It is but a stuffed nightingale
> With ragged plumes
> And an open beak,
> And its music is only the gold

That rattles in your purse.
Your youth is dead, To-Fo!
Dig a long perpendicular grave
In the center of your heart,
And bury it!"

"It is beautiful, Leonardo, and beautifully read!"

"*Grazie,* Niccolò!"

"And painfully true—for us—already. *Tempus edam rerum*
—"Time destroys everything!"

"Except art, Niccolò. I am finishing my *Last Supper.* It has
taken me years. I was uncertain about Judas. How shall I portray him? Is he a villain? Is he the scapegoat foreordained to
make the great drama of Jesus possible, and therefore, mankind's noblest friend? I asked my colleagues, but never received
an acceptable answer. One day I put the question to Madonna
Elisabetta—Monna Lisa. She is brilliant and more learned than
a cardinal—*Aspasia Rediviva.* You know her, Niccolò, do you
not?"

Niccolò nodded, his thin, ironic lips stretched. He was thinking of the lines he had written recently: "We see that women
have been the cause of great dissensions and much ruin to states
and have caused great damage to those who govern them." But
he would not interrupt his companion. Artists had childish notions about men and things. Only the historian and the politician
understood. "Whoever wishes to see what will be must look to
what has been. Men having the same passions will produce the
same results. . . . That is the alpha and omega of wisdom."

"Monna Lisa smiled," Leonardo pursued. "Never had I seen
such a smile on a human face. It solved all problems. It laughed.
It cried. It scorned. It pitied. I understood Judas now, but he
could wait. I had to paint her first. It is my masterpiece, Niccolò.
Should you wish to see it—"

"Leonardo, we are in the gravest peril. Watch the people
making merry. *They* are the crickets—the foolish, intemperate
crickets of Aesop's fable. Winter is sure to overtake them, and
they will have to dance to the tune of a tyrant—a barbarian who

will enslave us all. And your art will be carried off, destroyed. Art does not live among slaves, Leonardo. It needs freedom and freedom is not offered you on a golden platter. You must fight for it."

"Avoid the tempest, Niccolò!"

"You cannot avoid it, Leonardo. No one can avoid it. Italy has fallen to the lowest depths. Let us save Florence, at least. You know I've been appointed to establish a militia—"

"So I have heard."

"The first enemy we must conquer is Pisa—"

Leonardo laughed. "Poor silly Pisa—Mistress of the Leaning Tower! Do you think, Niccolò, that Tomaso Pisano constructed it on purpose this way to mock his compatriots? This is how you look, my fellow Pisani, forever leaning toward folly! Or maybe he said, Since you have nothing to boast about, I shall make you famous, and travelers will say, You must see the Leaning Tower of Pisa—nothing like it in the world! It has already stood, Niccolò, for two hundred years and with a deviation from the perpendicular of fourteen feet! Do you think, Niccolò, that anything our artists have created will last that long? And our names—will our names— ?"

"Pisa must be ours, Leonardo! Without Pisa Florence has no legs. She cannot reach the sea. And Pisa without Florence has no arms. She needs the gods which our genius produces. Separated, we are both at the mercy of the barbarians. Yet, the vain fools fight us, invite French, Spaniards, Austrians—any auxiliaries to help destroy us—and themselves. But what logic cannot accomplish, arms will—arms and strategy. Leonardo, you are as great an engineer as you are an artist—can you turn a river?"

"Turn a river?"

"Change its course—"

Leonardo's beautiful blue eyes scintillated with thought. "All things can be done, Niccolò. I've been planning a great bridge across the Mediterranean—a balloon with men inside to rise and fly to all parts of the earth—an engine with—"

"But the Arno, Leonardo," he interrupted, "can you turn its waters away from Pisa, so that her throat be parched as in a desert, and she is forced to surrender?"

Leonardo stroked his beard, his head lowered. "It could be done, Niccolò, but have we the right to inflict such misery upon others? We are no longer Christians, but as human beings—as Humanists—"

"Where the safety of a country depends upon the resolution to be taken, no consideration of justice or injustice, humanity or cruelty, nor even of glory and shame, should be allowed to prevail. The fatherland is well defended in whatever fashion— either with ignominy or with glory."

"But the morality of a state—" Leonardo mumbled.

"The State, Leonardo, is Power, only Power, and politics is nothing but the relation of Power."

Leonardo remained pensive.

"Come, Leonardo, let us watch our good river, which will bring us victory and safety."

They rose and making their way through the throng, bent over the bridge. For a long time, in silence, they watched the waters of the Arno, now silver-carpeted by the noon sun.

"Those two men didn't pay for their wine," the waiter complained to the innkeeper. "Shall I run after them?"

"No, *sciocco,* didn't you recognize them? The tall fellow is Leonardo da Vinci, the painter; the other is our own Il Machia, the Secretary. *He* will do the paying, when he gets the money. He owes me three florins already, but I'm not afraid. Besides, I charge him double the price, to make sure, so that maybe by this time I owe *him* money," he roared with laughter. "Nobody punishes you for deception, *ragazzo,* but for being unable to hide it. *Capito?*"

"*Sì, signor.*"

"We can't live except by stealing from one another, and mutual cheating is the best honesty. Remember that, *ragazzo.*"

"I shall remember, *patrone.*"

"And now clean the table, for I see customers coming. And

don't you try to put my philosophy into practice as long as you're with me, *caro,* or I'll tear the bowels out of you. Remember that, too."

"I shall never forget it, *patrone,* and put it into practice only after I leave you."

"You're a true son of Florence, *ragazzo,*" he laughed. "You'll be a better cheat than I am, just as I am a better one than *my* master. Each generation improves upon the previous one."

The young fellow laughed.

"The time may come when we'll all have to be honest, each one knowing all the tricks of the other. But don't look so sullen, *idiota,* it won't happen in your day."

"Well, Leonardo?" Niccolò asked.

"It shall be done, Niccolò."

Machiavelli pressed his arm. "And perchance our great Republic will at last take cognizance of you, Leonardo. It has ever been and ever will be the case, that men of rare and extraordinary merit are neglected by republics in times of peace and tranquility. But let me buy you a cricket, Leonardo. It will bring you fame."

"And I shall buy you one, Niccolò. It will bring you victory." *Et tempus edam rerum.*

Of Glory and Disgrace

Machiavelli's militia was now ready to prove its mettle. All the roads to Pisa were sealed and the soldiers, with mathematical precision, laid waste woods and fields, while from the sea the mouth of the River Arno was blocked by piles and stakes.

For a whole year, Pisans attempted to break the siege, but were unsuccessful and were now facing starvation. For the first time in her fifteen years of independence and defiance of Florence, Pisa found herself helpless and friendless. Her allies were bribed by the Florentines or were busy elsewhere. It became evident to her rulers that surrender was inevitable and negotiations were started with Machiavelli in a castle at Piombino.

Even self-preservation is defenseless against vanity, and the Pisan envoys refused to deal with a mere Secretary, coat untrimmed with gold, dagger unstudded with gems. "What are we," they demanded, "beggars, ragamuffins? We have lost the war, but not honor! We surrender only to the noblest!"

Enraged both at the impertinence of the envoys and at the nastiness of his masters, who depriving him of due honors belittled him even in the eyes of the vanquished, Machiavelli shouted: "Do you want peace or do you want war? If it is war you want you shall have more than enough!"

They wanted peace.

"Between an armed man and an unarmed one," Machiavelli later distilled his experience in an aphorism, "no proportion holds, and it is contrary to reason to expect that the armed man should voluntarily submit to the unarmed or that the unarmed should stand secure among armed retainers."

The treaty of peace which Soderini and Machiavelli drew up showed the conciliatory character of the former and the political wisdom of the latter. "Above all the victorious princes must abstain from taking property, for men forget more easily the death of their pater than the loss of their patrimony. . . . It is not prudent to wish always to have the last blow; it is injudicious to drive men to desperation, for they who are without hope are without fear."

No confiscations were made and no commercial privileges revoked. Amnesty was granted to all and the old rights, enjoyed previous to the city's secession in 1494, were restored. A model of a treaty, which, if imitated, might have prevented many a rancorous war in the grievous history of mankind. But Power is the alchemist who turns hands into steel and hearts into stone, befuming the brain with fantasies of glory.

On Corpus Christi day, June 8, 1509, a rider entered Florence waving an olive branch and reported to the Signoria that the treaty had been ratified by the Pisans and that there was peace in Tuscany. "Everyone is crazy with joy," a colleague of the Second Chancery wrote to Niccolò, who was with the triumphant troops marching into Pisa.

When Machiavelli returned to Florence, Soderini embraced him; the "Ten of Liberty and Peace" pronounced a "laudation" upon him in the name of the Republic, but neglected to add a little something in the nature of gold coins. The ceremony was quickly over—the little Secretary must not get a "swelled head." Only some of his colleagues feasted him in their favorite tavern on the Arno. Here he heard, mingled with the choicest obscenities, the love and esteem they bore him. They compared him to Hannibal and proclaimed him general.

"Time driving all things before it, may bring with it evil as well as good," said Niccolò Machiavelli, who had been watching intently the wheel of fortune turn and the calculations of men prove fallacious and preposterous. Time had already brought him whatever good it had in store for him, and now began to bring the evil. Save that as in fairy tales, the ugly witch is, in truth, the beautiful princess in disguise—the evil was, in reality, man's most cherished good—ransom from time —immortality.

Now started the saraband of nations and their perpetual perfidies. France, England, Spain, Austria, Venice, fighting one another, fighting the Pope, now allies, now enemies. Suddenly France achieved her greatest triumph at Ravenna—the most decisive victory of the century against the See of Rome. So the French believed, but they should have known, as Machiavelli knew, that "principalities acquired by Ecclesiastical Princes are acquired either by ability or by fortune, but are maintained without either, for they are sustained by ancient religious customs, which are so powerful and of such quality, that they keep their princes in power in whatever manner they proceed to live. These princes alone have states without defending them, have subjects without governing them. But as they are exalted and maintained by God, it would be a presumptuous and foolish man to discuss them."

Alarmed, Julius II invoked the "Holy League" to save Christendom. From Navarre, from England, from Spain the soldiers poured into Italy. Under the captaincy of the viceroy of Naples, Raymond de Cardona, they turned the great victory into an abysmal defeat, and Louis XII trudged back to France, relinquishing until the days of Napoleon the French dream of annexing Italy. On the other hand, Spain took this occasion to consolidate her conquest and under Charles V became the chief power of Italy. When Spain formed part of the Empire, she transferred her rights to the Hapsburgs of Austria, whose yoke the Italians could not throw off until the advent of Cavour in the middle of the nineteenth century.

Always in fear of the papacy, the Florentines, lured by the triumph of the French at Ravenna, made an alliance with them. How should they know that the spectacular victory would turn so quickly into a more spectacular defeat and that, therefore, they would be at the mercy of their mortal foe, Pope Julius II?

Julius was now determined to stifle that proud city once and for all. His Spanish troops had already taken Bologna and were on their way to Prato, a day's march from the Capital. Florence had her militia and Prato was well fortified, but the defending soldiers, terrorized by the mercenaries, allowed them to make a breach in the wall and rush into the city.

Now the Spaniards lived up to their reputation of being the cruelest as well as the most pious men of Christendom. It was this very ferocity, which, in lieu of discipline and training, made them the foremost infantry in the world. Soldiers, civilians, men, women, young, old—no one was spared. The victors boiled them in oil, quartered them alive, strangled them, blew their bodies full of air with bellows until they burst, blinded and roasted, and left not one coin or precious article in the city.

Florence sued for peace, which was granted in exchange for vast sums of money, the removal of the Gonfaloniere Soderini, and permission for the Medici to return. They had been in exile for eighteen years, since the days of Savonarola, and were ever plotting to re-enter and resume power.

Shrewd politicians, the Medici did not return as conquerors. They knew that the Florentines, accustomed to freedom, would plot against them and make their stay unpleasant and perilous. They returned as friends and patriots. They reminded the people of Lorenzo the Magnificent. Had any city in Italy been as happy and prosperous as Florence during his reign? Look at her now—poor, miserable, defeated. The time for reconciliation had come, and with it a renewal of the "good old days."

Suddenly, the city was full of Medici relatives and of Medicean followers, and those who had been vocal against dictators either tried to make their getaway as swiftly as possible, or hid in obscure corners and kept their mouths tightly shut.

Cardinal Giovanni de' Medici, while ostensibly upholding the constitution, began to cleanse the government offices of former enemies and of possible future ones—without ostentation and without apparent violence.

Now that Piero Soderini, symbol of honesty and democracy, had fled the city, seeking refuge in Ragusa, Dalmatia, it was inevitable that his chief aide could not remain in office long. Aware of this, Machiavelli attempted by means of flattery and fawning to convince the Medici that he would be their loyal servitor. But past master of cynicism and diabolism, as generations of preachers have described him, he found it impossible to keep truth from blotting the pages of his letters.

The Medici were not convinced and on November 9, 1512, Machiavelli received the fatal notice: "We remove Niccolò, son of Bernardo Machiavelli, from his office as Secretary of the Second Chancery, and we release him from all his other duties." Moreover, he was banished from Florence for the period of one year, but ordered to remain within Florentine territory.

Hardly had this misfortune befallen him, than a fresh one, more virulent yet, came rushing toward him. Two young Florentines of noble families, Agostino Capponi and Paolo

Boscoli, conceived a childish plot against the life of Giuliano de'
Medici, governor of Florence during the absence of his brother,
the Cardinal, who had gone to the conclave in Rome for the
election of a new pope, since in the interval Pope Julius II had
died.

The two young conspirators made a list of those whom they
considered faithful to the Republic and ready to help them, and
among them they included the name of Niccolò Machiavelli.
Had they only consulted him, their own lives would have been
spared, as well as the futile sufferings of the innocent ones
whom they embroiled. He would have told them of the countless
—and almost always the insurmountable—difficulties of con-
spiracy and the uselessness of assassination. He would have
explained that a nation does not free itself by the murder of a
dictator, for another promptly springs to take his place, but by
the people rising in mass, prepared to die, if necessary, to
achieve liberty. This, however, is accomplished only by long
preparation, by education, and by understanding the intricate,
inalterable dynamics of Power. But liberals understood Machiavelli as little as did the tyrants, and as in future generations,
the men of church, tribune, and university.

As it was inevitable, the conspirators were apprehended,
their list confiscated, and the men named upon it, arrested.
Machiavelli in vain protested his innocence. He was thrown
into the pestilential dungeon of Florence, where he was put to
the torture. Six shocks of the cord were inflicted, but not a word
escaped him in the bitterness of his agony which might incrimi-
nate others or serve as confession of his own guilt.

Still unconvinced, or their sadism unassuaged, the authorities
kept him closely chained in solitary confinement, week after
week. Yet his fortitude remained unshaken and while his mental
endurance puzzled his tormentors, it did not weary their
malignity.

To keep sane and in the vague hope of mercy, Niccolò wrote
sonnets to Giuliano, protesting his innocence and pledging
fidelity to the Medici—sonnets, half humorous, half tragic. He

spoke of "lice large as butterflies crawling on the walls"; of the
stench which choked him; of the filth; of the horror of hearing
the cry—*ora pro eis*—"pray for them"—as the condemned,
among whom young Capponi and Boscoli, were led to the gallows.

> Hor vadino in buonhora,
> Perchè la tua pietà ver me si volga,
> Ch'al padre et al bisalvo il nome tuo lag.

"But let them go, and God speed, provided that thy mercy
be turned toward me, that thou mayest outdo in greatness thy
father and great grandfather."

Was Giuliano amused? Did he think that a poor fool who
knew no better way of exciting interest in a ruler than writing
doggerel, must indeed be innocent? Take Francesco Guicciardini, for instance, only thirty years old, but how shrewd, the
rascal! That man might be guilty, but he was essential. Innocence—bah—*macchè*—in politics it might prove the greatest
crime. Oh, let the dog get out! He has already served as a
warning to all and sundry—to keep plume and tongue in check!
Let him wander about, a living witness to the greatness and
inexorable justice of the Lords of the Immortal House of the
Medici!

On the day on which Machiavelli was freed, the Florentines
were celebrating the election of Cardinal Giovanni de' Medici
as Pope Leo X. He was only thirty-seven, one of the youngest
men ever to occupy the throne of the Vatican.

Not even in the days of Lorenzo the Magnificent did the city
of Florence witness such a frenetic bacchanal of joy. Everything
was "on the house"—wine, meat, cake—brought in by oxcarts
in great barrels and enormous baskets. As in all fairy tales, the
celebration lasted for three days and three nights, and the relatives of the new Pope threw gold ducats from loaded sacks
into the crowds. "And when a sack was almost empty, the lords
and ladies threw it down. Wherever they saw the most people,

there they cast the most sacks." So wrote one of the eyewitnesses. Not only coins, but coats, hats, bonnets, silks, silverware. From the balconies of the palaces of the wealthy, gifts rained upon the wretched, who had been hungry and in tatters for so long. Only in the gorgeous dreams induced by hashish did such marvels occur.

Soon they would awaken and would find their gifts but broken bits of glass and rags upon which the sun had cast its treacherous rays, and the heavy yoke of tyranny would begin to cut into their flesh and fester. Alas, that generation after generation, deluded and famished Esaus barter their birthright for a mess of porridge to the shrewd, unscrupulous Jacobs, their false brothers!

It became known that at Rome, Leo X surpassed his ancestor, Lorenzo of Florence, in magnificence and in generosity toward artists and *letterati*. He proudly proclaimed that in his father's house, he had been raised among great books and wonderful works of art, and that he was determined to replenish the Vatican with the rarest of manuscripts and the most magnificent creations of paint and marble. He invited, as his guests, architects, poets, painters, archeologists, historians, musicians. The best Latinists he made his secretaries and Humanists were entrusted with the administration. "A stone could sooner fly into the air than the Holy Father save a thousand ducats," friends of Niccolò reported to him, "and poets sing: 'Leo gives gold for the silver tones of our lyres.' "

Big fish and little ones disported themselves in the glittering pond of the Vatican. Machiavelli alone was a fish out of water gasping on the sands of poverty and neglect. He was forty-four years old, jobless, and penniless, except for his little ancestral country home in San Casciano, eight miles from Florence. Thither he went. His wife, Marietta, was happy, for at last she would have him home. His children, too, welcomed him. Soon, however, he began to feel the awful burden of idleness. To Vettori, a friend who knew how to carve his own niche in the palace of the Pontiff, Machiavelli wrote: "As to putting a good

face upon my troubles, you may derive this pleasure from my
misfortunes, that I have borne them with such courage that I
can even find cause to admire myself, and I seem to be more
worthy than I had supposed. . . . But if nothing can be done
for me, I shall live as I first came into the world, for I was born
poor and learned want before I learnt to enjoy."

But hardly had he finished his heroic pose, than his desperation broke out again. "Thus, then, I must remain in my squalor
without finding any man to take thought of my services or to
believe that I can be of any use. But it is impossible to continue
long like this, for I am rusting away, and my family would be
much better off without me, since I am only a burden to them,
being accustomed to spend and unable to exist without spend-
ing. . . . And of what use is it to me the admiration of those
who like to see heroism in others, as they like to watch a fine
spectacle, from a comfortable seat and after a good dinner?"

A man of habits and punctuality, he could not live in the manner of è dolce far niente—"it is sweet to do nothing." He tried
to organize his daily routine. "Since my last misfortune I have
led a quiet country life. I rise with the sun and go into one of the
woods for a few hours to inspect yesterday's work. I pass some
time with the woodcutters, who have always some trouble to tell
me, either of their own, or of their neighbor." (He had decided
to have his tiny forest of oaks cut down, hoping thus to silence
his more clamorous debtors and pay his taxes.) "Bored, I betake
myself to the inn on the roadside, chat with passers-by, ask news
of the places whence they come. . . . This carries me to the
dinner hour, when in the company of my brood, I swallow whatever fare this poor little place of mine and my slender patrimony
can offer me—cheese, bread, beans, figs, pears, and smoked
meats. Nothing is bought in the city. . . . In the afternoon I
go back to the inn. There I generally find the host, a butcher, a
miller, and a couple of brickmakers. I mix with these boors the
whole day playing cricca and tric trac, which games give rise to a
thousand quarrels and much exchange of bad language, and we
generally wrangle over pennies, and our shouts can be heard in

San Casciano town. Steeped in this degradation, my wits grow mouldy and I vent my rage at the indignities of fate, and give free rein to all sorts of scurvy habits."

But when evening comes : "I return to the house and I go into my study. At the threshold I take off my peasant clothes dirty and spotted with mud; I put on my festive garments, and thus fittingly attired, I enter into the assembly of men of olden times. Welcomed by them, and feeling no weariness, forgetting all my troubles and no longer fearing poverty nor dreading death, for the space of four hours I live wholly with them. I feed upon the food which is my true nourishment and which has made me what I am. I dare to talk to them and ask them the reasons for their actions. Out of their kindness they answer me. And since Dante says, 'Knowledge consists in remembering what one has learned,' I have noted down what I have gained from my inter-course with them."

Still the days are long and hope becomes dimmer and dimmer. "I shall have to cower among my rags or retire to some out-of-the-way spot to teach children their letters, forsaking my own family as though I were dead. . . . I am wearing out and can-not go long in this fashion without being contemptible from sheer poverty."

Once in a while, unable to stand the monotony, he goes to Florence, but he may not visit the Chancery. And would his former friends, who escaped the axe, bother with him? How well he knows that nothing bores us as much as a friend's per-sistent misfortune. And so "I spend my time between Donato Del Corno's shop and La Riccia, the whore. But I think I am beginning to bore them both. The one says that I crowd up the shop, the other I crowd up her house. However, with the one and the other I try to pass as a sensible person, and up to now with so much success that Donato lets me warm myself at his fire and La Riccia sometimes lets me snatch a kiss. I don't think this happy state of affairs will last, because I have given them some good advice which they don't like. Today La Riccia said to her maid—in reality talking to me: 'Oh, these clever people, these clever people! I don't know what the idea is! It seems to me they just twist everything round.' "

As he gauges not only his misfortune, but that of his beloved city, once again in chains, he writes:

Io spero, e lo sperar cresce il tormento;
io piango, e il pianger ciba il lasso core;
io ardo, e l'arsion non par di fuore;
io temo ciò ch'io veddo, ciò ch'io sento;
ogni cosa mi da nuovo dolore.
Così sperando piango, rido e ardo,
e paura ho di ciò ch' i' odo o guardo.

"I hope, and hoping increases my torment; I cry, and crying feeds my tired heart; I laugh, and my laughter does not sink into me; I am afraid of what I see and of what I hear; everything brings a fresh pain. So, while I am hoping, I cry and laugh and burn, and I am afraid of what I hear or see."

Discourses—The Prince—Two Bottles of Wine

Of all the Roman authors with whom Niccolò Machiavelli held converse in his study, Titus Patavinus Livius (Livy) (59 B.C.–17 A.D.) spoke most eloquently and most intimately to him.

Under the title of *Decades*, Titus Livius, who was born in Padua, wrote the history of Rome from the foundation of the city to the year 9 B.C.—142 books in manuscript, of which only thirty-five are extant. An admirer of the past and an ardent patriot, Livius celebrated the grandeur of Rome. This being his aim, his style is brilliant and his facts are colored. It matters little, however, for always history creates legend and legend replaces history, while the balder and more numerous the facts the greater the chance of misrepresentation, and trees, even the leafless, have so often obstructed the view of the forest.

Niccolò had reached bottom, and he could sit comfortably, for nothing relaxes as the acceptance of one's total failure. His mind, now heavy with the honey of wisdom and the gall of experience, sought a vessel into which to pour them. He could not know it, but the moment had arrived which Fortune had prepared for him to start on his road to immortality.

He found the vessel—the books of Titus Patavinus Livius—upon which he would comment, expound, explain, relate the ancient days to his own, compare the heroes and the villains of two millennia past to those he had seen and known and watched, and point out to his disoriented contemporaries the activities of man which shape his codes of morals. For, history had little validity to him unless it revealed the perpetual struggle of man to extricate himself from the snares of his evil fate, even though he himself was generally their creator.

Machiavelli did not, like the Indians, believe in reincarnation; he barely knew of their existence, for the error of Columbus had not yet been entirely rectified. But he did believe in the eternal repetition of history and of men who make history, and in the cyclical fall of old civilizations due to decadence and corruption, and the rise of young ones, belligerent and unimpeded.

"Although the envious nature of man," he writes in the introduction to his book, which he entitled *Discorsi*—"Discourses," "so prompt to blame and so slow to praise, makes the discovery and introduction of any new principles and systems as dangerous almost as the exploration of unknown seas and continents, yet animated by that desire which impels me to do what may prove for the common benefit of all, I have resolved to open a new route, which has not yet been followed by anyone. . . . And wishing, as far as in me lies, to draw mankind from the error of ignoring the past—as though heaven, the sun, the elements, and men had changed the order of their motions and power, and were different from what they were in ancient times—I have thought it proper to write upon those books of Titus Livius that have come to us despite the malice of time. . . . In this way those who read my remarks may derive those advantages which should be the aim of all study of history. . . . I hope to carry it sufficiently far, so that but little may remain for others to continue it to its destined end."

Every chapter of the book, besides telling in an enticing manner a portion of the history of Rome, as evoked by Titus Livius, and dovetailed with related incidents in the current history of Florence and Italy, has a moral kernel—a maxim chiseled in form and luminous in thought—tinged with the bitter of truth and uncoated with the sugar of illusion, but seminal and liberating.

There are three kinds of government, Machiavelli agrees with the ancient writers of politics—the monarchical, the aristocratic, and the democratic. They are all good, but all of them are prone to speedy degeneration—monarchy into tyranny; aristocracy into oligarchy; democracy into licentiousness. How to avoid this perilous debasement and establish a free society comparable to the Roman Republic is Machiavelli's central occupation. And it is a republic which he favors, but to keep itself in a healthy condition, a republic should, in reality, partake of all the three forms of government, with the prince, the *aristoi,* and the people, restricting one another's powers within prescribed bounds. For the first time in political writing the modern conception of division of functions is foreshadowed.

"But whoever desires to found a state and give it laws, must start by assuming that all men are bad and ever ready to display their vicious nature, whenever they may find occasion for it. If their evil disposition remains concealed for a time, it must be attributed to some unknown reason; and we must assume that it lacked occasion to show itself; but time, which has been said to be the father of all truth, does not fail to bring it to light. . . . Since men act rightly only upon compulsion, poverty and hunger make them industrious and the law makes them good. . . ."

Ecce homo! It is safer to know his true nature than falsify it by pretension, ostentation, flattery, lies. For by knowing the truth, a society can be built in which men, despite their fundamental baseness, can live in peace with one another and to the general advantage. Indeed, the very evils may be utilized for the construction of good. What, in Nature, has not this dual possibility—water, air, fire, light, darkness—and the greatest of all, pain, which warning us of danger, makes life possible, and is, therefore, our greatest good?

"When the people are entrusted with the care of any privilege or liberty, being less disposed to encroach upon it, they will, of necessity, take better care of it; and being unable to take it away themselves, will prevent others from doing so." Thus they who, under pressure of hunger and need, labor and create, are superior to those who in idle futility consume and destroy. "Moreover, great troubles are occasioned by those who possess, for the fear to lose stirs the same passions in men as the desire to gain, as men do not believe themselves secure in what they already possess except by acquiring still more."

But "a republic must have laws that afford the masses the opportunity of giving vent to the hatred they may have conceived against any citizen; for if there exist no legal means for this, they will resort to illegal ones, which beyond doubt produce much worse effects. But just as useful as accusations are in a republic, just so useless and pernicious are calumnies. . . . Now, there is no more effectual way for putting an end to calumnies than to introduce the system of legal accusations."

Thus, the whims of the wielders of power and the vagaries of the tollers of tongues, could be eliminated.

"Princes and republics who wish to maintain themselves free from corruption must above all things preserve the purity of all religious observances and treat them with proper reverence. . . . And therefore everything that tends to favor religion (even though it were believed to be false) should be received and availed to strengthen it. . . . Such was, in fact, the practice observed by sagacious men; which has given rise to the belief in the miracles that are celebrated in religions, however false they may be."

The Renaissance was not a "rebirth" for all. It created an aristocracy of intellect, which in its scintillation and arrogance, viewed with contempt the common man who bore the burdens of life—tilled and mined and sewed, and with the ass and the ox pulled the carts and shared the stables. "The life of the many," said Hobbes, "is hasty, brutish, and short."

Such men—and they were the vast majority of the citizens of Florence—could not, in the opinion of Machiavelli, be tamed and be eager to defend their nation, save by a fear greater than that of the whip and a reward more delectable than that of a loaf of bread. Only a hell of perpetual torment and a heaven of eternal bliss, could make them accept without resentment and rebelliousness the indignities and injustices inherent in all societies. Human laws, therefore, without which chaos was inevitable, must be sustained by religious dogmas and fantasies even of the most preposterous nature.

Lies? What of that? Machiavelli was only interested in telling the truth, and the truth was that lies served mankind better than truths. Had not St. Augustine, in a flash of divine revelation, presented to the world the gist of all religions: *Credo quia absurdum* —"I believe because it is absurd"?

If the day comes when man can measure the skies and plumb the earth, and find there neither heaven nor hell, nor angels nor devils, will he, then, accept truths and discard lies? No. "For whoever considers things present and things past, will easily understand how the same appetites and humors are, and always have been, incident to all states and people, so that by diligently examining the course of former ages, it is an easy matter to foresee what is going to happen in a commonwealth."

The future? Remove this fragile moment, called the present, and the past and the future merge and are one.

"The great majority of mankind are satisfied with appearances, as though they were realities, and are often even more influenced by the things that seem than by those that are." And this characteristic is beyond the realm of time and the tide of circumstance.

"Men afflict themselves in evil, and become weary of the good, and both these dispositions produce the same effects. For when men are no longer obliged to fight from necessity, they fight from ambition, which passion is so powerful in the hearts of men that it never leaves them, no matter to what height they may rise. The reason for this is that nature has created men so that they desire everything, but are unable to attain it; desire being thus always greater than the faculty of acquiring, discontent with what they have and dissatisfaction with themselves result from it . . ." And thus arise revolutions, wars, and civil wars.

However, greed and ambition can be held in check, at least partially, by appropriate laws, "but there can be no worse example in a republic than to make a law and not to observe it; the more so when it is disregarded by the very parties who made it. . . . All evil examples have their origin in good beginning. . . . For this reason republics should make it one of their aims to watch that none of her citizens should be allowed to do harm under the pretense of doing good. . . . I think, and ever shall think, that it cannot be wrong to defend one's opinion with arguments founded upon reason, and without employing force or authority."

This, too, is possible only in republics, where men are equal and untrammeled before the law.

"We furthermore see the cities where the people are masters make the greatest progress in the least possible time. And this can be attributed to no other cause than that the governments of the people are better than those of princes. . . . Compared to princes we shall find the people vastly superior in all that is good and glorious. . . . Only cities and countries that are free can achieve greatness. Population is greater there because marriages are freer and offer more advantages to the citizen; for people will gladly have children when they know that their children not only are born free and not slaves, but if they possess talents and virtue, can arrive at the highest dignities of the state. In free countries we also see wealth increase more rapidly, for everybody gladly multiplies things and seeks to acquire those goods the possession of which he can tranquilly enjoy. . . . To usurp supreme and absolute authority in a free state, and subject it to tyranny, the people must have already become corrupt by gradual steps from generation to generation. For it is as difficult to make a people free that is resolved to live in servitude, as it is to subject a people to servitude that is determined to be free."

Two rattlers have always deafened the world—the rattlers of swords and the rattlers of gold, while muffled drums follow the triumphant armies. In the long run it is impossible to distinguish victor from vanquished, and the glory is ever to the worm.

"Everyone may begin a war at his pleasure, but cannot so finish it," warns Machiavelli. "And whoever impoverishes himself by war acquires no power, even though he be victorious, for his conquests cost him more than they are worth. But the ambition of men is such, that to gratify a present desire, they think not of the evils which will in a short time result from it."

Thus spake "Old Nick," the terror of those who glorify man, but brutalize him; the target of contempt, hate, rancor, and prejudice of those who preach man's liberty, but enslave him. In truth, however, Machiavelli's denigrators and denouncers have rarely read him or have simply caught on to a maxim or to a phase of his life, in search of a scapegoat or as a cloak concealing their own hypocritical plans.

While Niccolò held no office and his financial situation grew steadily worse, he was not entirely without honor in his city, and the gardens of the Rucellai family were open to him. Here foregathered the most distinguished citizens—poets, historians, Latinists, artists—discussing, reading, and doubtless quarreling, as men who hold opinions always will. For having expressed an opinion, however far-fetched, we straightway become its slave, ready to die defending it, and even ready to believe it. And many continue to be martyrs to causes which have ceased to exist, their crowns rusting upon their heads as tin wreaths rust upon forgotten tombs.

Cosimo Rucellai, the youngest of the family which was related to that of the Medici, in his sedan chair, paralyzed, ruled over the court. He listened with particular interest to Machiavelli reading chapters of his *Discourses,* as he brought them from San Casciano, where in his study, in the pleasant company of Titus Patavinus Livius, he composed them.

Doubtless, Cosimo must have lent—without hope of return—many a gold ducat to this man whose talent he praised, thus stirring envy in the cramped hearts of the professional scholars who considered him an interloper.

For the various courtesies shown him by Cosimo Rucellai and another friend, Zanobi Buondelmonte, Machiavelli dedicated his *Discourses* to them. "With this I send you a gift which, if it bears no proportion to the extent of the obligations I owe you, is nevertheless the best I am able to offer you; for I have endeavored to embody in it all that long experience and assiduous research have taught me of the affairs of the world. . . . Accept it, then, as one accepts whatever comes from friends, looking rather to the intention of him who gives, than to the thing offered. . . . Being good or bad, however, you wanted this work, and such as it is I send it to you. . . ."

Whatever friendship the two men had shown toward Niccolò, he repaid them handsomely, for he raised upon their vanished dust tombstones which time's hammers will never crumble.

Pope Leo X recalled Giuliano to Rome and appointed Lorenzo de' Medici, grandson of the Magnificent, governor of Florence. Lorenzo was a youth in his early twenties, who might have been surnamed "Inglorioso" to distinguish him from his ancestor.

Hope, which had for so long forsaken Niccolò Machiavelli, began to nudge him. The world had changed. The Medici were still around, to be sure, but the ruler now was not one of the old dogs, who hated and mistrusted him because of his republican ideas, but a pup, young enough to be his son. There was his

chance! He could be his father and more than his father—his
teacher! He could show him how to become as great a prince as
his grandfather—greater—capable of mighty deeds—perhaps
even unite poor Italy! He had but to indicate the true road to
glory, and surely he would follow it, for youth is ever ready for
glory, but few are there to point the way.

There were his *Discourses* he was working on, which kept him
busy, but of what good were they to him? How many hands applauded him? A dozen—two. He could return to them when
time was more auspicious, and he was in the mood. (He did, in
fact, return to them again and again for a decade.)

Erasmus' *The Education of a Christian Prince* had not yet
appeared, but Machiavelli had come across various books of the
Speculum Principis—"The Mirror for Princes," purporting to
teach young monarchs how to behave. He despised that type of
writing, for it dealt with men, not as they were, but as they
ought to be and with princes suitable for fairylands. "Many
have pictured republics and principalities, which, in fact, have
never been known or seen. . . . It is more appropriate to follow
up the real truth of a matter than the imagination of it."

He would write about men of flesh and blood and evil passions and about a prince, who, as their ruler, must hold both
reins and whip in hands of steel. His pupil would learn that
without the lust for Power no political structure can have validity or long survive, and that one's strength is derived from the
weakness of others.

His material was close at hand. He had but to extract from
his *Discourses* appropriate bits, history and maxims, simplify
them, sharpen them, and burnish them, until they glowed with
inextinguishable truth.

Yet, it was not to be pure gift to young Lorenzo. He would
expect appropriate reward. He needed money. He needed an
office to go to as in the good old days. He needed to be sent on
important missions. Who had had wider experience than he in
dealing with kings and generals? Who could report with greater

accuracy and depth—and truth—the intricate maneuvers of the subtle ones? There was nothing wrong in such exchange of goods. The great teachers of old were not only revered, but enriched, and Alexander took Aristotle along on his expeditions.

He would have to flatter a little. It was an ancient—and honorable—custom, not without value, when offered by a commoner to a prince. We often try to become what flattery claims we are, and thus the seed of lie may produce the blossom of truth. Nevertheless, since there are two sides to every argument, as to every coin, the young prince should be warned. "There is no way to guard against flattery but by letting it be seen that you take no offense in hearing the truth; but when everyone is free to tell you the truth, you lose their respect."

Prodded on by hope, Machiavelli wrote with furious speed and finished the book within a few months. "I have written a small book—*De Principatibus*. . . . It will undoubtedly be welcome to a prince and especially one who has newly acquired sovereignty. . . . My dire straits impelled the dedication." Thus he wrote to a friend. People might misunderstand. They might think that he had turned coat, that he had betrayed liberty by embracing the rule of the Medici, the tyrants, willingly and by conviction. But a man in need who had a family to support, was he not entitled to do or say anything, however reprehensible it might seem? The belly has no nimbus.

Niccolò soon found the Latin title pretentious, for unlike the orthodox Humanists, who disdained the new tongues, he was *italianissimo* and wrote only in the Tuscan dialect, which he helped to mold into the most musical of languages. He, therefore, changed it to *Il Principe*—"The Prince."

What did he tell Lorenzo de' Medici? Among other things— interwoven with examples taken from the annals of the Romans, greatest of conquerors, and contrasting them with the ways of their miserable descendants—the following:

"Men must either be caressed or else annihilated. They will avenge themselves for small injuries, but cannot do so for great ones; the injury, therefore, that we do a man must be such that we do not fear his revenge."

"It is necessary for a prince to possess the friendship of the people; otherwise he has no resource in times of adversity."

"When a prince can command and is a man of courage and does not get frightened in adversity, and by his own valor animates the mass of the people, he will not find himself deceived by them."

"It is the nature of men to be as much bound by the benefits they confer as by those they receive."

"A prince should have no other aim or thought, nor take up any other thing for his study, but war and its organization and discipline. . . . And one sees, on the other hand, that when princes think more of luxury than of arms, they lose their state. . . . But as to the exercise of the mind, the prince ought to read history and study the actions of eminent men."

"If one considers well, it will be found that some things which seem virtuous, would, if followed, lead to one's ruin, and some others which appear vices result in one's greater security and wellbeing."

"A prince must not mind incurring the charge of cruelty for the purpose of keeping his subjects united and faithful, for he will be more merciful than those, who, from excess of tenderness, allow disorders to arise, from whence spring bloodshed and rapine; these as a rule injure the whole community, while the executions carried out by the prince injure only individuals."

"From this arises the question whether it is better to be loved more than feared, or feared more than loved. The reply is, that one ought to be both feared and loved, but as it is difficult for the two to go together, it is much safer to be feared than loved. . . . Men have less scruples in offending one who makes himself loved than one who makes himself feared; for love is held by a chain of obligations, which, men being selfish, is broken whenever it serves their purpose; but fear is maintained by a dread of punishment which never fails. . . . I conclude, therefore, with regard to being feared and loved, that men love at their own free will, but fear at the will of the prince, and that a wise prince must rely on what is in his power and not on what is in the power of others."

"How laudable it is for a prince to keep good faith and live with integrity, and not with astuteness, everyone knows. Still, the experience of our times shows that those princes who have done great things have had little regard for good faith, and have been able by astuteness to confuse men's brains, and ultimately have overcome those who have made loyalty their foundation."

"A prince, and especially a new prince, cannot observe all those things which are considered good in men, being often obliged, in order to maintain their state, to act against faith, against charity, against humanity, and against religion. And, therefore, he must have a mind disposed to adapt itself according to the wind, and as the variations of fortune dictate, and not deviate from what is good, if possible, but be able to do evil, if constrained."

"The prince must avoid those things which make him hated or despised. . . . He is rendered despicable by being thought changeable, frivolous, effeminate, timid, and irresolute. . . . For a prince must have two kinds of fears: one internal as regards his subjects, the other external as regards foreign powers. From the latter he can defend himself with good arms and good friends, and he will always have good friends if he has good arms; and internal matters will always remain quiet, if they are not perturbed by conspiracies, and one of the most potent remedies that a prince has against conspiracies is that of not being hated by the mass of the people."

"Without doubt princes become great when they overcome difficulties and opposition. Therefore, a wise prince ought, when he has the chance, to foment astutely some enmity, so that by suppressing it, he will augment his greatness."

"Fortresses may or may not be useful according to the times.

The best fortress is to be found in the love of the people, for although you may have fortresses, they will not save you if you are hated by the people."

"A prince is further esteemed when he is a true friend or a true enemy. This policy is always more useful than remaining neutral."

"A prince must always show himself a lover of merit, give preferment to the able and honor those who excel in every art. And he should offer rewards to whoever seeks in any way to improve his city or state."

"The counsellors will all think of their own interests, and it cannot be otherwise, for men will always be false to you unless they are compelled by necessity to be true. . . . Only those defenses are good, certain and durable, which depend on yourself alone and your own ability."

"The wise man should always follow the roads that have been trodden by the great and imitate those who have most excelled, so that if he cannot reach their perfection, he may at least acquire something of its savor."

"A prince should never join with one stronger than himself, nor is it wise to form an alliance with a prince that has more reputation than power."

"It happens in all human affairs that whenever we seek to escape one mischief, we fall into another. Prudence consists in accepting a less evil as good."

"Let no prince complain of the faults committed by the people subjected to his authority, for they result entirely from his own negligence and bad example."

"There is a parable that says that in days of old young princes were sent to the Centaur for their education—the Centaur, half man, half beast. The parable of this semi-animal, semi-human teacher is meant to indicate that a prince must know how to use both natures, and that the one without the other is not durable. A prince being thus obliged to know well how to act as a beast must imitate the fox and the lion, for the lion cannot protect himself from traps and the fox cannot defend himself from wolves. One must, to be a fox, recognize traps and a lion to frighten wolves. Therefore, a prudent ruler ought not to keep faith when by so doing it would be against his interest, and when the reasons which made him bind himself no longer exist. Nor have legitimate grounds ever failed a prince who wished to show convincing excuses for the fulfillment of his promise. . . . Those that have been best able to imitate the fox have succeeded best. It is necessary to be able to disguise this character well, and to be a great feigner and dissembler; but men are so simple and so ready to obey present necessities, that one who deceives will always find those who allow themselves to be deceived. . . . They who wish to be only men and only lions do not understand power. Sooner or later, they lose both thrones and heads. He who is too concerned about means will rarely achieve his aims. He who accepts the end, must also accept the means, for the responsibility lies in the end, not in the means. And if a prince succeeds in establishing and maintaining his authority, the means will always be judged honored and approved by everyone."

The Prince caused a revolution in political thinking. It discarded sentimentalism, theology, morality, scholastic tradition, Humanistic idealism. It was the removal of cataracts from the eyes of man, even though the diseased skin afforded the mirage of utopias. What man saw now startled him, for he saw himself. Enraged, he began to cast rocks, but the rocks rebounded. There was no way by which he could escape the light Niccolò Machiavelli had shed. It preceded, it followed, it encircled. In vain "The Index"; in vain the thunders from pulpit; in vain the anathema by pedants and pundits. *The Prince* could not be removed, destroyed, driven into oblivion. If men were displeased, let them change their nature or their ways, but as long as they remained what they were and acted as they did, *The Prince* was their mirror which refused to flatter or remove the flaws. In truth, Machiavelli told nothing new; he only pointed out. And that is the function of all science and of all wisdom—pointing out.

"Having now considered all the things we have spoken of," Machiavelli begins his last chapter of *The Prince,* "I thought within myself whether at present the time was not propitious in Italy for a new prince, and if there was not a state of things which offered the opportunity to a prudent and capable man to introduce a new system that would do honor to himself and good to the mass of the people, it seems to me that so many things concur to favor a new ruler that I do not know any time more fitting for such an enterprise. . . . Almost lifeless Italy awaits one who should heal her wounds. . . . There is nothing now she can hope for but that your illustrious House of Medici may place itself at the head of this redemption. . . . This opportunity must not be allowed to pass, so that Italy may at last find her liberator. I cannot express the love with which he would be received. . . . This barbarous domination stinks in the nostrils of everyone. . . . May your illustrious House, therefore, assume this task with that courage and those hopes which are inspired by a just cause, so that under its banner our fatherland may be raised up, and under its auspices be verified that saying of Petrarch:

> Virtù contra'l furore
> Prenderà l'arme et sia il combatter corto
> Che l'antico valore
> Ne gl'Italici cuor non è morto.

> Valor against fell wrath
> Will take up arms; and be the combat quickly sped!
> For, sure, the ancient worth,
> That in Italians stir the heart, is not yet dead.

Machiavelli smoothed the parchment of the manuscript tenderly, fearfully, as a mother smooths the beloved head of her little son who leaves for school for the first time.

And sharpening a new goose quill and dipping it into the fresh ink, he wrote upon the best piece of parchment he could obtain, and with many flourishes, which are the calligraphic genuflection:

NICCOLÒ MACHIAVELLI
TO
LORENZO THE MAGNIFICENT
Son of Piero de' Medici

It is customary for those who wish to gain the favor of a prince to endeavor to do so by offering him gifts of those things which they hold most precious, or in which they know him to take special delight. In this way princes are often presented with horses, arms, cloths of gold, gems, and such-like ornaments worthy of their grandeur. In my desire, however, to offer to Your Highness some humble testimony of my devotion, I have been unable to find among my possessions anything which I hold so dear or esteem so highly as that knowledge of the deeds of great men which I have acquired through a long experience of modern events and a constant study of the past. . . . And although I deem this work unworthy of Your Highness's acceptance, yet my confidence in your humanity assures me that you will receive it with favor. . . . Nor will it, I trust, be deemed presumptuous on the part of a man of humble and obscure condition to attempt to discuss and direct the government of princes; for, in the same way that landscape painters station themselves in the valleys in order to draw mountains or high grounds, and ascend an eminence in order to get a good view of the plains, so it is necessary for a prince to know thoroughly the nature of the people, and of the populace to know the nature of princes.

May I trust, therefore, that Your Highness will accept this little gift in the spirit in which it is offered; and if Your Highness will deign to peruse it, you will recognize in it my ardent desire that you attain to that grandeur which fortune and your own merits presage for you.

And should Your Highness gaze down from the summit of your lofty position toward this humble spot, you will recognize the great and un-merited sufferings inflicted on me by a cruel fate.

His Highness was being groomed by his valet for the hunt, when a lackey entered with a small package. He informed the Prince that a man by the name of Niccolò Machiavelli had left it and begged that it be presented to him.

Lorenzo unwrapped the package. "Oh, a manuscript—" he made a gesture of displeasure with his nose and lips. The valet and the lackey exchanged winks. "What does the fool think I am—a bookworm? *Vabenne,* put it away and give the beggar two bottles of wine with my compliments."

The young ruler was weak, and vain, and interested in idle and licentious living. His chief concern was a royal marriage. An alliance with one of the great powers of Europe, via matrimony, seemed to him the only means of security. The sons and nephews of the popes had always been pursued by ill luck and he sought to avert disaster. At last his ambition was consummated. He married Madeleine de La Tour d'Auvergne, kinswoman to the French king. Now he became the tool—the willing tool—of France, for he was not at all interested in becoming the Prince of Machiavelli's dream.

Other men, in various lands, in various ages, would attempt it, would multilate Machiavelli's meanings, would grasp the evil surface but not the good essence of his words, would establish tyrannies and not democracies—his final goal—would wage wars for personal glory, not for the benefit of the people. His name would be the symbol of treachery, not of truth; of oppression, not of liberty. His "Prince" would become a monstrosity, a vile caricature.

Lorenzo died (some say he was assassinated on one of his nocturnal prowlings for women) at the age of twenty-seven, but not before he begat a daughter destined to be Queen of France—Catherine de' Medici—chief planner of the vast murder of the Night of St. Bartholomew. And for two bottles of wine, the rascal bought immortality—the biggest bargain on record!

Niccolò Machiavelli took the two bottles to the miserable hovel of La Riccia, the whore. "I have brought you princely wine, *cara.*"

"Always your jokes, Niccolò," she said, half-peevishly, half-pleased. *"Vabbene,* let's drink your princely *piscia."*

"To the long life of 'The Prince'!" Niccolò toasted.

"I thought you were against princes."

"So I was. So I am. So I shall always be. But this prince is not a man, but a book I've written."

"A book—" she spat. "Niccolò, you're no longer a youngster. Why don't you give up all that foolishness and do something which will bring in some money? Your poor wife and children certainly need it."

"How right you are, *cara!* But I can do nothing. I am not a businessman, I have no trade, I have no profession. My poor father wanted me to become a lawyer. I should have followed his advice—"

"In a word, you are nothing," she giggled, for the wine had begun to go to her head.

"True—I am nothing. I have written in water—or in wine," he smiled bitterly.

"Say, this *is* good—" La Riccia smacked her lips.

"It should be. It comes from the deep cellar of His Highness, Lorenzo de' Medici, Duke of Urbino."

"Stolen?"

"No—sent to me with his compliments."

Now she roared with laughter and slapped his shoulder. "Niccolò, you are the greatest liar in Florence."

"The greatest liar who does not know how to lie—that is the tragedy. In everything there is hidden an evil proper to it."

"I never know what you're talking about, but I love you," she jumped upon his knees.

"La Riccia, *cara putana,* pray that I become famous—and you will never die."

"I'll pray. But now take me to bed, *amore,"* she yawned loudly.

Whether it was La Riccia's prayer, or Fortune's caprice, Niccolò became one of the most famous men in history and *The*

Prince one of the most influential of books. It was published five years after Machiavelli's death, in 1532, and promptly caused a commotion, hailed and condemned as no other work has ever been.

Mandragola—Belfagor—Clizia —Storie di Firenze—Et Caetera

Niccolò returned to San Casciano, still hoping—for hope is the most fulsome of flatterers—that something would follow the two bottles of wine. Nothing followed. He could not endure his solitude and his idleness, and for the time being his *Discourses* did not entice him. However, he had other talents. He had written poetry and he would try his hand at plays.

But first he would explain himself in the Prologue, whatever the play which might follow:

> Scusatelo con questo, che s'ingegna,
> Con questi van pensieri
> Fare il suo triste tempo più suave,
> Perch 'altrove non have
> Dove voltare il viso;
> Chè gli è stato interciso
> Monstrar con altre imprese altra virtue
> Non sendo premio alle fatiche sue.

"Excuse him with this: that he endeavored to make this sad life less dreary with these useless thoughts, because he had nowhere else to turn, and because it had not been granted to him to show other qualities of his in other enterprises, there being no reward for his fatigues."

He could never understand that Fortune purposely blocked his path to mediocrity and oblivion by making it impossible for him to return to the petty post he had held. True, by doing this, she also made his life tough and unexciting, but that was the price she demanded, for she gives nothing for nothing. But she had already given him wisdom, and wisdom's function is not to make us happy, but to help us support misfortunes with equanimity. He was well provided for.

The play was *Mandragola*. Mandragola, or mandrake, is a plant of the nightshade family found in the Mediterranean regions, used in medicine for its narcotic and emetic properties, and since it has a human shape, in the days of Machiavelli it was considered in the nature of a phallic symbol witches employed for erotic purposes.

The story deals with a prosperous merchant by the name of Nicias, who is happily married to the beautiful and faithful Lucrezia, except that they have no children. Callimaco, a young blade, who has lived for a long time in Paris, sees the woman and falls in love with her. He asks Ligurio, a friend, to help, for he is in bad shape. "I try to be jolly, but succeed only poorly because I am assailed from every part of me with such a desire to be with that woman, if only once, that I feel myself changed altogether, from the soles of my feet to my head; and my legs tremble, my entrails shake, my heart jumps about in my chest, my arms hang down, my tongue is tied, my eyes swim, my brain turns."

Who would not help a man in such a desperate condition? And Ligurio is without conscience and without morals. He enjoys nothing better than proving man an ass, a matter which he finds rather easy in the case of Nicias, who has the air of grand wisdom and behaves with the assurance of foolishness.

Ligurio tells Nicias that he has come across a physician who could be of help to him in the matter of begetting a child, and since the poor man is interested, he introduces him to Callimaco. The latter informs him that he has been able to extract from the root of the mandrake a potion, which, if a woman takes, she is certain to conceive. He has tried it with great success on wives of royalty, and would be glad to offer it to him, since he is a man of great worth and wisdom. But there is one difficulty in connection with it. He who spends the first night with the woman dies within a week.

Nicias is very anxious to have his wife drink the potion, but he does not wish to die. Callimaco agrees with him, for what good would it do him if his beautiful Lucrezia gave birth to a child while he rotted in the ground? But Callimaco knows of a reckless young man, who, for love of adventure, would sacrifice his life. He would bring him over, if Nicias desires it. Nicias desires it and is willing to reward the youth with many gold coins. But the great problem is how to persuade Lucrezia, a woman of extraordinary modesty and virtue.

Callimaco's tool is Fra Timoteo, a greedy, impoverished priest, who traffics in the Church, the Madonna and purgatory. But people have ceased to believe in these things and the receipts are small, and he must use his wits. "Madonna Lucrezia is wise and good. But I will catch her through her goodness.... Women are the most charitable persons in the world, but also the most vexatious. He who drives them away refuses both the vexations and the profits, and he who has to do with them has both the profits and the vexations together. For the truth is, there is no honey without flies."

Fra Timoteo involves Lucrezia's mother, Sostrata, who always thinks with her confessor's brain. "She is a donkey," the priest says, "but I shall find her a great help in making Lucrezia do as I wish."

The friar, whose cupped hand has been filled with gold coins and who has been promised more still if he succeeds, works feverishly. "I have consulted all my books," he tells Lucrezia, who persists in having great scruples, "and I have learned that first, as to your conscience, you must stick to this generality— that where there is an alternative of certain good or uncertain evil, we must not lose the good for the fear of the evil. Now take the certain good—you know that you will bear a son and thereby gain a soul for the Lord God. Secondly, it is the intention rather than the act which creates sin, and the will rather than the body. You will sin if you refuse to obey your husband, who orders you to do this, but if you obey you will be pleasing him. You would sin were you to enjoy the deed, but you do yourself penance as you dislike performing it. It is nothing more serious than eating meat on a Wednesday, which is a sin absolved with holy water. Besides, we must consider the end in view. Your end is to create a soul for Paradise and make your husband happy."

Where in the annals of sophistry can one find a more consummate piece of sleight of hand? And where a shrewder, more devastating exposition of the corruption of clerics?

Sostrata, the mother, echoes the friar's words and adds her own plea for reasonableness. "Very well," Lucrezia finally says, "I shall do as you wish, but I am sure I shall not be alive tomorrow."

"Have no fear, *figlia,*" Fra Timotea consoles, "for I shall pray to the Angel Raphael, asking him to escort you. Go to bed early, both of you, and prepare yourselves for this mystery."

"And the young man—he will die within a week, and I shall be guilty—"

"Have no worry. The death of the young man shall be forgiven you."

The young man, who is, naturally, Callimaco, in disguise, spends the night with Lucrezia. The next day she is radiant. Has she not done the will of her husband and of God? Nicias is so delighted with Callimaco, who later appears as the physician to present his compliments, that he invites him to stay at his home as his guest indefinitely. He graciously accepts and Lucrezia smiles acquiescence. All ends as it should. Pretentious foolishness is punished. Clever unscrupulousness is rewarded. All are happy. Is not this the essence of morality?

Those who find Nicias an impossible character, do not understand the boundless gullibility of husbands, for, how else could it be since he has made woman's fidelity the symbol of his own honor? At any rate, the wit, the humor, the vivacity, the brilliant dialogue of one scene after another, have made *Man-*

dragola an immortal piece. Voltaire considered it better than the comedies of Aristophanes.

Mandragola was a huge success. It was played in villas, at banquets, by itinerant actors—in Bologna, in Venice, in Rome, and even the literary circles smiled upon Machiavelli as upon one resurrected from the dead.

The Cardinals laughed and the Pope was so delighted that he sent the author a fistful of ducats. What the Princes of the Church liked particularly was the denigration of friars, whom they despised, some for their dirty habits, ignorance, and petty thievery; others for their piety and their desire to imitate the Great Founder of their religion by embracing poverty and humility. Against the latter, the Hierarchy was particularly bitter. They were a perpetual condemnation of their own ways. From the ashes of Savonarola many a phoenix rose to plague them.

Yet, pity not Nicias, Machiavelli warns:

> Quanto felice sia ciascuno sel vede
> Chi nasce sciocco ed ogni cosa crede!
> Ambizione nol preme,
> Nol lo muove il timore,
> Che sogliono esser seme
> Do noia e di dolor. . . .

"Happy is he that is born a fool and believes all things. Ambition does not urge or affect him, which is usually the seed of trouble and of grief!"

Pity Niccolò Machiavelli!

Seeing his success with *Mandragola,* Machiavelli wrote another play, *Clizia.* This depicts the Florentine life of his day even more authentically. Nicomaco, a middle-aged, serious, decent man falls in love with a young girl, Clizia, who is also loved by his son. A plot which could by a twist of the wrist, become a gory tragedy, Niccolò presents as a farce with all the vulgarities and trickeries of the species.

Nicomaco's wife, with the help of her son, contrives to bring the paterfamilias to ridicule, the best cure for infatuated men past the zenith of romance, and a cure which, by its very potency, might also kill. It does not, because the wife who is reasonable, as good wives must be to cope with the vagaries of husbands who should stop prowling in forbidden fields, explains to him why she had recourse to such violent means. "I never wanted to make fun of you, *caro*. It was you who wanted to make fun of me and of your good son, which is a grave sin. We simply turned the tables on you. . . . But if you wish to become once more the Nicomaco you used to be, decent husband and good father, why, we shall forget what is past."

Nicomaco complains that he will become the laughingstock of his friends. Not so, the smart wife retorts. "No one need know anything of what happened. And if, by chance, any breath of it gets about, well, it is common enough for people to be foolish and later to see the error of their ways."

While less original than *Mandragola, Clizia* had sufficient wit and dramatic vigor to be applauded, and added to the reputation of Machiavelli as playwright, but left his purse as flat as ever. But that was Fortune's plan, for who knows what silly notions wealth might have put into his brain? In a palace men are midgets; in a hut giants.

The sap of inspiration continued to flow vigorously, and Machiavelli now wrote a novel, *Belfagor*, which became as famous as his plays. He was a born story-teller, as is evident in all his work. Even when he is technical, he conveys his meaning by incidents in history or from personal experience. Every maxim is surrounded by a tale.

The story of *Belfagor* begins with the vision of "a most holy man." In it he learns that the greater portion of mankind is doomed to go to Hell because of the evil habit of matrimony. The infernal lords hear of this and are intrigued. The Great Council is convened to consider the matter. Pluto, Supreme Master, appoints Belfagor to visit the earth, enter matrimony and report.

Belfagor is most reluctant. However, placated by a purse

of 100,000 ducats, he "set out for the upper world with a train of devils in guise of servants and made his entry into Florence under the noble name of Roderigo di Castiglia." He chooses Florence "as a city most suited to those who exercise the art of usury," and establishes himself "in a very fine house in the suburb of All Saints."

He marries Monna Honesta, a beautiful maiden of the noble but impoverished Donati family, "and celebrated his nuptials in the most splendid and ostentatious manner, being subject to vanity and all other human passions by the conditions imposed upon him when he left the infernal regions."

Unfortunately for Belfagor, he falls in love with his wife, who "brought such pride with her as her portion that Roderigo, who was a competent judge, being well acquainted with both parties, thought she excelled Lucifer himself."

Her extravagance is inordinate. "She laid aside all manner of affection and would call him the most opprobrious names she could think of whenever he deprived her of anything, however unreasonable her request." And he has "to content her with all the new fashions which is the habit of our city to constantly vary."

That is not all. "She grew so insupportable that neither man-servant nor maid-servant could bear to stay in the house above two or three days at most, and even the devils themselves whom Roderigo had brought with him deserted him and chose to return to Hell rather than live upon earth in the service of such a vixen."

Belfagor is reduced to bankruptcy. To avoid his implacable creditors, he flees the city, pursued by bailiffs. In danger of being caught, he bribes the peasant Giovanni Matteo del Bricca of Peretola to hide him in a dung hill, promising him riches if he escapes his foes. He does escape and bestows upon the peasant the power to cure women possessed of the devil. Only women, of course, for the devil knows where to find good lodging. This will certainly make his fortune since bedeviled women are plenti-

ful and their relations are so anxious for their cure that they
are willing to pay great sums to him who performs it.

Belfagor now seeks refuge in the wife of Buonaiuto Tebal-
ducci. She begins to indulge in philosophical disputations, infallible proof of the devil's presence. Nothing avails her—
neither holy water nor holy prayers nor holy relics. Matteo
offers to cure her for a respectable purse. "After having caused
certain devout ceremonies to be gone through to give good color
to the matter," he whispers into the woman's ear the words of
the pact and Roderigo must depart. The woman instantly becomes the goose she has always been, and all are happy, in
particular her husband who had felt as if cuckolded by a whole
university of philosophers, than which no greater affliction can
befall a good man.

Now Belfagor seeks refuge in the daughter of the King of
Naples. Matteo is brought over and again constrains the fugitive to depart. The daughter of the King of France is the next
hostess. His Majesty invites Matteo to perform his miracle.
The peasant whispers into the ear of the noble lady, but Roderigo this time refuses to leave. He had no necessity to read
Machiavelli's *The Prince,* Chapter 18, to know that one need
not keep faith when the reasons which made one bind oneself
no longer exist. It has been a very ancient custom among men,
devils and angels. At the time of the pact, Belfagor was deep in
manure; now he was deep in the bosom of a lovely princess. At
the time he was hounded by bailiffs; now it was only the breath
of a peasant. Blow, fool, blow!

But Giovanni Matteo del Bricca is no fool! He has a plan up
his sleeve. He asks the King to have a dais put up in the Cathedral of Notre Dame with musicians playing all sorts of instruments. The Hierarchy of the Church and the lords of the realm,
glittering in their Sunday attire, march in solemn procession,
leading the afflicted Princess toward the altar. The holy place is
full to the gills with commoners.

"What the plague is this scoundrel about?" mutters Belfagor. "Does he think he can frighten me with a parcel of

bishops and generals? Surely he must know that I have seen all the pomp and glory of heaven and heard all the noise of hell, and cannot be scared by mere earthly pomp and tumult."

Nevertheless, Roderigo *is* perturbed when suddenly the musicians strike up, trumpets blowing, drums beating, mob shouting. "What is the meaning of this, Matteo?" Belfagor asks angrily. Matteo, shaking like an aspen leaf, whispers: "Your wife is coming, Belfagor—your wife—your wife—"

In less time than it took the peasant to utter the word "wife" once, the alarmed Devil is out of the Princess and on his way back to Hell.

What happened when he confronted Pluto and the Great Council, Machiavelli does not say. Certain it is, however, that never again did an infernal citizen attempt marriage with a woman. But many a husband has complained that he was married to a devil.

There have been those who believe that Niccolò had Marietta, his wife, in mind as prototype of the vixen Belfagor married. Are they unaware of the fact that it is precisely the happy husbands of good wives who have the lightheartedness to banter about feminine foibles? The others plunge into the molasses of romantics, trying to escape reality in honeyed dreams.

The fact is that *Belfagor* is based upon a medieval legend, exploited by other writers, but never with the success of Niccolò Machiavelli.

L'Asino d'Oro—"The Golden Ass"—Machiavelli wrote in *terza rima,* but never finished it. In the poem he depicts his profound pessimism, referring not only to man's wickedness, but to man's inherent unhappiness. He uses Homer's myth of Circe, the enchantress, who turns men into beasts. In the Greek's poem, when opportunity presents itself, the men return gladly to their original human form. In the poem of the Italian, the characters refuse to assume again the image of God. They are both happier and better as beasts. Herein may lie the difference between the classic and romantic attitudes.

Two pieces which brought Machiavelli great prestige he composed in the year 1520: *Arte de la Guerra*—"The Art of War" and *Vita di Castruccio Castracani*—"The Life of Castruccio Castracani." *The Art of War* is a sort of supplement to *Discourses* and *The Prince*. In the form of a dialogue between "Fabrizio" and "Cosimo" and others of their friends, Machiavelli expounds his ideas of how wars should be conducted to bring victory. He reinforces his opinions by citations from the history of the Romans and the Moslems, as well as that of the Jews of the Old Testament, Moses being his great hero.

His chief argument is that a nation must be permanently armed and with its own citizenry. Seduced by the ancient warriors, Machiavelli ridicules artillery, since he claims that forty shots were needed to hit one target. He did not foresee the tremendous developments of that lethal tool, a most serious shortsightedness which dates his book and makes it principally a source of dialectic fallacy. Cavalry, too, he relegates to an unimportant position. Only the infantry has validity. The foot soldiers are the true warriors, for they meet their foes face to face, where courage and skill mean life, and the lack of them death. From this it follows that fortifications, too, are of little value, and generals should not shut up their troops and waste them in garrisons, where they lose "the spirit of courage," without which all is useless.

Castruccio Castracani was a prince of Luca during the early part of the fourteenth century—a medieval adventurer, who by personal ability and military skill raised himself to the tyranny of several Tuscan cities. To Machiavelli, he seemed to embody the *virtù* of the prince who could save Italy from her degradation and fragmentation.

"Castruccio was grateful to his friends, but terrible to his foes; just to his subjects, faithless to strangers; he never sought to overcome by force those whom he could overcome by deceit, for he was wont to say that victory brought glory and not the manner of securing it. . . . God is a lover of strong men, for one always sees that the weak are punished by the strong."

How like Cesare Borgia, whom Machiavelli could never forget. Not that Machiavelli would have considered Castruccio or Cesare the ideal ruler, acceptable to the people of a well-regulated, happy democracy, but he was always mourning the miserable status of his beloved *patria*—"this barbarous domination which stinks in the nostrils of everyone"—and pondered by what means, however reprehensible, to save it.

Vita di Castruccio Castracani purports to be a biography, but in reality, it is a story based vaguely upon that man's life, who had already become a legendary figure.

So pleased were Cardinal Giulio, who now ruled over Florence, and Pope Leo with the writings of Niccolò, that forgetting all the Medici rancor, they commissioned him to write the history of Tuscany, for which they would pay him a yearly stipend of a hundred florins.

Istorie di Firenze, modeled upon Titus Livius, is a study of the century—the Florentine-Roman Renaissance. Clear and honest it certainly is not a perpetual eulogy of the Medici, as the Cardinal and the Pope had expected. Yet, the two prelates to their credit be it recorded, accepted the work in progress, praised it, as it certainly deserved, and did not interfere.

The Story of Florence is doubtless one of the great works of the Renaissance, and in many ways unique for any century. Machiavelli was the first historian to give a luminous development of great events in their causes and connections. The style conveys his ideas with force and precision. There are no labored expressions or nicely wrought sentences, but the story flows on, concise in argument, clear and animated in description, reflecting every shade of his thoughts and opinions. How different from the emptiness of the Latinizing Humanists and the trivialities of the Italian purists!

For the first time one encounters live human beings. However, it is not the history of a people, of classes or of institutions, but the study of individuals, each of whom is a model lesson in moral-

ity, or rather, in immorality, for most of them are evil-minded,
treacherous, selfish, and only very few are capable of great
deeds, whether good or evil. And always there is *Fortuna* or
Accidente, altering, destroying the most elaborate calculations.
"Thus it was all in vain because of a trifling accident," says
Machiavelli, expressing his resentment that reason is treated so
cavalierly by the trivia of irrationality.

For a half-dozen years Machiavelli worked at his history and
in 1525, when he reached the end of Lorenzo the Magnificent's
reign, he presented the work to Giulio, who had recently been
elected Pope under the title of Clement VII. The book, however, was not published until 1532, five years after Niccolò's
death. Not one single book of his was published during his life-
time. The manuscripts, copied and often mutilated, read,
praised, and criticized, were by Fortune's care saved from perdition, the usual fate of unpublished works during the lifetime of
authors.

In Clement VII, Machiavelli found a firm and constant protector, and he would have been reinstated in his post and probably even promoted. But it was not to be. On May 5, 1527,
twenty-five thousand savages with torches lit and swords drawn
poured into the Capital of Christendom, shouting: "Empire,
Spain, Victory!"

"Then everyone had to die who was found in the streets,
whether young or old, layman, priest or monk." The churches
were turned into stables; the cardinals were made water carriers,
while noblemen and bankers were used as servants in their own
homes. The ladies of the highest rank were so manhandled that
ever after they were known by no other name than " 'the relics of
the sack of Rome.' " The soldiers in priestly garments rode to
St. Peter's accompanied by naked women and had themselves
crowned popes.

Everywhere one heard "shouting, the rumble of guns, the
screams and howls of women and children, the crackling of
flames, and the crash of collapsing roofs."

Clement and his entourage fled to Castel Sant' Angelo, but

presently this last fortress was also taken by the Spaniards aided by German mercenaries. Schärtlin, the German commander, reported to his dear ones in Wurtemburg. "There we found Pope Clement with twelve cardinals in a small hall; we took him prisoner. There was great mourning among them; they wept deeply. We all became very rich."

The grandeur that was Rome perished, but the Florentines jubilated, for they hoped to recover their freedom from the Medici, whom they drove out once more.

And Niccolò Machiavelli had high expectations.

Death and Transfiguration

The evil that men do lives after them,
The good is oft interred with their bones.

But how shall we recognize the good and how appraise the evil, since let but a little time pass and the good we were so valiantly fighting for withers into evil, and the evil we so strenuously rejected blossoms into good? The fruit of the Tree of Knowledge was both of good and of evil, and man has eaten of it irrevocably.

"In everything there is hidden an evil proper to it." If these were not his last words, they were nevertheless the ultimate reality that the man who died on June 22, 1527, would have pronounced had his lips opened for one more time after they had been forever locked.

Man raises arches to immortalize murder and temples to sanctify superstition, but enchains him who expounds the truth and would expunge his name from memory, or, unable to achieve it, does so besmirch it that the mouth which pronounces it is defiled.

There are those for whom life begins only after their death, and often they are among the profoundest thinkers and the most skillful artists. It is not necessarily because their generation is deaf to reason or blind to beauty, for there are contemporaries as difficult and as original, yet they are recognized and honored and rewarded; nor is it because they are ahead of their time, for they may, indeed, be ripe with the hours of their day. There seems to be a fiendish fate which will not allow their recognition by men until they have vanished from sight. They are, in a sense, condemned to death in order to attain deathlessness. No protestation avails them, and their clamor is answered by contemptuous silence or mocking laughter.

That success is achieved solely by sheer talent has its origin in the obstinate illusion that goodness and virtue must triumph. Talent, however, is not an abstract quality, eternal and immutable. Rooted in time and space it has validity only when these elements favor it—these and the amalgam of a hundred disparate trifles called luck. And of these, luck is the most essential ingredient. No gallery *claqueur* has such reverberating palms as luck.

Thus it happened that when Niccolò Machievelli, clerk and ambassador without title and without honors, delivered his ghost, the city he had so loved and for which he would have died (and in a sense did die), took no cognizance of the mournful event.

Skeptical in all matters religious and secular, by some atavistic bramble stuck in his brain, Machiavelli was of the opinion that important events were preceded by signs and portents. "Both ancient and modern instances prove that no great events ever occur in any city or country that have not been predicted by soothsayers, revelations, or by portents or other celestial signs."

He did not attempt to explain the phenomenon, but believed "that the air is peopled with spirits, who by their superior intelligence foresee future events, and out of pity for mankind warn them of impending catastrophes," by cosmic disturbances of the strangest order. For instance, in the year 1456, "dreadful tempestuous winds tore the roofs of churches and carried them away more than a mile, unbroken as when upon their respective

edifices. . . . The large oaks and lofty trees which would not
bend beneath its influence were borne a great distance." All this
fierce and miraculous prologue to foretell the tragic finale of one
Jacopo Piccinino, an officer, betrayed by his father-in-law, Duke
Filippo.

What is rarer and more formidable than the advent of genius,
of one who is about to light the all-consuming fires of truth?
Genius comes as an earthquake and many sacred edifices crumble
in his path. He wields a glowing sword and those who behold it
flee in terror, for no one can tell whose precious lie he intends to
slay.

Yet, the disembodied spirits, like the embodied Florentines,
were unperturbed, and performed no tricks, natural or supernatural, to warn the world of the ideas which would trouble, enrage, convulse, confuse, confound popes and emperors and
kings, topple philosophies, sacred and lay, make dead moralists
turn in their graves, and living ones shriek in agony. They were
less aware of the impending storm than an ancient peasant
woman's bunion foretelling rain.

Only the immediate family and a few office friends—Ac-
ciaioli, Strozzi, Luigi Alamanni—accompanied Niccolò Machiavelli on his last trip, which took place on the day he died, and
lowered his coffin into the mud of the cemetery of the Church of
Santa Croce.

The priest muttered the usual prayer and invocation, but to
please the mourners and to show off his erudition, he quoted
some verses from Dante and added the Latin proverb: *Lustra-
vit lampade terras*—"He has illumined the Earth with a lamp."

No occult oracle had ever uttered a more appropriate augury
—unwittingly, as all valid auguries are uttered—prompted by
the vagaries of the ironical gods who reign over the febrile des-
tinies of men.

Although "Machiavelli" had, in a very short time, become
both adjective and abstract noun, two hundred times did the
tragic Earth have to spin about the Sun before a monument was
raised upon his worm-eaten bones, and it was supplied by an

Englishman, Earl Cowper. Into it was carved: *Tanto Nomini Nullum Par Elogium*—"No eulogy would do justice to so great a name."

But Luigi Alamanni could not restrain his sorrow and, in the manner of the day, when verse, however deficient, was considered superior and more dignified than prose, wrote:

> Or poi che il nostro Segretario antico
> in cielo à l'alma e le membre sotterra,
> Morte, io no temo più le tue fieri armi.
> Per costui m'era il vivir fatto amico,
> Per costui sol temea l'aspera tua guerra;
> or che tolto me l'ài, che puoi tu farmi?

"Now that the soul of our former Secretary is in heaven and his body beneath the ground, Death, I no longer fear thy cruel weapons. Because of him I loved life and for his sake alone I feared thy bitter war. Now that you have taken him away from me, what more can you do to me?"

For his fidelity and tenderness, Alamanni was rewarded with immortality. Oh, how many would have dipped their goose feathers into ink and composed eulogies upon imperishable parchment, compared to which the wild songs of moonstruck poetasters would have sounded like the cawing of crows, had they but known! But man kneels before the candle, his back turned upon the sun.

Or, had Niccolò himself suspected what *Fortuna*—Fate—of whose inscrutable and irrational ways he was deeply aware—had in store for him beyond the meager number of his mortal years, how he would have taunted his foes, how he would have laughed at the grotesqueness of the strutters! For he was a true Florentine, with a tongue as sharp in his mouth as the dagger in his belt, and as he said: "Those who were most dexterous in wounding others with their words were held wisest and in the highest esteem."

And he was a great laugher with his cronies in the wine shop and in the "*chiasso*," the vulgar term for the poetic "*lupanar*."

He was of the opinion that a man of worth might do what he liked to amuse himself and would gain honor rather than blame for whoring and debauchery. He would be held gallant, sociable, and a jolly companion.

Not that he was happy. On the contrary, he played his life as a tragedian. He refused to be inebriated by religion or exalted by fictitious splendor, concealing the miserable destiny of man. Amid all the artifices of his day, the incomparable achievements of painters and sculptors and architects, he saw only man—the unchangeable man—the essence—the root. "People were born, lived and died, always by the same order of things. They have always had the same passions with the same effects. . . . Of men one may say this in general: they are ungrateful, voluble, pretentious, hypocritical, avoiding dangers, hungry for gains; and while you do them favors, they are all yours, offering you blood, life, and children, when danger is removed. But when it is near, they run away."

Yet, Machiavelli was not a misanthrope. He did not hate man. He understood him. Man, however, does not wish to be understood. He wishes to be glorified, to be loved, to be deceived. Machiavelli could not deceive, and since he could not deceive, he could neither love nor glorify. Nevertheless, he accepted deception as one of the most essential requisites for success, indeed, for survival. "Nature has placed riches in the world to be won rather by depredation than by industry, rather by evil than by good device. . . . Men's baseness can neither be conquered by time nor ameliorated by kindness."

We cannot both know man and love him, and it were better to lean toward ignorance. Machiavelli, however, was incapable of doing so. His intelligence had no opaque spots. Nor would he endeavor to close one eye, as most catechisms of morals advocate, for it was precisely the acknowledgment of man's perfidious nature which he believed would accomplish the aim he lived for.

Machiavelli knew that man's history was independent of his desires and was not concerned with the destiny of the individual.

And he was profoundly interested in history—in the history of Florence and of Italy—and the teachings of history by which Florence could remain free and Italy could be united.

Once *Italia* was the world's most glorious Republic, Mistress Supreme of the Earth, but now it was shredded into countless states and cities, one at the throat of the other, and all at the perpetual mercy of the barbarians. (All were barbarians— Spain, Austria, France, England—compared to Italy.) They sacked her and enslaved her and put her to the torch again and again.

All their battles for empire, dynasty, glory, they fought upon her lands, while the pontiffs at Rome invited king and prince and adventurer to help exterminate their own people, in order that their thrones might stay secure and their coffers be replenished with the gold of the credulous. "Nearly all the wars which the northern barbarians carried out in Italy, were occasioned by the pontiffs; and the hordes with which the country was inundated were generally called in by them."

Little wonder then that the pedestrian popes following the brilliant, humanistic ones, who accepted the facts, were incensed, and befouled the glorious name of Niccolò Machiavelli, even as birds befoul monuments of heroes. However, the rains of justice again and again washed it clear and "it illumined the Earth."

But even in his darkest moments, Niccolò could not have imagined that it would require more than three centuries for the union to be consummated and for Italy once again to be more than a spot upon the map and a contemptuous name in the councils of nations.

Yet, he died on time. For fourteen years he had been in partial exile, in poverty and debt, but now the tyrants had been driven from Florence and he was certain that the citizens, grateful for the many services he had rendered, would once more offer him his honorable post and allow him to enter public life again under more auspicious conditions.

He was mistaken. He had forgotten that he had said "men are more zealous in taking revenge than in showing gratitude, for the latter could only be exercised with some inconvenience to themselves whilst the former brings alike gratification and profit." The Great Council received his candidacy on June 10. Of the nine members who took the floor, eight berated him, spoke angrily against his morality, against his ideas, against his sharp wit which they called jeering. Only Luigi Alamanni defended him: "After countless missions, after decades filled with hard toil, Niccolò Machiavelli is among the most poverty-stricken of men. He is an honorable man from top to toe. To this day, in the fifty-eighth year of his life, he has betrayed no one and has always served faithfully."

And the members voted. Machiavelli received one dozen votes out of a total of six hundred! However certain we may be of man's rascality, we are, nevertheless, continually astonished to find that he is, in truth, a rascal.

But it did not matter. Machiavelli was never to know. He was gripped with violent cramps and took to bed. He had long been suffering from digestive troubles, a common malady of the age when drinking water mingled with the sewer and flies traveled from the offal in the gutter to the meat on the dining-table. Moreover, Machiavelli had been exposed in various military campaigns and on missions in Italy and beyond her frontiers, where most of the inns were pigsties.

Always he used special pills, which relieved his pains. The prescription is still extant: "Aloes, one and one-half drachm; cardamon, one drachm; saffron, one-half drachm; myrrh, one-half drachm; bettany, one-half drachm; pimpernel, one-half drachm; smooth paste to bind all together, one-half drachm."

This time the usual dose did not suffice, however, and he increased the number of the pills, which made his son, Piero, believe that he was poisoned. With death imminent, he sent for (or more likely, was unable to object to his presence) Fra Matteo, who administered the last rites. Whatever his quarrels with the church and his anger against the popes, he was now saved from the fires of Hell, in which he did not believe.

Machiavelli's last will and testament was a simple affair. He bequeathed his whole property to his sons, to be equally divided among them. But Piero wrote afterward: "You know that my father died in utmost poverty." To his wife, Niccolò left nothing, since her dowry had been made secure for her. He did mention her, however, with affection and made her executrix and guardian of his younger children. More than that would have been considered a gesture intended to scandalize and enrage the husbands of the world. A man should not show too great an inclination toward his wife, or how retain the mastery of the home? Or, as the Puritan Fathers in their wisdom put it—a woman's relation to her husband should be as humble and reverential as a man's relation to God.

Niccolò Machiavelli was dead. Three years later, Florence, the city which spurned him, died, too. She lost her liberty—lost her wealth—lost her culture—lost her art. Forever after she became a charming but insignificant town—a cemetery of glorious creations.

Niccolò Machiavelli was dead, but in less than a decade, *he* was resurrected. In fame and infamy, his name and his work have lived on generation after generation, century after century. . . .

Fortune had finished her work and

È FINITA LA COMMEDIA.

Justus ut palma florebit—"The righteous shall flourish like a palm tree."

MICHEL DE MONTAIGNE

The Witch's Cauldron

History is the incredible account of how man, despite his monstrous follies, still survives. Each generation views with horrified tenseness how near to the brink previous generations came, and each one carves its hoop of misery and of shame on the tree of time. Yet, each, however dark, however dense, however savage it may have been, can boast of a name, an idea, a deed, which exonerates its existence; and which, like a precious jewel, it bequeathes in token of atonement and as a sign that man does not deserve to be annihilated.

Noah and his Ark are the perpetual symbols of salvation. The flood recedes and returns, and many a dove of peace is drowned in its bloody waves, but the rainbow, the ever-broken covenant, serves as a momentary respite. If the respite is sufficiently long to allow men to repair, to build, to discover, to create, man hails the period as "the golden age" and glorifies it in song and marble.

The period in which Michel Eyquem, Sieur de Montaigne lived and which he enriched with his incomparable wisdom, was certainly not a "golden age." It was, in the opinion of many historians, a cruel, coarse, barbarous, bigoted, lawless age. It was, indeed, a witch's cauldron, filled with horrors without names, with prejudices, superstitions, nightmares. But out of the dregs, bloody and noxious, now and then magnificent flowers bloomed—new worlds, vast visions, daring conceptions, art, letters, science. Must man's good always be the residue of his evils? Must he first invent for murder and then beat his sword into a ploughshare? Must he first learn to heal the wounds on the battlefield before he may use the bandages for the sick-bed? Must he set the city aflame to learn the uses of fire? Must he first fill his heart with hate and then try to temper it with ethics?

Columbus had already sailed westward to discover a shorter road to the East and thereby established beyond any doubt that the earth had the shape of an apple and not of a pancake. The Grand Admiral discovered much more. He offered to the Old World a brand new one to corrupt or to exploit for the good of man. In time it would do both, for that is the way of men with worlds. Columbus also discovered what man does to his great benefactors. He was chained, imprisoned, robbed of his honors and titles, and died in poverty and obscurity. People have always demanded a sign of authenticity from their prophets and always discovered it in the shape of a cross on their backs, a rope about their necks, flames about their legs, scorpions ripping the flesh, and laughter ripping the soul.

The Old World was steeped in ignorance, but the dark curtain was being pierced—with extreme care, for the keepers were watchful. To make certain that it would forever encircle the mind of man, they had the rack and the pyre and excommunication.

Nevertheless, the printing presses moved and new words appeared on the paper—words which spoke of freedom, of ancient truths, long buried, of new truths burgeoning, of new methods of discovering truth rejecting the authority of Aristotle, the authority of any man, accepting solely the authority of one's own eyes, one's own senses, one's own judgment.

Latin, the lock upon the gate that led to the pastures of truth, was broken. The writers began to use the tongues of the people and thus gained the ears of the people, and in time, their masterpieces were superior to those written in the language of the clerics.

The Bible, the Book written by the hand of God—was it to be, like all other classics, talked about, debated, sworn on, but never read? How sad, indeed, is the fate of the author, mortal or divine. If popular, he is scorned; if acclaimed by the professors, he rots in his glory. But God was destined to become a bestseller, and His words were to be in the mouths of everyone, the mouths that uttered words in all the languages. Was it good; was it evil? At least it was open for inspection.

Luther had already broken the bonds of the Vatican, and other leaders followed suit, but the peasant was still a serf. And when he tried to free himself from his plundering master, Luther encouraged massacre. One hundred thousand of them perished, for the new prophet of God proclaimed: "To rebel against the princes is to rebel against God. A Christian should bear injustice patiently."

And now there were two camps of the Lord—the Protestant and the Catholic, and they fought without respite. Princes and kings took sides—with the Pope or against him. For they all sought more power, more land, more gold—the Earth in exchange for Heaven. They threw bits of Heaven to the poor as one throws bits of meat to dogs, and the poor tore one another to grab them. Meanwhile, like dogs, they lived in hovels, sided with rough boards and thatched with straw, without windows, without floors and ceilings barely higher than their heads. They were always hungry, had meat a few times a year, unleavened bread, goat milk, and windfallen fruit. Everything that was good and tasty went to those of the robe and those of the sword.

The cities were half-buried in mud and dung, and hogs and dogs were the scavengers. The medics, whose equipment consisted of Latin quotations, cups and clysters and a pharmacopedia in which figured the left foot of a tortoise, the urine of a lizard, an elephant's dung, a mole's liver, blood drawn from under the right wing of a white pigeon, the pulverized droppings of a rat, could hardly cope with the perennial epidemics, which vied with popes and princes for the souls of men.

In the midst of this vast squalor, there rose magnificent cathedrals dedicated to sacred illusions and gorgeous palaces dedicated to divinely-ordained rulers, most of whom were illiterate, stupid, barbarous, lecherous, vain, and whose chief passion was murder on a grand scale.

While the great majority of mankind was clad in stinking rags, walked barefoot or in ear-splitting sabots, the nobility strutted in resplendent gowns studded with gems and drove in

gilded coaches. From all corners of the earth, spices and rare
delicacies were brought to grace the banquet-tables of the rich,
while beggars by the thousands, many mutilated by the endless
wars, many self-mutilated to excite pity, prowled about the narrow, tortuous alleys, competing with the masterless animals for
the refuse.

Paris, the cosmopolis, was throttled by a perpetual cramping
stench, while the lords and ladies scattered with their fans of
ostrich feathers delectable perfumes, and in the churches the
fumes of frankincense rose from the censers to quicken the nostrils and deaden the mind.

To be sure there was beauty in Christendom, for man is ingenious, and as soon as he developed a thumb, he became an
artist.

France was a divided country. Francis I became the most
powerful of French kings, but he did not succeed in destroying
the well-entrenched nobles of the south, who, together with
many successful burghers, were followers of John Calvin, the
French Luther, and were known as Huguenots. These Protestants rebelled against the Pope and the tyranny of the Catholic
Church, but in their turn became tyrannical and intolerant.

Calvin was a rigid, merciless disciplinarian. He prepared a
catechism and a confession of faith which ruled life within and
without the church. He made laws regulating the furnishings of
houses and the pictures on the walls; laws as to stuff of which
different classes of citizens might make their clothes; laws as to
the number of courses which one might have at dinner; laws forbidding ladies to put grease on their hair or carry watches at
their waistbelts; laws commanding the housewife to make her
purchases in the market before 10 A.M. And, of course, the gibbet and the stake were always at his disposal for those who disobeyed or displeased him.

Yet, compared to the totalitarian rule of the Catholic Church,
Calvinism may be considered democratic, for the Calvinist was
encouraged to discuss religious matters and to follow his own

reason and conscience vis-à-vis God. This freedom led to freedom in matters of politics, trade, and science.

For almost a century the war between the northern Catholics and the southern Huguenots continued unabated. Enough blood was spilled to have cleansed the people of the kingdom of all evil humors, as the physicians called diseases, but the madness of man lies very deep within him and no science has yet discovered a means of exorcising it.

This, therefore, was the century in which Michel Eyquem, Sieur de Montaigne, made his bow to the world, and in which he penned words so wise, so true, so redolent of the good earth, that four centuries later, they are as fresh as this morning's violets and ring in the ear as soothingly as this dawn's voices.

Was Montaigne pleased with the period in which he lived? Hardly. He chastises its cruelties, its follies, its fanaticism, its superstitions, its hypocrisies. Would he have chosen another period? Hardly. He knew that a man who desired to lead the life of reason, would, everywhere and always, have as his implacable foes, the fools, the fops, the envious, the bigots. Moreover, had not his life been as full and happy as human lives can be? Had he not had love and friendship and health, at least until the age of forty-five, and had he not had an income and freedom, so that he might live among the masters of thought and himself write? What more could he have wished? He knew that however great and varied is the Earth, Man never finds a spot where he is quite comfortable, as one suffering from insomnia, who despite his tossing, always discovers an irritating lump in his mattress. The acid we splash at the world only burns our own faces.

But there was the civil war which was waged in his backyard, and which made him go to bed a thousand times, uncertain whether he would awake or be dispatched, his throat slashed or his heart stabbed. "A monstrous and unnatural war! Other wars act outwardly, this also against itself, eating away and destroying itself with its own venom. In its fury it tears itself limb from limb. . . ." Still, other times, other ills, "and disasters, after

SEVEN AGAINST THE NIGHT

all, were relative, and should not be exaggerated. . . . But to him who feels the hailstones patter about his ears, the whole hemisphere seems to be in storm and tempest."

Roots

In the year 1477, a man in his seventies, a merchant of the city of Bordeaux, bought a castle and the property of Montaigne, in the district of Perigord, famous for its truffles, symbol of all delicacies, but which only the snouts of hogs can unearth. (So near is the beautiful to the ugly and the delicate to the vile.)

Perigord was in the province of Guyenne, whose capital was Bordeaux. Already at the time, the city was famous for its wines, *vins de Bordeaux,* and carried on extensive commerce, situated as it is on the great river Garonne, which flows into the Atlantic. It had a university and beautiful churches, and its people, like the rest of the ancient Gascogne, were reputed for wit, boastfulness, loquacity, bequeathing to the French language the word "gasconnade," the composite of those characteristics.

The country was for a long time the battle-ground between the French and the English, each claiming it. It was definitely annexed to the crown by Charles VII who defeated the English in 1453. In 1469 Louis XI gave it to his brother, Charles, but at his death three years later, it reverted to the crown. Nevertheless, the pointless and endless war between the inhabitants of the place, who were chiefly Huguenots, and their northern Catholic neighbors went on and on. It required a sturdy and witty people to survive. Possibly the vineyards were enriched with the blood, and the grape was more luscious and its juice, as it coursed through the body, brought laughter and enhanced the joys of Venus. For, it would be a great pity that so evil a wind brought no one good.

The castle of Montaigne, as the name indicates, was situated upon a hill, and was so sturdily constructed that, despite the many storms, military and natural, which hammered against it for centuries, it still stands. With the castle, the old man bought the title as well—a humble title, to be sure, in the nature of "esquire," but something to separate one from the commonality. Besides, a foot on the ladder is like a foot in the stirrup. Who knows, one might even have a chance to swing about and mount. But the old man would leave that to his descendants. He would continue with his own name—and his own wine business.

What was his name? Ramon Eyquem. Ramon—a Spanish name and Eyquem, a Hebrew name. Was this little man, swarthy, with black eyes, a Spanish Jew, or a *converso,* a newly-converted Jew to Christianity? Was he perhaps a *Marano,* a Catholic practicing the Mosaic religion in secret? Had he but recently run into France to avoid the ever bitter persecution of the Holy Office of the Inquisition? Fifteen years after Ramon Eyquem bought the castle of Montaigne, all the Jews of Spain would be driven out, naked and empty-handed, after a millennium of service to the country. Those who were not cast to the waves or starved in the deserts managed to find asylum with the Mohammedan Turk, whom the Christian world cursed as infidel and dog. From which, one may conclude that there is more humanity in an infidel and more heart in a dog.

Ramon's son was, no doubt, in business with his father, and he, too, passed on without flaunting his title. He, too, may have been a refugee, and it is never prudent to excite the envy of the natives.

A century later, Michel, Ramon's great-grandson, was writing his *Essays* which were to make him immortal. In them he reveals himself as completely as any human being has ever done, physically and mentally, and although he speaks of the importance of ancestry and heredity, he never mentions the names of his great-grandfather or his grandfather, whom he probably knew personally, or his great-grandmother or grandmother, whom he certainly must have known, since women have a habit of outlasting their consorts. He never identifies himself with their peculiarities, except that they all detested physicians and drugs.

Why does he cut the roots that cling to his feet? He who tells the truth more fearlessly than any other man, fears to tell the truth about his immediate ancestors who had given him title and wealth—fears or is ashamed? Should the Sieur de Montaigne carry the stone of Jewishness around his neck? He would rather carry the "stone" in his bladder, "the most fatal, the most painful, the most irremediable of diseases," whose terrible symptoms he discusses for pages. Perhaps, after all, it was not as painful nor as fatal as the other stone.

In the year 1495, the third Eyquem, father of Michel, was born at Bordeaux. Pierre was probably duly baptized, for life is certainly worth a bit of sprinkling, and thus became the first of the family to be openly a Catholic and to speak French, or rather Gascon, without a suspicious accent. Nevertheless, he still looked Spanish or Jewish—"complexion inclined to be brown, a man of low stature, he bore himself with a pleasing, humble and very modest gravity." He was fairly well educated, but liked particularly to read Spanish. Why Spanish?

Pierre did not join his father in the wine business. He became a soldier. He would show the world that still whispered, perhaps, that no one was as loyal a citizen. He followed Francis I in the Marignano campaigns of 1515. The war was long and desultory and finally Francis was taken prisoner. He is the one who wrote to his wife that all was lost "save honor." He was freed, signed a treaty and promptly broke it, proving that honor has merit only when deprived of all earthly goods.

When we come across Pierre again, he is in Paris, the business partner of a Jew by the name of Louppes or Lopez, who came from Saragossa, and despite all pressures, remained a Jew. The man had a niece, who lived with her father, Pierre Lopez, in the city of Toulouse. Eyquem was already over thirty—a respectable age at the time—and his partner recommended that he go and see if his niece be to his liking. He followed Lopez's advice and soon after married her.

Michel says that "in the year 1528," his father, who had remained a virgin until then, married. And immediately after, Montaigne continues: "Let us return to our bottles." For he is writing against the evil of drink—a revealing thing, sobriety being a Jewish trait and a Spanish one. At any rate, although Montaigne wrote about everything and everyone, there is never a word about the woman his father married, and it would seem that as one great Jew was born sans father, another great Jew was born sans mother.

The marriage certificate and other documents have recently been found in the archives of Bordeaux, which tell that Pierre Eyquem married Antoinette de Lopez (Anthoynettes de Louppes) and received as dowry two thousand pounds, silver, and two thousand pounds to be invested in lands or for the purpose of revenue. Moreover, the bride who was of legal age, that is *plus de douze ans et moins de vingt-cinq,* more than twelve and less than twenty-five (how ancient this feminine coquetry!) would receive a becoming trousseau and other gifts. Eyquem himself contributed four thousand pounds, proving that the marriage was not one entirely "de convenance."

Antoinette was born a Jewess, but became a Protestant. After her marriage, she turned Catholic, and later on returned to Protestantism. We may safely say, therefore, that she remained a Jewess. Pierre and Antoinette seemed to have lived quite happily for forty years and brought into the world eight sons and daughters, Michel being the third. Due to the death of his two older brothers, however, he became heir to the castle and the title.

Pierre died in 1568 and left all his fortune to his wife, who, according to his will, was devoted and capable. In fact, the Montaigne estate prospered largely because of her intelligence and ability. Antoinette lived on for thirty-one years and survived her great son by five years. Indeed, she was in her nineties when she died, and her will as well as other documents prove that she remained until the end alert, a woman of character and understanding.

Never in literary history does a son write so lovingly of a father as Michel de Montaigne, and his father certainly deserved his praises for he was kind and gentle and self-sacrificing in an age in which fathers were brutal and haughty. Yet, whether Michel liked it or not, his genius derived from his mother, whom he so unjustly neglected, for it is not for the leaf to say which of the roots in the earth shall feed it, nor may it pretend that the branch on which it luxuriates has nothing to do with the trunk.

Education Is Not the Rod

Michel de Montaigne was born on the 28th of February, 1533. He seems to have been delicate, but in good health, and now the first son, since his two little brothers had died. A family at that time had to be well provided with children, if it expected to continue its line. Michel himself had six daughters, five of whom died in infancy. Infancy was a dangerous period in an age of swamps and witch doctors.

Pierre Eyquem, his father, did not wish his son to be either a businessman or a soldier. The Eyquem family had now reached a point when it could begin thinking of higher things. Michel, therefore, should become a true nobleman, a member of the royal household, a dignitary of the church, or a high councillor of state. But not by dint of money or flattery or evil deeds. The ancient Jewish tradition of learning, the tradition of the people to whom he no longer belonged, was still alive in Pierre. Although he himself had acquired little learning, a scholar, by dint of his knowledge, was always a most welcome guest at Montaigne.

In the general upbringing of the young lord of Montaigne, there would be inculcated honesty, truth, and in that cruel age, kindness. Are such weapons effective in a world of shame and greed? Would they lead to success? But without them, is success worthwhile? A man is successful only in the degree that he enjoys his success, so Michel's conscience should be clear and his heart not laden with regrets.

But first of all, the key to knowledge and culture—Latin. There are still people today who confound culture with Latin, even the Latin grammar. They consider its labyrinth of rules the means to metamorphose jackasses into gentlemen, and generally succeed only in stretching their ears. But at that time, for one who would study law or theology or read the best books, Latin was absolutely essential. Michel, when the day came for him to write, although he knew Latin as well as French, and perhaps even better (for he often fell into the Gascogne patois), preferred to use the language of the marketplace, the language which by his help, was to become the most beautiful since the days of Babel. "The speech that I like," he says, "is simple and natural, the same on paper as on lips : a succulent, nervous, short, and concise manner of speaking, not dainty and nicely combed so much as vehement and brisk . . . every piece to form a body in itself . . . not in the manner of the professor or the preaching friar or the pleading advocate."

Pierre made all possible inquiries about the best system of education, and finding them all wanting, he decided on a practical scheme. He imported a German scholar, a man by the name of Doctor Horstanus, who later became a famous physician, and who took the child, almost an infant, in his complete care. He spoke only Latin to him and everybody around was forced to use the ancient tongue. "In short we all became so Latinized, that it overflowed to our villages around, where to this day may be heard several Latin names of artisans and tools, which through frequent use have taken root. . . . And so, without artificial means, without any book, without grammar or teaching, I learned a Latin quite as pure as that of my schoolmaster."

Even as Moses smote the rock with his rod that water might gush out of it, so the pedagogue of those days (and of countless days that followed) smote the seat of the pupil that education might gush out of it. And there was water and sometimes there was education, but God punished Moses for having smitten the rock and would not let him enter the Promised Land, and the pupil whose seat was smitten abhorred the pedagogue and would not let him enter his heart.

Pierre, however, ordered Michel's tutors to teach him arithmetic and geometry by means of games, and to give him a relish for knowledge and duty, not by forcing his will, but by increasing the boy's desire to learn, and to train his mind in all freedom and indulgence, without rigor or constraint. He was so anxious not to injure the delicate mechanism of childhood that since a youngster is deeply plunged in sleep, Michel should not be awakened with a start, but by the sound of sweet music. For this, the father engaged a spinet player, who was never remiss in his gentle duty.

Did the father spoil the son? Perhaps, a little, but what are fathers for? But if the father spoiled the son, the son never said "father" without adding "dear" and "good" and "best" and "beloved" and "without compare." And many years later, when he was old himself and his father long dead, he would wear his father's faded cloak that he might feel him near.

Michel was not a prodigy. He did not, like Pascal a century later, discover at the age of twelve the propositions of Euclid without the help of any books or teachers, nor did he write poetry as so many did even before they were sure of their spelling, nor was he a slick little rascal, who could repeat so glibly what he heard that one mistook his words for original thinking.

He was, on the credit side, of a gentle and tractable nature, but for the rest "so heavy, so soft and sluggish, that they could not shake me out of sloth, not even to get me out to play." Still, "what I saw, I saw plainly, and beneath this heavy constitution nourished some bold ideas and opinions in advance of my age." Later, when these opinions and ideas would mature, they would be many centuries in advance of the age in which he lived. "I had a slow wit, that would go no farther than it was led, a tardy apprehension, a weak initiative, and with it all, an incredible defect of memory." All of which served as excellent fertilizer to the acorn that needed many years to develop into the great oak which would withstand the storm of the centuries.

His father became uneasy, however, for loving though his eye was, it could not detect in this duckling the magnificent swan he was trying to raise. And so, like other fathers, he decided to send his son to school. For despite the record of generations to the contrary, fond parents consider schools crucibles into which they cast their creations of clay and expect them to emerge vessels of gold.

At the age of six, Michel was sent to the Collège de Guienne, considered the best school in France, but with the express instruction that his boy be spared the rod and the harshness even of tongue and look.

In his essay "Of the Education of Boys," dedicated to Madame Diane de Foix, Comtesse de Guron, as a present "to the little man who threatens shortly to come happily out of you: (You are too nobly born to begin otherwise than with a male) and because the most difficult branch of human knowledge appears to be that which treats of the rearing and education of children," Montaigne describes the conditions in that "best of schools."

"It is a regular jail of imprisoned youth. They become undisciplined by being punished before they are so. Go there at the lesson time: you will hear nothing but crying and shouting, both of boys under execution and of masters drunk with rage. What a way to arouse an appetite for learning in those tender and timid souls, to drive them to it with a terrifying scowl and hands armed with rods! An iniquitous and pernicious system!"

All the pages of his books are strewn with appeals for kindness toward man and animal. It is his cardinal law of virtue. Even if a man is condemned to death, he urges that there be no torture, no mutilation. "All that is over and above simple death appears to me as pure cruelty."

The papal authorities in Rome censured this sentence while Montaigne was there, and although he was flattered by being made a citizen of the Eternal City, he defied the censure and even reinforced his statement by adding that "our justice cannot hope that the man who is not deterred from wrongdoing by fear of being hanged or beheaded, will be prevented by the idea of a slow fire or the pincers and the wheel."

At the age of thirteen, Michel graduated, "finished my course (as they call it) and in truth without any gain that I could at present put to my account." Even his Latin, now that it had gone through the mill of grammar, grew corrupt. His tutor, prompted, and perhaps bribed by his father, not to exert too much pressure on the youngster, pretended not to see that he was reading ceaselessly the Latin classics, and that he had become totally negligent in the study of his prescribed lessons. Thus whatever benefit he derived from his seven years' sojourn in that "prison," was merely coincidental.

He continued languorous and lazy. "The danger was not that I should do ill, but that I should do nothing. Nobody predicted that I might become wicked, but only useless; they foresaw a do-nothing nature, but not a bad nature."

In a world of murder, plunder, and treachery, it was no mean compliment to do no ill. The quarries of Carrara have been emptied to raise gigantic monuments to the doers—the doers of evil and of shame, but not a city in all history has ever considered it its duty to sculp even the humble bust of a man who has harmed no one.

Education, nevertheless, should not be entrusted to parents. "Their natural love makes them too soft and tender, even the wisest of them." But the tutor should be "one with a well-made rather than a well-filled head. He should have not so much learning as character and intelligence. He should not keep bawling into the pupil's ears as one pours water into a funnel, the pupil's business being merely to repeat what he has been told.

"The bee rifles the flowers here and there, but she afterwards makes honey of what she has gathered, which is all her own; it is no longer thyme or marjoram; so the things borrowed from others, the student will transform and blend so as to make a work all his own, to wit, his judgment. His instruction, labor and study shall have no other aim but the forming of his judgment." So speaks Michel de Montaigne—a century and a half before Rousseau and two centuries before Pestalozzi.

"We must let the pupil pass everything through a sieve, and store nothing in his head on mere authority and trust. To him Aristotle's principles should be no more principles than those of the Stoics and Epicureans; let their various theories be put to him, and he will choose, if he is able; if not, he will remain in doubt. Only fools are certain and cocksure."

A quarter of a century after Montaigne's death, Francis Bacon, who had read the Frenchman's essays carefully, published his masterpiece, *Novum Organum,* in which he inaugurates the modern spirit of research.

"This great world is the mirror wherein we are to behold ourselves, in order to know ourselves, in order to know ourselves from the right point of view. In a word, I should wish it to be my pupil's book." And what is the ultimate aim of education? "That the pupil know himself and how to die well and live a good life and choose the art which gives us liberty."

In the barbarous mid-twentieth century, timorous and fawning educators mistrust the youth and advocate divine fear and corporal punishment as the guiding posts in the march to civilization. For Montaigne, education concerns only man and the earth, and the "profit of our studies lies in having become the better and the wiser for them."

Nevertheless, the danger in nonconformity was very great and Montaigne urges his pupil to be strong and uncompromising in what he believes. "The pupil must be broken to the pain of imprisonment as well as torture. For he may even be in danger of the two latter, which, seeing the times we live in, threaten both the good and the bad. We are now experiencing this: whoever combats the laws threatens the best of men with the scourge and the altar."

Since we have localized virtue, vice has become ubiquitous. We have even forgotten the origin of the word, which means acting like a *man,* and that, Montaigne holds, includes for his pupil the joys of the flesh. "He shall laugh, he shall wanton, he shall live riotously, and if he refrains from doing ill, let it be, not from lack of power and knowledge, but from lack of will." Like Seneca, he considered it "a great difference between not wishing to sin, and not knowing how to sin."

The Sacred College of Rome was displeased with this paragraph and asked him to remove it. Montaigne promised he would, but he, though most punctilious in keeping his word, forgot.

While actors were still considered unworthy even to be buried among the good and dreary folk, Montaigne urged the opening of theaters in all localities. He would have professional mummers as well as youngsters perform gay and pleasant comedies. "Sociability and friendship are thereby increased. There is nothing like alluring the appetite and affections; or else we shall produce only asses laden with books." And he would like a man trained "to be able to do all things, and love to do only the good."

Sex and Law

Now Michel was a young man, and although his father had preserved his virginity until his marriage at the age of thirty-three, Michel lost his sometime during puberty. *Tempora mutantur*—"times change"; and *tal padre tal hijo*—"like father like son," does not always hold true. Perhaps the Hebraic rigid code of sexual morality still bound the father, but his son learned his lessons from the great pagan poets, and even more delectably from his compatriot, Rabelais, who died when Michel was twenty. They never met, for Rabelais was running from one safety zone to another, and it was only two years before his death, that he was appointed curé of Meudon. Even then he was an absentee shepherd of his flock, who seemed to have grazed well enough without his help, perhaps better, while he himself remained in Paris and continued writing the adventures of Pantagruel. There was also Boccaccio with his gallant stories. Michel knew Italian well enough to read them in the original, without the loss of flavor in translation.

Montaigne calls Rabelais "simply amusing." By pretending to see nothing deeper in Rabelais, Montaigne may have saved his skin and neck. For, in the year 1533, the year of Rabelais' death, Michel Servet, the great physician, was burned at the stake in Geneva at the order of Calvin, the Protestant, and seven years earlier Etienne Dolet, philologist and printer, was hanged and burned for his daring opinions, by order of the pope.

The martyr on the scaffold exclaims that his enemies may kill him, but not the truth for which he dies. This may be relegated to the realm of hope and consolation. While some truths have survived the suppression and annihilation of their advocates, who can tell how many have been forever exterminated together with those who conceived them and perished in their defence? The three Sirens—Illusion, Dream, Prejudice—make sailing on the Sea of Truth extremely perilous. Only a lonely Odysseus reaches shore, battered and without cargo, and few there are to welcome his arrival.

In fact, however, Montaigne was Rabelais' immediate successor, and in a subtler fashion carried on the old writer's ideas. But while retaining some of the ways, since known as Rabelaisian, he does no more than lift a corner of the fig-leaf. He does not propose to destroy the pleasure of Eros by portraying its coarseness, its cheapness, its banality.

He recounts his experiences, sometimes with tongue in cheek, sometimes moralizing a bit; sometimes sighing at the flight of the "golden days" which will nevermore return, but always there is merriment and charm and wit.

Montaigne was always fastidious of taste. "For my part I can no more recognize Venus without Cupid than maternity without offspring." Even the animals "will not have it gross and earthy. We often see that imagination and desire kindle and excite them, before the body; we may observe in both sexes that, among the herd, they make a choice and selection in their affections, and that their mutual intimacies and likings are enduring. Even those to whom old age denies bodily strength will still tremble, neigh, and thrill with love. We may see them, before the deed, filled with hope and ardor, and when the body has played its part, still gratified by the sweetness of the remembrance; and some there are that are afterwards puffed with pride, and though weary and sated, crow with triumph and glee."

Who has written more delicately, more tenderly about the mating of the innocents? As for himself, he wrote in the last edition of his *Essays,* a few years before his death: "I will tell this of the errors of my youth. Not only on account of the danger to health (and yet I did not manage so well but I have had two touches, slight, however, and transitory), but also out of contempt, I have seldom had recourse to venal and public connections. I preferred to whet the pleasure by difficulty, by desire, and by some vainglory . . . For the rest I used to set great store by mental qualities, but only provided that there was no fault to be found with the body. For, to answer conscientiously, if one or the other of these two attractions must of necessity be wanting, I would have chosen rather to renounce the spiritual: it has its uses in better things. And is it not reasonable that we should look upon pleasure with at least the same favor as upon pain?"

But now the years have put a "stone" in the bladder, and he, alas, has "not the faculty of that dreamer in Cicero, who dreaming he was embracing a young girl, found that he had discharged his stone in his sheets! Mine strangely diswenches me!"

Yet even now: "I have no other passion to keep me in breath. What avarice, ambition, quarrels, law-suits do for other men, who, like myself, have no fixed occupation, love would do more beneficially. It would wake me up, make me more sober, pleasing, and careful of my person . . . it would prevent the grimaces of old age . . . it would divert me from a thousand troublesome thoughts, a thousand melancholy humors . . . would warm up, at least in dreams, this blood that Nature forsakes, would raise the chin and stretch out a little the nerves and the gaiety in the soul of this poor man who is moving full speed towards disintegration. But I know well it is a blessing very hard to recover."

However, recalling how he used to give at least as much pleasure as he received, he is ashamed to be found among the young. "That germ of budding beauty will not be touched by such stiff old hands, nor won by mere material means." Always generous in all matters, he can be no less in this, particularly in this, for "it is a mean soul that would be beholden for everything." And as the final challenge to time, to pleasure, this descendant of hidalgos, who would rather die standing than live kneeling, exclaims: "I would much rather not live, than live on alms!"

And the essence he has drawn from his experiences, the gist of the comedy he has played, urged by a ravenous hunger until satiety had set in and the food had become as stone for his shaky teeth, is: "I say that the male and female are cast in the same mold; saving education and habits, the difference is not great. It is much easier to accuse one sex than to excuse the other; it is in the words of the proverb, 'the poker calling the shovel black.' "

There were periods in which woman was relegated to the status of the beast of burden and periods in which she was exalted to the beatific grandeur of an angel, and it is difficult to ascertain which was her more onerous yoke. But now, for the first time, perhaps, in the history of that fantastic creature who dares to call himself *homo sapiens* when he should call himself *homo stultus,* we come across the notion that the male and the female of the species are equal, and equally in need of much cleansing and mutual forgiveness.

The Earth carries in her womb not only the seeds of plants and trees, but the seeds of ideas, and these may be asleep for one hundred seasons or five hundred seasons, but when the time comes, they break through and grow and flourish and become part of the wealth of man. And Montaigne's idea slumbered for four centuries, and now wherever there is a modicum

of civilization, woman has been accepted as man's equal—
neither angel nor devil, but human, mother of man and man's
daughter.

Michel had been out of school for two years and his father
decided definitely to make a lawyer of him. Law has ever been
the last refuge of the rich son, who is willing to study, but not
too hard, and who, after receiving his degree, may work, but
not too strenuously. An ideal profession for Michel de Montaigne, who had for all time discarded the name of Eyquem.

Michel, then, began the study of law at the University of
Toulouse. There is no record of his scholastic efforts, but we
may assume, without embarrassment, that he was at the bottom
of his class. Even had he desired to achieve distinction, he was
thoroughly handicapped—his memory was atrocious. "I do not
think there is another in the world so marvelously defective as
mine. All my faculties are mean and ordinary, but in this I think
I am singular and quite a rarity, deserving of a name and reputation." He has no subtlety whatever. "I never set my mind
any problem, however easy, that it could unravel. Any idle subtlety will perplex me. Of games in which the intellect has its
part, as chess, cards, draughts, and others, I have only the
rudest idea." Nor is he quick-witted. "My apprehension is slow
and muddled." Does he know the multitude of trifles with which
people bewilder listeners? "No mind is so absurdly ignorant as
mine of many such ordinary things, of which it is a disgrace to
be ignorant. I can add up neither with counters nor with a pen.
Most of our coins are unknown to me. I can scarcely distinguish
between the cabbages and the lettuces in my garden. I know
still less of the mechanical arts, of trade, and merchandise."

Is this the man that you would engage to snatch you out of
the clutches of justice? Is this the man, who, so often needed
in court, can prove that black is white and white black? Can he
untangle law from justice, since law is so often the executioner
of justice? Can he show the court how often guilt is gravedigger
to innocence?

Why, this man is a fool! And so he is, and it is only because he is a fool—who knows himself—that he becomes a wise man, for wisdom is the sister of simplicity. Wisdom must not be entangled in the spider web of facts in which truth is strangled. Wisdom must not be dazzled by clever words which, like fireworks, burst in midair into false milky ways. The light of the sun suffices her. Wisdom is not shrewd, not sagacious, not skilled in proving the two sides of arguments, not glamorous. It partakes of the plainness of the roots of things. Since the honey of wisdom is gathered from the thorns of experience, the wise man must not mind the stings. The wise man cannot be vain, for watching fools, he sees how much he has in common with them.

Montaigne was fit by nature for wisdom. His mental drawbacks were absolutely essential—his lack of memory forced him to think for himself; his ignorance made him humble; his pains made him charitable; his follies gave him a sense of humor; his skepticism gave him tolerance. Wisdom is not one single element, but an amalgam of many—a strong drink fit only for clear heads and sturdy hearts.

Doubtless, Michel received his degree of bachelor of laws, *en droit*—of rights, as the French have it—and his good papa bought him a seat as Councillor of the Parlement of Bordeaux, according to custom. This was an easy matter since his father was mayor of the city—a good and honest mayor, a rarity among mayors of that time and this. For sixteen years Michel kept his seat in the Parlement, but his seat was generally vacant. Not only was he away from the Parlement, but away from the city as well. He had not yet begun his great voyages, but he often went to Paris, for which he had a deep passion. "I love her tenderly, even her warts and blemishes. I am a Frenchman only through this great city, great in its people, great in the happiness of its site; but above all and incomparable in variety and diversity of amenities, the glory of France and one of the noblest ornaments of the world . . . because it is really in my nature, and perhaps a little more than it should be, I look on all men as my fellow-citizens, and would embrace a Pole as I would a Frenchman, subordinating this national tie to the com-

mon and universal one. . . . Nature has given us to the world
free and unfettered; we imprison ourselves in certain narrow
districts...."

Internationalists—cosmopolitan—however deeply buried in
the mud, the roots flow with the rich, clear sap and feed even
the ungrateful branch.

Friendship versus Marriage

In 1556, Thomas Cranmer, Archbishop of Canterbury, because he helped abolish the supremacy of the Pope and insti-
tuted a number of ritual reforms, was tried as heretic and
burned at the stake by the order of Mary Tudor. The fires
were lit now here, now there, by Protestants, by Catholics, all
for the glory of the Jew who was nailed to a cross because he
spoke of love and brotherhood and the forgiveness of harlots
who brought pleasure to those who would stone them.

Michel de Montaigne, Councillor of the Parlement of Bordeaux, took no sides. He hated all bloodshed, all cruelty, and
therefore could take no sides. There was as yet no third side—
no side that would endeavor to rid man once and for all of the
poison of bigotry and liberate his mind of his ancestral fears.
There were individuals, to be sure, in all countries, who had
freed themselves, but they could not trust their neighbors, and
at best had to speak and write in parables, in gallant tales, in the
manner of the court's fools, but always protest loudly their
fidelity to prejudice, superstition, and chicanery. Montaigne will
become one of these later on.

Meanwhile, however, at the age of twenty-five, he spent his
days in indolence, wenching, and posing at court. He was a fop.
He dressed in fineries in order to make up for his size. He was
somewhat below middle height "This is not only an ugly defect,
but it is also a disadvantage, especially in those who are in office
and command. . . . It is very humiliating, if you are standing

among your servants, to be addressed by the question, 'Where is your master?' and to receive only the fag-end salute made to your secretary or your barber. . . . Other kinds of beauty are for the woman; beauty of stature is the only beauty of man. . . . When a man is small, neither a broad and round forehead, nor clear and soft eyes, nor an average nose, nor small ears and mouth, nor white and regular teeth, nor a thick, smooth, auburn beard, nor curly hair, nor a properly rounded head, nor a fresh complexion, nor a pleasant face, nor an odorless body, nor a correct symmetry of limbs, will make him handsome."

This is how he was at the height of his physical powers. Later, he became stone bald, thickset, a full face, without being fat, dim-eyed—"half a man." He wore then only black and white clothes to keep him warm in winter and cool in summer, and evidently, for no other purpose. But he was no longer miserable. He had grasped the meaning of things. "We commend a horse for his strength and speed, not for his trappings; a greyhound for his swiftness, not his collar; a hawk for her wing, not for her bells. Why do we not likewise esteem a man for that which is his own? Let him lay aside his riches and external honors and show himself in his shirt."

Whatever our age, we consider that particular period the most propitious for comprehending life. And always, as we live on, we discover that we were thoroughly mistaken. Thus the milestones of our career are carved with false symbols and the entire path may be called the Valley of Delusion.

But the period of insensitivity to vital conditions, the period in which it appeared that Montaigne's emotions would, like so many of his fellow courtiers, turn into sheer mockery, into sonorous, empty verbiage, ended abruptly, and he appeared as an exquisitely sensitive person—as if he had suddenly broken his stony chrysalis. At a town gathering and great feast, he met a man by the name of Etienne de la Boetie. He was Michel's senior by three years, but in seriousness and morality, he might have been old enough to be his father. De la Boetie was a poet and publicist, an upholder of liberty and a fighter against tyr-

anny. Quite possibly he would have ended on the gallows or
bound to a stake, if he had not died before achieving greater
popularity and importance. At any rate, at this first meeting
of the two men, "we found ourselves so taken with one another,
so well acquainted, so bound together, that from that moment
nothing could be so close as we were to one another."

Such friendship had never existed before, or if it had, it was
never recorded with such tenderness and such reverence as
Montaigne records it years later after it no longer existed, cut
short by the death of de la Boetie. "This friendship had no other
model than itself, and can only be compared with itself. This is
no one special consideration, nor two, nor three, nor four, nor
a thousand: it is I know not what quintessence of all this mixture, which, having taken possession of his whole will, carried
it to plunge and lose itself into mine, with a like hunger and emu-
lation. I may truly say lose, reserving as we did nothing to ourselves, that was either his or mine."

Philosophers have tried to explain the phenomenon of
friendship, but their words are cold and lifeless, and poets have
invoked its joys, but their verses are artificial. Montaigne presents his own heart, warm and pulsing, and his words course
like the mingled blood of the two men.

There are various types of loves—the love of a child for his
father, but there is too great a disparity between them. "For
neither can all the secret thoughts of the father be communicated
to his son, in order not to beget an unseemly familiarity, nor can
the admonitions and corrections, which are among the first offices of friendship, be administered by the son to the father."
There is fraternal love. "Truly the name of a brother is a beautiful thing, and full of affection, and on that model did he and
I form our alliance." (They became "frères d'alliance" and
called each other "brother.") But blood brothers have all sorts
of difficulties of "wordly goods, divisions, and the fact that the
wealth of one is the other's poverty," and these loosen the
"brotherly solder." There is our affection towards women. "Its
fire is more active, fiercer, and more fervent, to be sure, but sub-

ject to fits and returns. . . . What is more, in sexual love there is but a frantic desire for that which flies from us. Enjoyment destroys it, as having only a fleshly end and being subject to satiety. Friendship, on the other hand, is enjoyed in proportion as it is desired."

Then there is marriage. "Marriage is a bargain," whose purposes have many ends . . . a thousand extraneous entanglements to unravel, sufficient to break the thread and disturb the course of a lively affection; whereas in friendship there is no traffic or business except with itself."

But there are friendships and friendships, and even the most famous among them fall far short of the friendship between Michel and Etienne. "I cannot allow those other friendships to be placed in the same line with ours. I should not advise anyone to measure them with the same rule; he would be much mistaken." Nor can such friendship be shared by more than two. A third party, however devoted, would disturb the exquisite balance. "It is miracle enough to divide oneself in two, and they know not the greatness of it who speak of dividing oneself in three. And he who supposes that I can equally love each of the two, and that they can love one another and me as much as I love them, makes a multiple brotherhood of a thing that is the most one and united, and of which even one is the rarest thing in the world to find. . . . In the friendship I speak of, our souls blend and melt so entirely, that there is no more sign of the seam which joins them. If I am pressed to say why I loved him, I feel I can only express myself by answering—'Because it was he, because it was I.' "

De la Boetie died less than five years later of the cholera. He left to Montaigne his manuscripts, which Montaigne later published, and his libarary of more than a thousand books, an extraordinary collection for the times. But he left him much more —he left him the legacy of love, pity, tenderness, and the honest appraisal of courts and courtiers.

In fact, however, de la Boetie left him nothing. All had already been in Montaigne. It needed but ignition. Montaigne was by far the greater man, but he did not know it. Indeed, he was not to know it for many years after his friend's death. Shaken more deeply than he would ever be again by all the tribulations and miseries which were in store for him, Montaigne allowed himself two years later, "to be led to the marriage altar."

On the 25th of September, 1565, Michel de Montaigne married the daughter of one of his colleagues in the Parlement, for he was still there, doing nothing as usual. Françoise de la Chassaigne seemed to have been a good and capable woman, and moreover brought him quite a dowry—in modern money about one hundred thousand dollars. Like his mother, she barely appears in Montaigne's *Essays,* except indirectly in his study of marriage and love.

"Marriage," he says, "has for its share, usefulness, justice, honor, constancy—a flat pleasure, but a universal one. Love is founded on delight alone, and gives it, truly, of a kind more poignant, more caressive, more vital. . . . A man does not marry for himself, whatever people say; he marries quite as much, for his posterity and his family."

Nevertheless, Montaigne has a high esteem for marriage as an institution. "If rightly established and properly understood, there is no better institution in modern society. We cannot dispense with it, and we continue to dishonor it. It may be compared to a cage; the birds outside are desperately anxious to get in, and those that are in it, are equally anxious to get out."

There is no greater compliment to marriage than that we expect perfection in it, while in all other human relations, we are quite content with mere reasonableness. The painful dénouement in Eden was not the loss of the Garden, but that Adam found Eve only a woman and Eve found Adam only a man.

Had Montaigne followed his own bent, he would have shunned wedlock "with Wisdom herself, if she would have me. But say what we will, custom and the uses of everyday life carry us along." Why does he say "Wisdom," and not "Venus" or

"Cupid?" Already the seed is broken and it would not be long before the magnificent flower would begin to burgeon.

His marriage was reasonably happy, although he was not overfaithful to his wife, at least until the "stone" made him virtuous. But he says that he did not break his promise, or rather that he fulfilled it to the letter. He evidently told Françoise that he would be faithful to her in his own fashion, in the fashion of most husbands, everywhere and always. All formulas for wives to keep their husbands faithful must remain illusory as long as other women have also charms and circumstances favor their exploitation. There is, however, this mitigating situation—wives are also women.

Six daughters were born of the union, six minor tragedies, according to the mores of the times, but he was relieved of the burden, since five of them died in their infancy, and only one grew up, and in due time married. Montaigne was the kindest of fathers, even as his father had been toward him, but he says: "I do not know that I would not much rather have begotten a perfectly shaped child by intercourse with the Muses than by intercourse with my wife."

The house of Montaigne continued, but his daughter disposed of his books shortly after his death and of the more than one thousand, only seventy have been recovered. Nor was Montaigne luckier in the choice of his inheritor, for he named the youngest of his male descendants, which led to a lawsuit settled only two centuries later.

Adieu, Cruel World!

For the next few years, Montaigne continued his life of futile luxury and his visits to the royal court, where he was named Gentleman of the Chamber, but he found no savor in it. And now misfortune piled on misfortune, personal and general. His father died, his babies died, and everywhere wars, fanned by religion, flamed on.

In France, under the instigation of Catherine de' Medici, spirit of evil, the horror of fratricide reached its culminating point during the night of the 23rd of August, 1572, known in the black pages of history as the Night of St. Bartholomew. The marriage of Henry of Navarre, later Henry IV, to the sister of the reigning king, Charles IX, had been celebrated a day previously, and Paris was crowded with the cream of the Huguenot world, since Henry was at the time a Protestant.

The bells of the church of Saint-Germain-l' Auxerrois began ringing toward dawn, the signal for the soldiers to start their work, blessed in advance, by the Pope. Paris became a slaughterhouse. The Protestant noblemen, who had taken part in the joyous activities the day before and were now in the Palace of the Louvre, were strangled, beheaded, or shot, according to the place in which they were cornered. The blue blood oozing, the soldiers spread to all corners of the city, and pursued their monstrous business without regard to station or occupation—men, women, and children. The streets became bloody cemeteries, and the murderers, in the eternal tradition became plunderers and arsonists as well. The rest of France followed suit. The maniacal carnage continued for several days and did not cease until from fifty thousand to one hundred thousand had perished and the nation was plunged in misery.

But even as in the summer a thunder shower may cause great damage and yet not cool the parching air, so this blood shower only intensified the enmity between the two branches of the church of Jesus, and the civil war pursued its ferocious career for over a quarter of a century until the Edict of Nantes guaranteed, for a time, freedom of worship to all. Freedom *from* worship required the great Revolution, which would not come for two centuries.

The Castle of Montaigne was always in the very center of the vicious turmoil, and yet Michel would neither turn it into a fortress nor lock its gates. "Defense allures the enterprise, and distrust provokes it. I have baffled the designs of the soldiery by depriving the exploit of all danger and of all chance of military glory. The house is closed to no one who knocks. It is provided with no other safeguard but a porter with the old-fashioned ceremonious manners, whose office is not to forbid my door, but rather to offer it with the more grace and decorum. I have no other sentinel nor watch but what the stars keep for me. . . . The fact that so many strongly-guarded houses have been destroyed, whilst mine endures, makes me suspect that they were destroyed because they were strongly guarded. . . . All defense bears the aspect of war."

Would that the world's statesmen, who like hypnotized, mad ants raise mountains of weapons in the futile hope that thus they may find refuge behind them, read the words and fathomed the meaning of the good and wise man of the ancient Castle of Montaigne!

Montaigne was at the wedding festivities of Henry of Navarre, who was a personal friend of his, and had visited the castle on more than one occasion. He was twenty years Michel's junior, and it is quite possible that he learned much from him, particularly in the matter of treating the peasants well and in the meaning and function of liberty. As Henry IV he was one of the great kings of France, and invited Montaigne to come to his court as an adviser, but Montaigne, now afflicted with his painful disease and too deeply in love with his solitude and work, refused.

The massacre and cruelty which Montaigne witnessed on St. Bartholomew's Night shocked him profoundly, and his ambitions appeared infantile and preposterous. He decided to say farewell to the living barbarians and consort henceforth with the great dead, who had left to their undeserving descendants priceless treasures, now gracing his library in many rows and ever ready to offer themselves.

At the Castle of Montaigne there was a tower which stood somewhat apart from the building and dominated it. The library was on the third floor. On the first was a chapel which, if

Michel ever entered, he never mentions the fact in his *Essays*. On the second, a bedroom, and above the library, a large wardrobe.

The library was circular in shape, the only flat side reserved for his table and chair. Since it was round, he could see all his books at a glance. From this room he had three open and extensive views. He could see his garden, his farmyard, his courtyard, and most parts of his house. "Here is my throne; here I endeavor to make my rule absolute and to sequester this one corner from all society, conjugal, filial, and social. Everywhere else my authority is verbal and doubtful in reality. . . . Miserable, to my mind, is he who has not in his home a place to himself, where he may give all attention to himself; where he may hide!"

An ivory tower is an illusory refuge. When a man is not exposed to outer inclemencies, he exposes himself to his inner storms. We run away from society to seek haven in ourselves and run away from ourselves to seek haven in society. But there is no haven, no refuge, only conflict, precisely because we are the admixture of self and society, each claiming totality.

When Michel came to Montaigne, he thought he would find consolation in the books, but they only excited his imagination and proved no outlet for his nerves. He wrote marginal notes in his books, but he could not read them the next day. He did not know, as yet, that he was like the bee he would later write about, the bee who had rifled the flowers, and who returned to the hive to make the honey which was all its own.

Gradually it dawned upon him. He was not to be a mere reader, and his books could serve only to direct his thoughts into various channels. He now had experience and judgment and the knowledge of men, and he would merge that wealth, with something in him, which neither he, nor any other mortal would ever be able to analyze—genius—to flow out of him in the shape of words. And the words would cluster and the clusters would become thoughts, juicy with life, scented with wit, with humor, with grace—thoughts, ideas, impressions, opinions—flowing,

flowing. In time it would be as a river, a river gilded by the sun, silvered by the moon, tossed by the winds, cleaved by fleets of boats laden with precious cargoes, destined for a thousand **ports.**

Who Am I? What Do I Know?

Every writer writes about himself. He writes in the first person or in the third person, but always about himself. The skin imprisons not only our bodies, but our minds. Those writers who write in the third person hide behind the skirts of false objectivity. They try to deceive their readers, to divert their attention, to make them believe that they are reading something about other people than those named as authors. They even deceive themselves, for the symbols become unrecognizable like bad handwriting or a secret code whose key has been lost.

But who is this self? Who, writing about him, ever discovers him? Is the self only that particular entity, who, at the time of writing, breathes and functions in the manner of living things, or is he the guardian of the vast ossuary of his ancestors, to which he will, in due time, add his own ashes? Does he speak for that particular portion momentarily integumented in skin, or is he the spokesman for all?

If he pushes the pen himself and for himself and the ideas are the secretions of his own brain, why is it that so often he gazes at the words scrawled on the paper in incredulous astonishment? Who has thought them? Not he. He had meant quite something else. They may be better or worse than he had meant, but they are not his. Whence did those pictures come, those memories which had never been his, those passions which he had never entertained?

Montaigne started tapping the ground as one in darkness. His servants had sharpened many a goose's quill, for the master could not even do that, and placed them respectfully on his desk in the library near the immense bronze inkstand with two containers, one for the ink and the other for the fine sand to blot the wet pages. But Montaigne only walked up and down and in circles, uncertain how to start. Well, he mused, he was not a professional writer and had no professional obligations. He would simply try—*essayer*—and whatever came out of him, he would always call modestly—*un essai*—"an attempt," an experiment. Nobody could ever be angry with him then, nor consider him an impostor, that is, in the most unlikely event that eyes, other than his own, should ever scan the pages. And thus it was that Michel de Montaigne not only began the writing of a masterpiece, but created a genre of literature and baptized it —essay. More still, no one in the succeeding centuries surpassed him in the art, and few equalled him.

"Who does not see that I have chosen a path along which I shall wander, without cease and without labor, as long as there is ink and paper in the world?" This he wrote years later, after his *Essays* had gone through several editions. "I cannot keep a record of my life by my actions; fortune places them too low. I keep it by my ideas. So I know a gentleman who only communicated his life by the operations of his bowels; at his house you might have seen a row of chamber-pots of seven or eight days' use. That was his study; his conversation; all other talk stank in his nostrils. . . . Here, a little more decently, you have the excrements of an old mind. . . ."

Thus, the man who became more and more modest as his work was praised, meant, in an elemental way, to explain his creation. He meant to say—all you read is only myself and of myself. There are those who coyly claim to be ignorant and thereby expect to be considered learned and wise, for they heard it said that the learned and the wise are humble in their knowledge and not ashamed of their ignorance.

But Montaigne's very genius forced him into the channel. He could never have written impersonally or in the orthodox manner, classics such as he admired, poetry, history, philosophy. He was not a scholar or a thinker in the accepted sense. He did not possess the natural tools for such enterprises. He could only allow his mind to function as it listed, without labor, without falsification, without any *a priori* commitments. "It has been suggested to me that I should chronicle the events of my time, by some who regard me as one who sees them with eyes less impaired by passion than others, but I would never undertake such a task, sworn enemy that I am to obligation, assiduity, and perseverance. There is nothing so foreign to my style as a continuous narrative. I have neither composition nor exposition worth anything, for which reason I have undertaken only to say what I am able to say, accommodating the matter to my capacity."

But why, indeed, should he chronicle the events of his time, when he chronicled the essence of the events of all time? It has been said that it is easier to write about mankind than about one man. But in Montaigne's case, mankind merges with one man. He thought he was writing about himself, but he wrote not only about his ancestors and contemporaries, but about the endless caravan of generations which would follow his.

He was inconsistent, but how shall a man be consistent, if nothing in the world remains unaltered for the space of a second? *Panta rhei*—"all things flow." Had Montaigne desired to uphold a particular philosophic theory or political ideology, then he would have held on to it, and all the winds of time would have broken their horns against it to no avail. But he only wished to explain himself, and "he who examines himself closely will seldom find himself twice in the same state. I give to my soul now one face, now another, according to the side to which I turn it. . . . All the contradictions are to be found in me . . . bashful, insolent; chaste, lascivious; talkative, taciturn; clumsy, gentle; witty, dull; peevish, sweet-tempered; mendacious, truthful; knowing, ignorant; and liberal and avaricious and prodigal. . . ."

And yet, he *is* consistent. He is consistent toward the values which men have always held essential for their humanity, nay, for their existence—kindness, tolerance, justice, truth, courage, honesty. "Among other vices, I cruelly hate cruelty, both by nature and reason, as the worst of all vices. But then I am so soft in this that I cannot see a chicken's neck wrung without distress, and cannot bear to hear the squealing of a hare between the teeth of my hounds . . . I bring inwardly and from a natural propensity, an extreme dislike of deceit. . . . At all times and in all places my own eyes are sufficient to keep me straight; by no others am I watched so closely, and there are none that I fear more. . . . And so to train oneself to virtue that the very seeds of vice are rooted out. . . . No noble thing can be done without risk. Courage makes as magnificent a show in a doublet as in a chain armor, in a cabinet as in a field. . . . Lying is indeed an accursed vice. We are human beings and hold together only by speech. . . ."

And this is the foundation of Michel de Montaigne, deep, secure, immutable. But once he accepts these virtues, or rather shows them as part of his flesh and marrow, vascular and alive, he may resume to investigate, to see the contradictions, the seesaws of notions, the multitudinous, complicated antlers of dilemmas, the countless masks of truth. "Reason always walks crooked, lame and broken-hipped, and in the company of falsehood as of truth. Hence, it is difficult to discover her miscalculations and irregularities. I always call by the name of Reason that semblance of it which every man imagines himself to possess. This kind of reason, which may have a hundred counterparts around one and the same subject, all opposed to each other, is an implement of lead and wax, that may be bent and stretched to any bias and any measure."

How can a man pursue the Road of Reason since he is yoked to Hope and Fear pulling him now in one direction now in another?

Montaigne contradicts himself, because a man is the sumtotal of his contradictions, and he is anxious to know the full man and present him to the world. *Ecce homo*—but not as martyr, or at least not only martyr to his fate; also as comedian, as creator of beauty as well as of ruins. But if man is the master of his fate, then his history chronicles a monster. Man's sole exoneration is that he is the toy of his fate. Knowingly man sows what he will not reap and builds what he will not inhabit, and this is his redemption for the havoc and devastation which he spreads upon earth.

The society which protects animals from the cruelties of man no longer allows blinders on horses; when shall we have a society protecting man from the cruelty of having blinders forced upon him almost from birth, so that they grow into his temples, and to remove them becomes a major operation, frequently fatal?

Michel de Montaigne has been labeled "skeptic," and so he is, skeptic, doubter, but how shall a man learn save by doubting his own eyes and ears and the mouths of others? "Many of the delusions of this world, or to speak more boldly, all the delusions, are begotten of our being taught to be afraid to profess our ignorance, and thinking ourselves bound to accept everything we cannot refute. Whoever will be cured of ignorance, let him confess it. . . . If a man remembers how many and many a time he has been mistaken in his judgment, is he not a fool if he does not ever after distrust it? To learn that we have said or done a foolish thing, that is nothing; we must learn that we are but fools: a much fuller and more important lesson."

The wise man does not fear to appear as fool upon occasion, but the fool's perpetual concern is to hide his identity. The wise man may wear the dunce's cap as a merry-maker at a carnival, but on the fool's head it fits as an appropriate and solemn headgear. There is so much that those whom we call wise do not know, and so much that those whom we call foolish do know, that it is more reasonable to divide people into foolish and differently foolish.

What, in truth, are the disputes between men about, if not words? But words are mazes in which men wander, lost, and words are wantons and all hands maul them. "I ask what are

Nature, Pleasure, Circle, and Substitution ? The question is one of words, and with words is it answered. A stone is a body, but if you urge any further, 'and what is a body ?' 'Substance.' 'And what is Substance,' and so on, you will end by driving the respondent to exhaust his dictionary. To satisfy one doubt, they give us three."

Prolific words are like showers which sweep over the earth, but do not seep into it to feed the seeds and the roots.

Montaigne goes in search of truth, and only they should follow truth who are capable of changing their minds, or rather keeping their minds in suspense, for every truth carries within its texture the roots of its own denial, which, in time, cancer-like, flourish and throttle it. Truth must be as a bridge which allows for vibration, in order that time may pass over it without breaking it.

Meanwhile, the pen scrapes on. Montaigne has found his medium. He puts at the top of the page a title. It is to be the subject he will discuss. Soon he forgets it, on purpose generally, and wanders in all directions. What difference does it make ? An idea is a fire scattering sparks to all the winds.

He speaks about himself, about things that happened to him, excellent stories, short and all muscle; he retells stories that he has read in the ancients, and they are more alive and succinct now; he quotes from the philosophers, the poets, the historians. He has no memory, but somehow remembers an infinite number of things, or at least remembers where to look for them. But these are not extraneous, they are not studded as jewels of mere erudition. They seem to have been written especially for that spot; they form part of the pattern, never superimposed, never smudging. They were faded in some yellowed book, but now they have regained color and life.

Before too long, Montaigne will return to his topic, his arms full of the wonderful things he has gathered as he loafed about. Tomorrow he will put at the top of the sheet another title, and again pursue his merry way. Many are the roads he takes and many the treasures scattered upon them, but they lead him only to the Cave of the Ogre of Ignorance—QUE SAIS -JE ?—WHAT DO I KNOW?

What Is Man? Who Is God? What Now, Christianity?

Almost on his deathbed, Pierre Eyquem asked his son to translate a book he had recently come across, and which, he believed, would be of benefit to French readers. It was a drearily written theological treatise—Spanish with Latin terminations —by a Spaniard named Raimond de Sabonde, who had lived and professed medicine at Toulouse, two centuries before. Pierre had never lost his interest in things Spanish and maybe he suspected that Sabonde, or Sebond, as Frenchified, had belonged to those who had once frequented the synagogue.

At any rate, "being incapable of disobeying the command of the best father that ever was," Michel undertook the job, and his father "was singularly pleased with the result, and arranged to have it printed," which the son dutifully did after his death.

The book, Montaigne says, had for its purpose to stop the incipient movement against the Church of God, "which might easily degenerate into an execrable Atheism." And to that extent, Montaigne finds it excellent, for "the common people, lacking the power to weigh things by themselves, when once they have become possessed with the temerity to despise and criticize the beliefs they once held in the utmost reverence, they will shake off, as a tyrannical yoke, the laws or the reverence of ancient usage; resolved henceforth to accept nothing to which they have not applied their judgment and given their special sanction."

And thus, under the title of "Apology for Raymond Sebond," Montaigne composes his longest and most significant essay. In the manner of a *bonhomme,* of a simpleton, he writes a satire more devastating than those of Voltaire or Swift. He had to be shrewd indeed to survive. Those were very perilous days.

"What is it that unsettles the mind and most usually throws us into a state of madness, but its quickness, its subtlety, its versatility, and in short its own power? Wherein consists the most subtle madness, but in the most subtle wisdom? . . . . Would you have a man healthy, would you have him steady and well-balanced in mind and morals? Wrap him in the darkness of sloth and dullness. We must be made like the beasts to be made wise and blinded before we can guide ourselves."

He, Montaigne, makes it known to all and sundry, that he himself is healthy and well-balanced, because he accepts the teachings of that foundation of ignorance, blessed beyond all things, the Church, for God "chose simple and ignorant men, in order to impart to us His wonderful secrets; our faith is not of our own acquiring, it is purely the gift of another's bounty. It is not by our reasoning or our understanding that we have received our religion, but by outside authority and command. We are therein assisted by the weakness more than by the strength of our judgment, by our blindness more than by our clear-sightedness. By means of our ignorance, more than by our knowledge, do we become wise in this heavenly wisdom."

Because man has learned to walk on his hind legs, he has the temerity to believe that he bestrides the Earth; because he has learned to utter a great variety of sounds, he proclaims himself the interpreter of all creation. And yet, "is it possible to imagine anything more ridiculous than that miserable and puny creature, exposed to shocks on all sides, calling himself Master and Emperor of the Universe?" And "by what right does he separate himself from among the multitude of creatures, fellows, and comrades, the animals?"

Yahweh blew his trumpet, or more likely a ram's horn, and all the creatures of the Earth flew and crawled and walked and swam into line, and Adam reviewed them and gave each its name, and Adam was made their Lord and Devourer forever. Montaigne, too, reviewed them, or at least a portion of the descendants of those who were saved in Noah's boat, and spoke of their virtues and their charm and their intelligence with a tenderness and understanding rare in the annals of zoology. "So that their brutish stupidity surpasses in all their contrivances everything that we are able to do with our divine intelligence."

Yet, it is foolish to utter, as so many do, that we are "the only outcast animal, bare on the bare earth, bound and tied down." Man is not the stepchild of Nature. She has no stepchildren, nor illegitimate ones. She has children with various talents. "We are neither superior nor inferior to the rest. . . . Some difference there is; there are orders and degrees, but under the same aspect of one and the same Nature."

And God? Where is God in this menagerie? Every ten pages or so, Montaigne begins to be tickled by the tips of the flames which the bellows of bigotry keep ever ready for those who dare question, and he mumbles: "Glory to God!" "The mercy of God," "The bounty of God," and similar platitudes, for his original eloquence is devoted wholly to terrestrial matters. Thus he appeases the men with the sizzling pitchforks in whose image the devils were created.

Montaigne has no desire to become a martyr to opinions. We construct our opinions as birds construct their nets with disparate and incongruous bits and hold them together with the glue of vanity. Besides, is he not a martyr already to the stones in his kidneys? "You are sweating in agony, turning pale, red, trembling, vomiting your very blood, suffering strange contractions and convulsions, your eyes sometimes dropping big tears," and after two or three days' inability to pass water, "you pass water that is thick, black and dreadful to look at, or having it stopped by some rigged and sharp-edged stone that pricks and cruelly flays. . . . Once a month, if you do not embrace Death, you at least shake hands with him."

Why, suffering so cruelly, does he not pray? He would not disturb the Almighty, for see who prays and for what purposes: "The miser prays to Him for the safekeeping for his vain and superfluous treasures; the ambitious man for victories and the guidance of His ruling passion; the thief implores His aid in surmounting the dangers and difficulties that obstruct the carrying out his wicked designs, or thanks Him for the ease with which he has been enabled to cut the throat of a traveler. At the foot of the house they intend to scale or blow up they make their prayers, with their hopes and intentions, full of cruelty, lust and greed."

Why traffic with a divinity that listens and even responds to such villainies? Who is He, anyway? "Of all shapes the most beautiful is that of man; wherefore God is of that shape," so says man. But hearken to the gosling: "All things in the world concentrate on me; the earth serves me to walk on, the sun to give me light, the stars to communicate to me their influence; the winds benefit me in this way, the waters in that. There is nothing the vault of heaven looks on so favorable as myself. I am the darling of Nature. Does not man keep me, house me, and wait on me? For me he sows and grinds. If he eats me, so does he his fellow-man; so do I the worms that kill and eat him. . . ."

The Earth pullulates with divinites, and each is the true and only one, but at least the good animals devour one another for their own delectation, and only man tortures and slays his fellow-man for the glory and pleasure of his God. "Man is indeed out of his wits! He cannot create a mite and he creates gods by the dozen!"

Montaigne will say nothing further. The smoke of the crackling wood to which his colleagues in thought are bound, invades his nostrils. Wise people do not read lines, but what is between the lines, and between the lines all the gods, including *the* God have vanished. Montaigne is unfettered. He knows only what his senses reveal and judgment dictates. His senses reveal joy and pain and color and heat and cold and smells and sweetness and bitterness against the palate, and his judgment concludes that all these are due to nerves and flesh and blood and brain, which function for a while, according to their natures, and then cease, and man and animal revert to the elements.

Nature has no favorites and has no design for man, neither

present nor ulterior. She is neither kind to him nor cruel, and is unaware of his presence except as one of the particles in her vast totality, to be perpetuated or obliterated by the pressure and the reshaping of space.

And so the most illustrious Michel de Montaigne, Knight of the Order of St. Michel and Gentleman of the Chamber in Ordinary to the Most Christian King, as the Roman Senate wrote on its patent, when it granted him the citizenship of the Eternal City, was "the execrable Atheist," whom he flayed with a paper knife and tongue in cheek.

Not an "atheist," for that would convey little meaning to Montaigne—a deist perhaps,—a believer in the God of Marcus Aurelius or Socrates or foreshadowing the God of the great Lens Grinder of Holland a century later—impersonal, eternal, and infinite, beyond good and evil, beyond pleasure and pain, being both life and death and immortality, within whom the soul of man merges as a drop of rain merges with the ocean.

And Christianity? The Trinity he could not comprehend or accept, and as a prudent man, he makes the sign of the cross whenever necessary, and passes on to other matters. "How many cuckoldries there are in history, procured by the gods against poor humans! In the religion of Mahomet, through the credulity of the people, there are plenty of children without fathers, spiritual, divinely born in the womb of virgins, and bearing a name that signifies as much in their language." Poor Moslems, they have to serve as scapegoat for Christianity! As for himself, "of the religions that give a body to their Deity, as necessity requires in this universal blindness, I should, I think, more readily incline to that of the sun-worshippers."

More than that only a fool would dare say, a magnificent fool, whose burning body should serve as a torch for truth. Montaigne had never attained that glorious madness.

But what about that vaunted morality of Christianity? "There is no hostility that surpasses that of a Christian. . . . Our religion was made for extirpating sins; it screens them, it fosters them, it provokes them. Do you desire a proof of this?

Compare our ways with those of a Mohammedan or a pagan;
you will always fall short of them. Whereas, seeing the advantage our religion offers us, we ought to outshine them in
excellence at an extreme and incomparable distance; and people
should be able to say: 'Are they so just, so charitable, so good?
Then they are Christians.' "

The world is full of wonders and only the miracles are ridiculous. "Miracles are in accordance with our ignorance of Nature,
not according to the essence of Nature. Being accustomed to a
thing blinds the eye of judgment. I have witnessed the birth of
many miracles in my time. The private error first creates the
public error, and in its turn the public error afterwards creates
the private error. . . . There is nothing in which men are ordinarily more prone to push their beliefs; when ordinary means
fail us, we add command, violence, fire, and sword." And thus
Christianity has triumphed!

Since there is no personal God, He cannot have a specific
habitation, nor has He, as so many lords of castles had, wells
to cast victims into and towers to imprison them. The second
trinity, as well as the first, is unacceptable to Montaigne—
Heaven, Hell, and Purgatory. He does not speak about them,
except when he makes the Camel Driver of Mecca the Scapegoat
of Rome. "When Mahomet promises his followers a paradise
all tapestried, bedecked with gold and precious gems, peopled
with damzels of surpassing beauty, stored with choice wines and
viands, I see very clearly that they are deceivers who pander to
our stupidity, in order to sugar the pill for us, and allure us by
these hopes and ideas adapted to our mortal appetites. And
yet, there are some of our own persuasion who are fallen into
like error, promising themselves after resurrection a terrestrial
and temporal life, accompanied by all sorts of worldly pleasures
and comforts. . . . Moreover, what grounds of justice can the
gods have for noticing and rewarding the good and virtuous actions of a man, after his death, when it is they themselves who
led him to do them, and so brought them about? And why are
they offended with him, why do they avenge on him his wicked

actions, when they themselves have created him in the faulty condition, and when with a single twinkling of their will they can prevent him from erring?"

He does not say "God," he says the "gods." He always thinks in terms of the classics, and it is moreover an excellent alibi. Talk about Mahomet, talk about the gods, talk about the houris in a paradise of gluttony—but do not mention the Father, the Son, the Holy Ghost, angels, and even devils—and you have a loophole in the fearful net.

And so, with an ample gesture of his arm which gave the impression of describing a cross, the wily Sieur de Montaigne placed his lordly thumb to his *hidalgo* nose, his ultimate retort to all the arguments, polemics, mystifications, casuistries, quibblings, perversions, wranglings, dialectics of the pompous, intolerant, cruel, dishonest traffickers of false goods, false hopes, false fears.

Author, Traveler, Mayor

The first edition of the *Essays,* comprising two books only, appeared in two small volumes in 1580, eight years after Montaigne had climbed into his tower, at Bordeaux, doubtless at the author's expense. A second and augmented edition appeared in 1582; and a newer edition still, comprising a third book, in 1588. This appeared in Paris, but as crowded as all the rest, with typographical errors, which often changed Montaigne's meaning, and sometimes, as it happened, clarified it, since evidently the printer read the manuscript and tried to understand it. At his death, four years later, Montaigne left a copy of this latest edition with marginal notes and corrections, although he boasted that he never corrected, only enlarged. (Why this childish boast of a man who knew how words betrayed ideas and both betrayed the mind? Ah, Vanity, Vanity, thou wilt ever hang onto our coattails!)

While in Paris, in 1588, Montaigne met Mademoiselle Marie de Gournay, a *jeune fille,* a thorough classical student, and an enthusiastic admirer of the *Essays*. He was so taken aback by having a reader who thoroughly understood him, that he made her his daughter, *fille d'alliance,* and she called him *père* henceforth. Tongues wagged, but the waggers forgot his "stone" and the fact that for an author to actually come across a reader who understands him is a joy too rare, too pure, to desecrate by carnal defloration.

At any rate, Marie de Gournay proved to be a more faithful daughter than his natural one. She spent years after his death straightening out his manuscripts and deciphering his hieroglyphics, and the edition which she supervised in 1595 is the authoritative one, including his travel notes, which he dictated while on tour through Switzerland, Germany, and Italy. He traveled in high style with a retinue fit for a royal prince, and was often taken for such, a thing that thrilled him. So strange a creature is man, for Montaigne, as few others, knew the utter folly of distinction save that of merit. "So it is no use raising ourselves on stilts, for even on stilts we have to walk on our legs. And sitting on the loftiest throne in the world, we are still sitting on our behind."

Moreover, he was profoundly democratic. His father saw to it that early in life he acquired a fondness for the simple and the poor. "The good father that God gave me, whom I certainly can only repay with gratitude, for his goodness, sent me to be reared from my cradle in a poor village of his, and kept me there as long as I was at nurse, and longer. I was trained to the humblest and most common mode of life. His plan succeeded by no means badly. I generally feel drawn toward the lower class, whether on account of the greater credit, or by a natural compassion, a feeling which has great influence with me."

By what bizarre impertinence does one man claim mastery over another? Is he born by different means? Does he breathe, feed, sleep differently? Has he discovered the elixir of eternal youth and eternal escape from pain? Can he avoid old age and death? Nature is the eternal democrat. She mocks and confounds and despises the snob. The sun enters the pariah's hut and squats alongside of him. The rain washes all faces, of all colors, those shrunken with hunger and those plethoric with satiety. The wind reddens all noses, the disdainful and the pinched, and whistles into all ears. In the bowels of the earth all flesh turns to water and all bones are ground and mingled together, and empires sleep tier upon tier in their common shroud of dust.

While on his trip, Montaigne was elected mayor of Bordeaux. He tried to dodge the honor, but the King insisted, and he had to accept. He would not accept it, however, under false pretensions. "I portrayed myself faithfully and conscientiously, such as I feel myself to be: without memory, without vigilance, without experience, and without energy; without hatred, too, without ambition, without avarice, and without strong passions. . . . I have promised to take them in hand, but not into my lungs and liver; to take them on my shoulders, not to identify myself with them; to look after them, yes; to take them passionately to heart, certainly not. . . . My maxim is 'that we should lend ourselves to others, and give ourselves only to ourselves.' "

The Bordelaisians, shrewd with long experience, knew that only a good and wise man would so dare expose his weaknesses, would so humble himself, and were not deterred. And they were right, for so successful was his administration, that they chose him a second time for a period of two years, which was extremely rare.

He was honest, fair, just, and magnanimous. He was not blind to the laudable qualities of his adversaries. "Dare we not say of a thief that his hair is nicely parted? And because she is a prostitute, must she also be syphilitic? . . . . They also say that my term of office passed without leaving any trace or mark. That is good!"

Unfortunately, toward the end of his second term, the plague broke out, and he was forced to quit his office and take care of his family, since the Castle of Montaigne and its environs were particularly afflicted. He had to pilot the caravan for six grievous months, and was, in fact, a wandering beggar. Meanwhile his home was pillaged, and defencelessness proved no defence against cupidity and viciousness. He himself, however, was not too greatly troubled about himself. *Omnia mea mecum porto*—"I carry all my goods with me," so said the Latin philosopher. And Montaigne, a spiritual descendant, said: "I carry my antidotes within myself, which are resolution and patience."

It was during this dreadful disaster that he saw how courageous were the poor peasants, "though not a hundredth part of them had any hope of escaping . . . . expecting death that evening or upon the morrow, showing so little alarm, either in countenance or voice . . . . and had no other anxiety than about their burial. They were troubled to see the bodies scattered about the fields, at the mercy of wild beasts that immediately swarmed thither. Here and there a man, in good health, was already digging his own grave; others, still alive, lay down in theirs. And one of my day-laborers, as he was dying, scraped the earth over himself with his hands and feet; was not that like covering himself up in order to sleep more comfortably?"

The scourge at last subsided and Montaigne returned to his tower to add, correct, reshape his essays and his thoughts. He was not bitter and even the "stone" which seemed to have become a veritable quarry, never completely destroyed his equanimity. It was not the religion which he was forced to confess that ever gave him comfort or consolation. He never asked anything of it except not to molest him since he could not accept its hopes and terrors, and belief, he considered a matter of economy; it saved thought. And he wished to think, always think, for no fortress was as well manned as a thought. Not all the words in the vocabulary could surround a thought and conquer it.

Montaigne accepted the Earth with its mud and worms, because it also gave flowers and fruits. He accepted tragedy, because, hidden within its folds, he could discover understanding and compassion. And he accepted Man, for despite his cruelties and follies, he also knows love and beauty, and nothing has any meaning save in relation to Man. If we are contemptuous of Man, what shall we esteem? But if we do not scourge him for his baseness, what honor is left us? Yet, if we reject him, what can we accept?

Old Age, Death and Immortality

At the age of forty-five, Montaigne was afflicted with the "stone," a disease he had a particular horror for since childhood, doubtless because he had witnessed the torments of his poor father, who had also suffered from it. "Of all the misfortunes of old age, it is just the one I dreaded most." And it was already old age, since the life expectancy at the time was probably less than thirty.

He had always been of the opinion that a man should be cut short when sound and healthy, and that if "a man did not pay in good time, Nature was wont to exact a stiff usury." However, although he would not "put on a good face, a disdainful and indifferent mien, when suffering pain," he learned to accept the tormenting attacks without fear, and in time, he managed to ferret out from the hay-stacks of misery needles of compensation. Pain imprisons time and ransoms pleasure.

But the "stone" was, in reality, the milestone of old age, and *that* was the true disease, without hope of cure, save by annihilation. Terence wrote and Montaigne had read it: *Senectus ipsast morbus; hinc illae lacrimae*—"Age itself is a disease; hence these tears."

Montaigne could not accept the idea that the body and the mind were distinct entities. Cut into the flesh and you rip the mind; cut into the mind and the flesh quivers. Therefore, if old age was a breaking up of the body, how could the mind emerge unscathed? For a moment, he hopes he is wrong. "Seeing that it is the privilege of the mind to escape from old age, I advise mine to do so to the best of its powers; let it bud, let it flower meanwhile, if it can, like the mistletoe on a dead tree!"

However, he will not be fooled. "I fear my mind is a traitor; he has formed so close a tie with the body that he forsakes me at every turn, and leaves me to follow him in his need. I take him aside to coax him, I make up to him, but to no purpose. In his productions there is no joy if it is not shared by the body."

The art of growing old gracefully lies in the ability to relinquish without too much manifest pain the things we cherish most—dying, therefore, gradually, without violence, without clamor. For whatever man's machinations to ward off the blows of Time, they are labor lost. Time hammers away at the edifice, determined to tear it down. "Here is a tooth that has just come out without any pain and without any effort . . . and this part of my being, and several others are already dead; others half-dead, even those that were most active and ranked highest. Death even mingles and is confounded with all our life; decay anticipates its hour and thrusts itself even across the pass of our progress. . . . The final death will be less complete and hurtful; it will dispatch only the half or the quarter of the man."

As we live on, all the solid and stern realities turn to far-away echoes. Thus we may say that death is but a cacophony forever silenced. The worm is the most patient of hosts and whenever we arrive, we are welcome.

There may be no purpose in the life of Man, but he must find a purposeful living, and he who follows Reason can only discover it in pleasure, in reasonable pleasure, pleasure of mind and pleasure of body. To enjoy life in old age, one must husband one's resources. One should study, relish, and ruminate over one's contentment and well-being. "The shorter my possessions of life the deeper and fuller I must live. . . . I meditate over a thing that gives me pleasure; I do not skim over it, I go to the bottom of it." He will have none of those Christians "who scorn to give their minds to our beggarly, fleeting, doubtful goods. Between ourselves, I have ever observed that supercelestial ideas and subterrestrial conduct are singularly suited to each other. A man who can rightly and truly enjoy his existence is absolutely and almost divinely perfect. The most beautiful lives, in my opinion, are those which conform to the model of common humanity, with order, but with nothing wonderful or extravagant. . . . Now, old age needs to be treated more tenderly. Let us commend it to Apollo, that tutelary god of health and wisdom, but a gay and sociable wisdom."

Age gradually petrifies the mind even as it does the arteries, but while most minds turn into common rock, there are some which have layers of precious stones, and some, here and there, which may even become flawless diamonds, depending upon the original material and the thoughts which have ground it. And the mind of Michel de Montaigne became the Kohinoor in the crown of Wisdom.

Thus ends his third and last book of *Essays*. It is his gesture of adieu to the world. It ends with life. Of death he spoke on many occasions, for he had no other gauge for life. "Men are tormented by ideas they form of things, not by the things themselves. And if death frightens us, how is it possible to go a step forward without a fit of ague? Now one of the principal blessings of virtue is the contempt of death, by means of which our life is furnished with soft tranquility." But let us not be fearful of thinking about death, nor of speaking about it, nor of meditating about it. "Let us disarm him of his strangeness, let us become familiar and conversant with him, and keep nothing so frequently in our thoughts as death. Where death is waiting for us is uncertain; let us await him everywhere. Premeditation of death is premeditation of freedom. There is no evil in life for him who has rightly understood that privation of life is no evil."

Not all the pontifications of church nor all the babble of false philosophers ever approached these words in wisdom or courage or dignity.

And the day came. It was the 13th of September, 1592. Three days before, he rose from his bed of agony to take out of his strongbox the money he had destined for his laborers, a hundred or so in the castle itself, and distributed it personally to them. He feared, that however carefully made out, notaries had a way of mutilating a will, and in particular when dealing with the humble folk, who could neither read nor write. He himself, though scholar and lawyer, considered it his greatest piece of good fortune that he managed (sometimes even to his loss) to keep out of the arms of Justice and the claws of her representatives. Impartiality is the cloak which hides injustices toward the poor and the weak.

Montaigne despised and considered barbarous the deathbed scenes and "the appalling ceremony with which we surround death—the cries of mothers, wives, and children, a crowd of visiting friends numb and dazed with chagrin, and servants pale and blubbering, a chamber from which the sun is excluded, lighted by tapers. To sum up, nothing around us but horrors and bugbears. . . ."

As for himself, since there was no way by which he could attend the matter, he simply relied "on the discretion of the persons, whoever they may be, to whom I shall become a burden." He asked, however, to have mass said in his room, so that, since he had to submit to the last mummery, it might be without the added insult of pomp and parade. He dared not, however, dismiss the mummers, for it would have meant, no doubt, the burning of his manuscripts and books, the sequestration of his property by church and state, and the molestation of his family.

Montaigne was buried at the Commandery of St. Antoine at Bordeaux. In 1886, his remains were transferred to the University building of the same city.

"It would be excusable perhaps in a painter or any other artist, or even a rhetorician or grammarian, to labor to make

a name by his works; but the actions of Virtue are too noble
in themselves to seek any other reward but from their own
worth, and especially to seek it in the vanity of human estimation. . . . And yet, if this erroneous notion is of such service
to the community as to keep men within their duty, then let
it wax bravely, and let us nourish it to the best of our power!"

Thus Michel de Montaigne, skeptic, makes his bid for immortality. For he is both the upholder and dispenser of the
meaning of Virtue, and an artist—a great artist. And being
simply human, he would like, in some manner or another, not
to die. He knows that the body reverts to the dust whence it
came—*pulvis es et in pulverem reverteris;* he knows that the
soul, as a separate entity, is a phantasmagoric illusion; he knows
that names indicate, in reality, nothing, for each one of them
is owned by hundreds, thousands, of individuals. How many
Michels are there now in France, or slightly differently spelled
in many other countries; and Montaigne is, after all, the name
of a castle, and there were hosts of Eyquems!

And yet, he would like Michel de Montaigne, author of
Essays, not to die utterly, although he knows that once buried,
"he will have no handle by which to take hold of reputation,
nor will it have any means of reaching or touching me."

He knows, too, that "it is purely the work of Fortune if
actions are seen and become known. It is Chance in its heedless-
ness that fastens glory upon us." He repeats this idea upon
several occasions, as if to serve as an incantation to ward off
Fortune's evil ways, and force her not to pass him by, if he deserves glory and immortality. He wishes to put her to shame
before the Court of Man, should she attempt one of her cruel
tricks and sweep the name of Michel de Montaigne and his
Essays into the abyss of oblivion. And, indeed, it would have
been not only cruel, but a colossal injury to the mind of man.

This time, however, the Ancient Bitch was eminently fair and
just, and Michel de Montaigne achieved the only deathlessness man is capable of—his words have become the sap which

feeds the brain of man, and generation after generation, even those who have never heard of him, have been the wiser and the better because he had once lived and suffered and thought.

DENIS DIDEROT

Of Ducks and a Swan

In eastern France, in the Département of Haute-Marne, at an altitude of fifteen hundred feet, on a jutting promontory stands Langres, now a quiet, unobtrusive town of eight thousand souls, bent upon the quotidian chores of living.

Among its monuments there is the Cathedral of Saint Mammès, dating from the twelfth century; the Church of Saint Martin, built and rebuilt from the fifteen to the eighteenth, the ramparts protected by towers, most of them raised in the sixteenth; a museum; a library; the statue of a man who gave the town fame and immortality, appropriately done by Frédéric-Auguste Bartholdi, sculptor of the Statue of Liberty.

Langres is very ancient and its name in the days of the Roman conquerors was Andematunum. It saw many wars and much devastation. It was burned by the Vandals and by Attila, and its name appears often in military histories—an honor ever writ in blood and tears.

The inhabitants have the reputation of "learning from earliest infancy to turn in every wind. The man of Langres has a head on his shoulders like the weathercock at the top of the church spire. . . . Despite an amazing rapidity in their movements, their desires, their plans, their fancies, their ideas, they are cumbrous in speech. . . ."

In the year 1713, Langres was a prosperous town, noisy with the hammers and the anvils and bright with the flames of the forges. It was the center of the manufacturing of cutlery—the most famous in the land—including swords and surgical tools. There were also the barrel makers and the blacksmiths as an obbligato. And the tanneries unable to compete in noise, made themselves evident in smell.

In 1713 Didier Diderot was a solid citizen of Langres, a prosperous cutler whose surgical instruments were praised by doctors even a century after his demise. And it was as it should

247

have been, for long was the line of his ancestors engaged in the trade, and each generation taught the next the secrets of the art and the greatest of all secrets—conscientiousness and care.

Didier was upright, patient, and sensible. His life was simple—a long, hard-working day, and then the family reunion, where he, as husband and father, was lord and master. Thus did God, Nature, and Church command. "An excellent pillow is that of reason," Didier said, "but I find that my head rests even more softly on that of religion and the laws." This was his fundamental philosophy.

Angélique, his wife, deserved her name. She was sweet, submissive, and self-effacing, and totally devoted to her husband and her children. She was a Vigneron, an ancient family of tanners and priests.

In ornithological terms, Monsieur and Madame Diderot were normal ducks, strong of neck and wing and diligent in the pursuit of worms, while their quacking was in tune with that of the thousands of other ducks in the courtyard. Then how did it happen, by what mysterious combination of genes, did they find themselves the procreators of an "ugly duckling" who afterward became a swan of noblest neck and whose song added glory to France and immortality to Langres?

On the 5th of October, 1713, a male child was born unto Monsieur and Madame Diderot. It was the year in which Pope Clement XI issued his "Bull Unigenitus" (*Unigenitus Dei Filius*—"The Only Begotten Son of God"), which started a half-century of vicious and preposterous theological warfare between the Jansenists and the Jesuits and brought ruin to France.

The boy was christened Denis. At his baptism his cries were heard so loud and authoritative that the family was certain he was destined to follow in the footsteps of his maternal relatives and become a priest. A bishop—and more—Angélique thought, but dared not say it out for fear of being considered vain. To so simple a soul vanity was a mortal sin.

Denis was a handsome child and very intelligent. Gifted with an unusual memory, he managed to carry off all the prizes the local school offered. His father, seeing him laden with gifts, wept for joy. Weeping was not considered an exclusively feminine prerogative in those days, and Diderot says: "It is a beautiful thing to see a good and severe man weep!" He himself would weep copiously during his mortal career—sometimes for sorrow, sometimes for happiness, sometimes at the sight of human goodness, sometimes as a ruse when dealing with steel-hearted women, for tears in his estimation, were the strongest solvent.

Denis was a good child (and he would prove to be one of the kindest men in the history of letters), but he was a mischievous one. Not only physically, but mentally. His teachers—members of the Society of Jesus—shrewd, subtle, and experienced pedagogues without equal in their day, noticed something about him which troubled them. Denis was their favorite pupil and they wished him to join their order, but meanwhile they shoved their hands into the sleeves of their soutanes and watched, warily. Did they notice that the neck was growing longer, the plumage thicker, the down smoother—in short, that he was not developing into a duck, but into a swan, a beautiful but dangerous bird?

Their foreboding proved correct. The day was to come when Denis Diderot would turn a most formidable foe of monastery and convent, armed as he was by all the arts and wiles he had acquired at their feet.

Denis accepted, for the time being, the decision of the family to become a priest, and on August 22, 1726, at the age of thirteen, the Bishop of Langres conferred upon him the tonsure and he was addressed as "abbé." It was not an unusual procedure for youngsters who were committed to a church career. How proudly Denis paraded on the streets of Langres, his new, shining black cossack waving in the wind! And since man is valet to his uniform, the boy assumed the most pious attitudes.

Many years later, in *Jacques le Fataliste,* seeing life in perspective, Diderot wrote: "There comes a moment when almost all girls and youths fall into melancholy; they are tormented by a vague restlessness that affects everything and finds nothing to calm it. They want to be alone; they weep; they are touched by the silence of cloisters; the image of peace that seems to reign in religious establishments enchants them. They mistake the first manifestations of a sexual nature for the voice of God calling to them . . . and it is precisely when nature incites them most that they embrace a fashion of life contrary to nature."

Presently, however, Denis rejected the idea of priesthood but dared not reveal his thought. One night he prepared to run away to Paris. What his object was is obscure. Did he wish to join the Jesuits? Bored with the little town, did he follow the Pied Piper's lure to the City of Romance? He was fifteen and the tumult of life was in his ear and in his heart.

At any rate, his father caught him in the act. Instead of punishing him, as would have been normal, the good cutler not only permitted him to do as he desired, but accompanied him to the capital. There he registered him at the Jansenist Collège d'Harcourt. It is possible, however, that he was registered instead at the famous Jesuit Collège Louis-le-Grand. And also possible that, at different times, he attended both schools.

For a fortnight, the solicitous father remained in the city in seclusion, unbeknown to the son. Then he returned to the school. "*Mon fils*," he said to the astonished boy, "I have come to find out whether your health is good, whether you are satisfied with your teachers, with your food, with yourself. If you are not happy here, I shall take you back to your mother." But since Denis replied that he was quite happy, the father said: "In that case, *mon ami*, I have come to give you a word, to embrace you, and to leave you my blessing." They both wept. The son remained. The father returned to Langres.

Throughout his lifetime, despite quarrels and differences with his father, despite long years of estrangement, Denis Diderot had the deepest affection and respect for him and his death grieved him beyond measure.

Denis was a brilliant student, mastered Mathematics, Latin,

Greek, Philosophy, and later English, Italian, and the sciences. And while he refused to call himself a bookish man, he was never without a book in his pocket. On the 2nd of September, 1732, he received the degree of Master of Arts. Whether, thereafter, he attended the Sorbonne, at that time comprising only the Theological Faculty, is uncertain. Certain it is, however, that he knew all the intricacies of scholasticism, and this proved very useful later in his work and in his arguments with the Church.

Now he entered the office of Clement de Ris, a lawyer and also a native of Langres. For two years he was a recalcitrant and uncooperative clerk. The patient Maître Clement finally wrote to Diderot, *père,* informing him that he was about to dismiss his son, and also that his son refused to try the study of medicine as an alternative means of livelihood.

Denis returned home. "I do not wish to be a lawyer, *mon père,*" he said, "because I do not choose to do other people's business and I do not wish to be a physician because I have no liking for killing. I wish to be a man of letters."

"A man of letters!" Didier Diderot exclaimed, as he plunged the glowing blade into the acid.

"*Oui, mon père,* a man of letters," the young man repeated simply.

"*Mon fils,*" the father spoke gently and reasonably, "think it over. What is a man of letters but a vagabond, a Bohemian, ragged and starved, the enemy of God and society? I have seen them in Paris. I know what I am talking about. You do not wish to be a priest—*bien*. You do not wish to be a lawyer—*bien*. You do not wish to be a physician—*bien*. I am very much disappointed, but I am not a tyrant. You are a man of education and scholarship. You have a right to your opinions."

"*Merci, mon père.*"

"But you are a Diderot. Cutlery is in your blood. Let me teach you the trade of our ancestors. We have all of us been something of artists and inventors. I may say so without seeming to boast. It's an honorable trade for an honorable man. And it pays well. I do not have to beg or fawn. I do not have to steal or cheat. I never go hungry. I am well dressed. I have a comfortable home. I have money put aside for old age. People respect me. The police does not hound me. I do not fear the *lettres de cachet* of His Majesty." He waited while his son meditated. "You are my eldest, Denis. You will inherit the shop. You will also inherit the good name of the Diderots, master cutlers and decent citizens of France. Believe me, there is nothing in the world as important as a good name. Let the name of Diderot remain unspotted, *mon ami*."

"*Bien, mon père,* I shall learn to be a cutler."

"You are a good son."

Didier was wrong. Denis did not have cutlery in his blood. A few weeks of apprenticeship and he was bored beyond endurance.

"*Mon père,*" he said, "I can no more. I must be a man of letters."

"Be what you wish! But you shall not get another *écu* from me!" the angry father warned. "Not one *écu!*"

And Denis Diderot returned to Paris, where, in time, he became the most typical Parisian *littérateur* in French annals until the advent of Anatole France a century later.

His father was almost as good as his word. Once or twice he was constrained to pay debts his son had incurred in so wily a manner that he could not refuse, but he never sent him any money directly. His mother, however, with maternal solicitude, managed to dispatch a sum now and then with a trusted servant. Her husband was evidently aware of this bit of treachery and pretended blindness, as is often the case, for in his will the good cutler writes: "You well know, you Diderot, my eldest son, the great expense you have been to me for twenty years—I have sent you more than ten thousand *livres,* not including what your mother and sisters sent you. . . ."

But Diderot who wrote and talked so much about so many things, including his family, mentions his mother only a very few times in very few words. All honeyed, to be sure. Yet, one wonders. If virtue is its own reward, then all the rewards distributed must be for vice.

The Diderot family, however, was not deprived of a man of God, for Didier-Pierre, Denis' brother and seven years his junior, became a priest. The life-long feud between the two produced the bitterest letters ever exchanged. The elder was always ready for reconciliation, but all his *démarches* were frustrated by the younger man's intolerance. "He would have been a good brother, if religion had not bidden him to trample under foot such a weakness as this," Denis said. "Religion has made him cowardly and cautious. He is sad, circumspect, and peevish. He is a good Christian, who proves to me every minute of the day how much better it would be to be a good man."

But Denis' oldest sister, Denise, was his friend to the end of her days. She seems to have possessed the rough material of his own qualities. "She is a sort of Diogenes in petticoats . . . the most original and the most strangely marked creature I know. . . . I love her to distraction." Alas, the poor woman! When middle-aged, she developed "a pimple on her nose that became a cancer and completely destroyed that part of her face." She used false noses, and tried even one made of glass.

Still, the Abbé could not have been without love for his free-thinking brother, for he was jealous of the affection he showed their sister and often complained about it. Was his hate a poultice for the wounds of disillusion? We hate none more keenly than those whose pleasures are beyond our capacities, and none so violently as those who reflect our own weaknesses which we are anxious to hide.

Another sister, another Angélique, the youngest child that survived (for several succumbed in their infancy, as was common) became a nun and died insane in the convent. Pained and enraged, Diderot wrote *La Religieuse*—"The Nun." It was published in 1796, twelve years after his death—a powerful psychological novel with excellent characterizations and a vitriolic condemnation of convents, immoral because of enforced vows and anti-social because of enforced celibacy. Human dignity could only be achieved in society.

"It would be far more important to work at the prevention of misery than to multiply places of refuge for the miserable."

Apprenticeship

Was the man of letters in the middle of the eighteenth century in France the vagabond, the Bohemian, the enemy of God and society, that Diderot, the elder, portrayed to his son?

He was. He was a vagabond because the populace was ignorant and illiterate, and the nobles, imitating their masters at Versailles, spent their time whoring, hunting—bored and boring. Gone were the golden days of the *Grand Monarque* when the court was gracious host to genius and noblemen were anxious that authors dedicate their works to them in exchange for stipends and favors. Now many were the dreary and humiliating tasks that writers had to perform in order to gain their bread and often they went hungry and roofless.

They were Bohemians because the morals of the bourgeois seemed to them false and hypocritical and because they resented the monotony of conjugal life from which the savor of love had vanished and divorce was unobtainable.

They were the enemies of God because the men of God were cruel and corrupt and fought among themselves like drugged maniacs over futilities, and because science demonstrated that many theological assumptions about nature and man were anachronistic and baseless.

They were the enemies of society because the society in which they lived was rooted in injustice, rapine, violence, and vice. They were the enemies of society because countless innocent men rotted in prisons, dragged there by virtue of the *lettres de cachet*—the royal orders—vindictive, arbitrary, without explanation, without redress, and without date of release.

What was the aim of the man of letters? To teach. He would wrest from the hands of the ecclesiastics the power of information. He would popularize the new ideas based on science and on the senses. He would guide men to think for themselves and develop the spirit of mental discipline.

The man of letters was a propagator, scattering his seeds to all the winds. He used the various forms of literary art to interest and excite men's minds; to guide them empirically, judging each case of policy and conduct separately and on its own merits. He did not believe in universals. He knew, for instance, that tyrants approved of justice, provided it was universal, not particular.

He would enlighten the world, and the period in which he lived and functioned became known historically as the Age of Enlightenment.

And the *philosophe,* who was *he* and what did *he* wish? While he and the philosopher loved wisdom, as the word implies, the *philosophe* did not live in an ivory tower and formulated no system, since system was an iron frame into which one stretched or cramped truth to fit within its dimensions. The *philosophe* lived in society, was interested in his neighbor, was a good citizen, and acted according to reason. He combined the good mores of the people with cheerful ways. He was a man of probity and virtue—particularly virtue in the classic sense of *virtus* or manliness.

"I am a good citizen," Diderot wrote, "and everything that concerns the welfare of society and the life of my fellow-men is very interesting to me." A warmer attitude than that of Terence, the Latin: "I am a man; nothing that is human is indifferent to me."

The *philosophe* carried his ideas lightly like colored balloons at a fair in contrast to the pedant who dragged his like ponderous ladders through crowded thoroughfares. He was a *moraliste*—one who showed the world how men lived—and lied, and he knew that nothing in nature weighed so heavily as a moral platitude. When a bat proclaimed "I see!" night had fallen.

Many were the charlatans who called themselves men of letters because they could quote Latin and fill pages with obscurities and obscenities. Parasites upon the authentic men of letters, they often served as informers for censors. Their nefariousness led more than one author to the Bastille and more than one bookseller and publisher to the galleys. And many a worthy manuscript was cast to the flames because of their treachery.

And there were the half-baked who paraded as *philosophes,* loudly propounding absurdities, thus denigrating the serious thinkers, who were called *Cacouacs*—a perfect onomatopoeia for ridicule and persecution by the ignorant, the bigoted, and those in the saddle.

Now Denis Diderot, candidate for the title of man of letters and *philosophe,* began his apprenticeship. It was a long and arduous one, replete with hunger, homelessness, disillusion, pain, and crafty maneuvers which would have put to shame the wiles of the king of foxes. For he who lives by his wits is often at his wits' end how to live.

Not that Denis Diderot fed exclusively on misery. There was also gaiety and feasting on the Left Bank of Paris among the fraternity of aspirants to the laurels of the Muses. And Diderot was a man of cheerful disposition, whose voice boomed in the cafés as he recited, improvised, and harangued. He loved his food, his wine, and his women, and took them wherever and whenever he found them.

Diderot managed to survive this decade of apprenticeship. He taught privately, chiefly mathematics; translated; was a tutor to rich children; and even wrote a half dozen sermons for a missionary destined for Brazil. For this he received the incredible sum of three hundred *écus,* the equivalent of nine hundred francs—gold *francs,* since that luminous metal in those days was not hidden from sight, but delighted the eye by its sheen, and the hand by its friendliness, and gave to the miser a *raison d'être* for his passion.

There are, to be sure, many lacunae in this period of Diderot's life; whether on purpose dismissed from mind and tongue or forgotten in the debris of the years, we shall never know. We do know, however, that from the pains and tribulations, he extracted the rich essence of generosity.

"I promised to myself that if ever happier days come, and ever I should possess anything, I would never refuse help any living creature nor ever condemn him to the misery [I endured]."

No vow was ever kept more faithfully, and many aware of it took advantage of his purse, of his time, of his *sensibilité*—his sensitiveness to another's grief. The irony and doubt he entertained toward ideas were never translated into deeds toward men. Pity and affection and enthusiasm he offered all, according to their needs.

Jean-François Marmontel, author of many books, including his interesting *Mémoires,* who knew Diderot well for many years, says: "One of the most enlightened men of the century, Diderot was also one of the most amiable. . . . Never did a countenance better depict the goodness of the heart."

Three-fourths of Diderot's life was given to people who needed his knowledge, his talent, his good offices. Insolence and ingratitude, which were rampant, made no difference to him. "I turn mildly away from the bad; I fly to embrace the good. . . . *Faire le bien; connaître le vrai*—"do the good; know the true"—the rest for Diderot was mere commentary.

In his affluent old age, when he was regaled with expensive furniture for his den and an elegant dressing gown supplanted his beloved, comfortable, dirty, and ragged one, he tells the world: "My door is still open to want when it comes my way. I am still affability itself; I listen; I counsel; I pity. My heart is not hardened; my head is not carried so high, but that my back

is stooping and kind as heretofore. My language is just as frank;
I have the same fellow-feeling. . . ." He addresses God with
fictitious piousness, rolling his eyes heavenward. "If Thou
seest in the Eternal Decree that riches are to corrupt the heart
of Denis . . . lead him back to poverty."

This reflex motion to goodness, however, was not devoid of
folly, for Diderot squandered the energy needed for his own
writing and produced neither as much work nor as good as he
might have, had he had the strength of character to refuse
impudent and inconsequential beggars who robbed him of his
time. "It is not enough to have great qualities; a man must also
have the economy of them," says La Rochefoucauld.

Kindness is a dangerous adventure. It is considered the fool's
cornucopia into which everyone plunges his hand. We must
hide our kindly impulses, for they are our Achilles' heel and
archers have ever their bows taut.

And yet, what meaning has wisdom if its ultimate gesture is
not kindness? And who shall say what trauma of regret Diderot's soul might not have experienced had he disobeyed his
impulse to help and to console, and which might have proved
even more disastrous than the loss of time? Every man his own
stumbling block.

"I should rather be the dupe of a hundred hypocrites than
hurt a single good man. . . . More than once I have experienced
the inconvenience of such a morality, but I shall not change it."

There was an unconscious motive also. Diderot was an actor
without a stage, and he yearned for applause. He broadcasted
his generosity—in conversation, at home, in the cafés, in his
correspondence, in his books. He was a good man, a virtuous
philosopher. Why shouldn't the world know it?

And what was the root of his goodness? "How does it matter
whether I owe my estimable qualities to nature or to experience,
so long as they are solid and vanity never spoils them? I am
frank, gentle, just, indulgent, honest, charitable, obliging. . . .
I have simplicity; sincerity; warmth in the soul; a mind easily

kindled; an inclination to be enthusiastic; a love for the good, the true, the beautiful. . . ."

In truth, he was not vain. For, vanity conceals itself in the garb of humility, is coy, pretends to stuff its ears to applause. Diderot bowed to the audience and even added his own clapping to theirs. Childish? How should one be good unless one retained the ways of the child?

His appearance did not belie his soul. "He had the ideal head of a Greek philosopher. His brow was wide, lofty, open, gently rounded. The arch of his eyebrow was delicate; the nose proud; his eyes kindly and sympathetic, sparkling like fire when enthusiastic; the curves of his mouth had finesse, grace, geniality. There was much dignity in his carriage. Enthusiasm was the natural condition for his voice, his spirit, for every feature. . . ."

And this is how Diderot describes himself, as he watched his image in the mirror: "In a single day I had a hundred different countenances, according to the thing which affected me. I was serene, sad, dreamy, tender, violent, passionate, enthusiastic. . . . I had a high brow, expressive eyes, prominent features; my head was that of an ancient orator, with a kindly look that had something of the guilelessness of the rusticity of ancient times. . . ."

Meanwhile, his apprenticeship for his major work went on apace. He was a notable symbol of the universal spirit of the century. His curiosity knew no bounds. "It is this ambitious curiosity that leads us in spite of ourselves to examine things and thus in the long run dissipates all sorts of falsehoods."

He attended as many courses as he could and were available —chemistry, anatomy, physiology, biology. As for mathematics, he says in that typical *esprit Gaulois* which regards sex as the measuring rod of all things: "I always come back to it, as an unfaithful husband, tired of his mistress, returns to his wife from time to time."

The classics, Greek, Roman, and French and the Italian poets of the Renaissance, had always been with him, in his library, on his tongue, in his arms (for he was a mighty gesticulator), in his pockets. But the profoundest influence came from the English—philosophers, scientists, economists, and the novelists Richardson and his friend, Sterne. The English poets, too, he admired, and for Shakespeare he had esteem, although in the current judgment of the Latins, the Bard "was a Gothic Barbarian lacking in the graces, but possessed of unsurpassable flights of genius. . . . I will compare him to Saint Christopher of Notre Dame, an unshapely colossus, rudely carven, but between whose legs we could all pass without our brows touching his *parties honteuses*."

Voltaire had lived in the Tight Little Island for two years in a sort of exile, largely voluntary, and in 1723 wrote *Letters on the English*, a highly laudatory account of the various freedoms prevailing there. This became the beacon for the young man still in search of himself. Since it was possible for a people to be free, since authors could print and circulate whatever their talents produced without the perennial threat of a yawning Bastille, since religion was not a bloody battlefield, since a king was responsible to his subjects, since the peasant, the most pitiable of creatures, could raise his head proudly, unafraid of insolent and vicious nobles—why, then, could not a great nation like France, too, be transformed into a free and happy land?

He would have a hand in it—not in the arena of politics; not upon barricades; not with musket and sword and guillotine. These would be the means of the next generation. *He* was the child of reason and enlightenment. His contribution would be the word. A word is the essence of a thousand dreams. A word is a banner. With it aloft man goes forth to martyrdom and victory. A word may be the night or the torch in the night; evil or the challenge of evil.

Of all the English philosophers who at this time influenced Diderot—Bacon, Newton, Hobbes, Hume—Shaftesbury played the most significant part.

Anthony Ashley Cooper, third Earl of Shaftesbury, was born

in 1671 and died in the year Denis was born, 1713. He was an ardent lover of liberty, an enthusiast in the cause of virtue (as Diderot would be despite his sexual divagations), a man of unblemished life and untiring beneficence. In his generation he had no superior in philosophy and no peer in conduct. Considering his station in society it was as remarkable a phenomenon as the life and manners of the emperor-philosopher, Marcus Aurelius. Indeed, he was a keen student of the Roman and his influence is stamped upon his own products.

All the master minds of the generation—Leibnitz, Voltaire, Lessing, Mendelssohn, Wieland—found mental and moral pabulum in Shaftesbury, the gist of whose philosophy was:

Distinction between right and wrong is a part of the constitution of human nature.

Morality stands apart from theology, and the moral qualities of actions are determined apart from the arbitrary will of God.

The ultimate test of an action is its tendency to promote the general harmony of welfare.

Appetite and reason concur in the determination of action.

The moralist is not concerned to solve the problem of freewill and determinism.

The wise man discards the terrors of future punishments and substitutes the voice of conscience.

Cataracts of blood have rushed over the rocks of the centuries and yet these reasonable maxims have not yet become the rules of conduct of mankind. Indeed, in many parts of the Earth, they are still considered perilous and treasonable, which proves their continued vitality, for many an idea starts as a spirited bull and ends as a listless ox. Time is a sharp and cunning knife. In 1743, Diderot, as a tribute to the good thinker, translated his "Essay on Merit and Virtue."

Thus came to an end the turbulent, rich, gay, miserable, first three decades of the life of Denis Diderot. And thus ended the apprenticeship as man of letters and *philosophe*. Henceforth he would have to achieve or be ignored by his contemporaries and discarded by history—two misfortunes which he could not envisage—for he loved his neighbors and could not tear himself from the countless links of the endless chain of time.

The Daemon Stings—
A Bookseller Is Mesmerized

"L'homme est né pour penser de lui-même"—Man is made to think for himself—and nothing is more contrary to the progress of knowledge than mystery.

Yet, like private wells on private estates, for long ages, knowledge could only be drawn forth by small, leaky buckets and drunk only by those allowed on the premises. The mouths of men were parched and their words derived from the desert of ignorance. To tunnel the sources into a great rushing river of cool clear water at which all who desire could quench their thirst was the dream of many a thinker whose name has been erased by the sponge of time.

The Greeks made some valiant attempts, but their means of propogation were rudimentary and knowledge continued to be obtained in meager quantities and remained limited to students and their teachers—the ever-warring philosophers.

However, they invented a word (and that is no mean achievement) which was destined to assume, many centuries later, a far vaster and nobler significance than the masters holding forth in Plato's Academy had imagined—encyclopedia.

To the Greeks it meant "Instruction in the whole circle," or the complete system of learning—grammar, rhetoric, philosophy, arithmetic, music, geometry, and astronomy. At times, it even had an ironic tinge—ridiculing the sophists who went through all the arts and sciences as through a circle or a hoop, presumably an empty dance.

The word and the idea for which it stood vanished from the

tongue of man century upon century. Man slept the sleep of ignorance, which is a deep sleep, and from which he absolutely refused to awaken. Many were the tocsins and heavy the dousing ere he opened his eyes and ears, and he still yawns and the foolish phantoms of his dreams still hover about him and urge him to return to his couch.

In English the word "encyclopedia" seems to have been used for the first time by Sir Thomas Elyot (1490–1546), scholar and diplomat and friend of Sir Thomas More, author of *Utopia*, who was beheaded for his services to letters and to the State, and himself barely escaped the axe by a whimsical thread of fate.

In the manner of the great Humanist, Erasmus, who cheated the stake by a vulpine act of fictitious demise, Elyot popularized ethics and philosophy. In his Latin Dictionary considered the most authoritative of his day, he explains: "Encyclopedia, that lernynge whiche comprehendeth all lyberall sciences and studies."

Nearly two centuries after Sir Thomas' death, in 1728, Ephraim Chambers published his "Cyclopedia—or an Universal Dictionary of Art and Sciences, containing an explication of the Terms and an Account of the Things signified thereby in the several Arts, Liberal and Mechanical, and the several Sciences, Human and Divine—fol. 2 vols."

But the real ancestor of the encyclopedia was Pierre Bayle (1647–1706), great scholar, skeptic, and author of *Dictionnaire Historique et Critique*—a French Huguenot who took refuge in Geneva and then Rotterdam, where after much malignity on the part of colleagues and much persecution on the part of authorities, he died. Generations later, a statue was erected in his honor at Pamiers, city near the village where he was born as a *"réparation d'un long oubli"*—"reparation for a long forgetfulness." Man is consistent in the treatment he accords his benefactors—small stones for bread, large stones for honors.

After many maneuvers of questionable morality by book-sellers, which no longer have any significance and are obscured by contradictions, on October 16, 1747, Denis Diderot was appointed editor-in-chief to prepare for publication the Englishman's *Cyclopedia* in four volumes.

Diderot was putting shape and order in the work, but in the back of his mind his daemon (in truth the daemon of Socrates winging his way from the Elysian fields) began stinging him. (Daemons assume the shape and have the ways of gadflies.)

Why Socrates' daemon? Because Diderot was Socrates reincarnated—as much as a Frenchman of the middle of the eighteenth century of the Christian era could be an Athenian of four centuries before the crucifixion of the Jewish prophet. And strangely enough, he could be a great deal.

Diderot, like Socrates, was essentially a teacher. Most of his work takes the form of dialogue, and his questions and replies are as impertinent as those of the man who walked about the streets of the Greek capital annoying the citizens petrified in their illusions and prejudices and superstitions. Like Socrates, Diderot believed that virtue was teachable and that wickedness was the result of ignorance. Like the Greek, too, the Frenchman had misadventures with priests and courts, but died in bed (or rather at the dinner table) only because he had not lived some years longer. Assuredly, his head would have dropped into the basket, guillotined by those whom he tried to raise out of the morass of vice and ignorance. And like his spiritual ancestor he would have had wonderful things to say about death and immortality. One almost regrets that it had not happened. He, too, would have admonished the few faithful ones imprisoned with him, for the clamor about his and their own evil fate on the morrow. He would have ended his luminous harangue quoting from that wise Roman poet, descendant of Epicurus, Lucretius:

> Death is for us, then, a mere name
> For the mere noiseless ending of a flame.
> It hurts us not, for there is nothing left
> To hurt. . . .

And finally, to equalize the plates of the balance of the two men—Denis, son of Didier, cutler, and housewife Angélique, and Socrates, son of Sophroiscus, sculptor, and the midwife Phaenarete, both exemplary couples—had each a Xanthippe as consort, who outlived them.

In one matter, however, the careers of the two philosophers were quite distinct. Socrates talked, but wrote nothing, leaving it to his great pupil, Plato, to record his wisdom and his wit. Diderot talked, but he also wrote, not only his own stuff, but acted as ghost and half-ghost to many an author and a would-be author. And how delighted he was if the reward was gratitude, for oftener there were those who insulted and mocked him and brought him trouble. And there were also those (including the great Jean-Jacques Rousseau) who denied the hand and the mouth which had guided their pens.

Le Breton, the publisher, at least one-fourth charlatan (as were most of the better members of his guild of the day), was awaiting sheets from his editor. Instead, the editor appeared in person, empty-handed.

"*Alors, Monsieur Diderot?*" Monsieur Le Breton asked, a bit superciliously. It was a shrewd way of addressing an author who had not yet achieved fame. It forestalled a possible request for money. He was of the opinion that artists followed bags of gold as horses followed bags of oats. And what a race of improvident creatures they were! He was quite right about Denis Diderot in this. The way that man spent his money he should have been a millionaire or a pauper—and he was a pauper for most of his mortal years—a regal pauper. "How is the work getting on?"

"It would get on if—"

"If, what?" Now Le Breton was really worried. Had he not had enough trouble with the translators and previous partners, the German, the English? Had he not nearly committed murder by striking the Englishman with his cane over the head, when the Englishman made a gesture to draw his sword? Now he had believed that all things at last were settled and the work could

pursue its normal course. Diderot was known for his energy
and intelligence—and besides, he was getting a hundred *livres*
a month! A hundred *livres!* Was he not a generous bookseller?
Perhaps too generous. Authors, like hounds, were in best hunting shape when half-starved. "If—what, Monsieur Diderot?"
he asked again, ready for any battle.

Diderot smiled suavely. He knew that the publisher was
worried and he would assuage his fears. "I do not bring you
bad news, *mon ami*. I think, indeed, that I am bringing you the
best news you have heard in a long time—"

"Is that so?" He was skeptical of authors' enthusiasms. They
considered every stinking oyster a pearl-bearer and every
ragged carrousel-horse a winged Pegasus.

"Monsieur Le Breton, is it your opinion that France is a
barbarous nation?"

"Of course not, monsieur." He became wary. The fox was
the tutelary divinity of publishers—perhaps still is.

"Monsieur Le Breton, is it your opinion that the French
should be tattered beggars feeding on crumbs at the banquet
halls of knowledge of other nations?"

Le Breton made a vague gesture to be interpreted at will.

"Monsieur Le Breton, is it your opinion that there is not
sufficient knowledge, wisdom, understanding—?"

"Monsieur Diderot," the publisher interrupted, "I am not
a *philosophe*. Would it be possible for you to speak plainly,
without circumlocution, without empyrean flights?"

"Merci, monsieur. That is precisely what I wish to do."

"*Très bien.*" He was ready for any eventuality.

"Monsieur Le Breton, we are in the process of publishing the
Cyclopedia, translated from the English. The book has its
merits, naturally. Far be it from me to dismiss it as antiquated,
badly organized, lacking in universal grasp. Mister Chambers
was a very learned gentleman, but he tried to do what one individual is incapable of achieving. What *I* propose to you, monsieur, is not a *Cyclopedia* but an *Encyclopedia*."

"And what is an 'Encyclopedia,' Monsieur Diderot?"

"An 'Encyclopedia,' monsieur, is a book—many books—which will bring to mankind the whole gamut of knowledge—not written by one man, but by many, each an expert in his field—"

In utter bewilderment the bookseller heard unrolled the magnificent scheme of one supreme book which should be all books to all mankind. Science, art, literature, philosophy, mechanics, agriculture, trade, politics, archeology, history, religion —all things upon earth, on the breast of the sea, on the wing of the air—the present, the past, and the future which was the past plus the present—wisely interpreted.

Who has not seen and heard Denis Diderot has seen and heard nothing. "When I recall Diderot—the immense variety of his ideas, the amazing multiplicity of his knowledge, the rapid flight, the warmth, the impetuous tumult of his imagination, all the charm, and all the disorder of his conversation, I venture to liken his character to nature herself, exactly as he used to conceive her—rich, fertile, abounding in germs of every sort, gentle and fierce, simple and majestic, worthy and sublime. . . ." These are the words of a contemporary who *had* seen and heard him often.

"The aim of the Encyclopedia," Diderot now secure in his argumentation, since the publisher's smile and wide open eyes indicated an hypnotic condition, "is to gather the knowledge scattered over the face of the earth . . . that our descendants, being better instructed, may become at the same time more virtuous and more happy; that they may love peace and abhor the horrors of wars and their brazen glories; that we may not die without having deserved well of the human race.

"The Encyclopedia shall not be a peaceful, somnolent storehouse in which one may wander at leisure nibbling at facts. *Non,* monsieur, it shall be a gigantic siege-engine, an armory of weapons of attack—attack against the countless injustices around us, against the cruelties, against poverty and disease, against colonial tyranny, against the abominations of slavery, against the atrocious barbarities of the penal code, against all intolerances. And we shall not strike vague blows in the air. *Non,* monsieur! Not mere theory, but practice—not mere literature, but life—"

"*Ah, oui—ah, oui,*" the publisher muttered from time to time.

"It will not be a book of genealogical trees of ruling houses, nor will it list the vile conquerors who devastated the earth. *Non,* monsieur! It will record the great lives of the immortal geniuses who have enlightened it. The Encyclopedia will owe all to talents, nothing to titles—a history of the human spirit, not of the human vanity."

"*Ah, oui—ah, oui—*"

"Not only words, monsieur—although the words shall be the bravest and the noblest in our tongue—but pictures, drawings, volumes of plates depicting every art and trade and enterprise of our nation. I personally shall go among our people and learn how their hands, their eyes, their minds work. I shall have every part of every machinery designed and engraved and I shall write texts explaining the function of every thread, every wheel, every curve of wrist and finger.

"It shall be the animated scene of human life—the bustle, the dexterity, the alertness of foundries, of glass furnaces, of gun powder mills, of silk calendries, as well as the tranquil toil of the dairy-woman, the embroiderer, the confectioner, the compounder of drugs.

"It will show the importance, the incalculable value of the journeyman—the man who truly brings prosperity and happiness and virtue to our nation—and it will demand suitable rewards for him. How queer our judgments are, monsieur! We require that people should be usefully employed and yet we despise the useful man!"

"*Ah, oui—ah, oui—*"

"Nothing shall be lost to our children's children. Other encyclopedias in the future will improve upon our venture. We wish it so. Yet, the future generations will possess the roots, and therefore the blossoms will be more glorious. The world will understand that human nature is good and that evil is only the result of bad education and bad institutions."

"*Ah—oui, ah, oui—*"

"The Encyclopedia is not a dictionary like the *Cyclopedia*. It will be arranged alphabetically, to be sure, but we shall also classify our material and indicate cross references, so that a reader may obtain a circular knowledge—as the Greeks in their luminous intelligence implied in the word—enkyklopaideia."

"*Ah, oui—ah,—oui—*"

"The pyramids are not a greater glory to ancient Egypt than the Encyclopedia will be to modern France! It shall be the most monumental collaboration of intellectual enterprise in the annals of mankind!"

"*Ah—oui—ah—oui—*"

"And the editor for such an enterprise? The editor must be a man endowed with great good sense, celebrated by the breadth of his knowledge, the elevation of his feelings and conceptions, and his love for work; a man loved and respected both for his private and public character; never a frenzied enthusiast except for truth, virtue and humanity. . . ." (Oh, Denis Diderot, what price modesty!)

Diderot's gestures were ample, all-encompassing—rapping of tables, beatings of chest, rolling of eyes, arms flying in all directions, even as his words and thoughts. He was a ham—a noble ham—in quest of a noble aim.

"*Alors*, Monsieur Le Breton, will you publish the Encyclopedia?" Diderot, at last out of breath, asked.

The wily publisher tore himself out of the web of mesmerization which the writer had woven about him. He was profoundly interested, but he would curb his enthusiasm. Authors should be tamed or else they might demand who knows what clauses in their contracts. "Monsieur Diderot, you are a *philosophe* and your mind dances freely among the stars. I am a businessman and must step warily among glowing coals." He waited.

So did Diderot. He was not too poor a businessman himself,

as later deals proved. He would not flatter. He would not urge. Indeed, he pretended to eye the door.

"I *am* interested," Le Breton said, fearful now that Diderot might seek his competitors, "but there are a million items I should like to discuss with you, *mon ami*. Would you do me the pleasure of dining at my home tonight? I know that Madame Le Breton will certainly welcome you."

"It shall be *my* pleasure to dine with you tonight, and if I may say so, I find Madame Le Breton one of the most charming and brightest women of Paris."

"Ah, *merci, merci.* She must hear of this."

"I have already told it to her."

"*Voilà!*" the man laughed too heartily to consider himself on the road to cuckoldry.

In truth, Diderot did not like Le Breton's dinners. He wrote years later: "They are miserly and he sets too much importance on a miserable dinner for me to accept it at that price." But he did like to engage in gallant conversation with the flirtatious Madame Le Breton, and always considered her a good friend.

The publication of *Cyclopedia* was dropped and Le Breton received a fresh *privilège* from the government, permitting him to publish a book (of several volumes) entitled *Encyclopédie.* For a time he had some partners in the venture, but later became sole owner.

Denis Diderot was named editor. It was not the work for one man, however, as Diderot had said, but for many—for the best minds of the generation, he hoped. Meanwhile, he persuaded Jean Le Rond d'Alembert to be his co-editor.

D'Alembert was the natural son of the Marquise de Tencin and an officer of the artillery, Chevalier La Touche or Destouches. The Marquise, sister of the famed Cardinal de Tencin, was an author, a wit, and a thoroughly unscrupulous female. With a she-fish's maternal instinct, she deposited the fruit of her womb on the steps of the church of Saint Jean Le Rond, Paris, which supplied the infant with a name. (The surname d'Alembert he added himself later on.)

It was the night of the 17th of November, 1717. In an almost dying condition, the child was found by the beadle and entrusted to the care of a good woman, wife of a glazier, by the name of Rousseau (no relation to Jean-Jacques), who lived in the neighborhood.

His father, without disclosing his identity, settled an annuity upon the boy and he was sent to a boarding school. From there he was matriculated at the Collège Mazarin, a Jansenist institution. Before long, his brilliance in the general subjects and in particular in mathematics, became evident. His fame spread rapidly all over Europe. Enticing offers from Catherine the Great of Russia and Frederick the Great of Prussia to live at their courts were repeated on several occasions, but always rejected. D'Alembert remembered Aesop's fable about the Town Mouse and the Country Mouse, and how the Town Mouse spread before his guest figs, honey, raisins, and cheese, but as they were beginning to eat, someone opened the door of the cupboard and they had to flee for their lives. "Although you have prepared for me a dainty feast," said the Country Mouse, "I must leave you. It is surrounded by too many dangers. I prefer my roots from the hedge-row, so that I can live in safety and without fear."

At the age of thirty-seven, d'Alembert became a member of the French Academy. Always a valetudinarian, "born dying," poor, and disappointed in love (and love-making), he lived with the widow, Rousseau, in her humble home for many years until her death. She loved him as her son, but incapable of grasping his importance in the world, she taunted him: "You will never be anything better than a philosopher. And what is a philosopher? He is a madman who torments himself all his life, so that people may talk about him when he is dead."

D'Alembert, who had a keen sense of humor and a tongue stewed in vinegar, answered (or should have answered): "*Petite mère,* you have offered the best definition of fame—time's sole gift—a shadow horse which bears no scrutiny of mouth."

Madame Manon Phlipon Roland, famous for her virtue, her intelligence, and her good heart, and mistress of a famous salon in Paris, sat at one of the meetings of the French Academy in order to see and hear Monsieur d'Alembert. She was disillusioned by his small face and piping voice and came to the reasonable conclusion that it is better to know the writings of a philosopher than his "mask." Madame was guillotined during the Reign of Terror and on the scaffold pronounced the famous remark: "*O Liberté! Que de crimes on commet en ton nom!*" "O Liberty! how many crimes are committed in thy name!"

Her husband, Roland de La Platière, illustrious writer and Minister of the Interior, stricken with grief, committed suicide.

D'Alembert died at Paris on the 29th of October, 1783.

Encyclopédie

The labor of the *Encyclopédie* began. No travail in the history of parturation was as tormenting, as vexatious, as harassing, as thwarting, and in such perpetual danger of still-birth. And yet, by the constancy, the industry, the fidelity, the vision, the perspicacity, the near-martyrdom of one man—Denis Diderot—the vast project was consummated.

It took nearly a quarter of a century and when the *Encyclopédie* was finally finished, it consisted of seventeen folio volumes, eleven folio plates, four supplementary volumes, two index volumes, one supplementary plate—thirty-five volumes in all. Considering the means of printing and engraving in the middle of the eighteenth century, the very physical existence of such a collection of books was indeed of pyramidal magnitude.

The *Encyclopédie* was sold by subscription and the price of the entire set amounted to 980 *livres*—about two hundred dollars, gold, whose purchasing value today should be multiplied many times. Still, there were more than four thousand in Paris and the provinces able and willing to spend the money! (And there were several editions pirated in Italy and Switzerland.)

The total sum received by Diderot, for his many years' Herculean labors was about thirteen thousand dollars. "And to think," Voltaire cried out scandalized, when he heard of the humble wage, "that an army contractor makes two thousand *livres* a day!" Voltaire himself, shrewd and unscrupulous, had made a profit of more than a half million *livres* in the army contract during the war of 1734 and his yearly income derived from his various investments reached the sum of seventy thousand *livres*—something like seventy-five to one hundred thousand dollars in modern figures.

Diderot announced the advent of the *Encyclopédie* in a Prospectus detailing its purposes. So important was this in the political and intellectual history of France, that the French government published a reprint in 1950, a bicentennial national appreciation.

On July 1, 1751, the first volume appeared.

ENCYCLOPÉDIE
or
ANALYTICAL DICTIONARY
OF THE SCIENCES
ARTS AND CRAFTS
By a Society of Men of Letters.

Placed in order and published by M. Diderot, of the Prussian Academy of Sciences and Belles-Lettres; and for the mathematical portion, by M. d'Alembert, of the Royal Academy of Sciences of Paris, of that of Prussia and the Royal Society of London.

PARIS

Published by Briasson, The Elder David, Le Breton, and Durand.

MDCCLI
With Approbation and License of the King.

A fresh wind blew over Paris and thence over the rest of Europe. Two principles were to dominate the *Encyclopédie*—delving into the roots of philosophy and recasting man's notions of the true, the good, and the beautiful, based upon facts and not upon abstract logic, and rendering honor and admiration for all man's efforts in the fields of creation. Experience and Technique—these were henceforth the watchwords and the plumblines.

Encyclopedias were to spring to life in all countries, in all languages. Some of them were better than the *Encyclopédie* of Monsieur Diderot, better printed, better illustrated, better informed, but none could recapture the high spirits, the noble purpose, the heroism, the blaze of imagination, the indomitable will to achieve complete freedom of thought and freedom of man.

The "Preliminary Discourse to the Encyclopédie" was written by d'Alembert and it was also his address of admittance to the French Academy. This was a brilliant survey of the progress of science, thought, and letters since the Renaissance. It canonized the heroes of secular knowledge—Bacon, Descartes, Newton, Locke, Leibnitz. Not only did it excite hope and interest, but pressed the sterile propositions of dogmatic theology into a dim and squalid background, establishing a firm disregard for authority and a reluctance to concoct systems.

The articles of the *Encyclopédie* were written by the most illustrious authors of the Enlightenment—Voltaire, Rousseau, Montesquieu, d'Holbach, Condillac, Turgot, Buffon, Grimm, Helvetius, Marmontel, Duclos, Condorcet, Forbonnais, Quesnai, Morellet, Raynal—and Chevalier de Jaucourt (1704–1779) who was the slave of the *Encyclopédie* from A to Z and revelled in his drudgery. "God made him for grinding," Diderot says, "and if we have raised a shout of joy like the sailor who

espies land after a somber night . . . it is to Monsieur de Jancourt that we are indebted for it."

A high percentage of the articles were signed either by the
contributor's name or his symbol. Diderot's symbol, for instance, was *; D'Alembert's was *O;* Rousseau's *S;* Chevalier de
Jancourt's *DJ.*

Diderot wrote many of the most important articles as well as
thousands of lesser ones, often unsigned and without symbol,
but recognizable by tangential remarks, for always he inserted
his humor, his irony, his moralizations, his personal habits, all
deriving from his proposition of the centrality of man. "Why
shall we not make man the common center? Is there in infinite
space any other point from which we can with greater advantage
draw those immense lines that we propose to all other points?
. . . . Man is the single term from which we ought to set out
and to which we ought to trace all back. . . . If you take away
my own existence and the happiness of my fellows, of what concern to me is all the rest of nature?"

Many errors, much clumsiness, false assumptions, purposeful
deceptions, babblings, repetitions, in a creation of such vast
proportions and novelty were to be anticipated. Neither Diderot
nor d'Alembert denied their existence, but their pleas of exoneration should be largely accepted. Condorcet, philosopher
and mathematician, who committed suicide to escape the guillotine during the Reign of Terror, explained "that the true shame
and disgrace of dissemblings lay not with the writers, whose
only alternative was to leave the stagnation of opinion undis-
turbed, but with the ecclesiastics and ministers whose tyranny
made dissimulation necessary."

Historically, to have been an Encyclopedist signifies to have
belonged to that company of men whose minds catapulted the
walls of ignorance and superstition and intolerance and
crumbled them. That later, men of monstrous ambitions raised
the walls again and again, only proves that in the annals of man
the wise and beautiful things he has created are as startling as

the rare lucid moments of a raving maniac, and that his good is only the accidental residue of his evil.

The book was dedicated to Marc-Pierre, Comte d'Argenson, Chief Censor. It was a gesture of prudence—and of gratitude, too, for after all, had he not placed the seal of approval upon a work whose dangerous implications could not have escaped his vigilant eye? But dedicated also: "To Posterity—to the Being Who Does Not Die!"

No sooner did the first volume appear than the Jesuits, too shrewd not to be aware of the deadly armament which had made its appearance, began to clamor.

The first volume withstood the storm, and the next year the second volume made its bow. By this time the "devout party," as the enemies of the "philosophic party" were called, had been far better prepared for the combat. They won the ear of Versailles and on the 7th of February, 1752, the King's Privy Council issued an order to suppress both volumes of the *Encyclopédie,* forbidding further printing and distribution, and to seize the manuscripts.

"His Majesty has recognized that in these two volumes, the authors have presumed to insert several maxims tending to destroy royal authority, to establish the spirit of independence and revolt, and, beneath the obscure and equivocal terms, to raise the foundations of error, moral corruption, irreligion, and incredulity."

Diderot ran for cover, and in the dark recesses of his home— Rue Taranne, where he lived for the last thirty years of his life—he pursued his work, despite the urgings of friends to seek refuge at the court of Frederick, as others had done. He refused, not only because he disliked the Emperor, but because he considered him a tyrant, the eternal troublemaker of Europe, who said: "Do not speak to me of greatness of soul. A prince should only consult his interest. If there is something to be gained by being honest, we shall be honest; if we must deceive, let us be rogues." And, too, Diderot was a Frenchman and was publishing a work that would do great honor to his *patrie.* Why should he shame his people by hiding in the enemy's camp? "The most honest way is not to accuse one's self when one is innocent."

(The dislike of the two men was mutual. Frederick refused to read Diderot's books. "There reigns in them a conceited tone and an arrogance that revolts my instinct of liberty.")

Fortunately, at this time, the new *Directeur de La Librairie*—the Supervisor of Publications—Lamoignon de Malsherbes was an honest believer in the freedom of writers to print what they thought. This was doing the state a service, "for this liberty has always seemed to me to have many more advantages than drawbacks. . . . A man who has read only the books that, when published, appeared with the consent of the government the way the law prescribes, would be behind his contemporaries almost a century."

Since he had control of all printing licenses, Malsherbes found a loophole by which the *Encyclopédie* could resume publication and distribution. He did not issue a legal printing license—"*Avec Approbation et Privilège du Roi*"—but a "tacit license," which meant that the publisher could carry on secretly and that ample advance notice would be offered him to protect his property should scandal demand a search.

For doing noble service to the state, the honest and equitable Lamoignon de Malsherbes died on the scaffold in 1794 at the age of seventy-three.

Every year a new volume of the *Encyclopédie* appeared, always accompanied by fear of loss of property and loss of liberty, and on more than one occasion defection of friends and contributors.

"*We* swore to see it through," Diderot repeated, "but it really meant *I*." And the bitterness of the misfortunes heaped upon him forged the mind and the heart of the eighteenth century, and he became the tested leader of the Enlightenment.

To top it all, there was Le Breton himself, who secretly deleted portions of Diderot's articles and those of other contributors, taming and emasculating them and burning the original manuscripts. "You," Diderot shouted to his publisher, "you have

committed an act of vile hardihood to which nothing that has
ever happened in this world can be compared." And he wept
long and bitterly.

And yet how shall one blame too harshly the poor bookseller,
when after an attempt at assassination of Louis XV, the King
in rage proclaimed: "All those who shall be convicted of having
written or of printing any writing tending to attack religion, to
arouse opinion, to impair Our authority, and to trouble the order
and tranquility of Our States shall be punished by death . . .
authors, printers, booksellers, book peddlers, and all other persons disseminating such writings among the public shall be
condemned to the galleys for life. . . ."

"And so," Diderot sighed as he revised the last sheets of the
Encyclopédie on July 25, 1765, "in eight or ten days I shall see
the end of an undertaking that has occupied me for twenty
years; that has not made my fortune by a long shot; that has
exposed me so many a time to the risk of having to quit my
country or lose my freedom; and that has consumed a life that
might have been made more useful and more glorious."

He was weary and spoke out of the depths of disillusion that
follows success. In truth, however, he was aware that nothing
he might have done could have been more useful to mankind
and that glory would be his reward. It was, indeed, the greatest
single intellectual accomplishment of the century and the most
important work for a free and new society—forty-three editions
within a quarter of a century!

"This work," he had said, "will surely produce in time a
revolution in the minds of men, and I hope that tyrants, oppressors, fanatics, and the intolerant will not gain thereby. We
shall have served humanity; but we shall be reduced to cold and
insensible dust for many years before we have gratitude for it."

And in a more cheerful and more typical mood: "We have
seen that the *Encyclopédie* could be the effort of only a philosophical century; that this century has arrived; that renown
while carrying to immortality the names of those who will

finish it, will perhaps not disdain to take care of ours; and we have felt ourselves reanimated by an idea so consoling and so sweet, that we, too, shall be spoken of when we shall no longer exist . . . resurrected by this captivating murmur which gives us to understand from the lips of some of our contemporaries, what shall be said of us by men for whose instruction and happiness we have sacrificed ourselves, whom we have esteemed and loved though they are not yet born. . . . O posterity, holy and sacred! Stay of the unhappy and oppressed, thou who art just, thou who art incorruptible, who avengest the good man, who unmaskest the hypocrite, who draggest down the tyrant, may thy sure faith, thy consoling faith never, never abandon me!" Alas that all greatness must be in retrospect and that man should take such pleasure in chopping off heads and anointing skulls!

Of *Wives and Mistresses*

In the year 1742, Denis Diderot, twenty-nine years old, was still a Bohemian without permanent address, without certain means of livelihood except for occasional translations from the classics and the English; tutoring mathematics; and shrewdly deluding Carmelite Brothers into believing that he had in mind joining their Order (and he would have been a luminous star among them) in exchange for a little advance money to pay mundane debts, both of honor and dishonor. (His father, however, remained adamantine, his strong box locked and well hidden.)

But all in all, it was not a dreary life. There were the cafés where Denis scattered sparks of ideas, igniting the minds of artists and writers, some destined to become France's immortals. There were the Palais Royal and the Jardin des Tuileries, where he enjoyed the fresh air and watched the courtesans display their charms. There was the *Comédie-Française* which he frequented when a little flush with coins. And how he loved the theater! Had he not contemplated becoming a Thespian? Not entirely for the sake of the dramatic art, to be sure, but "to live familiarly with actresses, whom I found infinitely lovable and who, I knew, were easily obtainable." And was not so handsome a man, golden-tongued, welcomed to beds of modest maids and brazen wives?

Why, then, was he suddenly seized with the frenzied urge to turn into a domesticated bourgeois upon making the acquaintance of Mademoiselle Antoinette Champion, daughter of Marie Champion, née de Malville, widow of a country nobleman, Ambroise Champion?

True, Antoinette was a comely, dark-eyed demoiselle, but she was four years Denis' senior, and in those days, when life expectancy was forty or forty-five what with the perennial epidemics and the ills of the flesh due to bad hygiene and worse diet, a *pucelle* of thirty-three was definitely an old maid required by custom to pasture peaceably in the fields of the Lord—the shop, the home, and the church.

Nor was Antoinette wealthy, so that Denis' greed might be kindled and his hope for security of table and roof be materialized. Antoinette and her mother owned a modest lingerie and lace shop. They earned enough to keep body and soul together, to have a decent apartment and modish dresses and in the ancient tradition of Gallic parsimony to hide in stockings a small hillock of gold coins for a rainy day (and the clouds were already on their way). But a third mouth to feed—and it was the mouth of a gourmand—and coins for snuff and coffee to be consumed at the cafés and a suit of clothes and a wig—that, surely, would have been *de trop*.

Why did Diderot persist with the maniacal tenacity of a moonstruck adolescent to urge marriage upon the young lady? Oh, what magniloquent pleas! What torrents of tears! No candidate for sainthood at the foot of the cross ever pledged his soul into all eternity with more solemn vows! Was it love? Was it vanity? Was it, in truth, the need of hearth and progeny? Were the generations of Diderots, husband and fathers, calling in his unconscious mind: "Enough, Denis, enough of Bohemianism—propagate!"

"These are my feelings toward you, Antoinette," he wrote in endless variations of the same theme, "rather to die a thousand times than not to marry you as soon as you say the word; rather to die a thousand times than to think for a moment of any other than my Nanette as soon as she has crowned my love. It is to you that my last love letters were addressed, and may Heaven punish me as the most wicked of men, the most traitorous of all men, if ever in my life I write to anybody else. . . ." Fortunately he was no longer a believer and the lightning of Heaven could not, in honor bound, strike him. But was he a conscious liar? Was he deluded by his own eloquence? Was he unaware that his volatile nature would assuredly rebel against the self-imposed shackles and inevitably break them?

Alas, that time and love should be competitors in the race, and that time should ride upon the winds and love puff with the breath of words!

The Champions, mother and daughter, at first would not heed the tempestuous entreaties of this man full of sound and empty of purse. Then Mademoiselle began to waver. "After all, *maman*, Diderot is a man of great learning—"

"It is said, *ma fille*, that the Devil knows Scripture as well as a bishop."

"He says he loves me."

"Trust a wagging tail; never trust a wagging tongue."

"Shall I remain an old maid?"

"You don't have to, *ma chère*. There are still one or two well-to-do merchants who would gladly marry you and offer us security in our old age—and *entre nous*, you are not so young, *ma fille*, that you can afford to allow reckless passion to blind you."

"But I don't love those men—"

"Love—love—what has love to do with marriage? In our

Holy Church marriage is a sacrament, but love—" she pouted and shrugged.

Yet, as the days passed and the suitor invented one shrewd stratagem after another, the elder lady, too, succumbed. "He surely has a tongue of gold," she admitted. "Would he had instead a purse of gold—or even of silver!"

But marriage was not so simple. In those good old days, when a man was in truth the *paterfamilias,* a son below the age of thirty required the consent of his father or else many difficulties would ensue, including loss of patrimony. Marriage was not chiefly a personal concern. The family, the social status, the financial condition were paramount. There was also the little matter of the *dot*—the dowry. Moreover, it was considered safer for love to follow marriage than to precede it. Start with love and end with adultery; start with virtue and stay with honor.

But there was the rub! Denis had not returned to the bosom of his family for ten years—ten years during which time reports about the life he was leading in Paris were shocking to the sensibilities of the decent, virtuous Diderots, who now numbered among them an *abbé* of a rigid, inflexible, austere moral code.

There was, of course, the Biblical precedent of the "prodigal son," and his welcome. But that was part of the hospitality of the ancient Hebrews. Would Frenchmen of his generation toughened by a millennium of wars and the intolerance of Catholicism, react in the same manner?

But it had to be done. He had to go. The Champions—mother and daughter—made his father's approval and benediction (with all that it implied) the *sine qua non* of marriage. Still, after all, lovers in all ages, according to the rules of chivalry, had to endure grievous trials and perform arduous tasks in order to obtain the hand of their *inamorata.* And was not he a descendant of those noble knights? And did not his Dulcinea, the spotless, the faithful, the lovely Nanette, merit all the hazards? Moreover, although the knight had a sword to defend himself, he was not without a weapon—his tongue—and was not the tongue sharper and more deadly than the sword?

And so, whistling a tune he had heard in a recent Italian opera—oh, how much more melodious and pleasing to the ear than the French compositions—he mounted the stagecoach. The postilion cracked his whip and he was on his way—two hundred miles of pitted road!

"*Mon fils! Mon fils!*" his good mother exclaimed as he appeared at the door, and pressed him to her heart. "*Sois le bienvenu, mon fils!*" She was already aging and would die in another half-dozen years. "*Mon fils! Mon fils!*"

"Denis! Denis!" Denise, his sister, pulled him out of her mother's embrace and hugged him. She was always a little rough in her manifestations of love.

The father pretended that he was unaware of his presence, but soon could not restrain himself and he, too, kissed his son's cheeks and wet them with his tears. There was a lot of weeping all around.

And Didier-Pierre, the *abbé?* Fortunately he was at the seminary and out of the way.

The neighbors and friends of the family were constant visitors. How often had they the occasion to shake hands or kiss the cheeks of a man whose reputation rivalled that of Don Juan, plus many other horrendous distinctions? It was Paris transplanted to Langres. It was the vicarious thrill of the delights of vice for those burdened with the discomforts of virtue.

Denis became the hero of his native town, and his father, who had always missed him, took great pleasure in talking to him. He was religious, to be sure, and his son had the reputation of being a freethinker, but there were so many other things two men could discuss—two men irrevocably bound by blood and early affection. Didier-Pierre, the *abbé,* was virtuous and respectful, but frankly a bore. By much circumlocution this was the gist of his father's opinion of his younger son as expressed to his eldest.

As Denis was correcting proof of his translation of Temple

Stanyan's *History of Greece,* his father watched him with paternal pride, for culture and learning were greatly prized, and two centuries had to pass before their possession would be considered a disgrace, a misfortune, or a matter of ridicule.

"*Mon fils,*" he said, "I beg you not to be in a hurry to leave us. We are so happy to have you here. Your mother, the good soul, will fatten us all up like geese with the delicacies she is concocting every day to please you."

Denis laughed. "*Merci, mon père.* I shall stay on."

And upon a later occasion, the father said: "You know, Denis, I had always wished you to be a lawyer or a physician or a cutler, but I see now that I was wrong. I see that you have talent and will become a great writer—"

"Oh, *mon père,*" Denis made a gesture of modesty.

"I mean it. At any rate, if you wish it, you may stay with us always and do your work without worry. There is plenty of space here and you can transform one of the rooms into a fine study. Your brother, even when he does come on rare occasions, never stays with us longer than a day or two."

Denis made a motion of indecision. He had something else in mind. He wished to weaken the old man to the point at which he could beg him to assign to his credit a little income of, say a hundred *livres* or so per month, so that he might be able to support his Nanette until his pen became more productive. He did not like her to continue in her business where she met men, and he knew enough about men not to trust any of them. Frankly, he was jealous.

The father, too, had also something more up his sleeve. There was his old friend, the wealthy manufacturer, who possessed a marriageable daughter, and who had more than once intimated how appropriate and felicitous it would be for the two honorable families to become united. Denis was not unaware of the subtle maneuverings; indeed, the whole town—at least the more substantial portion of its citizenry—was beginning to flutter with anticipation.

It was time, then, to take the bull by the horn. *"Mon père,"* he said one day, "I am in love."

The cutler looked at his son queerly. "In love? Why, *mon fils,* from the reports I used to receive, you must have been in love dozens of times."

"As man to man, *mon père,* I was making love, but I was not in love. There is a great difference."

"I would not know," the father said, blushing a little. "To me they were the same. Your mother—"

"Yes, yes, I understand," the son said a little condescendingly, "but different generations, different *moeurs.* You see, this time I am in love and wish to get married."

And when Denis told him who the girl was and her financial status, the cutler was almost ready to plunge a knife into the foolish heart of his beloved son. *"Non et non et non et non!"* he shouted. "You shall not get married to that impoverished old maid!"

If Denis, in his *tréfonds,* harbored doubts about the wisdom of his marriage, the attitude of his father dispelled them all. Despite his apparent nonchalance, Diderot was a man of immovable obstinacy, or how else could he have withstood later, as editor of the *Encyclopédie,* all the slings, all the insults, the threats, the perils without taking recourse to renunciation or flight?

"I shall get married!" he hurled back at his father. "I shall get married with or without your permission!"

The outraged father had no alternative but to apply violence. According to the law of the land, he secured a *lettre de cachet* and Denis was carted away and imprisoned in a monastery. He would have to stay there until the fever of his love subsided, or his father, overcome with compassion, allowed his release. During the *ancien régime,* recalcitrant children could be flung into nunneries or monasteries by their angry fathers, and unfaithful wives to prisons by their cuckolded husbands, until they recanted and repented and vowed to reform.

As for the husband he was further protected by a royal edict which read: "Whosoever female shall draw into matrimony whosoever male subject to His Majesty by means of scents, oils, false teeth, or false bosoms or hips, shall be persecuted for sorcery, and the marriage shall be declared null and void."

One day, Madame Champion received a letter: "Dear Madame, . . . It is my duty to take precautions against a passion so fatal to your daughter and to my son. What will she do with a man who has no profession and perhaps will never have any? Is he rich enough for both? . . . No, madame, I will not allow him to make an unhappy creature of her, nor to make himself unhappy. . . . If you don't take a hand, it will ruin him completely, for you are not unaware that disinheritance is the usual result of such engagements. . . . If your daughter is as well born and loves him as much as he imagines, she will urge him to give her up. It is only at this price that he will recover his liberty, for with the aid of friends who are indignant at his boldness, I have had him put under lock and key, and we have more power than is necessary to keep him there until his sentiments have changed. . . . Put yourself in my place! Suppose that it was your daughter who acted like that with you, and what would you think, what would you say, what would you do? . . .

Your obedient servant, DIDEROT."

The monks knowing Denis' religious views and envious of his escapades, "employed against me all the determined maliciousness they could imagine," including the cutting of half his hair, to prevent his running away.

How long Denis remained in the monastery is unknown, but one night "I flung myself from the window," sheets tied together in the accredited manner of schoolboys and brides bent upon mischief. By walking many miles and by riding a portion of the way, Denis finally arrived in Paris in a most miserable state.

The poor man was confronted by three major difficulties—the minor ones were countless—to hide from his father's wrath, for he might hurl him back into prison; to find a lodging; to placate the Champion women who, certain now that Diderot *père* would disinherit his son, were not too anxious for the alliance, especially *maman*.

Denis fell suddenly ill, probably due to spiritual morbidity— psychosomatic miseries had been with man ever since he had allowed himself to be burdened with a psyche. He sent a mutual friend by the name of Duval—an appellation as distinctive in French as Smith in English—to inform Nanette that he was alarmingly ill, living in a filthy room, neglected by all mankind, penniless—a miserable *lazzarone!* And would she not have mercy upon him and pay him a visit, for his soul could not leave his fevered body without one last adieu from the beauteous being whom he would love into all eternity—here and hereafter. That he no longer believed in the hereafter and was even beginning to doubt the existence of mind and soul as separate entities was of no moment. After all, what is truth but the skillful adaptation of falsehood to circumstances?

Antoinette either fell for his lachrimose posture or reasoned that at her age a man was a man and it was foolhardy to persist in the haughtiness of futile virtue. The visit was consummated and the lovers, pledging eternal affection and unswerving fidelity, decided to marry in secret. At midnight, on the 6th of November, 1743, the knot was tied in a small church on the Left Bank which specialized in clandestine unions.

The chief problem of marriage is what remains when passion is spent—friendship or enmity, companionship or boredom. But there is nothing during the period of courtship which definitely foretells this, and marriage must remain, as all things dependent upon time, a matter of luck.

Ah, why did not Denis hearken to his father's warning? Why did he have the presumption to imagine that because he had "knocked about" in the cafés of Paris, he was wiser than the good cutler, who spent his days making knives and scissors and tools for surgeons to relieve unfortunates of their ills?

Only weeks passed before Denis and Antoinette began their

quarrels—quarrels which would not end until Denis died forty-one years later. And what quarrels! What brawls! Outbursts on her part that lasted for hours on end! "What advantage will that woman have, when she has made a blood vessel burst in my chest or deranged the fibers of my brain? Ah, how unbearable is life!"

Antoinette's ill-temper was not only directed against her husband, but against anyone who was unlucky enough to be around, including their servant, good and patient Jeanneton, who continually threatened to leave, but stayed on for the sake of her unfortunate master.

"That miserable woman, the most monstrous creature I know!" Diderot exclaims. And Jean-Jacques Rousseau adds his vituperation. "Antoinette is a shrew and a fishwife, sullen to her husband, impatient with her children, and exacting and unreasonable with her servants and her neighbors." And he wondered how in the world his friend could have been so deluded as to consider her a person of intelligence and fine character. But himself—what made *him* live on with his common law wife, Thérèse Lavasseur, whom Madame de Vendeul, Diderot's daughter and his biographer, called "that wench of a dishwasher?" And she bore Jean-Jacques six children, all sent to the orphanage. Is it required of a man who tells the world in the world's most famous books how to take care of and educate children, to also take care and educate his own? How shall life be balanced, unless humanity is divided into those who preach and those who practise? If we could live by reason, what reason would there be for living? Reason proposes; passion disposes.

But was Antoinette really a monster? Her daughter says: "My mother was a noble and proud soul, with a frankness that never knew the dissimulation of polite formalities. Solitude, the domestic cares to which she was condemned by a meager income, the chagrin of my father's love affairs, her ignorance of worldly manners, had all embittered her temper, and scolding became a habit. Had her tenderness for my father been able to weaken, her life would have been happier . . . but nothing was able to distract it for a moment."

And Angélique (named for her grandmother, and seemingly as good a woman) adored her father, and therefore toned down his faults, for Diderot was impatient and lacked delicacy and never bent a little that he might not tower over his wife and crush her. Nor was he grateful to her for her devotion. Often she would go hungry that he might have her share also. And somehow, she found every day a few *sous* for him that he might go to the café, sip his coffee, orate, and be applauded.

Even as his apostrophes to his love had ingredients of falseness, so his imprecations against his marriage had notes of hollowness. It is certain, that had his wife died before him, he would have poured a cataract of tears over her grave—and only partially of the crocodile. No dish is more universally eaten than one's own heart.

A couple of years after his marriage, Diderot sent Antoinette with their little daughter, Marie-Angélique, to Langres to meet his family in the hope of reconciliation—and a little purse. Antoinette was well treated and made a good impression, for after all, her marriage was *bona fide* and it is foolish to rage against a *fait accompli*. Being among simple, religious folk like herself, and relieved of the heavy pressure of coping with odds far beyond her capacity, Antoinette relaxed and was a pleasant, agreeable woman. She remained with the family for some time, perhaps reluctant to return, since she was becoming aware of the fact that her husband was infatuated with Madeleine d'Arsant de Puisieux, wife of Philippe Florent de Puisieux, lawyer and translator.

According to tradition, we seek in all our loves our first love and in the first love, our dream of love. Who was Diderot's first love? What was his dream of love? He loved Antoinette, a devoted, faithful, pious, ignorant woman. He also loved Madame de Puisieux, a selfish, unscrupulous woman, author of cheap, sophisticated novels. No one knows his first love, as no one re-

members the first step he took in the advent of walking, and all
the definitions of love are valid because love has countless facets,
but no face.

Madame de Puisieux demanded of her lover not only attention, but gifts and social activities, and Diderot in order to make
money, gathering all his talents, wrote several books, the most
notorious of which was the novel, *Bijoux Indiscrets—The In-
discreet Jewels,* based upon a *fabliau,* a French popular tale of
the twelfth century.

The story tells of a prince who possesses a magic ring which,
when pointed in the proper direction, makes a woman's "jewel"
speak out in public, revealing its secret love affairs. No one is
spared—wives and mistresses of kings, priests, magistrates,
authors, noblemen, academicians. Masks are ripped. Statues are
tumbled. Wings are plucked. Only Madame de Pompadour is
presented as the beautiful and incorruptible specimen of her sex.
As mistress of Louis XV, she often exercised an influence detri-
mental to France, but was patroness of artists and writers, and
perhaps Diderot hoped for a royal reward, which never materialized.

The novel is bawdy and licentious, but it is also replete with
profound observations, with valid criticisms of government,
religion, and the arts, and in particular the theater. Although
repetitious, (for a "bijou," after all, is but a "bijou") and its
escapades hardly varied, it is amusing as well.

The book appeared in 1748, and despite the cries of horror
of some of the friends of Diderot, and of critics at home and
abroad—or, perhaps because of this—the book was a success,
indeed the most successful of his books published during his life-
time, and many have been its editions in French and other
tongues, even up to the present.

It furnished Diderot with the money needed to entertain and
appease his mistress. What portion of it he dedicated for the up-
keep of his family is unknown, but they continued to live in the
same squalid cramped quarters.

The hectic affair lasted for some years, and he broke off—perhaps gladly—when he discovered with his own eyes that the lady was deceiving him.

If dead loves were decently buried, the whole earth would not suffice as cemetery, but they are cast to the vultures of forgetfulness and are promptly devoured.

Not long after its termination, Diderot, neither sadder nor wiser, met Mademoiselle Louise-Henriette Volland. Diderot was now forty-two years old and she was thirty-eight. Her physical charms seemed to have been slight. She wore glasses on a rather dried-up face, while her legs were disproportionately heavy and her fingers thin and dry. Moreover, she was sickly. But she possessed a fine intelligence and was well-read in all the departments of learning. She was a good conversationalist and had—a *rara avis* among ladies—a fondness for discussion of abstract questions. "Ah, Grimm," Diderot tells a friend, "what a woman! How tender she is, how sweet, honest, delicate, *sensible* (sensitive)! She reflects, she loves to reflect. *We* don't know any more than she, in customs, morals, feelings, in an infinity of important things. She has her judgment, her views, her ideas, her own way of thinking, formed according to reason, truth, and common sense; neither public opinion, nor authorities nor anything else can subjugate them. . . . Sophie is both man and woman, as her mood dictates." (What greater masculine compliment than hermaphrodism!)

Any wonder, then, that Diderot discarded all her names and daubed her Sophie, "the wise one" and thus immortalized her? Diderot's love for Sophie lasted until her death on February 22, 1784, five months before his own.

"My father consoled himself by the certainty that he would not long survive her," Madame de Vendeul, who had become Sophie's friend, writes in her *Mémoires*.

In her will Sophie left him seven volumes of the *Essays* of Montaigne (whom Diderot considered the wisest and best of men), bound in red morocco, and a ring "which I call Pauline."

Diderot was a fervent and constant lover, with the normal

changes from the physical to the spiritual. For a lasting love is a series of dissimilar loves superseding one another. Only one more woman appears in the tabulation of his amours—Madame Meaux, former mistress of his faithful friend, Damilaville, whom he supplanted after his death, which is an honorable bargain. But it was an unfortunate affair—Diderot's swan song with dolorous notes of self-abasement, jealousy, and cowardice.

To the very end of his days Diderot had an eye and a pinch for the charming members of what used to be known as the fair or the weaker sex. Alas, that only one generation should separate the great lover from the ridiculous *roué!* Yet, never to have sinned is the unforgivable sin, for then we learn neither the meaning of humor nor that of compassion.

Sophie would have vanished totally from the scene, had not Jeudy-Dugour, a French man of letters (who afterward became a naturalized Russian under the name of Gouroff, director of the University of St. Petersburg), sold to the publisher, Paulin, the letters that Diderot had written to her. How he had come across them no one knows, but when they appeared in print in the year 1830, they promptly became a document of great value, not only as a source for the more complete biography of Diderot, but also for the many tangential sketches of the period, for Denis Diderot was France of the eighteenth century.

It is a pity, however, that less than half of his letters have survived and not a single one of Sophie, although she had written nearly as many as he. Somebody in the Diderot family as well as in Volland's must have destroyed them in a spasm of moral indignation, since they are the ones written during the first three years of the affair which have completely and irrevocably vanished—the years of the careless rapture and doubtless of joyous carnal descriptions.

For, as Charles Pinot Duclos (1704–1772) author of *Mémoires Secrets,* comments: "The relaxation of morals does not prevent people from being loud in praise of honor and virtue; those who have least of them know very well how much they are concerned in other people having them. . . . The French are the only people among whom it is possible for morals to be depraved, without either the heart being corrupted or their courage weakened."

Guest of His Majesty

Denis Diderot was not a contemplative, meditative philosopher. Left to himself, alone with his thoughts, he would be lost in a maze of fugitive ideas. He became ablaze by another's intelligence. Contradiction excited his mind and in impassioned retorts he discovered the compass which guided him in orderly arguments, making it possible for him to create a global unity. Never could he have imagined and certainly never sustained any of his major—and even his minor—compositions without first encountering the sparks of an antithesis.

He was profoundly social and the mouth of man was the cornucopia wherein he discovered the raw material for his alembic. It was not essential for the mouth to be the wisest or the wittiest; it sufficed if it was merely vociferous. And thus it happened that even his own termagant wife, unconsciously, would be responsible for a paragraph or a portion of a dialogue.

While Diderot was getting the first volume of the *Encyclopédie* in shape, René-Antoine de Réaumur (1683–1757), inventor of the thermometer which bears his name, couched the eyes of a girl who had been born blind. It was the manner of treating a cataract at the time by forcing down the lens until it no longer intercepted the line of vision.

Diderot was anxious to witness the operation and to question the girl about her reactions to her new sense. He was becoming more and more convinced that all knowledge depended upon the senses and experience—a doctrine of Relativity which had already appeared in Greek philosophy—*Nihil est in intellectu quod non fuerit in sensu*—"there is nothing in the intellect which had not previously been in the sense."

Ideas are not born but reborn. However, they require the sun of reality to ripen and will not age into precious vintage in the cellar of mere speculation. But the Church of the eighteenth century in France was nervous about this theory, for it seemed to deny the supremacy of the soul—an entity independent of the body. Thus it was risky to propound it openly. Indeed, all ideas which were not in strict conformity with the teachings of theology had to be expressed obliquely and indirectly, and people were compelled to learn to read between the lines. It is a difficult and dangerous habit, for the lines themselves become blurred and unintelligible.

Réaumur refused to allow Diderot either to witness the operation or to interrogate the girl. In truth, he would have found it difficult to conduct an experiment of this nature. He himself later acknowledged that to prepare a person born blind to answer philosophical questions rightly would have been a feat requiring the combined talents of Newton, Descartes, Locke, and Leibnitz.

But he was angry at the famous physicist who snubbed him, and his mind became ignited. Now he sought the best medium for scattering its flames abroad.

In the month of January, 1682, Nicholas Saunderson was born at Thurlstone, Yorkshire, England. When a year old, he lost his sight due to smallpox. This, however, did not prevent him from mastering Latin and Greek and the mysteries of mathematics. In 1707 he began lecturing at Cambridge University on the principles of Newtonian philosophy; in 1711 he became professor of mathematics; in 1736 he was admitted a member of the Royal Society. The most prominent mathematicians of the period, including Sir Isaac Newton, were his devoted friends.

Having lost his sight, Saunderson developed to an extraordinary degree his sense of-hearing and his sense of touch, and he devised the "Palpable Arithmetic," a calculating abacus by which one could perform involved arithmetical and algebraic operations by the sense of touch. Saunderson died of the scurvy in April, 1739.

Here was a man and a situation that suited Diderot's pen and also afforded him the occasion of mystification, for Diderot was an actor and felt the need of playing "roles." Therefore, the dialogue form fitted him admirably. He appears in his name or the pronoun "I" or by a character easily identifiable as himself, discussing, debating with another—"He"—or a character, true or fictitious, mentioned by name. In reality, however, it is only Diderot talking to himself—to many selves—as in a hall of mirrors, since doubt was the first step to knowledge, and the profoundest doubt was the doubt of one's self.

And so, in the year 1749 appeared Diderot's "Lettre sur les Aveugles—A l'Usage de Ceux Qui Voient" ("Letter on the Blind—for the Use of Those Who See") purported to be based on the *Life of Saunderson,* by Doctor Inchlif. Of course, no such book had ever existed and no such doctor. The Royal Society of London took this hoax in bad part, since Saunderson is shown to be an agnostic. For this *faux-pas,* Diderot was excluded from the honor of admission to that learned body, just as he was excluded from the French Academy for similar reasons of "tactlessness."

The "Letter" shows a minister of the gospel, Mister Holmes, interviewing Saunderson on his death-bed, the place where the timid humbly make peace with their Maker and the bold speak their mind, unafraid of divine vengeance and unconcerned about terrestrial reputation.

Diderot puts into Saunderson's mouth a blind man's reactions to life and philosophy which he had, in part, culled from his conversations with a blind wine-grower at Puiseaux. To this he adds his own intuitions and ideas. "Why talk to me," says Saunderson, "of all that fine spectacle which has never been made for me? I have been condemned to pass my life in darkness, and you cite marvels that I cannot understand, and that are only in evidence for those who see as you do. If you want me to believe in God you must make me touch Him."

The minister replies that the sense of touch should suffice to reveal the divinity to him in the admirable mechanism of his own organs.

"The animal mechanism," Saunderson replies, "even were it perfect as you claim, what has it in common with a being of sovereign intelligence? It fills you with astonishment because you are in the habit of treating as prodigy anything that strikes you as being beyond your own strength. I have been so often an admiration for you, that I have a poor opinion of what surprises you."

Saunderson continues to expound his notion of the inexistence or, at least, of the insignificance of a god in the scheme of nature. "It is very important not to mistake hemlock for parsley; but not important at all to believe or disbelieve in God."

The blind mathematician propounds other ideas as well—as for instance, that the loss of one sense overdevelops the other senses as compensation—a novel theory at the time. More important still, and indeed startling, is the foreshadowing of the theory of evolution. "You," Saunderson retorts to Holmes' notion of creation according to the Bible, "you have no witnesses to confront with me and your eyes give you no help. Imagine, if you choose, that the order which strikes you so profoundly has subsisted from the beginning. But leave me free to think that it has done no such thing, and that if we went back to the birth of things and scenes, and perceived matter in motion and chaos disentangling itself, we should come across a whole multitude of shapeless creatures, instead of a few creatures highly organized. . . . I may maintain that some had no stomachs; others no intestines; some came to end through some fault of heart or lungs; that the monsters annihilated one another in succession . . . and those only survived whose mechanism implied no important mis-adaptation, and who had the power of supporting and perpetuating themselves. . . . The order is not even now perfect but that monstrous products appear from time to time. . . . I conjecture, then, that in the beginning, when matter in fermentation gradually brought our universe bursting into being, blind creatures like myself were very common. . . . Oh, philosophers, transport yourselves with me to the confines of the universe . . . seek across its lawless, aimless heavings some vestiges of that intelligent Being whose wisdom strikes you with such wonder here ! . . . What is this world? A complex whole subject to endless revolutions . . . a swift succession of beings who follow one another, press forward and vanish. . . . You judge of the continuous existence of the world as an ephemeral insect might judge of yours. . . . Time, matter, space—all, it may be are no more than a point. . . . Our most purely intellectual ideas result from the structure of our bodies. . . . It is absurd to imagine that there is on the surface of the earth a being, an animal, who has always been what he is now."

Thus Diderot reaches two conclusions of vast importance— refusal to separate the organic from the inorganic, which is the basis of modern biology, and the rejection of a psychophysical dualism, which is the foundation of our psychology.

Being of a practical turn and endowed with a sense of profound pity, Diderot suggests a means of helping the afflicted. "We have written characters appealing to the eye and ear, but none appealing to the touch. For want of such a language communication is entirely broken between us and those who are born deaf and dumb and blind. They grow, but they remain in a state of imbecility. . . . They would acquire ideas if we traced on their hand the same characters that we trace on paper and if we invariably attached the same significance to them."

A century later, Dr. Samuel Gridley Howe (1801–1876), American philanthropist, invented the alphabet for the deaf and dumb, while Louis Braille (1809–1852), the French blind professor, put into practice the invention bearing his name. Thus the eyes of the wanderers in the night and the ears of the lost in the desert of silence, were opened to the world.

With the publication of "The Letter to the Blind," Diderot was admitted into the worshipful circle of philosophers and promptly rewarded with the crown of thorns—man's custom, immemorial and inalterable. As he said later, in the *Interprétation de la Nature,* a small book of aphorisms : "Is it in my cen-

tury only and am I the only one against whom there are men
filled with ignorance and rancor, souls eaten by envy, heads
troubled by superstition? . . . If you introduce a ray of light
into a nest of owls, you will injure their eyes and excite their
cries. . . . We must all go through personal attacks or else we
shall have to give up telling the truth. . . ." And in *Pensées
Philosophiques:* "People have a right to demand of me that I
seek the truth, but not to find it. . . . Skepticism is the first step
toward truth."

This was the year of our Lord, 1749, when the Church and
the King were becoming more and more jittery. It was one thing
to say airily: "*Après moi le déluge,*" and another thing to discover posters on the walls of the Louvre menacing the King's
life and the life of his mistress, Madame de Pompadour. And
there were the satirical songs—by the dozen—lampooning
Court and Church. One pamphleteer dared to write: "Louis, if
you were once the object of our love [he had been known as le
"Bien-Aimé"] it was because all your vices were still unknown
to us; in this kingdom depopulated because of you, and given
over as prey to the mountebanks who rule with you, if there are
Frenchmen left, it is to hate you."

Alarmed, the government flooded the capital with *lettres de
cachet* and filled the Bastille to the brim with writers and scientists. Even the world-famous naturalist, Buffon, author of the
Histoire Naturelle, an epoch-making book, was forced to make
public retraction. "I have had no intention of contradicting the
text of the Scriptures; I believe firmly everything related there
about the Creation. . . . And I renounce whatever in my book
treats of the formation of the earth and everything in general
that might contradict the narration of Moses."

Denis Diderot, drunken with the wine of success, was holding
forth with his friends at the cafés. Little did he suspect that the
police had been on his trail for some time now and for adequate
reasons. In 1746, he wrote *Pensées Philosophiques,* in which he
said, among other things that tended to raise the goose-pimples
of the pious: "How ridiculous are they who castigate their flesh

to appease a God of love. . . . If the religion you preach to me
is true, its truth can be put to evidence and proved by invincible
reasons, instead of annoying me with miracles. . . . Faith is a
chimerical principle which does not exist in nature. . . . What
voices! What cries! What groans! . . . Who condemns them
to such torments? The God whom they offended. Who then is
this God? A God full of goodness. But would a God full of
goodness take delight in bathing himself in tears? . . . The
revealed law contains no moral precept which I do not find
recommended and practiced under the law of nature; therefore
it has taught us nothing new about morality. . . ."

Ten editions of this book were published, as so many other
books of the time, anonymously, under the imprint "The
Hague." But who, among the *cognoscenti*, did not know that it
was the work of Denis Diderot? On the 7th of July, 1747, the
Parlement de Paris condemned the work, accusing it of "presenting to restless and bold minds the most absurd and the most
criminal thoughts of which the deprivation of human nature is
capable, and by placing all religions, by an affected uncertainty,
nearly on the same level, in order to end up by not recognizing
any."

It was burned in effigy—an honor it shared with many another
good book and manuscript. Two centuries later, in a neighboring nation, flames consumed once more the best that man's mind
had wrought, and depraved youth danced about the bonfire the
dance of ultimate folly. History travels in diverse directions,
and it is fortunate if now and then it takes a step forward.

Praised by his cronies for his *Pensées Philosophiques*, Diderot
was emboldened to write a sequel to it—*La Promenade du
Sceptique*, an allegory—in which he obtains that the dogma of
the Original Fall is absurd and that the hypothesis of the Christian religion is without foundation and without import. "Asceticism is an aberration; it is senseless to impose upon people a rule
of life contrary to life."

Worse still, he attacks the priests, calling them hypocritical,
unscrupulous, cruel, and querulous. Any wonder, then, that his

parish priest (who had never spoken to him and who did not
know him personally) was incensed "at this man who speaks
with scorn of the holy mysteries of our religion, uttering blasphemies against Jesus Christ and the Holy Virgin that I would
not venture to put in writing"—this man who led an immoral
life and thereby corrupted the morals of the youth? (And Socrates, his ancestor, while promenading with his fellow-shadows
in the fields of Elysium, murmured: "Each generation is the
broken hope of the preceding one.")

In the morning of the 24th of July, 1749, as Diderot was already at his work on the *Encyclopédie,* whose publication was
lagging because of the pusillanimity of many of its contributors,
there was a knock at his door—a knock different from all other
knocks—the knock of might whose infallible touchstone is the
oppression of the weak. "Open in the name of the King!"

Tremblingly, he opened. "Denis Diderot, you are under ar-
rest, by order of His Majesty!" The Bastille being over-
crowded, he was hustled to the dungeon of Vincennes, a medieval fortress and former royal residence, in the suburbs of Paris.

For four weeks he was in solitary confinement, a most miserable man, in terror that he might have to spend the rest of his
days there. At the end of the first week, he had been interrogated
by the police inspector, Berryer, a shrewd individual, not devoid
of a sense of humor. Diderot denied the authorship of all his
books, save the manuscript *Promenade du Sceptique,* with which
he had been caught at home. And as exoneration, he offered the
excuse that he had since ordered it to be burned. (It was published posthumously.) *"Très bien,* Monsieur Diderot," the inspector said. "I fear me that you will be here for a time, a long
time."

The publishers, meanwhile, sent a heart-rending plea to
Comte d'Argenson, chief censor, to release the prisoner without
whose labors the encyclopedia could never appear. They had
already spent a quarter of a million *livres* for a book which
would bring glory to France and the respect of all men of worth
throughout the world. Moreover, they would take it upon

themselves to see that Monsieur Diderot would never again displease him, the King, or the Holy Church. Other prominent figures added their pleas.

On the 13th of August, Diderot sent Berryer a letter: "Monsieur, my suffering has gone as far as it can go; my body is exhausted, my spirit broken; my soul weighted with grief. . . . I yield, therefore . . . to the complete confidence that I have in your word of honor . . . that you will have consideration for my repentance and my sincere promise that never again shall I write anything without submitting it to your judgment. . . . I admit to you as to my worthy protector . . . that [my books] are debaucheries of the mind that escaped from me; but I can also promise you on my honor (and I do have honor) that they will be the last. . . .

"As for those who have taken part in the publicity of these works, nothing shall be hidden from you. . . . I shall disclose the names of both the publishers and the printers. I even undertake to tell them, if you require it, that they are known to you, so that they may, in the future, be as well-behaved as I have resolved to be. . . . I have the honor of being . . . your very humble and obedient servant . . . Diderot."

Alas for a nation that requires her citizens to be heroes in order that they may live! Yet, cowardice is the mother of all good. Trembling at the approach of storm, cowardice built the home. Fearful of the swift-footed beasts, cowardice invented the wheel. Dreading the claw of hunger, cowardice created society and law. Pursued by boredom, cowardice invoked the arts. In terror of the flashing sword, cowardice preached love and peace.

And cowardice saved Denis Diderot in order that he might bring forth the *Encyclopédie* and a number of masterpieces, most of which, recalling prison, Diderot did not publish during his life-time. It was the toll he had to pay for freedom. To console himself, perhaps, he said: "There was a time when an author anxious for the perfection of his work, preserved it in his portfolio twenty or thirty years. . . . He lived in the hope of leaving after him an immortal work, an immortal name. If this man is mad, all my ideas of wisdom are overturned."

Several years later, he wrote to Sophie Volland, trying to appease her mother who had been antagonistic to the attentions he paid her daughter: "Tell her that the greatest consideration in the memory of man is assured me. . . ." Diderot, disbeliever in the existence of the immortality of the soul, was allergic to posthumous applause. But all things have pressed into them the official seal of Time, Oblivion, and whatever Life signs Death countersigns.

These maneuvers, however, did not suffice to free Diderot. For the time being, though, he was removed from the dungeon and allowed to stay in the part known as the Château, where he was given a comfortable room, the right to walk in the gardens, receive visitors, and pursue his work on the *Encyclopédie*. Among the weeping visitors, he who wept most (being the high-priest of tears) was Jean-Jacques Rousseau, still unknown, but shortly to become world-famous, and for the nonce Diderot's dearest friend, even as in time he would become his most virulent enemy.

In his *Confessions,* Rousseau writes: "I found Diderot greatly affected by his imprisonment. The dungeon had made a terrible impression upon him, and although he was comfortable in the Château and allowed to walk where he pleased in a park that was not even surrounded by walls, he needed the society of his friends to avoid giving way to melancholy. . . ."

Between one embrace and another, Rousseau spoke about the "Mercure de France" in which a prize was offered by the Academy of Dijon for the best essay on the subject: "Whether the Renaissance of arts and letters had contributed to purify morals"; and that he decided to enter the contest taking the affirmative side. Denis laughed. "Everyone will take that side, *mon cher ami.* Only the other side will give you the chance to write something new and eloquent." Rousseau was convinced. What other practical suggestions Diderot offered his friend will always remain a matter of conjecture, but a fabulous career started, whose influence the centuries have barely dimmed.

On November 3, 1749, Denis Diderot was released from prison, but never released from the nightmare of its recollection.

Two years after the "Letter to the Blind," Diderot produced a parallel work, *Lettre sur les Sourds et Muets* ("Letter on the Deaf and Dumb for the Use of Those Who Hear and Speak"), a less brilliant work, but still interesting. Now he made certain that nothing impugning to Church and Crown would appear in it. As usually, the genesis of the essay was a refutation. This time it was "The Fine Arts Reduced to One Principle" by the Abbé Charles Batteux, which was famous in its day.

The essay abounded in many diverse reflections, as was his wont, sparks of ideas that would alight upon susceptible minds. Chief of his purposes, however, was to determine how words appeared into language. For the many centuries that Christianity dominated Europe, the origin of the varieties of tongues was reputed to have taken place on a plain in the land of Shinar. There the people said to one another: "Go to, let us build us a city and a tower, whose top shall reach unto heaven. . . . And the Lord said: "Go to, let us go down and there to confound their language, that they may not understand one another's speech. . . . So the Lord scattered them from thence upon the face of all earth. . . . Therefore is the name of it called Babel, because the Lord did there confound the language of all the earth. . . ."

Diderot's theory combines experimental and rational methods. "Language is the instrument by which man's mind decomposes its sensations and perceptions . . . the human mind being everywhere the same, should use the same logic of expression." Gestures, he considers, antedated speech, and are inseparably linked into it. "And there are sublime gestures that the greatest oratorical eloquence can never express."

Communication among primitives was based on cries and gestures, and the deaf-mutes corroborate the idea. Words do not merely convey ideas. They have values of their own, and their total effect far surpasses their literal meanings. Poetry, being the highest form of expression, is therefore often obscure. "Into the words of the poet there passes a spirit which animates every syllable. . . . Because of this, things are said and portrayed at the same time; the mind grasps them and the soul is moved by them. . . . I could say that all poetry is emblematic." Language is both a social and psychological phenomenon and has evolved into logical reasoning.

Pursuing his materialistic conception initiated by the "Letter on the Blind," Diderot published in 1754 *Thoughts on the Interpretation of Nature*—a small book of aphorisms in which he condemns philosophical systems. "The systematic spirit is injurious to the progress of truth. It builds plans and forms systems of the universe to which it consequently desires to adjust phenomena willy-nilly."

He predicts that the progress in physics will eventually reveal the essential unity beneath all natural phenomena, and even ventures to foretell the breaking of the atom "by some artificial operation further than that of nature working by herself"—an uncanny intuition of the atomic theory.

The tone of the *Interpretation* was considered arrogant because with the severity of a pedagogue, he starts the book with the command: "Young man, take this and read it!"

Frederick, surnamed the Great, because historians need milestones to guide them in the wilderness of events, walked up and down the great hall of Sans-Souci, filled his nose with snuff tobacco, sneezed, and snorted: "There is a book I shall not read. It is not made for an *old* fellow like me."

Sensibilité—Paradoxes—Plays

The age was the Age of Reason—reason not as an abstract method for weighing problems of logic or a property of innate ideas prior to experience, but the main force of the mind impelling it to investigate, to discover, to grasp the mechanism of the universe. In another generation the Goddess of Reason would be installed in the Cathedral and worshipped in lieu of the cross. Yet, so strange and inconsistent is *homo sapiens* that precisely at this juncture *sensibilité* was, if not discovered, dissected, analyzed, rejected, embraced, loved, and despised. And the high-priest of *sensibilité* was Denis Diderot.

If *sensibilité* could be adequately translated into English it would mean sentiment, sentimentalism, sentimentality, and *its* high-priest in the Anglo-Saxon world was the Vicar across the Channel, Laurence Sterne, contemporary and friend of Denis Diderot.

It is in his *Paradoxe sur le Comédien* that Diderot expounds most eloquently his ideas about *sensibilité*. "*Sensibilité* is hardly the quality of a great genius. . . . It is not his heart, but his head that accomplishes everything. . . . His whole talent consists in *not* feeling, but in rendering most scrupulously the exterior signs of sentiment. If it were otherwise, the condition of the actor would be unfortunate indeed. . . . Extreme *sensibilité* makes mediocre actors; mediocre *sensibilité* makes the multitude of bad actors; and the absolute lack of *sensibilité* is the preparation of sublime actors. . . . The tears of the great actor fall from his brain. . . . He may not even die as one dies in bed, but a different kind of death in order to please us . . . since nothing takes place on the stage as in nature. . . . *Sensibilité* is the quality of second-rate people who are ever at the mercy of their emotions. . . ."

Presently, however, Diderot has quite other things to say about that emotion. "It is the characteristic of the goodness of the soul. . . . Among all men, nature has chosen some to whom she has granted this quality of heart, exquisite but dangerous. These men are prone to enthusiasm; they love virtue; they feel as intensely the horror of an evil deed as the beauty of a disinterested one."

And to Sophie Volland, Diderot writes: "The sight of an act of injustice makes me sometimes so indignant that I lose my reason and I am ready to kill, to annihilate." On the other hand, he continues that at the sight of a good deed, he experiences "an immediate and delicious sensation, and it seems to me that my heart dilates within me and I can hardly breathe. . . . The entire surface of my body shivers . . . and in particular the top of my forehead and at the roots of my hair the emotion becomes most intense, while the evidence of admiration and pleasure mingles on my face with that of joy and my eyes over-brim with tears. . . . He who is deprived of *sensibilité* consecrates his existence to mediocrity, without savor, without nobility, devoid of adventures of the heart, niggardly, fearful of all risk, mistaking boredom for happiness and selfishness for wisdom. The mediocre man without strong passions lives and dies like a brute . . . nothing remains to talk about when he is dead; his name is pronounced no more, the place of his burial is unknown, lost among the grasses. . . ."

Diderot had forgotten what the wisest of all the wise, Solomon, King of the Jews, had said: "For that which befalleth the sons of men befalleth beasts; even one thing befalleth them; as the one dieth so dieth the other; yea, they have all one breath; so that a man has no preeminince above a beast; for all is vanity. All go unto one place; all are of the dust, and all turn to dust again. *Hevel hevalim hakol hevel—vanitas vanitatum et omnia vanitas!*"

"Reason without the passions, is as a king without his subjects. Therefore, long live the man of passion, the man of *sensibilité!*" So concludes Monsieur Denis Diderot.

Diderot's chariot was ever hitched to fiery steeds: reason-*sensibilité;* logic-passion; heart-brain; dashing in diverse directions, a vertiginous race, which bewildered both his own generation and their descendants and was again and again the cause of his dismissal from the Sanhedrin of venerable philosophers. But precisely because of this, Diderot was one of the most colorful figures of the eighteenth century and one of the most seminal.

His analysis of *sensibilité* in the *Paradoxe sur le Comédien* turned into an angry exposition of the state of the theater in his day. "The stage is a last resort, not a profession of choice. Never does one become an actor because of the taste for virtue, because of the desire to be useful to society and to serve one's country or one's family, because any of the honest motives which prompt a person of rectitude. . . . An actor a gentleman, an actress a pure woman . . . these are the rarest phenomena. . . ."

The trouble was that the actors were not properly taught and parents did not bring up youngsters for the stage. And how could they? "Actors are excommunicated. The very people who cannot get along without them despise them. They are slaves. . . ." Ah, if actors were brought "to the stage as people are brought to the army, the palace, the church—by choice or by taste— what an influence the theater would have on the *bon goût* and the customs!"

It was not only the miserable status of the actors and the theater that Denis Diderot lamented, but with even greater vehemence he inveighed against the playwrights and their products. Diderot did not disdain the classics—Corneille, Racine, Molière. On the contrary he had found respect—reverence— for them. He would have considered it a national calamity to see their plays swept off the boards, although it is also true that the manner in which they were presented, revolted him.

Where in the world, he shouted, did men and women ever speak as those actors declaimed? Why should princes and kings walk differently from other men who walk well? Did they gesticulate like raving maniacs? Did princesses, when they spoke, utter sharp hissings? It was not better than a Serbonian bog in which generations of comedians were drowned.

"To every thing there is a season, and a time for every purpose." The ridiculous *bourgeois gentilhomme* of Molière had long disappeared and the present middle-class, rich, educated, and self-conscious demanded not only social and political recognition, but artistic as well. Why, then, should scribblers, under the colorless banner of neo-classicism, try to imitate the old masters? Was this anything but ludicrous monkeyism and parrotism? Where could it lead save to literary bankruptcy?

Diderot declared war against this travesty of art. He proposed a new genre of play—the *drame*. It would deal with the realities of the day, with the problems of the people who did not dwell in palaces and were concerned with futilities. The theater should be a school, but not for petty amours—a school for virtue, a school to teach morality more convincingly and more radically than the church or the collège—a school "offering us such regulations of conduct and motives as would make men tender, pitiful, simple, and contented."

The day of art for art's sake was still more than a century away; now it would be art for virtue's sake. "Truth in art is morality." The *drame* would be realistically portrayed. The language should be proper to the characters, to their professions, and their trades, and the action should be simple and direct, even including the violent moments—as in life, which the play would simulate. Every gesture should be appropriate to the word. No more declamations; no more addressing the audience always. "Be as true on the stage as off the stage," was the motto he offered the players. "But especially remember that there is no general principle; I do not know a single one of these that I have indicated, which a man of genius cannot infringe upon with success." It is safe to assume, however, that men of genius are as rare as white blackbirds, and that modesty becomes all.

Diderot would now put into practice what he preached. He would show the world what a *drame* should be, as expounded in the *Paradoxe*. He presented two plays: *Le Fils Naturel* ("The Natural Son" or "Virtue Put to the Test"), A Comedy in Five Acts and in Prose, with the True History of the Piece, which appeared in 1757; and *Le Père de Famille* ("The Father of the Family") in 1758.

Both pieces proved that an artist, like a spider, spins his web out of his guts and that his theories are but the scaffolding to hang the threads upon.

The Natural Son is the tale of a man wholly dedicated to virtue who sacrifices love and fortune for his companion, saves his life and the happiness of all concerned, despite the awful fact that he is only "a child of love." The play ends happily, for virtue must be rewarded. It was not presented at the Comédie-Française until 1771, and the *première* was its *dernière*. In print, however, from its first appearance until the beginning of the nineteenth century, it had thirty-two editions in France and many in other Western countries, not to mention the uncounted pirated ones.

The Father of the Family—a play based upon his experience with his own father regarding his marriage—was first produced in 1761 and then revived in 1769 when it became the hit of the year. By this time, the public had become accustomed to realistic plays. A hundred of them had appeared in different parts of Europe, chiefly in Germany, where Diderot was acclaimed as one of the great writers of the generation, and men like Goethe, Lessing, and Schiller translated his books, both before and after his death. And Diderot was often called the most German of the French authors, sometimes as a compliment, but more frequently as denigration, since there is in certain of his works a pedestrianism characteristic of much of the Teutonic output.

Both are of the "*larmoyant*" type—the "weeping" theater. "This very pathetic *drame*," writes Louis Petit de Bachaumont (1690–1771) in his *Mémoires Secrets,* after witnessing the performance of *The Father,* "has produced the usual effect, the tightening of the heart and causing abundant tears. You could count as many handkerchiefs as there were spectators; women became ill, and never did a Christian orator in his pulpit produce so theatrical an effect." Thus it accomplished what the author considered the chief purpose of a play. "I believe that a dramatic composition should inspire among men a love of virtue and a horror of vice."

Even Antoinette, Diderot's wife, who had never read any of his works, was finally persuaded to attend a performance, and while she would not give her husband the satisfaction of praising it, her daughter, Madame Marie-Angélique de Vendeul, says that she had wept as much as anyone else. And Diderot says: "There was a frightful crowd and people hardly remembered such a success. . . . My friends are at the height of exultation. My daughter came home intoxicated with wonder and delight."

The plays enhanced Diderot's reputation, but he profited little by them. "Whatever success my work has had, I have scarcely received anything but embarrassement and I expect nothing but vexation," he wrote to Rousseau. Still, he was not the man to regret having been of service by disseminating knowledge. "Had I but one secret for all my stock in trade, it seems to me that if the general good should require its publication, I should prefer to die honestly on a street corner, my back against a post, than let my fellow-men suffer."

Père de Famille was published at the end of 1758, accompanied by the *Discourse on Dramatic Poetry*—poetry, in the Greek sense of "doing" or "making," and therefore including prose as well. It dealt with plot, dialogue, characterization, costumes, decorations, gestures—a veritable *vade mecum* for aspiring playwrights and actors.

The book was dedicated to Her Serene Highness the Princess of Nassau-Saarbruck, and concerned the education of her children. Among other bits of advice, Diderot makes the Princess say: "I shall take very good care not to speak ill of sensual pleasure and not decry its allure. Its purpose is too august and too universal. I shall speak to you, my children, as if Nature herself were listening. Would not Nature have the right to reply to whoever shall speak ill of sensual delight—'Be silent, foolish one! Do you think that your father would have concerned himself with your birth, that your mother would have risked her life to give you yours, were it not for the unutterable charm that I have linked to their embraces? It was pleasure that brought you forth out of nothing.' "

The Princess was horrified, and since she was lucky to have read the manuscript of the dedicatory epistle, she urgently begged the author to have this passage suppressed in print.

Although the plays of Diderot are admittedly weak, undramatic, subjective, and verging on the romantic melodrama, they had an incalculable influence, and generally for the good, not only during his life-time, but more especially during the nineteenth century. Ibsen, Strindberg, Dumas fils, Shaw, Echegaray, Brieux, and many others, knowingly or unwittingly, gratefully or disdainfully, benefitted from the lessons Diderot taught.

Each generation serves as fertilizer for the succeeding one, and each is crucified by its favorite idea. The future is a wide-open mouth laughing uproariously at the past, but in the tunnel of time all things fuse—and vanish.

Dialogues and Monologues

Whatever the judgment passed on the plays of Diderot, it has been universally conceded that *Le Neveu de Rameau*—"Rameau's Nephew"—is a masterpiece, and the finest work of the author. It was favorably compared to Hamlet and Don Quijote, and Goethe called it "the classical work of an astounding man."

Jean-Philippe Rameau (1683–1764) was considered, a generation after the death of the great but scoundrelly Lulli, the foremost composer of France. He contributed several important innovations to the science of harmony and in his own operas—twenty in number—he gave much more prominence to the orchestral accompaniment than had been customary.

He became conductor at the Opéra-Comique and composer to the Court. In 1764 Louis XV granted him a patent of nobility and the order of Saint-Michel, but these were received on the eve of his death on the 12th of September. It is not known whether the Ferryman Charon considered it a choice obolus for crossing safely the Styx, the Hateful River, into the Land of Shadows, since it is rumored that there is no hierarchy of the dead.

Diderot knew Rameau well and had great regard for his

musical genius, although later in the *Nephew* he wrote disparagingly of his character and personality. But it might have been due to pique for his refusal to contribute an essay on music for the *Encyclopédie* and for ridiculing in several pamphlets the musical contributions of Rousseau, who dared to say: "The French have no music and cannot have any. . . . If ever they do have any, it will be so much the worse for them."

Rameau also chided Diderot for his negligence in editing Rousseau's articles, but Diderot, although sufficiently well grounded in music to have caught some of the errors, had been too harassed by work and other troubles, to bother. Moreover, it was perilous to criticize Jean-Jacques, the most sensitive of men. One could never tell what form his fury might assume, but a cataract of tears was sure to flow, and it could easily drown a friendship.

All this made part of the "Querelle des Bouffons," which had reached its highest peak of violence about this time. Paris—and other cities—was divided into two camps warring with words, pamphlets, and foils. Even the royal couple became involved— His Majesty taking one side, Her Majesty the other. And the momentous question? Who were the better opera composers, the Italians or the French—and which music sounded sweeter to the ear—the Gallic or the Roman? There was, of course, no victory and no unconditional surrender, and time is a sea in which all passions are extinguished and all problems are solved by being proven superfluous or ridiculous. Yet, there is a glow of satisfaction to realize that the hearts of men could be stirred by music as well as by superstition, prejudice, and the periodic urge to murder one another for the glory of kings and in the name of the Divinity of Peace.

But who was this nephew of the famous maker of music? Jean-François Rameau's name does not appear in the register of the *état civil*—the vital statistics—but on the register of the police as having been baptized on the 31st of January, 1716 in the parish of Saint-Michel of Dijon. There is also a record of marriage at Saint-Séverin on the 3rd of February, 1757. On January, 1761, his wife died and his child followed her in June of the same year. To be a clown one must have one's roots in tragedy. Rameau's own death, however, is recorded nowhere and no one knows the date. But what matters it, since the dead own no calendar and the Earth is hostess to all? In the end the spider crumbles in its own web and its speck of dust mingles with the shivering wings of the devoured fly and the wind carries it off together with the dust of the emperor and the dust of the empire.

But in the archives of the police there is another item dated 7th of November, 1748. "The sieur Rameau, nephew of the sieur Rameau of the Royal Academy of Music, a character of little sociability and difficult to tame, insulted while in the theater, the directors of the Opéra." Obviously the opera performed must have been that of his uncle, who, naturally, did not lift a finger to pull him out of jail. Never had he bothered to help this man destined to be called always "The Nephew of Rameau" rather than by his own Christian name. And he had talent, but how should the puny sapling thrive under the massive shadow of the great tree?

How much better for him had his uncle been a little shopkeeper, who would say proudly to his customers: "My nephew Jean-François—he knows music—he can compose songs—and you should see him act! What a *comédien!* He can make you laugh until your belly hurts and your eyes tear!" Maybe, then, Jean-François, his vanity soothed, would have tried to climb a few rungs of the ladder of success. But how should one climb chained to a hod weighted with a spine-breaking name?

Every village has its "Character"—its fool, its eccentric, its vagabond—whom it fears, ridicules, despises, but whom it would not relinquish. Paris was a metropolis, but l'Ile de la Cité —the Latin Quarter—was in a sense a village, a charming, brilliant, disputatious, learned, wicked, glamorous village, as it would remain for all the centuries. In the 1750's it found its "Character" in the shape of the Nephew of sieur Rameau of the Royal Academy of Music. One encountered him in all the cafés, in all the promenades, in many of the best homes, now in rags, now in fineries, now pinched with hunger, now plethoric with food and wine, now laughing uproariously, now weeping copiously. And always dramatizing, clowning, parodying, enthralling, and repelling.

"I am my own interlocutor, discuss politics, love, taste, and philosophy. I give my mind full fling; I let it follow the first notion that presents itself, be it wise or foolish. . . . My forehead is high and wrinkled, my eyes are keen; I have a prominent nose, large cheek bones, black, thick eyebrows, a big slit of a mouth, full lips, and a square face. If this large chin were covered with a long beard, do you know it would look very well in bronze and marble?"

Who is this—the Nephew of Rameau or Denis Diderot? He is both. He is one and the same. He is the caricature and the painting. He is he who looks in the mirror and he who stares back. *Moi* and *Lui*—"I" and "He," as the two protagonists are called in Diderot's masterpiece. But it might just as well have been *Moi* and *Moi*.

An author must fragment himself in order to capture himself, and in particular a Diderot who belonged to a period— nay, he was the symbol of that period—in which all values were changing, a revolution far more significant than the one following the fall of Bastille.

Rameau's Nephew lives by his vices. He is a liar, a cheat, a glutton, a coward, a fawner. "I am never false as long as it pays me to be true; never true as long as it pays me to be false." Had not Diderot been that in his youth? Is there not a tacit understanding that every man is entitled to a certain amount of folly, roguery, falsehood, prejudice, superstition, baseness, treachery—ingredients essential for survival? Only the discrepancy between the individual's estimate and that of society forms the basis of all law and morality.

But Rameau's Nephew is also a free spirit, an adventurer, a laugher at human pretensions, and because he owns nothing, he owns everything. Diderot, however, has become a bourgeois tied down to his labors and social commitments, and because he owns bits of furniture and a purse of gold and silver coins, he is a moralist, and because he possesses a wife and daughter, he is the grand voice of virtue.

"If it is important to be sublime in any field," says the Nephew, "it is most of all in evil. You spit on a petty thief; but you cannot refuse respect to a great criminal." And he points to countless cases, including the elegant loafers at Court, the King himself and his mistress, who plunged France into disastrous wars. And does not the world bend knee to them, including the dignitaries of the church which preaches peace, poverty and humility?

And so the duel of wits continues page after page, always scintillating, always revealing, always dramatic—the one tearing masks, the other healing faces.

I—You call vanity defending one's country?

HE—Vanity! There are no more countries. From one pole to the other I see only tyrants and slaves.

I—Vanity to serve one's friends?

HE—Vanity! Do we have friends? And if we did, should we make ingrates of them? And according to you, we should be virtuous?

I—In order to be happy, certainly.

HE—I see an infinity of good people who are not happy and an infinity of wicked people who are. . . . Virtue is an old word devoid of meaning. Virtue is often vice and vice virtue. . . . Drink good wine, gorge yourself with delicious food, roll over pretty women, sleep in soft beds—the rest is vanity.

I—It is infinitely sweeter to me to help an unfortunate person—to write a fine page—to perform the duties of my profession. . . .

"He" is not the Bohemian of the Latin Quarter, nor is "I" Denis Diderot. "He" and "I" by the genius of the author emerge as two Titans, far greater than the living individuals of their day. They have become the two forces of Man forever struggling against each other—Ahuramazda, the Good, and Ahriman, the Evil, and must forever be locked in combat. When their struggle is over, Man vanishes from the Earth.

What a burden man has taken upon himself—not only to live, but to know life's meaning; not only to cultivate the earth, but to pry open the universe; not only to master time, but to harness eternity. Even if he breaks under the burden, who, throughout all eternity and throughout all infinity, has been like unto him?

The manuscript of *Rameau's Nephew,* which was not published during Diderot's life-time, had a most extraordinary career, was lost, found, lost, and found again in most unlikely places. It reposes now in state for all to see in the Pierpont Morgan Library in the City of New York, and a film has been made by the New York Public Library, Ratio 12, 1948.

There were other "Dialogues"—the less dangerous ones published during Diderot's life-time. In 1773 appeared *The Conversation of a Father with His Children*—a tribute to his own father's compassionate and just nature and to the kind and generous impulses of his sister, as well as a condemnation of the rancor and the violence of the *abbé,* his brother. But the old cutler had already said: "I have two sons. One will surely be a saint and I fear that the other will be damned, but I cannot live with the saint and I am happy with the sinner."

The Supplement to Bougainville's Travels is a sort of epilogue to Bougainville's *Voyage Around the World.* Louis-Antoine de Bougainville (1729–1811), a celebrated sailor, accomplished the first circumnavigation of the globe between 1766 and 1769 and gave an account of his visit to the Island of Tahiti, which created a great stir on the Continent.

In the *Supplement,* published a quarter of a century after his death, Diderot, as was his wont, expounded his ideas on many things, emphasizing the hypocrisy and ugliness of the sexual mores of his own country, and marriage only as a species of slavery based on the idea of property. In Tahiti, however, there was honesty and simplicity, and there was neither jealousy nor

rape nor crime of passion—therefore no sin. Love was, as Car-
men sings a century later, *"un enfant Bohème"* who never knows
any laws. Yet, Diderot wrote to his own dear daughter that the
very suspicion of her infidelity to her husband (who deceived *her*
many times) would crush him with grief. "I should die to have
to blush for it. . . ." (Always the inevitable dichotomy in Diderot's personality—Bourgeois—Bohemian.)

This encomium of the civilization of the uncivilized became
the leitmotif of countless books during the next century, until
serious scientific anthropologists visited "the noble savages" in
their own habitat all over the world, and reported their vast
miseries, their countless superstitions, their cruel taboos, possessing neither liberty nor equality, but being, in truth, abject
slaves to unconscionable tyrannies. Thus illusion transmutes
base metal into gold.

Jacques le Fataliste which, like other manuscripts of Diderot,
found its way into Germany long before appearing in print in
France, is purported to be an imitation of Sterne's *Tristram
Shandy.* That Diderot was influenced by Sterne is quite evident,
but both he and Sterne were great adepts in taking other men's
writings as points of departure, and yet creating works
thoroughly personal. All things have been said, but who has
heard them? Many an artist adds his personal smoke to the general fog and calls himself original.

Boisterous enthusiasm, eccentric geniality, buffoonery were
characteristic of both Sterne and Diderot. They knew that
man's existence is possible neither by wisdom nor by folly, but
by their admixture—a pontifical tiara tinkling with the jester's
bells. *Jacques,* condemned by some critics as vile and salacious,
because Diderot, who considered sex as a normal and worthy
urge in the scheme of nature, wrote frankly about it. He received
warm praises from Goethe. "A real first rate dish—a very fine
and exquisite meat prepared and served with great skill."

Among many castigations of both writers and readers, Diderot presents in *Jacques* his chief argument—the denial of
predestination. In all cosmos he finds nothing but chance, which

people, prejudiced by religion, mistake for divine, preordained order. *"Il était écrit là-haut"*—"it was so written up above"—Kismet—Fate.

Le Rêve d'Alembert—"The Dream of d'Alembert"—a boldly, imaginative piece of work, was published in 1830, nearly a half-century after the author's death. By that time much of the scientific discussion carried on in the dialogue had become obsolete, and the influence the book might have exerted had evaporated. Still, because of its artistry, humor, and bonhommie, and despite its earthiness—or perhaps because of it, too—the book is entertaining and stimulating even now.

Diderot's last major work, *The Essay on the Reign of Claudius and Nero,* had originally been conceived as the life of Seneca, but Diderot soon realized that he could not abstract him from his environment and pass honest judgment. (Ah, if only his own carping critics for the last two centuries had been willing to recognize that each man is the fruit not only of his mother's womb, but of the womb of the generation in which he plays his little part!)

Diderot therefore reconstructed the period in which Seneca flourished, during the reigns of the two emperors—one the best, the other the worst of Rome's rulers. As always, he identified himself with the ancients, and this time he was Seneca *redivivus.* He was the *philosophe* of his day as Seneca had been the philosopher of his. And both were pedagogues—Seneca to Emperor Nero, Diderot to his generation; and both strove to inculcate virtue. And their reward? Seneca was condemned by his pupil to open his veins, and Diderot's generation imprisoned him, hounded, and ridiculed him, forced him to live most of his life in poverty and fear, while his principal works had to be locked in his drawer to be published when he no longer ran any peril—after his death.

The *Essay* offered him the opportunity to vent his spleen on the contemporaries who had made his life miserable, under the guise of scourging the enemies of the Roman, including Rousseau, now his most virulent foe. No hammer can twist iron as time twists man. Once Diderot said: "I flew into the arms of my friend Rousseau. . . . With a single bound I pressed his face close to mine. . . . I clasped him tightly in my arms without speaking to him save by tears and sobs. . . . I was choking with tenderness and joy. . . ." And now, as the years had passed, he said: "I have lived fifteen years with that man. Of all the marks of friendship that a man can receive, there is none he has not had from me, and he never gave me any in return. . . . This man is false, vain as Satan, cruel, ungrateful, hypocritical, and bad. . . . Truly this man is a monster. . . . Detest the ingrate who speaks evil of his benefactors . . . detest the atrocious man who does not hesitate to blacken his old friends. . . . When I compare our friendships to our antipathies, I find that the former are thin, small, pinched; we know how to hate, but we do not know how to love." This was the conclusion of a man for whom friendship was the right, the duty, the privilege of rendering service, and who practised what he preached.

The writing of the *Essay* is tumultuous, rambling, and often incongruous, but as with all Diderot's works, it stimulates the mind and illumines many dark alleys en route to truth and justice. He is not a lamp on the table, but a torch in the wind.

Diderot wrote several smaller pieces, among them the famous and delightful *Regrets for an Old Dressing Gown.*

"Why did I not keep it? It was just made for me and I was made for it. . . . The new one, stiff and starched, makes a mannequin of me. . . . There was no call to which the old one did not lend itself. . . . If a book were covered with dust, one of its flaps was a ready duster. When ink on my pen was thick and would not flow, its side was ready. . . . These long stripes announced the man of letters, the writer, the toiler. . . . At present I look like one of the idle rich. No one knows who I am. . . . Friends, keep your old friends, fear the touch of wealth. Let my

example teach you. Poverty has its freedom, luxury its restraint. . . ."

*The Conversation of a Philosopher with the Maréchale
de . . .* considered by many critics as the purest jewel in Diderot's casket, is a brilliant protestation against persecution
and futile self-sacrifice.

La Maréchale—Are you not Monsieur Crudeli?
Crudeli—Yes.
La Maréchale—The man who believes in nothing?
Crudeli—Yes.
La Maréchale—But your morals are the same as a believer's.
Crudeli—Why not, if that believer is an honest man?
La Maréchale—And you put that morality into practice?
Crudeli—As well as I can.
La Maréchale—What! You do not steal, or kill, or pillage?
Crudeli—Very rarely.
La Maréchale—Then, what do you get out of not believing?
Crudeli—Nothing; but does one believe in order to get some-
thing out of it?
La Maréchale—I do not know. But a little self-interest comes
in useful both for this world and the next. . . . Do you think
man can get along without superstition?
Crudeli—Not as long as he remains ignorant and timid.

On Women: "I have seen love, jealousy, superstition, and
rage developed in women to a degree beyond the experience of
man. The contrast between the violence of their gestures and
the sweetness of their features render them hideous. . . . Address yourself to women; they absorb quickly because they are
ignorant; they expand easily because they are shallow; they
remember long because they are obstinate . . . impenetrable
in dissimulation, cruel in vengeance, persevering in their
schemes, unscrupulous in the means they employ. . . ." But is
it their fault? "They have been treated like imbecile children.

In organized countries there is no vexation man cannot practice on women. . . . When we write of women, we must needs dip our pen in the rainbow and throw upon the paper the dust of butterflies' wings. . . . The only thing they are taught is to carry well the fig-leaf they have received from their first ancestress. . . . When women have genius, I think their brand is more original than ours."

Thus, Diderot tries to portray that strange creature with whom man cannot cope, since she is only an incident in his career and his knowledge of her remains rudimentary and amateurish; but a woman's chief interest is man and her knowledge of him is deep and professional.

The *Salons* are criticisms of the biennial art exhibitions at Paris which Diderot commenced in 1759 and carried on until 1783, one year before his death. However, only his friend, Grimm and Grimm's correspondents in Germany (the nobility, including King Frederick and King Stanislas of Poland) had seen them. The first of the nine *Salons* was published in 1795 and the last in 1857.

With a show of selflessness, Diderot explained to his friends who were anxious to see the criticisms, that he would not publish them for "humanitarian reasons." Might not those artists whom he denigrated lose their means of livelihood? This pose of virtue incarnate—a favorite one of his—was only partially valid. The police, it is true, would not have molested him, but a horde of infuriated artists would have trampled upon him and the prison at Vincennes would have seemed to him the Garden of Eden whence he was driven.

"What with their unrivalled clearness, painting the picture over again for us, so that we, too, can judge it; what with their sunny fervor, inventiveness, real artistic genius, they are the only Pictorial Criticism we know of worthy of reading." Thus Thomas Carlyle, the dispeptic genius, so chary of praise, so quick to impale.

The point of departure for Diderot's analysis and judgment
of the arts was that the True, the Good, and the Beautiful were
three facets absolutely essential in any work. Lacking any of
them, distortion and corruption were sure to ensue. "What does
it mean? Where is its interest? . . . Two qualities are essential
to the artist: morality and perspective. . . . Touch me,
trouble me, make me weep, provoke my enthusiasm and my
anger!" he calls out to the painter. "If I have not been moved,
you have missed your objective!" And to clench his argument, he
points to one of the canvases of Jean-Baptiste Chardin (1699–
1779). "You could take the bottle by the neck if you were
thirsty; the peaches and the raisins waken your appetite and
draw your hand. . . . His paintings will be sought after some
day. . . ."

There is in the *Salons* a zeal, a vivacity, a brilliance which the
French criticism of art had never before achieved and Diderot
may be considered the father of the great works that appeared
a century after him—father, although it is quite probable that
he would not acknowledge many of the present practitioners as
his legitimate sons and daughters, but regard them as bastards
spawned by confusion, ugliness, immorality, and inhumanity.

Diderot who tackled all forms of the written word has also
produced two short stories—two masterpieces—*The Two
Friends of Bourbonne* and *This is Not a Tale*. They suggest
strongly that he was the innovator of the modern short story,
though not of the recent form. He discarded the abstract, the
crowded background, the belabored psychological analysis, for
one single concentrated effect fused into action.

Diderot was ever of the avant-guard, but not in the specious
and obscurantist use of the word nowadays. He sought, on the
contrary, to simplify and clarify ideas. Writing was not a private affair, but a social function. In order to achieve his aim, he
removed from the French language the shackles of classicism,
clipped its weighty wings, and supplied it with strong, trim legs
to run in all directions—science, literature, philosophy.

With the naive vanity unbecoming a *philosophe* (but normal in a ham, and he was both), Diderot boasted that writing was the simplest of all occupations, that he never bothered rewriting, that, in fact, he cared little for literary glory. Accepting the judgment of himself, friends and foes alike, from one generation to the next, called him diffused, disorganized, careless, and in truth, unworthy of glory.

Few of the critics, however, bothered to read his works in their entirety or without bias. "Diderot's contemporaries, even his friends," Goethe said, "used to reproach him for knowing how to write fine pages without knowing how to write a fine book. This kind of talk if repeated, takes root, and thus without further scrutiny the glory of an eminent man is weakened."

The truth is that Diderot was a conscious artist, and that there is nothing haphazard about his work, that, indeed, his better books were rewritten many times, as the manuscripts lay in his drawer year after year.

In his less histrionic mood, Diderot said: "It is the style which assures a work of literature its immortality; this is the quality which charms the author's contemporaries and which will charm the centuries to come." Always posterity, holy and sacred! But Time's most gracious gesture is to make of our career a legend or a fable, and even legends lose their charm and fables their lessons.

Diderot was not the master of delicate irony, of sprightly wit, of fictitious naïveté—the French graces, particularly evident in Voltaire and in his spiritual son, Anatole France. Nevertheless, he did possess qualities capable of keeping a work of literature fresh—sincerity, vivacity, intensity, swiftness, enthusiasm.

Realizing that many of his contemporaries, even among the well-wishers, were not loath to push him off Olympus, and that the future generations might take their cue from them, Diderot says: "People will be tempted to take me for some sort of eccentric; but what matters it? Is it such a great fault to have been able to conserve, while tossing about in society, a few vestiges

of nature, and to distinguish oneself by a few angular characteristics from the mass of those uniform and well-rounded pebbles
which abound on all shores ?"

The "Synagogue" of Rue Royale— an "Angel" Beckons

The lean years were over. Denis Diderot, past middle age,
was a solid citizen with an income of over four thousand *livres*.
He was no longer fearful of the stentorious knock at the door,
for his chief enemies, the wily Jesuits, disgraced and despised,
had been expelled from the country and the austere Jansenists
would shortly follow them into oblivion, while the government
had accepted a *modus vivendi*. *It* ignored his existence and *he*
kept his manuscripts in his drawer, to be rewritten, annotated,
polished for the delectation of those creatures he loved so dearly
—the ones who never die—the ladies and gentlemen of posterity.

As for the *Encyclopédie,* it was now a standard and honorable
work, which found its way into the very boudoir of the mistress
of the King, where noble ladies looked up ancient prescriptions
for pomades, powders, and rouge and the latest instructions for
embroidering kerchiefs for lovers and sometimes for husbands,
too, since one had to placate whom one could not eliminate.

Freed from the drudgery of editorship, Diderot had time on
his hands and wisdom on his tongue and he needed ears to hear
and palms to applaud. The salons he shunned. Their hostesses—
Madame Deffand, Madame Necker, Mademoiselle De Lespi-
nasses, Madame Geoffrin—were charming, witty, generous with
their food and wine, but there was too much intrigue around
them. Authors were made and unmade, politicians found their
way to the Throne or to La Bastille—machinations which were
abhorrent to the essentially naive Diderot. "I was not made for

society." And although Madame Geoffrin admired and was fond of Diderot (she had bought him the new dressing gown and new furniture for his attic), she was not anxious to have him around. She considered him too bold and too venturesome in his ideas and feared "his impetuosity, the rashness of his opinions, supported when aroused by a fiery and stirring eloquence."

But there was the "Synagogue" of Rue Royale—the six-story mansion of the rich and scholarly Baron d'Holbach. Paul Thiry, Baron d'Holbach (1723–1789) was born in the Palatinate, but was raised in Paris. Among his many works on science and philosophy, he published in 1770 *Le Système de la Nature*, in which he categorically denied the existence of a deity, scorned the notion of immortality, and lashed at Christianity and all religions as the root of human evils. Amid the various degrees of disbelief of the enlightened ones—deism, theism, pantheism, agnosticism—d'Holbach stands alone as the unequivocal atheist, the knight of absolute freedom of conscience.

Here Denis Diderot was ever the welcome and honored guest, the dear friend. Here the famous French and foreign intellectuals (men only, which gave the place its nickname of "Synagogue") foregathered twice a week, dined on choicest foods and drank of the costliest wines. Here neither fear nor hypocrisy nor false modesty hindered one from expressing debatable opinions and condemning theories including those of the host, considered one of the most learned men of the day.

Here came d'Alembert, Condillac, Buffon, Hume, Garrick, Wilkes, Sterne, Jean-Jacques Rousseau, Benjamin Franklin, Helvetius, Turgot, and Jacques-André Naigeon, the tenacious, indefatigable and fervent disciple of Diderot, whose "Boswell" he became, but without the Englishman's genius and wit.

And here, too, came Diderot's *alter ego,* Friedrich Melchior Grimm, Baron of the Holy Roman Empire (1723–1807). Grimm was born at Ratisbon and moved to Paris about twenty years later, as secretary to Count Frieson. It was Jean-Jacques Rousseau who introduced Grimm to Diderot and before long the inevitable triangle traced itself—the cross of love and

friendship. Diderot, who so admired Montaigne, did not heed
the advice of that wisest of Frenchmen, who held that friendship, the rarest of all human emotions, was only possible between
two persons, a third one disturbing the harmony and breaking
the subtle chain that bound them. And no one could have known
better, for there never was a nobler friendship than that between
Montaigne and Etienne de la Boetie.

It is likely that the eventual fierce enmity between the two
encyclopedists started at this time, for Jean-Jacques, jealous of
the German, detested him and the bile began to gather. Diderot's friendship for both men was rooted in his unconscious
need for natures foreign to his own, thus deriving comfort and
balance. Diderot was brash, self-confident, and overbrimming
with generosity, while Rousseau was shy, brooding, and vindictive and Grimm was elegant, cool, hard, and brilliant, a career-
ist and later the confidant of kings and princes. Ambassador
Thomas Jefferson found him "the pleasantest and most convers-
able member of the diplomatic corps."

In 1755, Grimm issued the *Correspondance Littéraire,* a sort
of gossip sheet about art, literature, politics, and society of the
Paris of his day. Appearing twice a month, and strictly confiden-
tial, it found its way to all the courts of Europe. When the
Correspondance was first published in 1812, it became a famous
document, an important source-material of the thoughts and
opinions during the most crucial years of the eighteenth century,
immediately preceding the Revolution.

Grimm, with a keen eye for his interests and for the use he
could make of other people, was not loath to take advantage of
Diderot. Many days and many nights did the latter slave at the
Correspondance to help out his friend, who was too busy to attend to it. No gratitude was expected and none was offered. Yet,
Diderot's goodness was rewarded. Via the *Correspondance* he
had the opportunity to write and circulate his *Salons,* and his
manuscripts hidden from the eyes of his compatriots, were,
thanks to Grimm's efforts, translated and printed in Germany,
thus saving them from probable loss and oblivion.

Maria-Angélique, daughter of Denis Diderot and apple of his eye, was growing up. Advocate of pagan and sinless love for all the world, he reverted to the most Christian of virtues for his own child—modesty, fidelity, purity. Angélique was obedient and repeated her father's catechism, albeit often with tongue in cheek, and still preserved her treasure intact.

And now the time had come to look around for a suitable match, but a suitable match could not be obtained with a flattened purse. Despite his share in the legacy of the good cutler and his income from his literary labors, Diderot had saved very little. Too many beggars, too many café lizzards and aspiring authors knew his weakness and no one ever left empty-handed.

How to sweep together a nice pile of gold coins with which to entice a worthy young man of a worthy family into whose hands he could entrust his rare jewel? For a quarter of a century as editor of the *Encyclopédie,* Diderot acquired what was considered an extraordinarily large private library, needed for his research in the various fields of knowledge, and in accordance with his contract with Le Breton, the publisher, it remained his property. Diderot made it known that his library was for sale. But where in the Land of the Franks on the shaky bridge between the old regime and the nascent one, was there a patron— a Maecenas—willing and able to purchase the treasure?

Grimm wrote to the Empress of All Russias about the plight of his friend, and Catherine replied that she suffered greatly to think "that this philosopher so famous in the Republic of Letters found it necessary to sacrifice to his parental love the object of his delight, the source of his work, and the companion of his leisure," and immediately instructed her Paris agent to buy Diderot's library and pay him whatever price he asked. The author mentioned fifteen thousand *livres* and the deal was promptly sealed. The Empress added a codicil to the contract— that Monsieur Diderot retain the library until it pleased her to send for it and that he be its custodian at the salary of one thousand *livres* a year to be paid in advance for twenty-five years—a gracious wish that he live far beyond the Biblical allotment of time to mortal men.

Any wonder, then, that Denis Diderot, foe of autocrats, wrote to the Autocrat of the Steppes: "Great Princess, I fall at your feet; I stretch out my two arms toward you!" In due time, after Diderot's death, the library was sent to the Hermitage in Saint-Petersburg and there occupied a special room. Years later, however, to the dismay of scholars and historians, the library vanished. Not one single volume of the 2904 nor one of the many manuscripts has ever been discovered in any part of the world, and the mystery of their disappearance has never been solved.

With forty thousand *livres* bulging his pockets, Denis Diderot, *père* without peer, set out in search of a son-in-law. He avoided Paris, the Seat of Enlightenment, where the young men had been suckled on his philosophy, imbibing the milk of freedom more heady than all the wines in Bacchus' barrels, and wended his way to where his ancestors for countless generations had been pure and virtuous and honest, and where, doubtless, at least some shreds of these qualities still persisted.

At Langres the family Vendeul, friends of his late father, possessed, providentially, a youth of marriageable age and marriageable timber. There was much haggling and bargaining about the dowry and other pertinent matters, and even about love—a proper and natural procedure when dealing with an affair which should last, despite life's vicissitudes and tribulations, throughout all the days of one's years. Finally, Caroillon de Vendeul was affianced to Marie-Angélique Diderot, and on the 9th of September, 1772, the couple was united in holy matrimony, but without the blessing of the bride's mother or that of the bride's uncle, the abbé.

The abbé resented his niece's education and his brother's pride, but what grievance Antoinette bore is not known, save that time sharpens the tongue and tightens the heart of the termagant. At any rate, she refused to allow any of Diderot's friends to attend the ceremony and embarrassed the good man no end.

Now Denis Diderot was lonesome and found no surcease in his home. "Parents who lose their children," he says, "find each other again, talk to each other, and solace each other. . . . We wander about, Madame Diderot and I, one around the other; but we are nothing to each other. How can you speak to a woman full of ill-humor and ready to burst out for a trifle?"

Was the marriage a happy one? It certainly was an improvement upon that of Denis Diderot. Angélique remained pure and unblemished; Caroillon had some love affairs. The new family grew and prospered. Caroillon made several wise investments and established a sizable fortune for his descendants, who became pillars of conservatism. They were ashamed of their radical ancestor and his papers were relegated to the secrecy of a moldy backroom, where many years later, by a rare good fortune, they were rescued from the teeth of rats by Doctor Herbert Dieckman of Harvard University.

Angélique never wavered in her love and admiration for her doting father. She wrote his biography to the best of her ability, inexact in many places, uncritical in others, but generally understanding and always forgiving—not only toward him but also toward her mother who had so often turned their home into a hellish cauldron.

Catherine, the Semiramis of the North, was anxious to see the Philosopher of the West and from his mouth, so eloquent, as she had heard, gather knowledge and wisdom and learn of the ways of justice and truth. Again and again she invited him to be her guest at the palace at Saint-Petersburg, offering to pay all expenses and provide special coaches to make his trip agreeable and safe.

A typical Frenchman of that day—and this—Diderot hated to leave his *patrie*. "What would you say of the owner of an immense palace, who should spend all his life-time in going up from the cellars to the attics and down from the attics to the cellars, instead of sitting quietly in the midst of his family? That is the image of a traveller." A deeply-rooted chauvinism, which considers France the center of the universe, mistress of all the good and all the beautiful. What shall one seek elsewhere? What can one find? Let the rest of the world come to France—and the rest of the world comes!

At last, however, Diderot had to bow to the will of the generous Monarch, who would accept none of his excuses as valid. And so, at sixty, considered old age in his day, and already suffering from some of its disagreeable symptoms, Diderot undertook the formidable trip to that icy lair of the Lioness on the shores of the Neva River.

He stopped for some weeks at The Hague, capital of the freest republic of Europe, where he was entertained by many admirers, then set out for Saint-Petersburg. Forty-one days! "Try to imagine, if you can, the state of a man tormented by a violent colic, rolling over the worst roads in the world. At each jolt—and every moment brought a more or less strong one—if they had plunged a knife into my stomach and sawed through my intestines, they would not have hurt me more."

He arrived at the Capital on October 9, 1773. Catherine's court was a hot-bed of corruption, intrigue, jealousy, violent hates, and violent murders—a mixture of barbarism and refinement, culture and illiteracy, slavery and elegance. But the Empress? Ah, the Empress! "If she is great on the throne, her charms as a woman would turn thousands of heads!" Her shady and cruel history, her notorious amorous adventures, did not interest the French *philosophe,* who had reached the age of ideas untinged with passion. The older a man grows the more virtuous the women become.

Diderot kept aloof from the doings at the court. "Am I made for court life and is court life made for me?" he explained and complained again and again. But his Imperial Hostess he met daily for a few hours to compare notes. Their notes did not always dovetail and the two would explode. "You are a hothead, and so am I," the Empress said. "We interrupt each other, don't hear each other and say silly things."

"With this difference," he answered, "that when I interrupt Your Majesty, I commit a great impertinence."

"Between men, are there impertinences?"

Ah, if only his wife, Antoinette, had been as amiable and understanding as this beautiful, crowned head! And yet, they say that the simple are simple! "Of all Russia I saw only her!"

The seminars were not without physical violence. "I never come away from our conversations," the Empress wrote to Madame Geoffrin, "but my thighs are black and blue. I have been compelled to put a table between us to protect my limbs and myself from his gesticulations."

Catherine's reactions to Diderot's opinions varied from silly to profound, from valuable to preposterous. "Monsier Diderot, I have listened with the greatest pleasure to all your brilliant intelligence has inspired. . . . You forget in all your plans of reform, that you only work on paper, which endures all things. . . . But, I, poor Empress, work on the human skin, which is irritable and ticklish to a very different degree."

Again and again Diderot tried to say goodbye and return to his home—even to Antoinette. He needed his Paris, his attic, his friends at the "Synagogue." The Empress would not hear of it for five months, when she finally consented. Laden with gifts, Denis Diderot started on his way homeward—a journey even more replete with pain, fatigue, and dangers, despite all the care and attention of the Empress' men and her powerful horses.

When he finally reached his destination, Diderot began bragging about his unequalled experience at the court of the most magnificent of all monarchs. The episode became the greatest adventure of his life, affording him a subtle soupçon of aristocracy, so relished by a democrat.

As a sign of friendship for her, Catherine asked the *philosophe* to write a system of education which she should promulgate in her nation. Delighted with the task, Diderot composed his

Plan of a University. Generations had to pass before his ideas were put into practice, not only in Russia, but throughout the Western World.

"Education," Diderot wrote, "should be free, compulsory, and universal. It should not necessarily make a man profound; it should rather give him the knowledge he will need to fill his role and vocation in society. Not the savant, but the citizen. . . . Education should start with mathematics, followed by physics and mechanics, astronomy, natural history, chemistry, and anatomy. In later forms, logic and grammar and the language of the country. Only in the eighth and last form Greek and Latin. . . . As for religion, if the Empress thinks that the total small advantages produced by belief outweighs the total of evils wrought by sectarianism and intolerance, then she might introduce it . . . with caution."

But all this is futile, if there is no liberty. "Liberty alone can lead the individual and society to the greatest happiness they desire." Diderot tells Catherine that she is a despot and urges her to set up a constitutional government. The people must have the right to depose and punish the tyrant who violates their rights. "A benevolent despotism is the most dangerous of all because people lose the right and custom of criticizing the government, falling into a sleep of death." He warns her against witch-hunting and thought control. "Without realizing it, people begin avoiding a certain kind of dissenting ideas, as they would avoid an object that would hurt them. . . . They get used to that cautious gait, and it is difficult to return to a frank and outspoken way."

Many have rotted in dungeons, have dangled from scaffolds, have been riddled with bullets, not only in the land of the Czars, but in all lands, not only in the past, but in the ever present, for proclaiming the truth of Diderot's words and for trying to harden them into realities. History records only one eternally recurring phenomenon—that might is dislodged by greater might and right always takes lodging with the victor.

And what was the judgment passed on the *Plan* by Catherine

the Great, Empress of All the Russias? "This piece is a true
Babel in which there is neither knowledge of things, nor prudence, nor clairvoyance. . . . It would have turned everything
topsy-turvy."

The *Plan of a University* was not published until 1814—
eighteen years after the death of the Empress, thirty years after
the death of the *philosophe,* and one year before the ultimate
defeat of the Glorious Tyrant born of the Great Revolution.

History is a long cry.

Finale

Who shall capture and imprison Time, the implacable thief
whose master key opens all doors? We stand sentinels to our
days, while our years slip by.

Denis Diderot was home again in his attic. Again he went to
his favorite café to sip his coffee and watch the chess players,
brows knit, move their men of wood with far greater concern
than the Fates move their men of flesh. Again, twice a week, he
visited the "Synagogue," and now and then spent a longer vaca-
tion at d'Holbach's country seat at Grandval.

Gradually, however, the salt of life began to lose its savor.
The mind became sluggish, the body honeycombed with aches.
"We are all ailing," he said about himself and his cronies.
"When we meet each morning at lunch, one has slept badly, the
other was more tired when he got up than when he went to bed;
it's the stomach, it's the back, it's the chest, it's the teeth, it's the
eyes. We are dragging a miserable carriage in which there is
always something loose and those loosenings will only increase,
until the happy or unhappy moment when the carriage and its
driver will go to the devil. . . . The earth is as light in Saint-
Petersburg as in Paris; the worms have as good an appetite, and
it is quite indifferent in what part of the earth we fatten them."

One by one his friends died or worse still cooled toward him,

or he toward them—even his "other self," Grimm, now
weighted down with decorations, would be too busy to pay him a
visit when in Paris. Old friends, like old wine, turned sour. Poor
Job, he was on the crest of his fame, but the hill was manure and
the birds that pecked at it were crows cawing the rasping litany
of futility.

"The greatest crime of man is that of having been born," says
Calderón de la Barca. Was it a crime or a misfortune? It might
be both, but it was something else, too, for Diderot, unlike the
great Spaniard, was essentially an optimist—not toward the
present, but toward the future. The horizon, for him, was not an
optical illusion, but a real demarcation, and beyond it there
would be justice and truth and peace among men of all nations.
"What does it matter to me if a man is born on one side of the
strait or the other?" How should he know how distant the horizon would be and what dreadful specters would thrive beyond
it—he who lived in the Age of Reason and had the certainty that
man was a reasonable creature?

No one was better prepared for Humanism than Diderot. He
had a classical education (the point of departure of the movement two centuries preceding his own); he had the taste for the
great adventures of intelligence; he discarded authority, and in
particular, revealed religion which makes something outside of
man superior to man. And he loved people. He even loved the
aged, the pathetic refugees from time and the strangers in
space. "They seem to me some singular creatures that have been
spared by the caprice of fate."

He had an immense pity for man, his brother, laden with
tribulations, subject to a thousand ills, so frail and yet so avid
for immortality. The man that Diderot conceived and for whom
he fought, was not a philosophic concoction, but a creature of
flesh and blood and senses, and therefore his Humanism is truer
and richer than that of all the other philosophers of his century.

When he learned of the American Revolution, his heart was
filled with joy. "After centuries of general oppression, may the
revolution which has just broken out beyond the seas, by offering

to all the inhabitants of Europe a shelter against fanaticism and tyranny, instruct those who govern men on the legitimate use of their authority!"

Years previously, Diderot had already written in the *Encyclopédie:* "No man has received from nature the right of commanding others. . . . Power acquired by violence is only usurpation. . . . The Prince holds from his subjects the authority that he holds over them. . . . The government is not a piece of property, but is public property. . . . It is not the state which belongs to the prince, but the prince who belongs to the state. . . . What is intolerable is to have slaves by calling them citizens."

The authors of the American "Declaration of Independence" as well as those of "Les Droits de l'Homme"—"The Rights of Man" of the French Revolution were profoundly influenced by Diderot's "Droit Naturel"—"Natural Right." And when Diderot wrote the words, he braved the fires of fanaticism still crackling around the stake and the wilful authority of the masters at Versailles who were dancing a saraband in which the masks had lost their faces.

Diderot's heart was weakening and one day he suffered a mild stroke. Antoinette, his wife, was worried. If Denis refused the last sacraments, a religious burial would be denied him. She begged Monsieur de Tersac, the curate of Saint-Sulpice, to try to persuade the deluded man to return to the fold before it was too late and the flames, which by sheer good fortune he escaped upon the surface of the earth, would consume him beneath it forever. He had not been a good husband, but she still loved him, in her own annoying way, and she was anxious to spare him.

Monsieur de Tersac was a gentleman and a scholar and he spent many hours wandering with the *philosophe* in the mazes of theology. Diderot, however, had always his Ariadne's thread to lead him out safely—his Jesuit masters had trained him well. And so, the good curate, unable to trap him, tried to excite his civism. "Think of it, Monsieur Diderot, what a salutary effect upon the world a little retraction of yours would have."

"I believe so, Monsier le Curé, but I would be saying an impudent lie. And you know, monsieur, that only the truth saves. The Church refused to bury Voltaire because he did not believe in the divinity of the Son. *Bien,* monsieur, when I am dead, they can bury me wherever they wish, but I declare that I believe neither in the Father, nor in the Son, nor in the Holy Ghost, nor in any member of the family."

Diderot recovered, but he found climbing the stairs to his attic an exhausting experience, and perhaps some day, it might prove a fatal one. He would have to be nailed to his chair. The Czarina, who despite the black and blue marks on her legs and the impudent suggestions in the *Plan of a University* and the brazen remarks about her court and her despotism, had a soft spot in her imperial heart for Denis Diderot, the good man. Voltaire she admired, but he was not a good man. Many might be clever and brilliant and profound, but few were good. She who lived within evil and had achieved her exalted rank by evil, appreciated this *rara avis*—the good man.

Thus when she heard that Diderot had been ill and was becoming immobile, she was scandalized. How long should the great philosopher, the good man, continue to live in that ancient, dilapidated house? Had not thirty years of his life been sufficient? She ordered her agent in Paris to rent immediately a beautiful apartment and furnish it comfortably—all at her expense.

Just as Diderot had been unwilling to discard his old robe for the new one, but had to give in, so now he objected to leaving his garret, but how could he disobey his wonderful benefactress? And so, on July 18, 1784, he moved from Rue Taranne to a "superb apartment" in the fashionable Rue Richelieu.

He was aware, even more than those around him, that Fate Atropos was about to snap the thread of his days, but the only way to lend dignity to life was not to fear death. "You desire the end of life, just as after working hard you desire the end of the day." And a coffin, what is a coffin but a bed from which one forgets to rise?

It was the evening of July 30, 1784, twelve days after the

Diderots had moved into their "palatial" residence. Diderot was eating his dinner with his family, and having ever a sweet tooth (although toothless now), he was indulging in his dessert. He had been eating an apricot and moved his arm to take some stewed cherries. Antoinette told him to desist. "Why should I?" he retorted. She turned her head for a moment and when she faced him again, ready doubtless to offer him a reply, his head had fallen upon his chest. "He passed away as if mastered by sleep."

Caroillon de Vendeul, his son-in-law, anxious for the good name of his family, promised the priest a lavish funeral, and moreover, would not a pompous church burial give the impression that Diderot had recanted? Whether the latter argument or the vision of the purse convinced the priest is not known, but he agreed.

As Diderot had always desired, an autopsy was performed "for the good of the living." His brain was found perfect, as well preserved as that of a youth of twenty, but the rest of his body was a roster of pathology.

The emptied corpse was carried to the parish church of Saint-Roch and lowered beneath the slabs in the Chapel of the Virgin. In later years when it was looked for, it had disappeared and nevermore was discovered. Who played this macabre jest upon him, and why?

Denis Diderot was hated by the villains, denounced by the bigots, ridiculed by the fools—yet he loved man. Let this be his cenotaph!

PIERRE-AUGUSTIN Caron DE BEAUMARCHAIS

1750

Every age is an age of transition. Man is forever at the cross-roads of yesterday and tomorrow. Each generation breathlessly awaits the birth-cry of the millennium, while time broods upon a marble egg and prophets crow.

1750—Louis XV, great-grandson of the Sun King, known as *Le Bien-Aimé*—The Well-Beloved—ruled over France, himself ruled by his courtesans, wily, corrupt, and tyrannical. His reign of twenty-four years was France's most disastrous. She engaged in futile wars, lost her colonies, was on the verge of bankruptcy. Famine stalked the land; prisons were overbrimming with innocent victims; bigotry indulged in vile and foolish battles. The Jesuits fought the Jansenists and both hounded the Huguenots. There was no new St. Bartholomew massacre, but enough cruel injustices were perpetrated to make the annals of this period reek with blood and shame.

"I am your master," His Majesty thundered from his throne sunk in the mire of folly, "and I intend to be obeyed. All rights I hold from God. It belongs to none of my subjects to limit them or to decide the extent of them. They who question my authority are wicked, blasphemous, and traitorous."

And what of the cries, Sire, and the grumblings and the voices in the wilderness which are beginning to echo in the cities?

"I shall outlast all that."

And later, the Well-Beloved said: *Après moi, le déluge*—after me, the deluge. Or, if he did not say it, it was said in his name. And what a deluge it was! And how long it has lasted! The dove has not yet brought the olive leaf nor has the rainbow appeared in the clouds.

When at last he delivered his royal ghost in 1774, he was buried secretly at night, for fear the people might take it into their heads to drag the hated carcass through the gutters.

341

France celebrated his departure for three days and three nights in mad revelry.

But this was only the *apéritif* and the full feast was to take place nineteen years later with the beheading of his grandson, Louis XVI. This Louis, although obese and dull, was a man of virtue and was welcomed by the people with enthusiasm, hoping that he would purify the government and bring about justice. Nothing is so expensive as hope, for nothing gives so little in exchange for so much, and despair is the toll it must pay to truth.

Louis XVI attempted the reconstruction of his nation, but the *ancien régime* was too heavy with corruption for his poor shoulders to sustain and there was no Atlas among the men he gathered about him, while his spouse, Marie-Antoinette, flighty, imprudent, and prodigal, hastened the inevitable *dénouement.* If she did not say: "They have no bread? Let them eat cake!" it was in tune with her personality and her contempt for the French—she the daughter of Maria-Theresa, Empress of the Holy Roman Empire, hereditary enemy of France.

But if Marie-Antoinette did not know how to live, she knew how to die. Mounting the scaffold with dignity and pride, she lost her beautiful head under the admiration and applause of the audience. And Louis XVI paid for the sins of his ancestors, he the least guilty of them all.

1750—France was divided between the privileged and the unprivileged. The former were the nobles and the clergy; the latter, the peasants, the artisans, the bourgeoisie. The privileged owned two-thirds of the land, monopolized most of the higher offices of the government, and held all the commissions in the army. They were not warriors, however, and rarely visited their regiments. Sufficient for them the burden of their gorgeous uniforms and the weight of their medals. The menial work of fighting and dying was delegated to the subalterns and the soldiers drafted from the peasantry and the bourgeosie.

The privileged possessed the hunting rights. Game preserves

were maintained for their benefit and the peasant who killed an animal which destroyed his crops was himself killed or mutilated. Nor was there any redress against the wanton trampling of the crops by the galloping horses of the vainglorious riders. It was safer to weep in one's sleeve or mutter an imprecation in the privacy of one's hut, for to offend a lord was to offend the Lord and he who ventured it forfeited body *and* soul.

The privileged enjoyed exemption from the *taille*—the tax on land and income from industries. And by special favors from the collectors, they managed to escape all the indirect taxes as well—tax on salt, tobacco, wine, cider, and the import and export duties levied on goods sent from one district to another.

Many of the nobles entrusted their estates to stewards and spent their days in revelry and cuckoldry at the royal court of Versailles, where twenty thousand of them were entertained from the public treasury.

1750—The peasant was the ass on whom rode the nobleman, the soldier, the monk. He paid all the taxes, his own and theirs, the direct and the indirect—the *taille,* the *vingtième,* or the twentieth, and the *capitation,* or the poll, to the state; the *tithe* or the tenth, to the church—altogether three-fourths of his earnings. He paid in *cens,* or money, and in *champart,* or grain.

Even though serfdom had virtually disappeared, there were still vestiges of it in the feudal dues the peasant was forced to pay to the lord—tolls for the bridges he crossed, tolls for the roads he drove on, and presents on holidays and special occasions. And there was the *corvée*—the hated *corvée*—forced labor without payment on the highways or in the lord's domain, one day a week. And when the peasant died, his sons, before being allowed to inherit the farm, had to pay a fee to the lord.

The curse of Adam was upon the man who tilled the soil that others might have food. Like his forefathers he used a rough wooden plow, which he drew himself, and a spade. He sowed his grain by hand, reaped it with a sickle, and tramped it out with his heavy sabots. He lived on vegetables and black bread and only upon rare feast days, tasted meat or eggs. He dwelt in a one-room house, dressed in rags, was illiterate and despised. "All other classes of society stood aloof from this one, and perhaps in no other part of the world had peasantry ever lived so alone," says de Tocqueville. "A French village was a county of persons, all of whom were poor, ignorant, and coarse; its magistrates were as rude and as contemned as the people; its syndic could not read; its collector could not record in his own handwriting the accounts on which the incomes of his neighbors and himself depended."

"Certain savage-looking beings, male and female, are seen in the country, black, livid, and sunburnt, belonging to the soil which they dig. They seem capable of articulation, and when they stand erect, they display human countenances. They are, in fact, men." This is the judgment La Bruyère in his *Caractères,* the incomparable gallery of literary paintings passed on the French peasant. Although written a half-century earlier, the picture was as vividly true in 1750.

A century later, Edwin Markham, the American poet, inspired by Millet's paintings of the French contemporary rustic, wrote his famous "Man with the Hoe."

> Bowed by the weight of centuries he leans,
> Upon his hoe and gazes on the ground,
> The emptiness of ages in his face,
> And on his back the burden of the world.
> Who made him dead to rapture and despair,
> A thing that grieves not and never hopes,
> Stolid and stunned, a brother to the ox?
> Who loosened and let down his brutal jaw?
> Whose was the hand that slanted back his brow?
> Whose breath blew out the light within his brain?

1750—France had a population of twenty-five million—the vast majority, peasantry. There were only eighty cities with ten thousand each, besides Paris which had over six hundred thousand and Lyons over one hundred thousand.

The business in towns was largely controlled by the merchant guild and the trades by the craft guilds, each a separate organization—spinners, weavers, armorers, goldsmiths, bakers, brewers.

The Guild of Booksellers was limited to 360 members and thirty-six printers. They were on the lowest rung of the economic ladder, disreputable and hardly better off than beggars. Harassed by grievous regulations and always at the mercy of the police, most of their transactions were done surreptitiously, and many a one was sentenced to the galleys for life for printing or selling a condemned book.

1750—*Cujus regio ejus religio*—a man's religion must be that of his ruler. And the ruler of France was a Roman Catholic with Gallican variations. After fierce wars and horrendous massacres, Henry IV issued the Edict of Nantes in 1598, granting the Huguenots—the French Protestants—equal, or nearly equal rights with the Catholics. Despite the fact that the Huguenots were among the most industrious, the most prosperous, and the most intelligent of the population, or rather because of it, they were hated and their freedom was begrudged.

In 1685, Louis XV, in a pious spree, revoked the edict. As a result the Huguenots were forbidden to worship in public. Their ministers were exiled. Their schools were closed. They were in perpetual danger. Thousands escaped to Holland, Germany, and the English colonies in America. Many others were killed, imprisoned, and sent to the galleys. Saint-Simon (1675–1755) in his *Mémoires,* in which he describes with admirable penetration the thousand incidents at the royal court, where he as duke often dwelt, writes: "The revocation of the Edict of Nantes . . . depopulated a quarter of the kingdom, ruined its commerce, weakened it in every direction." Injustice is the gibbet from which the judges in time will swing.

1750—There were 150,000 clergy of the Catholic Church— bishops, abbots, monks, and parish priests. They owned one-fourth of the land, paid no taxes, controlled education, censored

346 SEVEN AGAINST THE NIGHT

books. They had their own special courts of justice and were in most ways a state within a state—*imperium in imperio*.

1750—Torture was in bloom and the chief amusement of the populace. In the public square men, women, and children were thrilled by the slow agony of the wretches condemned to the wheel which broke their bones and the red-hot pincers which tore their flesh. Upon gala days they could applaud decapitation, quartering limb from limb, and the stake's gay flames roasting alive.

How pleasant to the nostrils was the smoke mingled with the spluttering lard! How delicious to the ear the crackling of the skin! How comical the screaming and the writhing! What thunderous laughter at the jests about the tripe and the privates! And then—when it was all over—how comforting the bishop's benediction! Now they could go home purified and purged and ready once more to accept cheerfully tyranny, poverty, and the thousand miseries which beset them. There is no measuring rod for one's good fortune more accurate than the evil fortune of others.

1750—PARIS. Two centuries earlier the celebrated chronicler and jurist, Michel de Castelnau, said: "Paris is the capital of all the kingdom and one of the most famous in the world as well for the splendor of its Parlement (which is an illustrious company of thirty judges attended by three hundred advocates who have the reputation in all Christendom of being the best seen in human laws and acquainted with justice) as for its faculty of theology and for other tongues and sciences, which shine more in this town than in any other in the world, besides the mechanic arts and the marvelous traffic which render it very populous, rich, and opulent; in such sort that all the other towns of France and all the magistrates and subjects have their eyes directed thither as the model of their decisions and their political adminstrations." And in 1750, Garrick, the great Shakespearean actor said: "London is for the English, but Paris is for the world."

Paris, however, was not yet *la Ville Lumière*—"The City of Light"—but it was destined presently to spread enlightenment to all parts of the earth and the Americans were the chief inheritors. The population was marked off into groups with a definiteness impossible in modern cities. There were the members of the various guilds, merchants and tradesmen; there were the professionals—lawyers, notaries, doctors, teachers, and the quarrelsome professors of the Sorbonne, center of tumultuous theological disputes. There were the men of letters and the men of the theater, for the moment both shabbily treated, both hounded by police and church. There were the small shopkeepers and the laborers. There were the speculators and the bankers, whose ambition was to enter the noble caste by some back door —bribery, dowry, chicanery. They built themselves fine homes in the Capital and splendid country houses, and squeezed the rents from the peasants with a more merciless grip than the old nobility. They had not even the ragged panoply, *noblesse oblige.* And they knew, being self-made men, that no ladder of success rises as high and is as solid as that whose rungs are the necks of the people.

In their turn, the *nouveaux riches,* and particularly those who managed to buy or steal a title, were infinitely more hated than the members of the old aristocracy, whose vulgar origin was concealed in the protective folds of time. For no form of hatred is as keen as envy. Envy strikes a double blow. It magnifies the importance of our enemy and belittles our own.

One-fifth of the population was servants, topped by a small army of lackeys, insolent and rascally. There were thirty thousand professional beggars and how many of them were also thieves is not recorded, but hunger creates impatient fingers. The *filles de joie,* euphemistic appellation of the daughters of misery, were legion, in lupanars and on the streets at the mercy of their procurers. They were "a band of chosen women sacrificed to the superior interests of the family life, who cater to the countless men stricken by nature with an insatiable hunger

for love . . . but in the commerce of women, men are punished.
. . ." And so it was, for the devastating disease named by the
eminent Italian poet and physician, Girolamo Fracastero, for
his miserable hero, the shepherd Syphylus, was ubiquitous—
from the royal boudoir to the rustic hayloft.

1750—Paris was the gayest capital of the Western World.
London had vestiges of Puritanism. Rome had lost its ancient
luster. Florence had fallen asleep. Venice wept into the canals as
she recalled her former glory forever gone. Berlin was but an
administrative and military outpost. Vienna was not yet aware
that the Danube is blue and would have to wait another century
for the Strauses to lift hearts and legs in joyous dances. New
York, Boston, Philadelphia were overgrown villages and their
inhabitants were laden with blue laws, since the key to the gate
of Heaven was wrought from the iron of earthly miseries.

The silver waters of the Seine flowed as through a vast artery
within the body of Paris giving the city vigor and cheer. Across
it spanned fine bridges and the Pont-Neuf, the queen of them
all. Over it carts and carriages and pedestrians streamed without
interruption. Peddlers offered fruits and flowers. Mountebanks
turned somersaults and juggled balls, while shrewd little monkeys passed cups among the laughing—and rarely generous—
audiences. Barbers with enormous forceps pulled teeth and
pressed them back into the torn bleeding gums promising a
third dentition to the howling, swollen-cheeked victims.

Velvet-tongued, black-robed quacks offered herbs and liquids
certain to cure all the diseases that human flesh is heir to. It
was a period in which three-fourths of the children born were
doomed before reaching the age of five, and epidemics of typhus,
small pox, and diphtheria plagued mankind in constant rotation.
Physicians chattered in Latin and prescribed blood-letting, cup-
ping, and clysters to relieve the patients of their humors. For
the rich they also recommended "potable" gold, for what thing
on earth has greater merit?

Drink, therefore, monsieur—madame—the filaments of gold

and your health shall be as radiant and as enviable. For you, the poor, we recommend crushed sow bugs and incinerated toads, for God-given misery should be redoubled by man-made offense. Diseases of the poor had their origin in sin, and expiation must be accompanied by means of suffering and disgust.

MacAdams, the Scottish engineer whose invention, the macadamized road which transformed the surface of the earth's highways, had not yet been born in 1750, and the streets of Paris, like the streets of all other cities, were either cobblestoned or "left to nature" to splash their mud or choke with their clouds of dust.

Paris was a city of open-air stalls—haberdasherers, jewelers, butchers, cobblers. Hawkers, baskets on their heads or swinging from bars across their shoulders, called out their wares—fish, hot pies, flowers—each with a distinct chant. There were voices among them which, if trained, would have graced the boards of the opera.

There were the perennial chestnut vendors and the vendors of apple fritters and potato chips. And rushing in all directions the water boys with brimming pails. Housewives, waiting at their doors, bought the minimum quantity needed for cooking and washing. Was water made for drinking? Not since the days of Noah and his vineyards. And who would pour into his belly yellowish liquid swarming with flies and floating with wisps of hay and feathers of birds? Bathing? What a foolish, and indeed, harmful habit! Wise physicians warned against its hygiene and good priests thundered against its immorality. The body should be hidden from view, even as much as possible from its owner, for who did not know that the Devil was ever ready to pounce upon the naked body, particularly when freshly washed?

Healthy nostrils welcomed life's stenches: the mounds of manure of passing horses, oxen, mules, and grunting hogs; the ever-running, filthy waters splashed out of doors or poured out of casements; the streams of urine which flowed from underneath the kiosks against walls and fences where modest men eased themselves (the more brazen ones required no such protection) ; the acrid fumes of ancient sweat and garlic and wine. In sum, all the wholesome manifestations of living.

The finicky, decadent nostrils belonging to the wealthy and the nobles could stifle the stench—as they stifled truth—by drenching their kerchiefs in perfumes and incense. But this was strictly a matter of taste, *Chacun à son goût.*

At night Paris was romantic and mysterious with the moon and the stars hanging over the Seine and the flickering lights of the torches piercing holes in the dark, circuitous streets without sidewalks. Boisterous gay blades coming from the Opéra-Comique or the Comédie-Française sang an aria or recited from Racine or Corneille. Sedan chairs and hacks, carrying masked ladies, dashed in all directions. Pedestrians to save feet and necks pressed against walls and shouted imprecations, while the prudent bourgeois fastened doors with iron shutters. Lovers walked in the gardens of Luxembourg and the Tuileries. Writers, artists, hangers-on played chess, read newspapers, declaimed, disputed, and talked, talked—for never had the art of conversation reached such a phenomenal pitch—in the famous cafés Procope, Régence, and Gradot. And wild parties lasting until dawn took place Chez Landès.

1750—The stately majesty of the baroque was surrendering wistfully to the frivolous grace and charm of the rococo. Gentlemen wore wigs and three-cornered hats and ladies pasted on beauty spots and pancakes of rouge to hide the withered pallor that autumn paints upon leaf—and cheek. In halls gleaming with crystal and gold and dazzling with mirrors couples danced the minuet to the music of the harpsichord, the recorder, and the viola, while whispering words of love and places of assignation.

1750—The storm was gathering. Small fists of clouds—in the shape of pamphlets printed in the cellars of Paris, of books smuggled into France from Switzerland, Holland, and England; of philosophers talking, uninhibited in salons; of scientific theories expounded at the academies—fists of clouds which will merge and spread and cover the skies and before the century unwinds its years, there will be such an upheaval as never recorded in previous annals—a tearing forth—a parturation—and the birth of a new world!

Treaty of Peace at Rue Saint-Denis, Paris

One day in the year 1750, André-Charles Caron, Maître Horloger—Master Watchmaker—shoved aside his work and tools, cleared his table, and began writing on a long sheet of paper with heavy black lines. Every now and then he stopped, creased his brow in thought, then dipped again his pen, a goose's feather sharpened to a fine point, into the ponderous silver inkwell, the sole object inherited from his father, Daniel Caron, also a watchmaker, who had plied his trade in Lizy-sur-Ourcq, a town of fifteen hundred souls.

Daniel was an honest and industrious man, severe in his morals in the Huguenot tradition, for being a member of a minority group one had to make up for physical weakness by superior spiritual rectitude. Daniel's wife, Marie Fontain, bore him fourteen children, who despite their modest means, or perhaps because of it, managed to live happily together, or at least peaceably, which, considering the usually deep-seated familial jealousies and animosities, was a matter of pride for the parents and served as a model lesson to the neighbors.

When Daniel died in 1708, the widow took her brood to Paris, where there was a greater chance to scrape together a living. Presently the older ones left the nest and began scattering about, as is the nature of birds and of children. André, breaking the ancient custom of pursuing the parental trade which had raised the crafts in France to an artistic pinnacle, joined the dragoons under the elegant name of Caron d'Ailly.

His eye was enticed by the magnificent uniform and his brain by dreams of glory and of love. To be sure, as a commoner one could not rise above the rank of sergeant-major, but that sufficed to make one strut proudly, twirl one's mustachios, and captivate any woman, maiden, or mistress. And if, by good luck, His Majesty declared war on any of the many foes of France, one could gain an officer's épaulettes for bravery on the battlefield, and what was more natural than bravery to a noble-hearted youth?

Alas, the abysmal difference between dream and reality, poor André! The dreariness of the barracks, the coarseness of his fellow-dragoons, the endless monotony of drilling, the harshness and cruelty of the officers made him wish he were a simple bourgeois like his father and his father's father. But that was not so easily accomplished. One could not shed a uniform, symbol of allegiance to His Majesty, by simply reporting one's wish to the commandant.

Destiny, however, in the shapely form of Marie-Louise Pichon, daughter of a Parisian bourgeois, led him out of the maze, but not without bewildering meanderings. Marie-Louise was Catholic, André Protestant. Monsieur Pichon, the girl's father, was an honorable man, but poor. He could offer no dowry. André had no trade.

"Angels cannot sing more beautifully than you, Marie-Louise," the timorous soldier said, when she finished singing some "Bergerettes," accompanying herself on the spinet.

"*Merci*, André," she answered, her cheeks two red roses in bloom.

"I cannot live without you, Marie-Louise," he continued. "What good is religion, if it separates me from the woman I love? I am willing to become a Catholic."

On February 5, 1721, thanks to clerical intervention, André received an honorable discharge from the army. On March 7, the Cardinal of Noailles confirmed the fact that André-Charles Caron had renounced Calvin's false religion in the "Church of the New Catholics." As is frequently true of converts, in order to still their consciences, overcome their doubts, and prove to the world their honesty and their sincerity, André became more dogmatic and inflexible than those born to the fold. This proved a source of friction between him and his son later on.

At about this time, too, André Caron (he had discarded d'Ailly with his uniform) was accepted as apprentice by the Watchmakers' Guild of Paris, an unusual procedure, since he was already twenty-three years old. To top this, only one year later he begged the Conseil d'Etat to grant him the rank and title of Maître Horloger. This he asked by virtue of his conversion, having in mind the words of Jesus, since in his Protestant days he had read the Bible. "How think ye? if a man have an hundred sheep, and one of them be gone astray, doth he not leave the ninety and nine, and goeth into the mountains, and seeketh that which is gone astray? And if so be that he find it, verily I say unto you, he rejoiceth more of that sheep, than of the ninety and nine which went not astray."

His request granted, André married his beloved Marie-Louise Pichon, harbinger of so many good things, on July 13, 1722. André was born among watches and clocks and many of the mysteries of the trade must have been partially familiar to him, which helped him greatly in the mastery of that meticulous and complicated work. He scraped together some money and opened a small shop on Rue Saint-Denis in the center of Paris. He had a large sign painted with the inscription: ANDRE CARON, MAÎTRE HORLOGER, which in time became a matter of embarrassment to his ambitious son.

His pride, however, was tempered by the knowledge that he had acquired his master's degree after too short an apprenticeship. Unwilling to remain mediocre, André borrowed all the books he could on the technics and physics of that marvelous bit of live machinery, which told the hours and warned of the passing of the days, and studied them diligently. Before very long, André Caron became a craftsman highly esteemed by his

fellow-members of the Guild and patronized by satisfied customers in many walks of life.

Meanwhile, in the ancient manner of things, Marie-Louise
began bearing her husband one child after another to the tune
of ten—not quite so many as his mother bore his father, but
thank the Lord for His bounty. As was the pathetic condition
of the period, four of the offspring died in their infancy and only
five girls and one boy remained. The boy arrived on January 22,
1732, and was christened Pierre-Augustin after his godfather, a
candlemaker. Perhaps there was a cryptic symbolism in it, for
this male child was destined to brighten the world as with a
vast candelabrum.

André Caron continued writing for a while longer. He liked
to make ornate capitals and he used capitals as his mood dictated
—nouns, verbs, and even the little prepositions. At last, he
sprinkled ashes over the paper to dry the ink, for the miracle of
the blotter had not yet been revealed.

He stood up. He was tall and good-looking, and his military
training gave him an air of assurance and a bit of cockiness,
which his female customers interpreted as gallantry toward
them, particularly the Spanish ladies who regularly came to
Paris to purchase fineries. The French capital, then as now, was
famous for its artistic products, and they brought their precious
timepieces to Monsieur André Caron, Maître Horloger, for
repairs.

"*Enfin!*" André sighed with satisfaction. "*Voici, monsieur!*"
He handed the paper to a youth of eighteen, who had been
waiting respectfully. "Read it! No! Wait! Let your mother
and your sisters hear it as well. Marie-Louise!" he called into
the interior.

"*Oui, mon ami!*" the woman waddled into the shop. She was
fat now and worn and had not many more years to live, but she
still had traces of that gentleness which had captivated her
courting soldier and could still sing and play the spinet tolerably
well. And her children, and in particular, her son, had inherited

her musical talent, but also from their father, since he, too, loved music and could turn *vers gallants*. She looked at the young man with a mixture of maternal pride, for he was handsome, almost as tall as his father, with a mobile face, regular features, vivacious blue eyes "which did not gaze only at the Heavens," and with commiseration, too, for he was in trouble.

"And now your sisters!" André said. "Where are they? La Grande!"

"Ici!" she answered.

"Lisette!"

"Ici!"

"Fanchon!"

"Ici!"

"La Bécasse!"

"Ici!'

"Tonton!"

"Ici!"

The five girls, who had been watching from behind the curtain which separated the shop from the rest of the house, rushed in and placed themselves in line, according to size, serious, heads high, as if on inspection, since their father insisted upon a military discipline, compatible, of course, with their sex. Now that he was no longer a soldier, he thought of the time when he wore the uniform with nostalgia, and often related anecdotes and incidents, some true, some partially true, some invented, all glorifying the profession of arms, and incidentally himself. He was something of a braggart, but much less so than his son would be.

"I am the vainest of men," said Pierre-Augustin many years later, as he took stock of himself. "What annoys the imbeciles, is not that one is vain, but that one has good cause to be."

"*Mes amies,*" André addressed his wife and daughters, "you are all aware of how your son and brother has been behaving, mortifying us all. I need not tell you how much I counted on him, my only son. I sent him to the best school I could afford in the hope that he would become an honor to the family. He would advance beyond his father, would not be a little shopkeeper, although I am not ashamed of my trade or my position. An honest, hard-working man doing honorable work is, after all, the backbone of a nation, her defender, even as a soldier. But one cannot deny that there are higher rungs to the ladder, and it is a matter of great joy to a father—and to a mother—and to sisters—if one of theirs climbs and climbs.

"*Eh, bien, mes amies,* I spent my money, which I could ill afford, since the rich hate to pay their bills and the poor cannot, and one works fourteen hours a day to keep one's family well fed and decently dressed—I spent my money on an ungrateful son. What did he learn at the school? Almost nothing. A little grammar and less Latin and his spelling and even his punctuation of his own tongue are full of errors. And what you do not learn when you are young you will never know when you are grown-up. I can assure you of that, *mes enfants.* His good teachers advised me to take him out. He was not only a miserable pupil, but also a nuisance. The pranks he played demoralized the whole school.

"And so, after four useless years, I brought him back home. He was already thirteen years old—in my day considered a man. Nowadays with all the coddling that's going on everywhere, no one seems to ever grow up. *Eh bien, mon fils,* I said, since you cannot or will not be a man of learning, I shall make a good watchmaker of you, and God willing, you will outdo me and become wealthy and honored by the trade. For I have never had such a teacher as you will have, of that you may be sure. You will not have to spend years groping for a bit of knowledge. You will be given it on a platter, so to say, and from that point you may go on and on, and I shall never be so happy as when I notice that you have outranked me.

"You know, *mes amies,* how it turned out. My son worked little enough during the day, and as soon as the sun set, he dashed out of the house and consorted with the lowest of the apprentices of the district and together they annoyed our neighbors by their brawling, their shouting, their rowdyism during all the hours of the night. I was patient. I pointed out his error. I tried to reason with him. *Mon fils,* I said, the name of Caron has been a respectable one for generations—centuries—and are you going to make it now a word of shame and hate? For I cannot raise my head, and the neighbors complain bitterly that they cannot sleep in peace, and say to one another, 'that young Caron is a menace—Caron—Caron—'

"*Eh bien,* did he hearken to my words? He sulked and muttered and his work became more and more worthless. And then one day—think of my distress, my dear wife, my sweet daughters—this son of mine proved himself a thief! Not only did he steal the money from my drawer, but he had also kept the money customers left with him for my work during my absence. What could I do? What could any honorable man do?"

By this time, the six women had been wiping eyes and blowing noses into their handkerchiefs and aprons.

"I chased him out of his paternal home. And if you think that this is an easy thing for a father to do to his only son—his only son whom he loved and for whom he would have sacrificed his life, you are grievously wrong.

"What manner of life he led after leaving our house, you are aware of, *mes chères.* We may believe it or not, but I hear it said that he became a mountebank performing on Pont-Neuf—that he was a beggar singing on the streets—that he tried to join the Théâtre de la Foire, and you know what a shameful hole that is reputed to be—that he borrowed *sous* from our friends and acquaintances. . . . Oh, I shall not go into further details nor demand from him a strict accounting of this shameful period. Let the past bury the past.

"He has declared himself completely vanquished, surrendered unconditionally, and is ready to sign the treaty of peace which I have just formulated, and which I wish you all to hear from his own mouth, that you may witness his abject submission and contrition. Read, monsieur!"

Pierre-Augustin had a well-placed voice. Before many years would pass, he would recite for princesses and even the King himself. His audience now was sympathetic and his father was vain about his composition. He would read it, therefore, with dramatic fervor. "Know you, Pierre-Augustin Caron, the conditions I place upon your return. I require full and complete submission on your part, and I demand that you show me great respect in your words, in your deeds and in your entire behavior. Not only do I wish to be obeyed and respected, but I also wish that you anticipate my desires in anything that you think may please me.

"ONE. You must make nothing, sell nothing, cause nothing to be made, directly and indirectly, except for me alone, and you must no longer give way to the temptation of appropriating anything which belongs to me. You must have absolutely nothing but what I give you. You must not even sell an old watch key without accounting to me for it.

TWO. You shall rise in the summer at six o'clock and in the winter at seven. You shall work until the hour of supper at anything I may give you to do, without showing any displeasure for your task. You must work cheerfully. I furthermore mean that you employ whatever talents God has given you that you may become famous in your profession.

THREE. You must not go out anymore for supper parties, nor indeed, go out at all in the evenings. Such parties and entertainments are too perilous for you. And I recommend to you from this day never to ask permission to break this rule, and I should advise you not to take it upon yourself to do so. I consent, however, to your having dinner with your friends on Sundays and holidays, on condition that I know where you are going and that you return home not later than nine o'clock.

FOUR. You must give up your wretched music, and above all, the company of young men, for I shall tolerate neither. They have been your ruination. However, in consideration for your weakness I shall allow you to play the violin and the flute, but on the express condition that you play neither instrument except after supper on working days and never during daytime and that you do not disturb the neighbors' rest or mine.

FIVE. I will avoid sending you out as far as possible, but in case I am obliged to do so for business reasons, remember above all things that I shall never accept any of your poor excuses for being late, and you know beforehand how much a break of this rule would annoy me.

SIX. I shall allow you board and four *livres* a month which suffice for pocket money and enable you by degrees to pay your debts."

The young man stopped and looked about as if in expectation of applause, or as on his beggar's days for the drop of a coin. "Are you ready to sign it?" the father demanded, delighted with the sonority of the words and certain that his woman-folk admired his composition. As soon as his son signed the document, he would show it to them that they might also admire his calligraphy. "*Oui, monsieur,*" the son replied.

André Caron pointed to the stool and the pen. Pierre-Augustin signed and added: "It is fitting that I suffer this humiliation, which indeed I have deserved, and if this, in addition to my good behavior, will put me back in your good graces and win me your friendship, I shall consider myself as happy, indeed." He would show that he, too, could compose, and besides that his manners were worthy of a Caron.

It was the father this time who read aloud the paragraph, and pleased, shook the young man's hand. The women surrounded him, each seeking his cheeks to kiss. "We are so happy, Pierrot!" his mother said, her face muddied by tears, for she had come out of the kitchen and had had no time to wipe the soot and the grime of that ever-smoking oven. And all the girls chirped: "We are so happy, Pierrot! We are so happy!" And the happiest of them all was Marguerite-Julie, nicknamed *La Bécasse—The Woodcock*—signifying in French "the idiot," probably because, as a matter of fact, she was the brightest of them all, but alas, also the homeliest. Her affection for Pierrot, her brother's nickname (since they never used among themselves their names, only nicknames) was so profound that she remained a spinster in order to be with him always and take care of his house and of him. She was his best friend, defender, and advisor throughout her life, which terminated one year before his.

Purveyor to the King

It took a wise father to know his son, Pierre-Augustin mused as he scanned the entrails of a watch. His father was intelligent and educated and perhaps did not lack wisdom, but certainly he did not possess enough of it to understand him. How comical the way he made him sign formally the "Treaty of Peace of Rue Saint-Denis," historians would say some day. He could not get over his military attitude—a miserable career according to his mother. He had never risen even to the lowly rank of corporal, but now he acted as a conquering *maréchal*. Unconditional surrender, he laughed silently, his taut, athletic belly shivering.

Still, he had to acknowledge, it was a wily way of degrading him before his mother and sisters and he could not tell how many of the neighbors had read the document. He had seen several grin contemptuously as he passed them by. As for his friends, they turned their backs upon him as a traitor.

He could not deny that he was guilty of discourtesy toward his father, and was, as he said, an ungrateful son. Yet, was this the way to admonish him, make him feel like a schoolboy at the collège, his pants down and birched? This was something one found hard to overcome, and perhaps could never forget.

And the system of fines he imposed on him mercilessly for punctuality at High Mass. If he arrived late and after the Epistle, twelve *sous* deducted from the monthly allowance; if after the Gospel, twenty *sous;* if after the Elevation, all four *livres*. Why, he had been in debt three *livres* some months ago. And did this make him more devout? Hardly. He had begun to hate the church, because it meant loss of wages and of dignity.

No better than the way his teachers made him kneel on sharp-pointed logs for oversleeping.

Definitely, his father was unwise, although he might as definitely be right. This difference between "right" and "wise" he would try to unravel some day, because he had found the two in conflict, not only at home, but abroad. Oh, he had witnessed a lot (a great deal more than his father suspected) and garnered much wisdom from the folly of his conduct. As he saw things now, in perspective, he was glad he was not always a "good" son or a "good" scholar or a "good" neighbor. "Good" meant to conform, to accept prejudices and injustices without thinking for yourself and without daring to rebel. Of course, one was loved for being "good" and hated for being "bad," but maybe it was as necessary to be hated as to be loved. This, too, he would have to think out.

"*Mon père,*" Pierre-Augustin said, raising his head from his work, "the trouble with these watches is the escapement. It's too complicated and cumbersome."

"*Et alors?*" André Caron shrugged, without looking up.

"I intend to invent an anchor escapement which would make it possible for a watch to be as thin as a leaf and small enough to be worn in the ring of a lady."

"You do?" the father asked ironically.

"While the teeth of the little wheels should keep regular time," the youth continued his idea.

"Is that so?"

"You don't believe me, *mon père*—"

"Seeing is believing, *mon fils.*"

Yes, that was the way out of the disgrace, Pierre-Augustin thought, indignant at the incredulity of his father—invent something wonderful, surpass his father, surpass them all, all who doubted him, all who considered him a coward, all who saw in him nothing but a little watchmaker on Rue Saint-Denis, trembling before his father's wrath.

"Meanwhile," André said, "make sure that you have the watch of Condesa de Fuen Clara ready. She wrote me she would leave Madrid in a week and it's nearly two weeks now. She'll be here any day. We must not disappoint her."

"Why not? She hasn't paid any of her bills for nearly two years now—"

"That's true. Nevertheless, she belongs to the high nobility and we must consider ourselves flattered that she patronizes us."

"What did she do to belong to the high nobility, except take the trouble to be born? Does not the value of a man depend upon his intelligence and virtue?"

"Take care, *mon fils!* These are the words you must have heard in the cafés—the words of those subversives—Diderot and Rousseau—"

"But isn't it true?"

"Who are we to decide what is true? We have superiors for that. And anyway it's dangerous. The Carons have been law-abiding people for generations. Not one of us has ever seen the inside of a prison. I warn you, Pierre, stick to your last. I am a good deal older. I have seen many more things than you."

"*Oui, mon père.*"

"Live so that you are not suspected—that's the highest wisdom."

"*Oui, mon père.*"

"Ask no questions. Questions are often more dangerous than answers."

"*Oui, mon père.*"

"If things don't go right, laugh so that you may not weep."

"*Oui, mon père.*"

"And while we are at it, *mon fils,* watch your step with women, because a man goes hunting a girl and catches a family."

"*Oui, mon père.*"

"And remember it's as easy to fall in love with a rich girl as with one who has no dowry. I don't regret having married your mother. There is no better woman in the world, but poverty is a long road that rarely has a turning. And after you've spent a quarter of a century in a hole like this, you lose all sense of joy and beauty and you act like a boor at times—even to your own—"

Pierre-Augustin looked sharply at his father, who sat beside him behind the green-tainted shop-front, and realized that he was getting old—his hair thinning and turning grey—his cheeks crossed with deep furrows. And now the youth's anger and contempt changed into pity, and he understood that whatever variety of emotions he had entertained toward him, the foundation was love.

His father was a good man and his harshness was a cover for the love he bore his son. He feared that if he showed tenderness, the son might turn into an immoral tramp. And maybe also he had to counteract his mother's tendency to spoil him, and the sisters, too, and in particular Julie who made so much fuss over him. It was difficult to raise an only son, but he would show him —some day—that the son, in the final count, was not an ingrate. Some day—

In its issue of September, 1753, the *Mercure de France,* the country's most influential magazine, published a full-length account of the principles of the great discovery which would revolutionize the entire watchmaking industry, based upon a new theory of escapement for timepieces, the *Lepaute System.*

Pierre-Augustin cried out in anguish, when he read the article. "Betrayed! I've been betrayed!"

For some time now he had confided his plan to Jean-André Lepaute, one of the leading members of the Watchmakers' Guild and a prosperous merchant. The young man needed books to consult and the older one placed his well-stocked library at his disposal. Finally, after many months of intensive labor and study, Pierre-Augustin told Lepaute, whom he considered his patron, under vow of absolute secrecy, that he now was ready to put his theory into practice.

"*Très bien, mon ami, très bien,*" Monsieur Lepaute said, "let's try it on this clock. It's Monsieur de Julienne's, and if it doesn't come off right, we'll throw it out. I can do nothing with it in any case."

The experiment proved a triumph! The false friend immediately sent a communication to the French Academy of Sciences describing the escapement which *he* had invented and which would be called henceforth the *Lepaute System*. The news caused such excitement in the Capital that the *Mercure de France* considered it a patriotic duty to all Frenchmen, and indeed to the whole world, to spread it.

"As I have told you many times, *mon fils*," André Caron tried to console Pierre-Augustin, "the great always take advantage of the little, and nothing can be done about it!"

"Something *can* be done, and I am going to do it!" the young man declared, shaking his fist in all directions.

"I would not advise you to start up, Pierrot. That man Lepaute is dangerous. You can never tell where this may lead to," the father insisted. "There is no greater crime than that of being innocent. The weak are always guilty. A good Christian should turn his cheek."

"So that the criminal may slap both?" the youth asked sarcastically.

"In any case, he who barks should also have teeth."

Pierre-Augustin lent a deaf ear to his father's philosophizing. He would not accept so colossal an injustice. He sent a petition to the Academy of Sciences, stating his grievance, appending documents, sketches, calculations, as proof that the invention had been a long and steady growth, and challenged Monsier Lepaute to also present proof of a similar order. At the same time, he wrote to the *Mercure de France*:

"I have read with the utmost astonishment your number of September, 1753, in which Monsieur Lepaute, watchmaker to the Luxembourg, announces his invention of a new escapement for watches and clocks and which he says he had had the honor to lay before the King and the Academy.

"It is important to me in the interest of truth and my own

reputation to claim this invention as my own and not to remain silent over a great breach of confidence.

"I will not publish any of my proofs. They must first be placed before the Commissioners in all their strength. The discerning public will be kind enough to suspend judgment until then.

"I venture to flatter myself that you will consent to insert this letter in your next number.

"Caron, *fils*, Watchmaker, Rue Saint-Denis, near Saint Catherine's. Paris, November 15, 1753."

Little David challenged big Goliath and little David won again! Might is right, now and forever, only it is sometimes difficult to know whether might is a well-aimed stone or a huge sword clumsily wielded. The fly makes sport of the lion's tail.

On February 23, 1754, the Commission read its findings before the French Academy of Sciences, and the conclusion was unequivocal: Monsieur Pierre-Augustin Caron was the sole inventor of the escapement.

And Monsieur Jean-André Lepaute? A scoundrel trying to rob an ingenious young man of his valuable discovery. A scoundrel, who by his miserable effort at traducement, achieved immortality. Many a man's fame is rooted in infamy.

And so started four decades of almost perennial battles against insolence, lie, perjury, defamation, calumny, scandal, which Pierre-Augustin Caron, Sieur de Beaumarchais, encountered at every step in his astounding career.

One day, as Pierre-Augustin was sitting at his working-table, a messenger entered the shop and informed him that His Majesty commanded his presence at the Court of Versailles. All Rue Saint-Denis was astir, and since success determines values, the young watchmaker was now addressed with respect and ill-concealed flatteries. And some there were who, in order to minimize his importance, belittled royalty. We often endure our own evil fortune with more becoming grace than the good fortune of our friends.

Dressed as a young nobleman, Pierre-Augustin presented

himself to the King, who was well impressed with this handsome, modest, and intelligent young man. He deigned to ask him about the invention and Pierre-Augustin answered with scientific precision, yet adroitly enough to interest the monarch who, upon hearing that he could build a watch tiny enough to fit into a lady's ring, instantly ordered one for Madame de Pompadour, second of his notorious mistresses (the first being the Duchesse de Châteauroux, and the last Madame du Barry).

The work proved a success. The little shop on Rue Saint-Denis hummed with orders from the courtiers, and Pierre-Augustin Caron began calling himself "Purveyor to the King."

De Beaumarchais—Husband and Widower—Four Princesses

A strange bird appeared at the Court of Versailles, handsome of feather and pleasant of song. Such was the young man from Rue Saint-Denis, near Les Halles, inventor and maker of beautiful watches for the rings and the bracelets of ladies of high degree. And the ladies—they could, without being chided, pinch the downy pale cheeks and deposit, when especially well pleased with the work, pecks upon them. The gentlemen laughed at the antics of their females and the embarrassment, real or fictitious, of the stranded creature.

Madeleine-Catherine Francquet, however, did not look upon the "Purveyor to the King" either as an intruder or as a youth who could be treated with lack of formality. He was, in her opinion, a vital man, and her intuition told her he would become a remarkable one. She invited him to her house and introduced him to her husband, whose name happened to be—Pierre-Augustin. No gambler could find in any system of numerology a more auspicious number to bet on.

Monsieur Francquet was old enough to be the watchmaker's

father and he took to him, as all would who were not envious of his accomplishments or jealous of his successes. Monsieur Francquet was, among other things, a Contrôleur Clerc d'Office de la Maison du Roi, a sort of bookkeeper (one of sixteen) who checked the expense accounts of the royal kitchens at Versailles. Besides, upon solemn occasions, such as banquets and feasts, a contrôleur had the honor of joining the nobles in the long procession of serving the meat at the royal table. An honor not to be disdained, for everything that concerned the physical manifestations of His Majesty—sleeping, arising, eating, evacuating, fornicating—was of vast concern to his entourage, and he who had the honor and privilege of witnessing the performances was considered a favorite with the highest expectations. No hungry dogs ever fought so viciously over a bone as the lords fought over this juicy prerogative.

Monsieur Francquet had the gout, was bored with his commission, and was ready to sell it to his young friend and namesake—for a profit, naturally—in the ancient and accredited tradition of business. Thus, on November 9, 1755, Pierre-Augustin Caron was appointed Contrôleur d'Office and thereby became a courtier.

To further oblige him, Monsieur Francquet died suddenly of a cerebral hemorrhage, according to the reports of the physicians. Years later, when Caron had become a man of great wealth and international renown, the dogs that always dash after the victor on horseback barked wildly that he had murdered the old one.

Ten months after the demise of the former contrôleur, on November 1756, Madeleine-Catherine married Pierre-Augustin. She was several years older than he, but still pretty and charming and Caron *fils*, still tied to his mother's apron, preferred maturer women. When he grew old, to balance the burden of the years, he took to the very young, as is the nature of man.

Pierre-Augustin could at last leave the parental roof which, truth to say, had long pressed uncomfortably upon his head, and moved into the lovely home of his bride. Furthermore, to do things properly, he gave up the name of Caron and assumed that of Beaumarchais, after a small wooded property which had belonged to his wife, but which now, according to the law, was his. It was the common practice of the day to adopt estate names. Presently everybody addressed him as Beaumarchais, except those who wished to denigrate him and remind the world of his lowly origin.

To further establish himself as a man of consequence, on December 9, 1761, he bought for the solid sum of eighty-five thousand *livres* the office of Secrétaire du Roi, a position entailing neither work nor salary, but which removed him from faceless *hoi poloi* and raised him to the rank of *écuyer*—"squire"—the lowest rung of the ladder of nobility, to be sure, but still a nobleman. It gave him the legal right to add the glittering preposition *de*—de Beaumarchais.

This would be his dilemma throughout his mortal career—to be a lord and yet to be of the people—to be a lord and show up the weaknesses, the injustices, the futilities of the nobility, and to be a simple Frenchman and glorify the intelligence, the honesty, the goodness of his fellow-citizens. To be elegant and yet unaffected; to be haughty and yet modest; to be of the Court and also of Les Halles—the Market Place. And he was always pierced by one horn or the other.

And this, too, would be the quandary of his contemporaries. Who was Beaumarchais? The nobles rejected him; the populace mistrusted him. In the end, he reverted to his roots—he fought for freedom and equality on the two continents, and still he would not relinquish his ancient dream of rank.

His marital life was blissful, but alas, so short. For the gentle and loving Madeleine fell seriously ill. All the efforts of the ablest doctors of the day were futile and she died on the 29th of September, 1757. From the records extant her illness must have been an acute attack of typhoid fever—a common affliction in an age in which open sewers ran through the streets and the origin of all diseases was the intractable humor, blood, phlegm, choler,

or yellow bile, and melancholy, or black bile. A new and pretentious nomenclature for Satan and his hordes, who found the
body of man so pleasurable a habitation, teasing, tormenting,
and often ejecting its lawful, preordained tenant, the soul. But
why a pure spirit should choose ordure as its home has not yet
been convincingly explained.

The young widower was profoundly grieved by his loss and
perturbed by the insinuation that he had been the cause of his
wife's death, since he wished to obtain her wealth. As a matter
of fact, he inherited nothing and even gave up his house to the
members of her family.

But time brought consolations, chief of which now was the
friendship of the four Mesdames—Louise, Sophie, Victoire,
and Adelaïde, ranging in age from twenty-two to twenty-seven,
daughters of Louis XV, *le Bien-Aimé,* who had cute nicknames
for them—Logne, Coche, Chiffe, Graille.

Louis XV, great-grandson of Louis XIV, was born in 1710
and was five years old when he became heir to the throne. At
thirteen he attained legal majority and at fifteen his first minister repudiated his betrothal to a Spanish princess and procured
his marriage to Maria Leszczynska, daughter of the exiled king
of Poland, then resident of Alsace. She bore him seven children,
of whom four daughters and one son survived, but the son was
to die before mounting the throne and the Salic Law forbade
the succession to go to any female descendant. What, under the
circumstances, should a father do with four daughters—a father
who had a legal wife, accredited mistresses, and a reputed
seraglio at Parc aux Cerfs? What, but protect them from the
carnal embrace of the male—make them nuns, if not *de jure,* at
least *de facto,* and coil them with such chains of reverential etiquette that they would be virtually walled in a cloister?

The four Mesdames were rarely seen at court, and those who
caught glimpses of them reported that they were rather unprepossessing, stout, morbidly timid, and slow-witted, the natural
outcome of so virtuous and pious an existence.

Their father, pleased with their conduct, visited them when-

ever the plethora of passion rendered him chaste and worthy of
encountering purity. Always, at such times, he was a fond parent
and ready to satisfy their whims. In the year 1759, their whim
was to learn how to play the harp properly. There was not at
court or out of it a man better suited for the job than Monsieur
Beaumarchais, charming, handsome, courtly, yet one who would
know "his place."

The Princesses saw him and instantly accepted him. For four
years, Beaumarchais visited them every week. For the sole
pleasure of being with them, refusing all other compensations,
he not only taught them the harp, the guitar, the tambourine,
but composed musical pieces and sang songs to soothe their
nerves and relieve them from the perpetual boredom of their
seclusion. More still, to make their playing easier, he invented
a new pedal arrangement for the harp, which was promptly
adopted by all the harp makers.

Once His Majesty listened to his daughters' performance,
and particularly pleased, not only kissed their foreheads, but
tapped the shoulder of their teacher amicably. *"Très bien, monsieur, très bien."*

The fops witnessing the incident could no longer endure the
agony of their envy and began pinpricking the intruder. The
words "watch," "watchmaker," "Les Halles," always struck
his ears as he walked about the gardens or the salons. It was
easy to understand their far-from-subtle strategy. It meant that
although he had honestly bought his title and wore his costume
and sword with appropriate elegance, and although the four
Mesdames granted him their friendship and the King was pleas-
antly aware of his existence, he now and forevermore would remain a commoner, a watchmaker, son of a watchmaker.

Certainly, not all his annoyers had themselves been born of
aristocratic loins, and even more owed their existence to wombs
unsanctified by holy matrimony. What irritated them, however,
about Beaumarchais was not only his good luck, which they
knew could not last long, since the life expectancy of the favorite was that of a butterfly in the spring and could be terminated

in one instant, but his solid merits, his abilities, and it must be owned, his cockiness. If one borrowed feathers, one should not display them for all to behold.

Sensitive though Beaumarchais was, he accepted their pettiness with cold hauteur which only intensified their hatred. One day in the month of March, 1763, the Chevalier des C . . . renowned for his swordsmanship, asked a conundrum of a gathering of nobles: "What has hands, but does not tick?" "A watchmaker!" they all exclaimed, roaring with laughter. Beaumarchais, who was present, could not retain his position at court and accept the insult. And what meaning and savor would life hold for him if he returned to Rue Saint-Denis? He challenged the Chevalier to a secret duel, as was the custom of the day.

More than a century before, Richelieu, worried that duelling was decimating the aristocracy (the commonality was too insensitive to indulge in the luxury of mutual murder—a slap or a fist sufficed to redeem honor), forbade, under heavy penalty, its practice. Nevertheless, it persisted. As a propitiatory gesture in which only a "pink" spot is required, it still persists. To appear honorable, we are ready to commit all sorts of dishonorable deeds.

Beaumarchais had taken lessons in fencing, but what chance had he vis-à-vis so clever a wielder of the saber? Was the Chevalier too sure of himself? Did he first wish to tease his antagonist as a sarcastic cat teases a doomed mouse? Did he mock the watchmaker's clumsy, unorthodox gestures? At any rate, while dancing and prancing, suddenly to his vast amazement, he felt the deep thrust of steel into his entrails. He lingered for a few days, but would not name his adversary. "I got what I deserved. To please persons for whom I have no esteem I challenged somebody who had never given me offense."

His gallant last words, however, would not have saved Beaumarchais from the clutches of the police, for it was common knowledge who had dispatched the Chevalier's soul to its reward. Terribly worried, Beaumarchais confessed to the Princesses what had transpired, and how he, a man who harbored a profound respect for his fellow-man, unwillingly, and one might say, unwittingly, killed a member of an ancient family which, in all likelihood, would take a barbarous revenge.

Thrilled and delighted, the Princesses complimented him both for upholding his honor and for his skill in ridding himself of a brazen foe. Moreover, they spoke to their father about the incident, embroidering it so as to portray their teacher as a brave and spotless knight, the kind one found in the *Chanson de Roland* and in the *Roman de la Rose*.

Louis agreed with his daughters that the young man had done his duty by defending his honor and that the sword was a gentleman's natural means of retaliation to insult. Instantly, the monarch's words were relayed to all and sundry and neither the police nor the victim's relatives took any action against the incredible little watchmaker. The vilifiers, henceforth, were more circumspect, but at times, when envy could not summon facts against him, evil gossip could whisper that he had murdered three—a friend, a wife, and a nobleman. And how should one recognize truth since lie knows all its passwords?

Riches—Adventure in the Land of Don Quijote

At the age of seventy-five, Joseph Pâris-Duverney was not happy. He had been born a poor boy, son of an innkeeper in the village of Moirans, in the Département of Isère, and was now the head of a vast financial empire and the richest man of France. Richer than the King, for the King, who, in theory, was the owner of all things and all persons in the land, was in actuality forever in debt and forever fearful, for there is no slave so abject as a man in total power. Where a tyrant is there a dagger is being sharpened, and all sounds have the ominous echo of the rasping whetstone.

Pâris-Duverney was not happy, for he would die before long and be as quickly forgotten as the poor men who pullulated all about. What was wealth if it could not buy a century or two of memory among the living? He had, however, done something which might grant him posthumous glory—built the magnificent military college, l'Ecole Militaire on Champs de Mars. There five hundred cadets were receiving splendid training to become the heroes of France whenever enemies dared to attack her. But after his death what would become of this? Nothing! His faithless heirs would let it rot and spend their inheritance in an orgy of folly—of that he was certain.

This could be obviated on one condition only—that the King officially accept the school. He had tried on several occasions to get those near the monarch to broach the question, even including Madame de Pompadour, whom he had known when she was only Mademoiselle Antoinette Poisson. Labor lost. The potential interceders, either jealous of him or fearful of the response of the King, or aiming at other more profitable favors, rejected his proposal or promised and forgot.

Like everybody else at court, Pâris-Duverney had heard of a young man, a mere Contrôleur Clerc d'Office, who was a welcome guest in the quarters of the Mesdames and whose shoulder was tapped by the gracious hand of the King. Pâris-Duverney had not succeeded so spectacularly without "hunches," as the uninitiated call the ability to see the forest despite all the trees.

The financier informed himself minutely as to the young man's ways, his character, his abilities, and he was satisfied that he had come across an unusual personality. He made it his business to meet him as if by chance, which is the most elaborately calculated way, and as tangentially, he held out a possible affair that might be profitable to him—something in the nature which had made the fortune of Voltaire. "I am a man of business, Monsieur Beaumarchais," Pâris-Duverney said, "but I like to encourage and let us say, patronize, men of talents—literature, philosophy, inventions. In the final count, they are the ones who make the reputation of a nation, and I may even say, make her existence possible."

And incidentally, the old man mentioned the fact that his military college was flourishing, but it needed the official baptism to achieve permanence and validity. He said nothing more. If this handsome, bright-eyed young man could do that most difficult of arithmetical problems—put two and two together—then there would be no end to the favors he might bestow upon him. But he would not offer him the solution ready-made.

Beaumarchais *was* an excellent mathematician. One day, when the Princesses seemed more bored than ever and even his playing and singing could not soothe their spirits, he said: "Mesdames, there is in Paris, on Champs de Mars, a building, a beautiful building where handsome young officers parade on foot and on horseback in a most elegant manner, and their *marches militaires* are the most stirring in France. Would Mesdames care to visit the place?"

They clapped their hands. "*Oui! Oui! Oui!*"

"And may I have the honor to accompany Mesdames?" the wily teacher asked.

"*Oui! Oui! Oui!*"

It was a triumphant expedition. He did not have to instruct them to relate their marvelous adventure to their royal *papa* that evening. They marched and pranced about, as if they had been the officers *and* the horses. His Majesty laughed. He did not wish them to ever grow beyond blessed and simple-minded girlhood. "You should go and see the place, *mon père!*" Madame Adelaïde, the smartest of the girls and often their spokesman, suggested. "*Ah, oui! Ah, oui!* You should, *mon père!*" the other trio chimed in.

And so it happened that on August 18, 1760, eight years after its construction, His Majesty, King Louis XV, visited the Ecole Militaire and officially recognized it as a royal school. Thus Joseph Pâris-Duverney had his wish fulfilled. Two centuries have passed and his monument still stands and within its walls young men still learn the great art of magnificent murder.

"I swear I shall treat you as my son, Pierre-Augustin," Pâris-Duverney embraced him. And he kept his vow. For ten years they collaborated on many important affairs, and soon Beaumarchais was a very wealthy man. At the age of thirty-one he bought a spacious home, which he furnished in grand style. He hired several servants, a chef, a coachman, a groom, and a personal valet. He had carriages and horses. He had traveled far and fast since his father had made him sign "the treaty of peace."

And his prophecy had come to pass. He would show his father his filial love and consideration. First of all, the old man should give up his dark hole of a shop and come to live in this comfortable mansion, and with him all his sisters. From now on and until the end of his life, he would support them, their husbands, their children, as necessity demanded.

"From the bottom of my heart," his father said, "I bless Heaven for finding, in my old age, a son with such an excellent nature. . . . My soul rises and warms itself at the touching idea of owing my happiness, after God, to him alone. . . . You are the honor of my gray hairs, and I pray the Almighty every day to bless you, to recompense you, to preserve you from all accidents. . . . These will be the wishes of your good friend and affectionate father."

Sister Julie, still unprepossessing, but cheerful and vivacious, and moreover worshiping her brother, became the lady of the house. To identify herself the more with him, she discarded the name of Caron and henceforth called herself Mademoiselle de Beaumarchais, a title to which she had no legal right. But she dared anyone to dispute her *moral* right, due to the great love she bore her brother.

"Our house [No 26 Rue Condé]," wrote Julie, "is a regular dovecote where everyone lives on hope and love. I am the one who laughs most because I am the least in love." Beaumarchais himself was smitten with Pauline Le Breton. The young lady was born in Santo Domingo of a wealthy family of French planters. Seventeen and unsophisticated, she could not cope with the vagaries of this eternally romantic man, who leaped from one mood to another like a young goat. "Beaumarchais is a naughty fellow who worries Pauline by his levity," Julie wrote.

However, in the end, it was this timid maiden who made sport of her tormentor by jilting him and marrying another—a Chevalier de Séguirand. Unfortunately, the Chevalier died one year after the marriage, and the poor widow became involved in the most intricate financial difficulties which pestered her for the rest of her mortal career.

The son of Mercury and Venus, the clown Cupid, did not limit himself to the young members of the household, but aimed one of his arrows at the heart of the ancient dragoon, poor André Caron, widower for the last half-dozen years. The lady in the case was the dowerless but decent widow, Madame Henry. Even as the father had once moralized the son, so the son now showed his displeasure at the ways of his father, who, in his estimation, should have remained faithful to the memory of his sainted mother until the end of his days. But he reasoned that time was not a weaver of laurels and old heads lacked both the crown of wisdom and the crown of hair, and accepted the inevitable. André Caron married for a second time. As modesty demanded, the couple moved into a small house of their own, expenses all paid by the son who, however, would avenge himself upon his father's lack of virtue by making him the prototype of a lecherous old fool in his play.

Two of Beaumarchais' sisters had left France and made their residence in Madrid. Marie-Josèphe, married to a Frenchman, was doing fairly well as the owner of a millinery shop. Marie-Louise, however, was in difficulties. A spinster at thirty-four, she was in love with a *hidalgo* from the Canary Islands, Don José Clavijo y Fajardo. How platonic the relationship between these two was will always remain a mystery, but when Clavijo finally obtained an excellent position as editor of *El Pensador,* and did not marry her, the Madrileños, famed for their malicious gossip, began to cackle in all the cafés.

Lisette, in her distress, called to her brother for help. Don Quijote, Knight of the Sorrowful Face, thy sons are not limited to those born on the soil of Spain! In all lands, in all climes, speaking all tongues, they are born. Many are unaware of their immortal Father, but thy sign is upon their foreheads, ineradicable, glowing with glorious folly. And Pierre-Augustin Caron de Beaumarchais called back to his sister: "Thy brother is coming to save thee and thy honor!"

Beaumarchais took leave of the four Princesses, and when he told his friend, Pâris-Duverney, of his intentions, the aged fox said: "*Mon fils,* while you are on a journey to rescue a maiden in distress, which is quite laudable, why not add to it—on the side —a little practical business which also is not without its merits?" With a letter of introduction from the Prime Minister of France to the Prime Minister of Spain and Pâris-Duverney's two hundred thousand *livres* in his pockets, Monsieur de Beaumarchais started out by stagecoach on the first of May, 1764, and arrived in Madrid a fortnight later.

The maze-like plots of his own comedies are as straight paths compared to the tortuous dealings with that rotund little Don José Clavijo y Fajardo, slippery son of the Fortunate Isles. Madrid held its belly from laughter. Beaumarchais would not give up. Don José signed papers and vanished, signed more papers and vanished again. He wept and vowed and recanted, then took refuge with one friend, then another.

Finally, in desperation he went to the police and complained that the Frenchman, at the point of a gun, forced him to sign a promise of marriage to his sister, Mademoiselle Caron. Now Beaumarchais was in peril, and he was warned to desist or risk imprisonment. Indeed, it was safer for him to return to France. The French Ambassador would gladly put a carriage and six mules at his disposal for the purpose. But Beaumarchais who had fought the man who stole his invention and won, and fought a duel with the smartest sword-wielder at the Court of Versailles and won, was not the type to turn tail in a struggle with a swivelling little trickster who had made his sister the laughing-stock of the Spanish Capital.

He managed through the efforts of a Señor Wahl, a man of high prestige in Spain, to secure an audience with His Most Christian Majesty, King Carlos III. He was accustomed to the ways of kings and knew how to flatter—an art beyond the capacity of most who try it, for there are flatterers whose tongues strike like the tongues of snakes. The shrewd flatterer discovers our Achilles' heel and he strokes it and salves it and scents it; the clumsy flatterer praises our evident qualities and stifles us with superfluous incense. Beaumarchais emerged triumphant from the palace and the Canarian was promptly dismissed from his important post as the Keeper of the Crown Archives (for he was a man of talent and ability) and declared henceforth ineligible for any position in His Majesty's government.

Now gossip altered its direction, and the tongues, like weathercocks, turned in the fresh wind. Beaumarchais was not the ridiculous Frenchman who was outwitted by the crafty Spaniard. He was the noble knight who defended the honor of his sister and the prestige of his country.

No longer did they offer him carriage and mules for retreat in ignominy, but begged him to be the honored guest. The mangy dog was now transformed into the noble lion, a hair from whose great mane was as a feather in one's cap. There was, among other delights for Monsieur de Beaumarchais, his affair with the Marquise de La Croix, described by contemporaries as "the essence of majestic beauty and the ideal of a Roman empress." At any rate, she was pretty and what is even more important, accessible. But the crowning glory was his introduction of the Marquise to His Majesty, who granted her a substantial pension, raised her husband to the rank of Commander of the Order of Santiago, and pinned upon his valiant, cuckolded chest a diamond cross, symbol of salvation. And Carlos III, widower for the last four years, was no longer lonesome and melancholy.

Beaumarchais, meanwhile, had not forgotten his second mis-

sion—that of Pâris-Duverney. For months he tried to interest
the responsible agencies and authorities in various enterprises
which would make Spain once more rich and powerful—trade
monopoly in Louisiana; transporting African slaves on French
ships to American colonies; repopulate the Sierra Morena re-
gion; revive Spanish agriculture. But Spain was the cricket of
Europe and she preferred to sing on. Oh, she would have to
dance—and it would be a dance of death—but that was—ma-
ñana.

And Clavijo—what had become of the wretch who would
rather suffer so many indignities than become a husband? Clavijo, terrified by the Frenchman who associated with royalty,
took refuge in a monastery. But he longed to return to life and
to work—as a bachelor. He wrote to Monsieur de Beaumarchais begging his forgiveness and imploring his mercy. That was
all that was needed. Beaumarchais was not the man to harbor
animosity or to take pleasure in hurting an enemy who was
ready to throw away his sword. "He was right to count upon
it," Beaumarchais wrote at a later date. "I hated him no longer.
Indeed, I never hated anyone in my life." And that was the
fundamental characteristic of the nature of the man. He never
hated. There was no malice in his heart. Bitter foes who had
sought to ruin him he forgave and when they were in distress,
he helped, often unbeknown to them. One of them cried out: "I
looked for a man, I found a god!" Not only did Beaumarchais
forgive the man he had come to Spain to punish, but was instrumental in rehabilitating him, and Clavijo lived long and had a
brilliant career and remained a bachelor.

Beaumarchais left Spain at the end of March, 1765. What
had he accomplished? Nothing. Clavijo never married his sister.
He had been unable to interest anyone in his business, despite
the heavy bribing and the fabulous promises. The adventure
with Marquise de La Croix left a taste of ashes in his mouth, for
in retrospect it took the shape of a procurer's deed.

"Nothing—nothing—" he mused as the mules pulled his
coach across the frontier. "Nothing." How was he to know that

his visit would lay the foundation for his renown and his immortality? How was he to know that permeated with the spirit of Spain, he would write his two masterpieces, redolent of that mysterious nation which is neither Europe nor Africa, but something unique and forever elusive to logic and to criticism?

Le Barbier de Séville

Charles Lenormant d'Etioles was the husband of the Marquise de Pompadour, official mistress of Louis XV. The horns he wore, therefore, were of pure gold, and what husband of the realm would not have considered it an honor only slightly less grand than that of a crown? Still, that he might not cause envy —and perhaps also laughter—among the noble loafers at Versailles, he retired to his castle, the Château d'Etioles.

To drown whatever sorrow he might have secretly endured at the loss of his beautiful wife, he spent his time in almost incessant revelry—banquets, masquerades, shows. Frequently, the actresses were the lesser luminaries of the Parisian theaters, and it is an ancient fact that often the stage is but the hallway to the boudoir.

After the death of his wife, Madeleine-Catherine, in 1757, Beaumarchais sought assuagement at the Château d'Etioles, where he proved not only a merry guest but an excellent master of ceremonies. He improvised sketches, witty and ribald, composed tuneful songs, caricatured personages of the world of politics and nobility. It was, in short, a laboratory where he learned many of the tricks of the art which was to make him famous.

When he returned to Paris after the brilliant but futile adventure in Spain, Beaumarchais found everything changed— and for the worse. Even the gaiety of the Château d'Etioles no longer appealed to him. His mind sought refuge from the disillusions and difficulties. Having seen Diderot's play, *Le Père de Famille,* he decided to write one himself in that same vein.

The plot of *Eugénie* is in the tradition Diderot had made famous—the *drame*—a play dealing with the common folk, their struggles, their tragedies, and their triumphs. Eugénie is an innocent and pure girl, seduced by a rascally nobleman who deceives her by contracting a fake marriage. Abandoned and miserable, Eugénie confides in her brother, a noble man, not of title but of heart. He forces the deceiver to repent and "since the soul of a libertine is unfathomable," the girl forgives him. Now he marries her "for good," and so finds peace with himself and the esteem of decent people.

Fearful of offending the French aristocracy, Beaumarchais laid his plot in England, but it was too evident that the characters were French and that the impudent watchmaker had dared to insult and ridicule his betters. Little did the glittering gang guess that this was only the beginning and that in his future plays, those which were not to die with the passing generations, he would flay them and grill them with the fires of sarcasm, and even—but this unwittingly—smooth the path of the Revolution and their annihilation.

As was to be his literary fate, Beaumarchais was also assailed by the playwrights and the critics. To them, Beaumarchais was a turncoat, and since he became rich into the bargain, he was presumptuous and had no business in their business. Beaumarchais himself never felt comfortable in the society of the *philosophes* and men of letters, such as Diderot and d'Alembert, conscious as he was of lack of formal education, while these men were eminent scholars and scientists. That his plays would outlive the works of all the others, neither he nor they could know, or knowing would alter their attitudes—they of contempt, he of disdain.

Eugénie was presented at the Comédie-Française on June, 1767, and died in the storm of ridicule after a few performances. Seven years later, however, the play was revived and was a hit. Only to the most naive success and merit run parallel. The others know that the fortunate moment determines all; that luck is the most persuasive of barkers and wherever his finger points there the crowds gather.

Disgusted with both the aristocracy and the society of letters, Beaumarchais decided to become a full-fledged man of business. For the time being lumber was the most profitable of investments. In partnership with Pâris-Duverney, as he would be until the death of the old man, Beaumarchais bought a great forest in Touraine. He went personally to supervise the felling of the timber and lived the rough and wholesome life of an overseer. Like Figaro, his great creation, he had to be the factotum and as such he dealt both with laborers and representatives of various businesses. There was a decency and reliability among these people that he had never found among the nobles with their cynicism, craftiness, and corruption.

Back in Paris, Beaumarchais wrote *Les Deux Amis*—The Two Friends—a *drame* portraying the uprightness of the new world he had been in. Two friends, merchants, placed in an embarrassing situation financially, are ready to sacrifice their honor and their lives for each other. The play, as by prescription, ends happily, the heroes rewarded for their nobility. The plot is surcharged with the technicalities of the trade, which bored the spectators. The play was presented at the Comédie-Française on January, 1770 and was still-born. An enemy with a sardonic sense of humor wrote on the posters announcing the performance of *Les Deux Amis*—"The Two Friends" By One Who Has None.

In gossipy Paris the wag's remark caught on quickly and for a long while persisted in annoying the poor author. At this time, Beaumarchais had no friends and a multitude of enemies, but in the final count the quality of a man's enemies rather than the number of his friends indicates the true measure of his success. And among his enemies, Beaumarchais could name the luminaries of his day.

One man, however, remained his perdurable friend until the end of his mortal days—thirty years—during which neither

Beaumarchais' successes nor his grievous failures nor the perilous adventures which brought him to the brink of the scaffold altered his love and his admiration or the readiness to sacrifice himself.

Paul Philippe Gudin de La Brenellerie, of Huguenot ancestry, had studied for the ministry at Geneva, but the city of Calvin, murderer of Servetus, had not yet, two centuries later, quite dissipated the unrelieved harshness of that unrelenting man of God. Gudin, breathing the leaden atmosphere, lost his religious faith and decided to become an author in the manner of Voltaire, whom he met at Fernay. Not that he had dared to aspire to the dizzy eminence of that immortal, but his books should ridicule and chastise intolerance and bigotry.

The works of Gudin had little merit and less success, but his artistic vanity was assuaged by the fact that one of his tragedies was burned with pompous solemnity by the Inquisition.

Some years earlier, Beaumarchais had witnessed the performance at Etioles theater of Noland de Tautouville's play *La Précaution Inutile,* which inspired him to write a similar comedy. *Le Barbier de Séville,* a sketchy affair only adumbrating the final form of the masterpiece, was nevertheless well received by the audience at the Château, always indulgent toward its habitués. Now idled by the current bad financial situation in France which was defeated, dishonored, and impoverished by the futile Seven Years' War, Beaumarchais returned to his play. His hand was steadier and his understanding of mankind deeper. He breathed life into his characters and barbed the dialogue with wit and satire against the nobility which had screwed up its nose at his presence and whose folly and presumptuousness had ruined the nation.

The plot of the *Barber* has no element of the avant-guard, for Beaumarchais was not interested in novelties of intrigue. He even used the subtitle, *La Précaution Inutile*—"The Useless Precaution," borrowed, without permission, from the play of De Tautouville—a gesture common among authors of the day. Plagiarism had a much less immoral connotation. An author was chiefly concerned with doing better, rather than innovating. A plot was used again and again and the creation which finally achieved perfection remained as a permanent piece of literature. Authors and artists were not afraid to compete with past masters, which is the basic reason why extreme innovation is sought by the moderns.

The plot of *Le Barbier de Séville* is a very ancient one—youth versus age, with youth emerging triumphant. Count Almaviva comes from Madrid to Seville in search of a maiden by the name of Rosine, whom he has seen in the Capital and with whom he has been smitten beyond cure. The young lady, however, is now practically a prisoner in the house of Doctor Bartholo, her ward, who not only is arranging to keep her fortune entrusted in his care, but also to make her his wife.

And who is this Doctor Bartholo? He is "an old libertine, covered with pimples, boring, wrinkled, bleary-eyed, jealous, silly—a poor devil, in turn coughing, spitting, growling, whining. A widower for the second time and no longer a gallant novice, he wants to play the lively young blade all over again."

Critics have it that the picture is that of Beuamarchais' own father—revenge on the man, who at the age of seventy-six, again a widower, was on the lookout for a third bride. He discovered her in the shape of his housekeeper, whom he married despite his children's disgust and displeasure. Love's strain, however, ended his mortal career a half-year later. But the evil he left behind did not end, for the widow, an unscrupulous female, produced a document, signed by the ancient dragoon, in which he promised her a substantial sum. And the son, to avoid any more scandals—he was stewing in several—paid the woman six thousand *livres* and saved the soul of his father from the crackling fires of hell, where all debtors are hurled.

How achieve the release of the incomparable maiden, Rosine, from the ugly ogre's cave and claws? Alas, the glorious days were no more when a knight stormed a castle, put to the sword the wicked keeper, and galloped away with the beauteous prize! Count Almaviva walks up and down in front of the house, catching sight now and then of the unfortunate damsel gazing at him through the barred casement, mutely imploring deliverance from the horrible fate awaiting her.

But he is helpless. He is but the degenerate descendant of the great *hidalgos,* lacking both their skill and their strength. He, too, is locked in the prison of his impotence. Suddenly he becomes aware of a man strumming a guitar and singing couplets. The men stare at each other. "Monseigneur!" the guitarist exclaims. "Figaro!" the Count replies.

Figaro had been the Count's valet, but he left in order to better himself. Despite his many talents and abilities, however, he found the world a tough, unresponsive, and wicked place for one unsupported by titles and wealth, and now was engaged as barber and factotum to Doctor Bartholo, nastiest of humans.

"From what I remember, Figaro," the Count says without malignity, "you were rather lazy, unreliable—"

"My faith, Monseigneur, they expect the poor to be without fault. . . . Considering the virtues demanded of a servant, does Your Excellency know many masters worthy of being valets?"

They reminisce and philosophize, in good Spanish fashion, a while longer, and the Count confesses his objective and the insurmountable difficulties he is encountering. Figaro promises to bring about the consummation of his passion, provided the Count follows his instructions to the letter, which, of course, is accepted with alacrity.

This delights the Barber's soul, for it emphasizes the superiority of the vital bourgeois over the decadent aristocrat. For who, in truth, is Figaro but Pierre-Augustin Caron before he appended "de Beaumarchais" and tried to crash the worm-eaten gate—Pierre-Augustin Caron, shrewd, inventive, courageous, cheerful—and honest—in the manner of one of the characters of the play, Bazile, who says: "In cases difficult to judge, a purse filled with gold pieces seems to me an argument which brooks no retort. . . ." Or as Figaro himself explains to the Count: "I shall not employ grandiose phrases of honor and

devotion. . . . I have but one word—my interest answers for
me . . . weigh this in the balance."

The play is one day in the lives of the characters, but never
had the stage witnessed such a day of gaiety, frivolity, tenseness,
near-tragedy, and surprises without end. The trite and artificial
plot seems a story newly-minted in the vast repertory of comedy.
There is the picturesque setting of Spain with its romantic ex-
aggeration. Ever after, no foreigner could write a novel, a
play, an opera with Iberian background in a sober, terrestrial
manner. Not a single character is waxen, however hackneyed he
may be. And Figaro—Figaro, half Don Quijote, half Sancho
Panza, would never die—Figaro, the amalgam of good and
evil, wisdom and folly, truth and lie, tear and laughter.

Besieged by Figaro and his accomplices, some bribed, some
unwitting, and flanked by the Count and Rosine, who despite her
innocence, possesses the usual feminine wiles, Doctor Bartholo
battles heroically to free himself. On more than one occasion it
seems that he will succeed, but always there is Figaro with his
battery of traps to turn him back. And the audience sits on pins
and needles. Not until the last few moments of the last scene is
it certain that the play will end happily—that is, unhappily for
the old man. "The pieces are old, but the game is entirely new,
for although one of the players advances ceaselessly, his success
is compromised at each move by the defensive skill of his op-
ponent, and we do not breathe freely until the latter is check-
mated."

Finally, Bartholo surrenders, but he is not completely defeated. He is allowed to keep the money that had been entrusted
in his care as dowry for his pupil, for Almaviva is wealthy and
noble and scorns the "filthy lucre." He obtains the maiden and
marries her right there and then. The couple lives happily for
three years, when there is trouble in the Count's household, and
again Figaro will come to the rescue—but of this in due time and
place.

"Let's face it," Figaro tells the dazed Doctor Bartholo,
"when youth and love conspire to deceive an old man, all he

may do to stop it may properly be called—Useless Precaution."

Le Barbier de Séville or *La Précaution Inutile,* after many
hitches, was finally presented at the Comédie-Française on
February 22, 1775. The première was a flop. When the play
was first conceived, some years previously, the climate of the
country was one of despair and anger against the Court of Versailles and the aristocracy in general which had plunged France
into war and misery. But in 1775 things looked brighter. Louis
XV was dead; Louis XVI would rule justly; and even the nobles
no longer seemed such monsters. The audience seeking only
amusement was bored and resented Beaumarchais' satire,
barbed with sarcastic comments.

Beaumarchais instantly understood the cause of the failure
and overnight altered the tone of the play by removing the bitter
and ironic remarks (which he kept for a future work, for he was
still full of bile), leaving only the delightful comedy of loving
youth defeating hated old age. The play as shown on February
23 was an indisputable hit.

The cabal, however, was at it again. "The reputation of Sieur
de Beaumarchais has certainly fallen; and the good people are
at last convinced that, if one should pluck out his peacock's
plumes, he would remain but an ugly black crow with his ef-
frontery and voracity." Such was the tone of the critics, but the
public applauded and was delighted and would applaud and
be delighted generation after generation. Beaumarchais joined
the ranks of the leading playwrights of France and found a
permanent niche in French letters.

But he was enraged and in an introduction to the published
play, he pilloried and slashed and quartered his critics as few
authors have done and fewer still as ably. Dressed modestly,
back bent, the Author presents his play TO THE READER:

"Monsieur,
I have the honor to offer you a new little work in my own
way. I hope to meet you in one of those happy moments when
relieved of cares, content with your health, with your business,

with your mistress, with your dinner, with your stomach, you may take a moment of pleasure in reading my *Barbier de Séville;* for one needs all that in order to be willing to be an amused and indulgent reader. . . .

"Plays, Monsieur, are like women's children. Conceived in voluptuousness, borne with fatigue, delivered with pain, and rarely living long enough to repay their parents of their cares, they cause more chagrin than they offer pleasures."

Beaumarchais takes up item by item which displeased the critics and "those illiterates" who wrote to him and to the actors, shrewdly pointing out their stupidity, their crudity, their malignity, meanwhile deftly praising his own work. "The play, one of the gayest ever presented in a theater, is written without the least equivocation, without one single thought, one single word which might do violence to modesty . . . which is something, Monsieur, in a century in which hypocrisy toward decency is carried almost as far as looseness of morals."

And now the melancholy plaint of all the authors in all the ages, in all the tongues: "A bad play is not an evil action, and the punishment to be meted out to a bad man is not proper to a bad author." Beaumarchais pleads with the public to discount the critics and judge for themselves. A long, helpless cry in the wilderness, for the people ever follow the critics as the mesmerized children followed the Pied Piper, and like them, are lost in the woods and devoured.

Before long composers began to recognize in *Barbier de Séville* a peerless work for the opera. A dozen or more tried their hands at various times, but either their music did not convey the spirit of the drollery, the cockiness, the depth of sentiment, or else the librettist squeezed the living juices out of the characters, making them limp about the stage like puppets pulled by strings not too-well oiled.

It was not until Gioacchino Rossini (1792–1868) that the book found at last its master composer. At twenty-four, gay and successful, Rossini was precisely the man to respond to the vivaciousness and feel the emotions of the Beaumarchais master-piece. *Il Barbiere di Siviglia* was first presented in Rome on February 20, 1816. Strangely enough, it suffered the same fate as the première of *Le Barbier de Séville,* at the Comédie-Fran-çaise, forty years before. It was a total flop, due in this case to petty untoward incidents, such as the snapping of a cord of the guitar and its tuning on the stage, and a black cat running be-tween Figaro's legs, which made the gallery mew and snicker and strum. And as with its forerunner, the next night *Il Bar-biere* was an extraordinary triumph.

Even as the play had placed Beaumarchais in the forefront of dramatists, so the opera crowned Rossini as one of the world's great composers. Rossini never created a masterpiece equal to this, but Beaumarchais wrote a greater play still—*Le Mariage de Figaro.*

Le Mariage de Figaro—An Author Spanked

Three years have passed since Count Almaviva with the as-sistance of the inimitable Figaro outwitted old Doctor Bartholo and married the incomparable maiden Rosine. The couple now live in the Castle of Aguas-Frescas, three leagues from Seville and Figaro is the devoted valet and concierge. Among the many people who take care of the great estate—peasants, servants, shepherds, there is Suzanne, first lady's maid of the Countess, a pretty and provocative wench, fiancée of Figaro. Because of his love for Rosine, Count Almaviva officially relinquished the *Jus Primae Noctis* among his villagers—the lord's right to the bride's first night—but he has taken a fancy to Suzanne and would like to make her his mistress.

Doesn't he love his wife anymore? "I love her very much, but three years of marriage makes love so respectable!" What does he want of her? "I do not know . . . less uniformity, perhaps, something more piquant in her ways, a *je ne sais quoi* which makes for charm; a refusal now and then . . . *que sais je—* what do I know? One is surprised one fine evening to find satiety where one sought happiness. . . ."

Suzanne, however, despite all the inducements, desires to remain faithful to her fiancé, who is informed of the Count's maneuvers. Rosine, too, is duly warned. And so the trio set out to outwit Almaviva, as once Bartholo had been outwitted. Involved with the trio there is a fourth character—Chérubin—the Count's first page and the godson of the Countess. Chérubin is thirteen or fourteen, neither man nor boy, possessing the wild-eyed innocence of the latter and the baser promptings of the former. All in all, a charming little rascal, full of deviltry, a poetic tongue, and deeply in love with Rosine—in short, a creation as eternal as Figaro.

"I do not know any more who I am," he explains his vagaries to Suzanne, "but for some time now I feel my chest agitated; my heart raps at the very presence of a woman; the words '*amour*' and '*volupté*' make it tremble and trouble it. The need to tell someone 'I love you,' has become for me so urgent that I say it running through the park, alone; I say it to your mistress, to you, to the trees, to the clouds, to the wind which carries my lost words. . . ."

Useless to state that Chérubin is Beaumarchais himself during that fragile dawn of life, for no author was as personal as he. Indeed, he was a little of each character and the members of his family were all included in the cast. His efforts at detachment in the grand manner of the sophisticated aristocrats proved ludicrous and only emphasized the expansive nature of the man of the people.

To what extent Rosine reciprocated the youth's passion is difficult to fathom, for she, too, like her husband, experienced that normal need for the refreshment of love, but she could conceal it under the cloak of maternal feeling. (Years later, in the third play of the Figaro trilogy, we discover to our discomfiture that upon a certain date Chérubin and the Countess had had an affair with disastrous consequences.) In *Le Mariage de Figaro*, however, Rosine is chaste, but the awkward, yet delightful love-making of Chérubin renders the Count jealous, for every man desires fidelity in one woman and infidelity in all the rest—and that is what generally happens.

Other personages, too, are caught in the dragnet. There is Marceline, middle-aged *femme de charge*—caretaker of laundry, silverware, and other valuables. She is in love with Figaro and is determined to marry him, as per a contract he has signed. He borrowed a considerable sum of money from her on the basis of repayment or marriage. He is unable to fulfill the former and unwilling to do the latter.

There is Bartholo again, much attenuated, but essential to the dénouement. There is Antonio, a real man of the people. By his honest remarks he causes consternation and embarrassment all around. His philosophy is simple: "To drink without being thirsty and make love in all seasons—that's the only thing that distinguishes man from all other animals."

And there is Don Gusman Brid'Oison, the judge, whose ignorance, formalism, and pomposity have made him the ridiculous man of the bench in French life and letters. Beaumarchais himself had been a judge for twenty years—Lieutenant Général des Chasses aux Baillage et Capitanerie de la Varenne du Louvre—a post which he bought, as judgeships generally were. His judicial duties concerned the enforcement of game laws, particularly those in the royal preserves for a radius of fifty miles around Paris. The statutes harked back to the Middle Ages and the penalties meted out were extremely harsh.

In the ridiculous person of Brid'Oison, Beaumarchais exposes the cruel injustices perpetrated in the courts of France during the reign of Louis XV, the foolish technicalities and the hollow verbosity. From sheer self-importance Brid'Oison stammers. "Let us sp-speak verbally. . . . I-I—un-understand—etcetera—etcetera—and the rest. . . . You see—you see—the

fo-fo-form. As for me, I do not know wh-what to say—that's
my fash-fashion of thinking."

Figaro, as his wont, challenges the aristocracy (much more
openly than he did as the Barber) and this time in the person of
Almaviva, to whom he is faithful, but with whom he does not
wish to share the marriage bed. "Because you are a great lord,
you believe you are a great genius! Nobility, fortune, rank,
position, all that makes you so proud! What have you done to
enjoy so many advantages? You have taken the trouble to be
born—and nothing more! While I, *mon Dieu,* lost in obscurity,
I needed more science and skill to merely survive than were
needed to govern Spain for a hundred years. . . . You need
intellect to advance? My lord mocks me. . . . Mediocre and
crawling, and you succeed in everything. . . . Pretend not to
know what one knows and to know what one does not know; to
understand what one does not understand and not to hear what
one understands; appear profound when one is empty and
hollow . . . spread spies and pension traitors . . . try to ennoble
the poverty of means by the importance of objectives—that's
all there is to politics."

However, Beaumarchais is not primarily a critic of society
and will be surprised to find his plays construed as theses for
the Revolution. He is interested in the theater chiefly as a means
of entertainment, and he is supremely successful in *Le Mariage
de Figaro,* a comedy comparable to the best of Molière's. Within
the space of one "mad day"—the play has appropriately as its
second title, *La Folle Journée*—by means of a cataract of
sparkling dialogue and countless twists, gay and barbed with
suspense, Beaumarchais presents characters, full-blooded and
three-dimensional in the throes of variegated emotions—love,
hate, jealousy, ambition, vanity—the wisdom and the folly of
man.

The labyrinth Daedalus built for King Minos of Crete to
house the Minotaur was a simple toy-house compared to the
intricate edifice of *Le Mariage de Figaro*. In the end, however,
the exit is found, for the author has held on valiantly to the

guiding string of his plot and sub-plots. The Count is thwarted in his disgraceful effort to betray both his faithful servant and his faithful consort. He falls in love all over again with the woman whom only three short years before he had desired to the point of committing capital crime for her possession, and Figaro gets his Suzanne. But not without a coincidence acceptable in life, though hardly tolerated in art. Nature may allow herself the luxury of fictitiousness, but art must at all times be natural. Yet, the *deus ex machina* served the wily Greek playwrights without tarnishing their golden laurels; why not Beaumarchais?

Marceline, who was so eager, and according to the contract lawfully entitled, to marry Figaro is suddenly proved to be his mother! He had been kidnapped as a baby—the bastard son—one must use the harsh word, for alas, it was the truth—of a young innocent girl seduced by a conscienceless rascal whose name is—Bartholo!

"Deplorable fault," Marceline admits, "and greater than one would believe!... But how hard it is to expiate it even after thirty years and an honest life! I was born to be decent ... but in the period of illusion, of inexperience, and of needs, how can a child defend herself against so many enemies gathered about her? You men are worse than ingrates, who despise the toys of your passions, your victims! It is you who should be punished for the errors of our youth—you and your magistrates! Even in the highest ranks, woman obtains from you only a trifling consideration. Ah, under all conditions, your conduct toward us is horrible and pathetic!"

Bartholo, who at first is reluctant to accept the marital yoke, finally is convinced of its justice. Figaro becomes legitimized and the spectators, purged of evil thoughts and feelings, leave, ennobled for a fragile and fugitive moment of their lives.

As was his habit, Beaumarchais wrote only intermittently when the afflatus urged him or the pressures of affairs and the phlegm of rancor demanded relief. The first draft of *Le Mari-*

age de Figaro was finished in 1777, but the play was not produced at the Comédie-Française until April 27, 1784. Between those dates, however, Beaumarchais read the play in all the salons, and everywhere it was applauded. Chamfort, who also had heard the play read said that he had never known such a magician as Beaumarchais—Chamfort, the great *moraliste,* whose maxims rank only below those of La Rochefoucauld, and who later, during the Terror, committed suicide to escape the guillotine.

Queen Marie-Antoinette herself and her intimate friends heard the play and were delighted with the witty dialogue and the biting criticism of the aristocracy made them roar with laughter. They were the sophisticates and enjoyed watching the foibles of their class ridiculed so brilliantly. It was in the nature of gossip, and since it concerned all, no one in particular took offense. So pleased, indeed, were they that they were very eager to have the play produced in the Royal Theater of Versailles. But first they must obtain the permission of the King. It was, they believed, a mere formality, for the Monarch in the first place was not a connoisseur of letters, and besides, as the most pecked of henpecks, the Queen's wish would be his command.

The courtiers engaged Madame de Campan to read *Le Mariage de Figaro* in the presence of the King. Jeanne-Louise de Campan (1752–1822) was the principal of La Maison d'Ecouen, a school for the orphans of the members of the Legion of Honor. She wrote several books, among which the usual *Mémoires.* And in her *Mémoires* she says that the King, to the painful amazement of all present, suddenly burst out in anger. "It is detestable! It shall never be played! If this play were to be performed, the Bastille would have to be pulled down! That man dares to mock everything that should be respected in the government! It shall never be played!"

The poor man was right. Simple-minded, he sensed the danger which the sophisticates took lightly, unwilling to show that anything deserved too great a concern. These were the last few years of the *ancien régime* and one could afford the luxury of laughing at all things. The Revolution was approaching? Let it! It could be quenched by sprays of perfume! Not even Figaro of real life realized the depth of the meaning of his words which he put into the mouth of Figaro of the stage. How could he foresee the extent and the consequences of the Revolution? How could he foresee the unquenchable, maniacal lust for power of the protagonists? And to judge a man, newly appointed, by his past, is a grievous error. They were all children playing with fire. Later he wrote: "They owe it [the Revolution] to me, to me. My struggle for my own small career, which I achieved after I failed to make a really great success, developed into a mass struggle, which I did *not* desire."

When Beaumarchais was informed of the King's decision, his reply was almost treason. "The King does not want *Le Mariage de Figaro* played—therefore it shall be played!" First trumpet call to the Revolution!

Months passed, but the people did not forget Beaumarchais' challenge, while many of the noblemen regretted that so delightful a play had to be locked in the drawer of the author. With the tacit approval of the Queen, who had always been on the side of Beaumarchais, the play was performed in the Salle de Menus Plaisirs with much success, and since the King did not object this time, the actors of the Comédie-Française began rehearsals.

The date of the performance, June 13, 1783, was announced and the crowds gathered to buy tickets. A half-hour before curtain time, however, a messenger from the King informed the actors to desist "under the pain of incurring His Majesty's wrath." The actors had no alternative. They obeyed. The public, infuriated, rioted the whole night, shouting: "Oppression! Tyranny!"

"These words had never before the fall of the throne been pronounced with greater passion and greater vehemence!"

wrote Madame de Campan. The fall of Bastille was only six years, one month, and one day away. The mobs had begun the rehearsal.

In September of the same year, the Comte de Vaudreuil had the play shown at his own château. Beaumarchais received a wild ovation. The King continued to be obdurate, but the pressure grew ever greater, until finally he gave way and *Le Mariage de Figaro* was performed at the Comédie-Française. What a triumph! Seventy-three consecutive presentations and receipts equal to twenty-four million *francs* in modern French money! And seven times that sum eventually as royalties for the author!

The critics, as ever, buzzed like maddened wasps after the play. "The success of *Le Mariage de Figaro* is the greatest scandal of the day." Beaumarchais retorted: "Provided I do not speak in my writings of authority or religion or politics or morality or people in office or of anybody who belongs to anything, I am at liberty to say what I please, under the watchful eye of some two or three censors. . . . But I am not the enemy of my enemies. By saying evil of me, they have not done evil to my play; and if they have felt as much pleasure in tearing my play as I have had in writing it, no one would be grieved. . . . I know some amateur authors who have lost weight since my success with *Mariage*. Let us forgive them, therefore, their wrath."

But their envy was unassuaged. Unwittingly, Beaumarchais insulted the King's brother, one of his foes. The Comte de Provence complained to Louis, whose anger against the author had left some bile in his gall, and he ordered his imprisonment. To add a mock dramatic note, the Police Commissioner in person appeared at the fashionable Hôtel de Hollande where Beaumarchais was entertaining some friends of high social rank, presented the royal warrant, and bade him follow.

"*Adieu, mes amis!*" Beaumarchais waved to his guests. "La Bastille!" he exclaimed, not without elation. At long last the world which doubted him, maligned him, scorned him, would hail him as martyr in the war against tyranny! He would have his name carved into the golden tablet and he would join the immortals who had preceded him, including Voltaire! "de" Beaumarchais was but a hollow title compared to "de" La Bastille!

Alas, poor Pierre-Augustin Caron, the Monarch had a sense of humor! The Police Commissioner did not drive him to La Bastille but to Saint-Lazare! Saint-Lazare, the prison for juvenile delinquents who had committed petty crimes. There they would be detained for one night in solitary cells, given a spanking on their *fesses,* and released. Saint-Lazare for him—the great merchant, the great author, the great patriot! Had anyone ever endured so mean a disgrace? A heavy cross and nailed to his derrière!

Paris rocked with laughter. "Beaumarchais has much wit, but Monsieur de Beaumarchais is a fool." Such was the estimate of the populace. "High time he had received a good spanking! Bravo for His Majesty!" Some shouted: *"Bis! Encore!"* A few days later, however, public opinion made another volte-face. Antoine-Vincent Arnault, poet and writer of fables, says that the people now rebelled against the arbitrary power of the Court. "Everyone felt menaced in his own liberty."

Meanwhile, Beaumarchais refused to leave the prison, then changed his mind, went home, and shut himself in a self-imposed jail. He sent a *mémoire* to the King in which he easily proved that he had not meant to insult his brother and certainly was not guilty of *lèse-majesté*. The good-natured Monarch, on his part, promised never again to meddle in literary feuds, sent Beaumarchais the eighty thousand *livres* the government owed him, which, it seemed, would never be paid, accompanied by a very flattering letter.

Moreover, the King allowed the Queen to organize at Trianon a presentation of the *Barbier de Séville,* with the music recently composed by Giovanni Paisiello, the Italian master, and which remained the standard operatic work until Rossini com-

posed his, relegating it to oblivion. The Queen took the part of
Rosine; the Count d'Artois that of Figaro and Vaudreuil that
of Almaviva—a dazzling cast rarely equalled in the annals of
letters. No more adulatory reparation of the affront received by
Beaumarchais could have been made.

Twenty days before *Le Mariage de Figaro* was presented at
the Comédie-Française, on April 7, 1784, it was shown in Vienna
with much success. At that time Wolfgang Amadeus Mozart
was twenty-eight years old. He had had already much fame and
much misery and seven years later would die and be cast into a
pauper's grave, unmarked and indistinguishable. It is well. His
body became part of the vast Earth, even as his music.

Mozart had already tried his hand at the *opera seria* and the
opera buffa, but despite the glow of genius apparent in all his
work, it was not until he composed the music for *Le Nozze de
Figaro,* that he achieved the wonderful combination of *seria*
and *buffa,* and created, as the librettist, Lorenzo da Ponte, wrote
in the introduction to the printed form, "a new type of spectacle."

The satiric barbs were extracted, the revolutionary significance attenuated and the characters were modified to fit into
the musical conception of the composer, yet the play with its
wit, its charm, its marvelously intricate pattern, remained intact. In 1786 Vienna witnessed Beaumarchais' work in its Italian
libretto form, and despite the cabal led by Mozart's mortal
enemy, the fellow-composer, Salieri, and Emperor Joseph the
Second's prejudice, *Le Nozze* had a fair success, and at Prague
a prodigious one.

Not until 1793 was the opera produced in Paris, and it fell
flat. It was four years after the fall of Bastille, the year in which
Louis XVI and Marie-Antoinette were beheaded, two years
after the death of Mozart, and Beaumarchais, though still alive,
was in exile. Truly time was out of joint, and music graceful
and charming and a play witty and spirited were decidedly out
of tune.

The day would come, however, when the marriage of Beaumarchais' words and the notes of Mozart would bring perennial joy to ear and eye and heart the world over.

Of Many Things—Mémoires—Royal Messenger

There never was a dull moment in the fabulous life of Pierre-Augustin Caron de Beaumarchais. Tragedy and farce, pleasure and pain, honor and disgrace chased one another in a perpetual merry-go-round. But always he kept his emotional balance. "I am happy. A happy man is detested—a man whose happiness nothing may trouble—since happiness appears insolent—nothing, neither chagrin nor worry nor—good fortune!"

Beaumarchais had been a widower since 1757, assuaging his sorrow with many fugitive amours, since the best treatment of the malady of love is the homeopathic. Eleven years later, Beaumarchais now in his middle-thirties, felt the need of permanence. Good fortune placed Geneviève-Madeleine Watebled, widow of Antoine Lévêque, wealthy merchant, in his path. She was in her early thirties, rich, sweet-tempered, pretty, and lonesome—ingredients beyond cavil.

It was love at first sight—or almost. At any rate, Beaumarchais married Geneviève-Madeleine on April 11, 1768. Some months later (whether due to premature birth or premature love, the gossips never positively decided) a son was born unto the couple. He was christened Pierre-Augustin-Eugène.

Now Rue Condé seethed with life again. Beaumarchais' sister, Julie, as an exception in family annals, got along beautifully with her sister-in-law. To complete the merry picture, *papa* Caron, now twice widowed, returned to the hearth.

Alas, poor Geneviève, devoured by tuberculosis, gave birth to another child and both died in November, 1770. Pierre-Augustin Eugène, the older son, did not long survive them.

Troubles come linked in progression like the plates of giant snakes, clanging their ominous approach. Within some months of Geneviève's death, Pâris-Duverney, Beaumarchais' friend and benefactor, passed away at the age of eighty-six. His death brought in its train disgrace, loss of fortune, prison, and turmoil. Only Beaumarchais' tenacity, good humor, and wit made it possible for him at last to extricate himself from his foes' net of lies and libels. Comte Alexandre Falcoz de La Blache, grandnephew of Pâris-Duverney, unscrupulous and violent, managed to inveigle the tired old man into naming him the sole testamentary executor. "I hate Beaumarchais," he said, "the way a lover adores his mistress."

Great sums were involved in the dissolution of the partnership, and La Blanche was determined to lay hands upon them. His machinations were intricate and foul with libelous overtones, including the reprehensible rumor that Beaumarchais killed his second wife, as well as the first, as well as the husband of the first and a nobleman. Precisely because this was preposterous, it tickled the tongues of the gossips, who each added a fistful of yeast to the ugly dough.

The judicial system in France was in a period of transition and reformation, but still largely run by ignorant and prejudiced judges and scheming advocates, and would not achieve a more or less inviolate condition until after the Revolution. The case of Sieur de Beaumarchais versus Comte de La Blache would hang fire, and cause much scorching, for eight years, when by an unexpected turn of good fortune Beaumarchais won and recovered a great sum of money, while La Blache, in utter disgust, vanished from the scene, leaving behind him a stench of sulphur.

Meanwhile Beaumarchais became embroiled with Duc de Chaulnes whose mistress, Mademoiselle Ménard, a minor actress of the Comédie-Française, transferred her affections to him. The "triangle" met to discuss the affair in a civilized manner, and in the manner of the civilized a violent warfare between the two males ensued. To keep the record straight and assure its survival for the instruction and delectation of generations to come, Beaumarchais wrote to the nobleman, *inter alia:* "I wish to pass in silence over the scene, horrible for her [Mademoiselle Ménard], disgusting for two men like you and me, where you so forgot yourself that you reproached me with being the son of a watchmaker. Since I honor my parents—even in the face of those who imagine they have the right to outrage their own— you must certainly feel, Monsieur le Duc, how much more advantageous my position was at that time, than yours." (And how infinitely more advantageous two decades hence, when being the son of a duke was a capital offense and one's head tumbled into the basket!)

The fights by sword and fist between the two gentlemen and their aides and servants would make a delightful cinematic enterprise, but it ended in the imprisonment of Monsieur de Beaumarchais in For-l'Evêque on Rue Saint-Germain-l'Auxerrois— a miserable, damp jail used for debtors and delinquent actors. It was demolished in 1780, seven years after it had housed its most distinguished guest in all its vile history.

Comte de La Blache, hearing of Beaumarchais' imprisonment, started a vigorous campaign to have the lawsuit brought to the Parlement de Paris at once. The advantage would be enormous, for a litigant had the privilege of talking over the case with the judges, and very often influencing them. However, thanks to Mademoiselle Ménard, who invoked the help of Antoine de Sartines, Lieutenant General of Police, a gentleman susceptible to feminine graces, Beaumarchais was allowed to confer with the *rapporteur*—the man in charge of the case. The *rapporteur*, Louis-Valentin Goëzman, grasping, impudent, disreputable, had the habit of accepting, indeed, demanding *pourboire*. He was in league with his wife, Gabrielle-Julie Jamart, whose palm must also be greased. "It would be impossible for us to live decently on the salary we get, but we know how to pluck the fowl without making it cry," Madame Goëzman, herself a goose, confessed.

The case soon became the most celebrated in the annals of the French courts before the Dreyfus affair, for here, too, an innocent man was held prisoner, his honor besmirched and his property confiscated. Beaumarchais, checkmate, took to his pen. He composed his *Mémoires*—pamphlets presenting his case to the public.

The first *Mémoire* stated the legal and factual aspects of the affair, but even here, Beaumarchais brought his natural liveliness of style, and the people were beginning to be impressed. It was not yet a personal triumph. "I have no illusions," he said. "The public is less concerned to see me justified as to watch how an isolated individual can stand against such tremendous attack and repel the attack all alone."

His dramatic instinct awakened, he dropped the mere legal entanglements and in his next *Mémoires* he created theatrical characters of his enemies, condemning themselves out of their own mouths, and since they were theatrical, they appeared more real than nature. Why, these enemies of his, La Blache, Marin, the censor, Dairolles, the banker, Goëzman, Madame Goëzman, were the villains in his *Barbier,* and he—he was Figaro! And as Figaro he would outwit them all, while at the same time he would shake the rotted pillars of law and justice and point his accusing finger at the corruption of judges and barrister. "Cursed be the generation in which they imprison people in the hope of finding at last the reason for which they deserved it!"

By the time Beaumarchais published his fourth *Mémoire,* Paris and even the capitals beyond the frontiers were convulsed with laughter, and the applause was an endless thunder. Beaumarchais was the idol of the people. The *Mémoires* sold by the tens of thousands and the cafés became the improvised stages where customers took the parts of the characters. His Majesty himself read them and Madame du Barry—poor, frivolous comtesse, who would lose her beautiful, light head during the Terror, had her actor friends perform in her apartments some of the scenes that had taken place in the court-room, particularly the confrontation of Madame Goëzman with Beaumarchais, which proved her a she-fox caught by the tail and him a trapper without equal.

Voltaire, stifling his congenital jealousy, said: "No comedy was ever more amusing, no tragedy more touching. . . . What a man! He unites everything—humor, seriousness, argument, gaiety, power, emotion, every kind of eloquence. . . . He confounds his enemies and gives lessons to the judges. . . ."

Bernardin de Saint-Pierre (1737–1814), naturalist and author of the famous *Paul et Virginie* (once upon a time the Bible of the romantics), compared—and favorably—Beaumarchais to Molière. In Germany, Goethe was so impressed by the fourth *Mémoire,* in which Beaumarchais writes his autobiography, an unidealized portrait of an imprudent, impulsive, adventurous man, but generous, warm-hearted, and lovable, that he based one of his best-known plays, *Clavigo,* upon it.

Beaumarchais, who saw it produced at Augsburg, was shocked at the liberties the poet had taken with the facts. "That German," he wrote, "has spoiled the anecdote contained in my *Mémoire* [about Clavijo, his sister's recalcitrant suitor in Spain] by adding a duel and a funeral to the action—which showed him more empty-headed than talented." Goethe was only twenty-four at the time and had not yet published *Die Leiden des Jungen Werthers,* which took Europe by storm, and Madame de Staël had not yet made him the symbol of freedom. After that, who would dare question his genius?

The circus in the court-house continued for many days and finally on February 26, 1774, the verdict was rendered. Defendants and plaintiffs alike were fined three *livres* each and were put *au blâme*—that is, they were deprived of many legal abilities and rights. The four *Mémoires* were to be torn and burned by the public executioner, and as a special punishment for having written them, Beaumarchais was fined twelve *livres* more. No publicity could have been better calculated to make them immortal. The public was enraged at the verdict, despite the fact that Beaumarchais was morally vindicated, and the judges barely escaped with their skins intact.

The deprivation of his rights irked Beaumarchais, but he knew that only the King could lift them. Louis, who had at first enjoyed reading the *Mémoires,* now began to realize that in a subtle way, they were directed against the monarchy. Any criticism of the nobility, the Parlement, the law, sooner or later struck at Versailles. Moreover, the adulation of the populace of any individual except the sacred person of the royalty, was an indirect condemnation and a violation of the first Commandment: "I am the Lord, thy King, thou shalt have no other gods before me."

Beaumarchais sensed this, and since, in truth, he was not a *révolté* and considered the King the sacred symbol of France, he could, in all sincerity, write to him: "The thing that more than anything else in this sinister event has broken my heart is the unfavorable impression created about me in the King's mind. . . ."

Louis remembered him well when he was the teacher of his daughters, and was rather fond of him. He agreed to grant him a reprieve. Beaumarchais was overjoyed and very grateful. His Majesty, however, desired, in return, an indisputable proof of his loyalty. Sartines, the Lieutenant General of Police, invited him to discuss the matter. A man, by the name of Charles Theveneau de Morande, he explained, who called himself a French political refugee, residing in London, but who, in reality, was a professional blackmailer, published a sheet, *Le Gazetier Cuirassé*—"The Journalist in Armor"—dealing with scandalous stories, true or fictitious, of prominent figures in France. He never stopped his scurrilous attacks unless adequately bribed.

Morande, it seemed, had just printed a pamphlet with the umbrageous title of *Mémoires Secrets d'Une Fille Publique*— "Secret Memoirs of a Prostitute." And whom did the scoundrel mean but the charming mistress of His Majesty, Madame du Barry? And the worst part of it, discovered from secret reports, was that much of the material had a solid foundation of fact.

The King was worried, and as for the poor lady, one could imagine her distress. His Majesty had sent agents to kidnap the wretch and bring him back to France before the pamphlets were put into circulation. Ah, if the operation had been successful, the Royal Shepherd would not have been troubled for long by this *brebis galeuse*—this scabby sheep, the Chief of Police neighed, and drew an invisible knife across his throat.

But the woman used as decoy proved a traitress and the English, with their silly notion of freedom and the offer of sanctuary for refugees from political tyranny, were up in arms against the French government and warned that there would be trouble if another attempt was made to "invade" their country.

"Monsieur de Beaumarchais, the King has a high regard for your ability and he considers you the only man who could relieve him from this embarrassment." Finally the Lieutenant General of the Police made clear the purpose of the interview.

"Be a secret agent—I ?" Beaumarchais felt disgraced.

Sartines contradicted him. "It is an honor and a privilege to serve our King, monsieur."

Beaumarchais asked for an audience with Louis, which was granted, and the King persuaded him easily. Indeed, by this time he was quite excited about the whole affair. Spain all over again !

It was a masterly piece of work, evoking the admiration of the King and the gratitude of his *amoureuse*. After much spying, counterspying, and near-misses, Beaumarchais gained the confidence of Morande and for the sum of twenty thousand *livres* cash and a promised annuity of four thousand, all the pamphlets were destroyed, and their author not only vowed to desist henceforth from his disgraceful occupation, but to become a faithful agent for the King and France.

Alas, Beaumarchais' triumph did not last long enough for him to receive the reimbursement of his expenses plus, as he had hoped, a purse in the form of a perennial annuity. As he returned from England and landed in Boulogne, he learned that Louis XV had been stricken with the smallpox and was dying. And in effect, he died on May 10, 1774.

Beaumarchais' position now was unenviable. Marie-Antoinette, the new Queen, hated Du Barry and her clique, and a man
who had succeeded in saving her honor would not be welcome at
court. Nevertheless, Madame Du Barry was not cast upon a
dunghill. She was permitted to retain an ample estate and keep
her friends, and she had many, for she had never, even in her
heyday of power been malicious, vindictive, or treacherous.
Whatever her early life may have been, she was faithful to the
King and even to his memory, and her liaison with the great
noble, Cossé-Brissac, was dignified and honorable. During the
period that she was mistress of Louis XV she had squandered
great fortunes and had become too profoundly identified with
the "smart set" to escape the guillotine, but she was not without
merits—beauty, charm, dignity, reticence—priceless jewels of
femininity.

And Beaumarchais, on the perennial see-saw, once again
struck bottom.

New Loves —Male or Female?—
Le Pauvre Homme!—
The Wandering Jew

"Do we make love because we love each other or do we love
each other because we make love?" Beaumarchais asked again
and again as the occasions arose, and they were not infrequent.
The replies are not recorded, but one generation passeth away
and another cometh; and the question abideth forever. The embraces of the Don Juans are like prestidigitators' knots—elaborate and seemingly forever fixed, but one pull—and all is undone.

Before Charles Theveneau de Morande began seriously to
threaten the reputation of Madame Du Barry, and while Beau-

marchais was still at the height of his popularity, the harp, which like the watch, had once brought him fame, now brought him love. Marie Thérèse Amélie de Willermaulaz, a beautiful young lady of twenty-three—when he was forty-one—was in need of a harp, since hers was being repaired, and sent a messenger to beg him to help her out of the difficulty.

He offered her harp and house, which she accepted with joyous alacrity. It was to be a long affair culminating in marriage on the 8th of March, 1786, when Beaumarchais, fifty-three, began to feel the sting of conscience. As in his new play, which he was contemplating, he spoke both for his protagonist and for himself: "I shall be lavish with the attributes of the most austere morality, and I shall thunder against the vices I have treated with too much considerateness in the past."

His marriage legitimized his beloved daughter, Eugénie. However, this was to be only the penultimate affair, for at the age of fifty-eight, although both stout and deaf, he retained sufficient charm, which, added to his reputation both as scoundrel and hero, stirred the heart of Amélie Houret de la Marinière. She was in her twenties, pretty and an expert in the ways of Eros. The affair lasted to the end of his days, but the lovers were so careful and so considerate that Madame Beaumarchais never discovered it, despite gossip. Or, perhaps, she knew, but pretended ignorance, which in such matters, is the height of wisdom. As the proverb goes: "Blindness for sweetheart—deafness for wife—priceless the gifts of the Goddess Life."

Louis XVI was slow-witted, modest, moral—excellent qualities for a constitutional monarch whose chief occupation is to hold a loose commonwealth together by the glow of his crown and sign the papers that his ministers put upon his desk. But for an absolute ruler, these were cardinal faults, which eventually brought him to the scaffold. The absolute ruler must be unscrupulous, vain, ambitious, versed in deceit and hypocrisy—attributes which people dream in secret and respect in the open.

France was again in need of a secret agent of a high degree of intelligence, ingenuity, and reliability. Charles Geneviève Louis Auguste Timothée d'Eon de Beaumont was one of the most notorious characters of the century. This ex-advocate, ex-dragoon, ex-secretary of the French Embassy in London, redoubtable duellist, a chevalier de Saint-Louis for his exploits in war—was a woman! She was pretty, had soft, gentle features, and no beard. She had been at the Court of Versailles for years and in 1775 Louis XV sent her to the Tzarina Elizabeth of Russia, daughter of Peter the Great, on a very important mission. She succeeded. Later she was sent to London with the promise of an eventual ambassadorship which never materialized. Embittered, the lady began to plot.

Louis XVI was privately informed that his grandfather had bequeathed him not only the throne, but documents of a very dangerous nature. They were now in the trunk of Chevalier d'Eon, and she demanded an exhorbitant price for them, under the threat that they would be delivered to the Foreign Office of His Majesty George III. Fearful that the strained relations between England and his country would once again flare up in war, Louis sought to appease the would-be traitor. Only one man in all of France, he was told, would know how to wheedle the papers out of her trunk for a reasonable sum—Sieur de Beaumarchais.

Like everybody else in the kingdom, Louis had heard of the man and his exploits, good and evil, but was reluctant to meet him. He was too brilliant for him, too witty—how could he cope with him? *Force majeure,* however, demanded the encounter, and it proved mutually agreeable. The King found Beaumarchais charming, simple, wise, and ready to serve him faithfully, and Beaumarchais found the Monarch a man of honor and good-will.

And so, Beaumarchais went to London to meet that strange being, on whom the English, always gamblers, were betting— "Is it a man or a woman?" But no one dared approach her— him—for his—her—fame as a wielder of the sword scared even the most intrepid. The circuitous dealings of the two artists in deception are largely hidden from the annals, but ultimately Beaumarchais succeeded in persuading the Chevalier to accept a pension of twelve thousand *livres* annually and live in France as a woman, for women in those chivalrous days were considered irresponsible creatures, unmolestable, and therefore, her shady history would be relegated to the sorceries of the boudoir—and oblivion.

What was Beaumarchais' opinion in the matter of the gender of d'Eon—masculine, feminine, neutral, or, as it is writ in Genesis, the two in one? We shall never know for certain. "Who the devil would have fancied," Beaumarchais wrote to Count Vergennes, the famed Minister of Foreign Affairs, with whom he was in constant touch, "that to serve the King I would have to pay court to a former captain of the dragoons?" This would indicate that he believed the character to be a man. Yet, upon a later occasion, he wrote: "Everyone tells me that this mad old woman is crazy about me. She thinks I have treated her with contempt, and women never forgive such an offense." Ergo—a woman.

Be that as it may, d'Eon, who first admired Beaumarchais, later hated him fiercely. An old fat female, she returned to England in 1783, thus escaping the Revolution and the Terror, and keeping her head upon her neck she lived until 1810, aged eighty-two—rich in years, in hates, and in disillusions.

Now the time had come to know the truth. What had not been verified in the boudoir was verified in the morgue. Thomas Copeland, the operating surgeon, wrote in his report: "Male organs of generation perfectly formed in every respect." The case was closed. Yet, it is a pity that Charles Geneviève Louis Auguste Timothée d'Eon de Beaumont, Chevalier de Saint-Louis, had not like so many Frenchmen, written his *Mémoires*. They should have been witty, ironic, cruel, pitiable—a eunuch Casanova—an Imperial boy-favorite—in a wrong world, at a wrong epoch.

"*Le pauvre homme!*"—"the poor man"—Marie-Antoinette wrote to her mother, referring to her husband, Louis XVI. Maria Theresa was empress of Germany, queen of Hungary and Bohemia, and mother of five sons and eleven daughters—a career unequalled by any feminine crowned head in recorded history. She had taught her daughter that being a French queen did not mean that she must ever forget that she had another capital besides Paris—Vienna. And the daughter never forgot and that was one of the reasons why she lost her head. "*Le pauvre homme*" meant that there was so much to do, so many frontiers to defend, a nation in the throes of multifarious passions, that the King regretted the burden of the crown.

The people, however, interpreted "*Le pauvre homme*" in their own fashion, and changed the sentence to "*Est-ce un homme?*"—"Is he a man?" The question was barbed with mockery. Louis had married Marie-Antoinette when he was the dauphin, in 1770, but still no heir four years after the nuptials. What could it mean, except that he was a husband in name only and that the poor Queen might be forced to do like the daughter of Jephthah, "who went up and down the mountains" bewailing her virginity?

The sterile bed of the royal house was not merely a matter of satirical interest, or of compassion, for Louis XVI, at this time, was still well-liked by his subjects. It was a condition which might precipitate a bloody crisis, since the Spanish branch of the Bourbon family, claiming that it had been cheated by the will of Louis XV, might attempt to put one of their members upon the French throne, who would assure the perpetuation of the dynasty.

A pamphlet purported to state the Spanish case to the world, peppered with many intimate details of the private life of the royal couple, was printed in London by an Italian Jew named Guillaume Angelucci (alias William Atkinson), a blackmailer of the lowest type, and was ready for publication. The information was offered by Beaumarchais to Sartines, who had retained his post as Lieutenant General of the Police after the death of Louis XV. Sartines promptly instructed Beaumarchais to go to the English Capital and once again save the honor of France, while the Monarch gratefully supplied him with a royal document. "The Sieur de Beaumarchais, entrusted with my secret orders, will leave as soon as possible for his destination. The discretion and energy that he puts into their execution will be the best proof he can give me of his zeal in my service. Louis."

And Beaumarchais answered: "I have had a large, flat, oval gold case made. I have enclosed Your Majesty's order in it and suspended it about my neck with a gold chain, as the most necessary thing in my work and the most precious possession I have."

Was this pamphlet together with its author a cock-and-bull story invented by Beaumarchais? Was he in such desperate straits that he needed such desperate means of making money? Was he, in truth, the faithful servant of his Monarch? Was he Figaro making sport of the high and the mighty? Was he the eternal adolescent in search of excitement and adventure?

Beaumarchais was an extremely complex character. Idealistic and practical, he had a keen sense of honor, and yet he was not troubled by scruples, and if necessary, was ready to stifle them. He was brilliant, witty, flippant, and capricious. He was steadfast, too, and when his ideas were challenged, he could become stubborn to the point of martyrdom. His versatile and supple understanding quickly moved from grave to gay, from surface to depth. He was industrious, yet indolent. Master debater, he rose to a high plane of original thinking, and readily tumbled into the trivial and commonplace. Ambitious, he was ever forging his way to the front, yet would not harm those whom he elbowed out of his path, and always he yearned to be conspicuous.

In London, according to his report to Sartines, he had met Angelucci, paid him fourteen hundred pounds for four thousand copies of the infamous pamphlet, which he burned in the suburbs of the Capital upon a moonless night.

That should have ended the episode and Beaumarchais should have returned to France to present his respects to His Majesty and receive the reward. But Angelucci, whose name should have been Diavolaccio, had a copy of the pamphlet which he meant to print somewhere in Germany, and had fled the coop. So now Beaumarchais was constrained to follow the rascal, capture him, and get a hold of the libelous material. The search for that son of Abraham foreshadowed all the tales of the Wandering Jew. From town to town he chased him—Amsterdam, Clèves, Düsseldorf, Cologne, Frankfurt—until the 14th day of August, 1774, when he reached the forest of Neustadt.

He ordered the coachman to stop, while he dashed into the woods. Many minutes passed, and the coachman, worried, followed in his tracks. When he discovered his customer, he was in a pathetic condition, clothes ripped, face and hands spattered with blood. Since Beaumarchais knew no German and the coachman knew no French, he explained in signs that he had been waylaid by robbers and wounded. And now, he ordered him to drive to the nearest city, Nüremberg, at top speed, for help.

Anxious about his traveler, the coachman, a while later, looked through the window and saw him wipe the blood off a razor and put it carefully into his bag. In his profession, the coachman had seen many things, and he promptly understood that the French nobleman's wounds were self-inflicted. Later, when interrogated by the Burgomaster, he so deposed.

Confident that all things were in order, Beaumarchais took passage on a boat going to Vienna, which he reached on August 20, 1774. Immediately upon arrival, he asked to be granted an audience with the Empress, bringing very important news from the Court of Versailles. He was received at once, and revealing his identity as de Beaumarchais (which he concealed all along under the fictitious name of Chevalier de Ronac, his *nom de guerre*) whose fame had doubtless traveled as far as the ancient Capital of Austria.

Maria Theresa admired the courage and shrewdness of this

man so devoted to the interests of her daughter, but her Minister began to find flaws in the narration, and the deposition of the coachman had percolated, also with variations, to the police of Vienna. Admiration changed into suspicion and to avoid possible dangers to the state, Beaumarchais was thrown into jail, where, despite his ruffled protestations, he remained for several weeks.

Finally, he was allowed to leave and the Empress offered him a purse to compensate him for his expenses. Beaumarchais promptly rejected it. He would not accept money from a government that had acted so shamefully toward him! Later, to show her regret for the treatment so chivalrous a man had received at the hands of her misguided Ministers, she sent Beaumarchais a ring with an enormous diamond, which he wore to the end of his days—this man who made sport of royalty, but fawned upon it—this man of the people, whom he glorified, but with whom he would not mingle.

Sartines, whether taken in by the strange tale of Beaumarchais, or not, accepted it officially, including the statement that he had finally caught the Jew and tore the last ugly pamphlet, which he had found on his person. The Jew disappeared again, naturally, and would nevermore be heard of, except in various disguises in literature. The good-hearted King Louis XVI, touched by Beaumarchais' fidelity, ordered the royal treasury to pay at once the 72,000 *livres* which he asked as his fee. It was a great sum, but the price determines the value—something which Figaro-Beaumarchais knew so well.

Emperor Joseph II, brother of Marie-Antoinette visited France and as a good brother-in-law offered some important hints to Louis XVI, which he evidently took to heart, for the Queen became enceinte and gave birth to a girl, Marie-Thérèse-Charlotte, later the Duchesse d'Angoulême, in December of 1778. Only a female, but better than nothing. On October 22, 1781, Marie-Antoinette gave birth to a son—a dauphin—Louis-Xavier-François! The people were wild with joy! Two more children were born to the King—a son and a daughter.

And the people no longer said: *Este-ce un homme?* but: *Quel homme!*—"What a man!"

My Friends, the Free Men of America—Ingratitude Thy Name's Man!

Beaumarchais' frequent trips to London served, in the perspective of time, a far more significant purpose than the saving of Madame Du Barry's reputation or the hindrance of Chevalier d'Eon's treason or the burning of the imaginary pamphlets of the Incredible Jew. They afforded him the opportunity of meeting Englishmen in high public office and liberals of all shades, including Americans who still were more or less loyal Britishers. He became the best informed Frenchman of the political climate of the Island.

In the month of April, 1775, he heard "the embattled farmers . . . fire the shot heard round the world," on the battlefields of Concord and Lexington. England was filled with consternation, but the French government, thoroughly informed by Beaumarchais' letters to Vergennes, was delighted. This was not, he wrote, a passing phase, an angry gesture against one tyrannical act, but the struggle of men to break their chains and become free. It was, indeed, the practical application of the teachings of the French philosophers and poets for two generations. And it was both natural and well that the New World should be the first to do it. The Old was suffering from ankylosis of traditions—social, religious, economic. The joints of the New were still elastic. Its history had not yet hardened into morbid prejudices. Virginal was their country and virginal the mores of its inhabitants—decency, frugality, neighborliness.

The Old World could write and moralize, but the Young World must act.

The Huguenot—the Protestant—long asleep in Beaumarchais awakened with a start. What had he done all these years, save aping the overweening lords and gathering the withered laurels of vanity and personal profit? Arise, Pierre-Augustin Caron, son and grandson of noble fighters for truth and freedom! The hour has struck, Pierre-Augustin! The hour had, indeed, struck and henceforth until the end of his hectic days, Beaumarchais would never cease battling for the liberation of man from slavery and political tyranny. He would become the champion of the American Revolution, though harassed, vilified and robbed, yet ever—"My friends, the free men of America!'

His undying love and admiration for America and the Americans was fortified by his patriotic fervor. France, glorious France, upon what evil days she had fallen! Defeated by the English, stripped of her colonies, she had become a timorous nation ruled by a timorous king. But now—the moment was at hand to avenge herself, recover her luster by belittling her perennial foe, by pulling the steely claws of the lion whose roar frightened the whole earth!

He wrote to his Monarch and urged him to help the insurgents from beyond the Ocean. He should send guns and shoes and officers and engineers, and if for the moment it was impolitic to do so openly, then, it should be done by devious ways. "The Americans, Sire, are resolved to suffer anything rather than yield, and filled with enthusiasm for liberty, I say, Sire, that such a nation must be invincible."

The King replied indirectly, informing his Minister, Vergennes, that he would take no action against the English—of all things on religious grounds. "Love your enemies, bless them that curse you, do good to them that hate you. . . ."

Beaumarchais was dumbfounded. Could a state be run on such a philosophy? What would happen to France if her neighbors believed it? How long before she would be obliterated

from the face of the earth? It was no wiser than for a flock of
sheep to invite to partake dinner with a pack of wolves. "I en-
treat you, Sire, in the name of your subjects, to whom you owe
the best of your endeavors. . . . This lamentable excess of
justice toward your enemies would be the most flagrant injustice
toward your subjects, who would soon have to pay for scruples
so out of place."

Why, these were the words that would cast prophets into
wells! In the glorious days of the Roi Soleil or his great-grandson, Louis XV, the black jaws of La Bastille would have opened
wide to swallow the impudent villain whose mouth had dared
to utter them. But now—what power had the King? Mention La
Bastille and the mad, stinking rabble would march on Versailles.
This was the true reason why the bewildered King took refuge
behind the skirts of religion—very wide skirts of many colors
for most diverse purposes. He feared England and would gladly
take revenge for the humiliations his country had suffered at her
hands, but he feared the Americans more—the Americans with
their hatred of kings who ruled by the grace of God—the Americans whose ambassador, a man by the name of Thomas Jefferson, could write: "The kings are despicable fools without mind,
from whom let him perish who does not say 'Good Lord, deliver
us!' And who also said: "A little rebellion now and then is a
good thing." If those barbarous insurgents dethroned George
III, how long before the French insurgents, taking a hint, would
dethrone Louis XVI?

If he was slow in perceiving this truth, there was always
Marie-Antoinette to point it to him. She had learned much from
her shrewd mother and more still from her shrewder father-
confessors. No mistress stood behind the throne of Louis XVI,
but there was a wife with the ways of a mistress and she led her
man by his hooked Bourbon nose as well as any of her predeces-
sors had led his ancestors. During the greater part of the eighteenth century, France was a matriarchy—not the type of the
humble, ageless rocker of the cradle nor that of the blatant
virago of two centuries later, but one which ruled by the subtle

graces of pleasure, the intoxicant perfumes of sex, rendering man docile and obedient. Women have ever chosen the Cinderella or the Delilah role, but both Princes and Samsons remain to grind in the prison house.

Beaumarchais now had the tenacity of a fanatic—America must be victorious and France must aid her. He bombarded the office of the Foreign Ministry, headed by Vergennes, with warnings and pleadings. "Ah, Monsieur le Comte, as a favor to me . . . some powder and a few engineers! It seems I have never wanted anything so much. . . . I can pledge my sacred faith to make any sum reach them through intermediaries, by way of Holland, without any risk and without any other authorization than that which exists between us. . . . But engineers! Engineers and gunpowder!"

And to the King: "You will only maintain the peace you desire, Sire, by preventing at all costs peace between England and America, and the only means of attaining this end, is by giving assistance to the Americans."

Gradually he wore down both Minister and King and they were ready to help—but still *sub rosa*. For Beaumarchais that was sufficient. Instantly he informed the secret agents of the Colonies of France's determination. The American Army at this juncture was in a pitiable shape and there were many, even in the higher échelon, who clamored for surrender and peace with the Mother Country. Without foreign aid it would be impossible to carry on the struggle. But the good news from France galvanized the people and they dared to launch the Declaration of Independence of the 4th of July, 1776.

Thus Beaumarchais became a cog in the great wheel which influenced world history. "I say, Sire," Beaumarchais wrote joyously, "the colonies are lost to England." But how administer the help without (for the time being) getting involved in the war—that was France's dilemma, which Beaumarchais resolved. He established the firm of Rodrigue Hortalez et Cie., a Franco-Spanish concern. His partners were a ship charterer of Nantes, a businessman from Le Havre and a Jewish financier from Bordeaux, Joseph Peyrera. (Joseph Peyrera, at a later date, was imprudent enough to visit Spain. He was caught in Cádiz by the Inquisition, and for the sin of being a member of the race of Jesus of Nazareth, he was condemned to be burned at the stake. . . . He succeeded in sending Beaumarchais a note telling him of his predicament. "When I received it," Beaumarchais wrote, "my hair stood on end. I ran to Versailles and went down on my knees crying to Monsieur le Comte Vergennes, the Prime Minister. I tormented him so long that I obtained from him the claim that Pereyra belonged to France." The Jew was saved, and according to Beaumarchais proved to be the most grateful man he had ever known, since he who did so much good knew so much ingratitude.)

To start his business, the French government offered Beaumarchais a million *livres,* gold, and later the Spanish ambassador in Paris added another million. The partners soon became hazy and he alone was virtually Rodrigue Hortalez et Cie.

Throughout the year 1777, Beaumarchais shipped to America the vast supplies which made eventual victory possible. Forty boats plied the Atlantic, carrying hundreds of field guns, thousands of muskets, hills of kegs of gunpowder and clothes and shoes to cover the shivering bodies and protect the bleeding feet of thirty-thousand men. This was not all. Beaumarchais was instrumental in selecting volunteers for the American army, including Marie-Joseph Marquis de La Fayette and Baron Friedrich Wilhelm von Steuben and three of his nephews, one of whom fell on the American battlefield. Von Steuben was penniless and Beaumarchais lent him the money necessary for their passage, nearly six thousand *francs,* gold, which, of course, was never repaid.

And no one worked harder to persuade France to recognize the young Republic and sign a treaty of commerce and friendship with her. When his efforts finally succeeded, the French government reproduced verbatim passages from his *Mémoire* written for the purpose, in order to justify the step she had taken according to international law.

The recognition was, before long, followed by war between France and England and made certain the final triumph of America. Silas Deane, Chief of the American Secret Agents, wrote to Beaumarchais: "After the perplexing and embarrassing scenes you have had to pass through, it must give you the greatest pleasure to see at last the object of your efforts fulfilled, and a large fleet ready to sail, which will convince the whole world of the sincere friendship of France and her absolute determination to protect America's freedom and independence. I once more congratulate you on the glorious event, to which you have contributed more than anybody else."

And La Fayette said to him: "The venerable Doctor Franklin has asked me to tell you that the decisive victory of Saratoga would never have been accomplished without you. The Americans will never forget it."

"Provided," Beaumarchais answered wistfully, "they will first remember it." They did not remember. "I propose to serve America as though it were my own country, and I hope to find in the friendship of a generous people the true reward for the work I take pleasure in dedicating to them. But whatever happens, one thing can never change or decline—my ardent desire to serve America to the utmost."

Now that France had become an ally and her great fleet was put into the service of the States, Rodrigue Hortalez et Cie. had lost its importance, but Beaumarchais had already spent more than five million *livres,* gold, whose value in dollars, banknotes, would have to be multiplied many times. On the verge of bankruptcy, he asked the United States Congress to repay him. "A people that has become sovereign and powerful may perhaps be allowed to consider gratitude a virtue good for individuals, but beneath the realm of politics. But nothing dispenses a state from being fair and particularly from paying its debts." There was no reply, and the red tape began to strangle him.

"We have as many intrigues and cabals here as you suffer from in the Continent. And why not? Are we not sovereign states and are we not friends and allies of Louis XVI?" William

Carmichael, Secretary to the Commissioners in Paris, now back in America, disgusted, wrote to him.

Heartbreaking were Beaumarchais' *démarches,* until at last in the year 1793, Congress, by devious and dishonorable calculations, fixed the debt at 2,280,000 *francs.* "*Soit!* So be it!" Beaumarchais accepted the verdict. But the money never came. Political complications and endless machinations stopped the payment.

In 1795, exasperated, hurt to the core, Beaumarchais wrote to the American people: "Americans, I have served you with indefatigable zeal and I have received only bitterness as a reward for my services. I die your creditor. Allow me, therefore, now that I am dying to bequeathe you my daughter, and that you may endow her with a portion of what you owe me. . . . Adopt her as a worthy child of the state. . . . If this is rejected I shall come to America and I should have to be carried to the door of your National Assemblies; and there, holding out the liberty cap—which no one on earth helped you to wear more than I—cry out: 'Americans, give alms to your friend. For all his services to you you have brought him naught but this reward. . . .' "

America was deaf. She remembered nothing. And the years passed. There was the French Revolution. There was Napoleon. There was the War of 1812. There was Waterloo. There was the Monroe Doctrine. There was the Revolution of 1830. America doubled its population and became a world power. Still, she remembered nothing.

Not until Beaumarchais had been dead for thirty-six years, in the year 1835, did an impatient and impolite Congress offer the third generation of the Beaumarchais family, on the basis of "take it or leave it," eight hundred thousand *francs*—by this time only one-tenth of the real value of the debt due. The family, having no choice, accepted.

There is no portrait of Beaumarchais in the Halls of Congress, nor mention of his name in the school books, nor is there a statue in any square or park amid all the proud horsemen riding to victory. Nations have ever been ingrates, but rarely has one neglected so long a man who contributed so much to her very existence. The dead need no honors, but the living not honoring their memory, dishonor themselves.

The Whirlwind—Interludes— The Summing-Up

Once when Louis XV deigned to chat with Sieur de Beaumarchais, the former teacher of his daughters ventured to express an opinion on the angry temper of the Parisians.

"What shall I do to calm them, monsieur?" His Majesty asked.

"A symbolic gesture, Sire, might suffice."

"What, for instance?"

"Order La Bastille to be torn down."

Louis laughed. "You are jesting, monsieur."

"No, Sire, I am serious. And it is pressing. Some day it will be demolished, but in a fury."

"Tear down La Bastille, and to free how many, monsieur?" His Majesty asked ironically, knowing that the number at that particular time was small.

"To free those who are *not* there, Sire."

"They tell me, monsieur, that your comedies rival those of Molière and that you have a great sense of humor. My compliments."

Whether Beaumarchais regarded the King's flattery a sufficient reward or felt that it was futile—and dangerous—to enlighten royalty, is not known, and would be difficult to determine considering the man's complex nature. He was not a doctrinaire, and a man of irrepressible optimism, he probably smiled at his role as prophet of evil. Moreover, he knew that events were stampeding buffaloes crushing under hoof the trim gardens of prophets and philosophers. And events were precisely the things which one could not anticipate.

"They have sown the wind and they shall reap the whirl-wind." Never in history had there been a more unconscionable sower of evil winds than Louis XV. And never a fiercer whirl-wind followed. But he was not the reaper. He had been at peace in the bosom of his God for fifteen years when it raged.

Beaumarchais had recently built himself an immense home with two acres of land, two hundred windows, a sumptuous gar-den, a pool, marble columns, statues, in the heart of the poverty-stricken district of Faubourg Saint-Antoine, a few hundred yards from La Bastille. Why there? To show off? To tell the world that he, in truth, was always Pierre-Augustin Caron, one of the people? To repent for his folly of pretending to be Sieur de Beaumarchais? To show the reward of industry and genius? Who knows? He could not have extricated himself from the many strands of his many emotions.

But on the 14th of July, 1789, he beheld from the windows the vast fury of the people as they tore down the symbol of tyranny and injustice—La Bastille. Did he recall his conversa-tion with the King? Was he pleased with the fulfillment of his prophecy? Had he not battled for American freedom and jus-tice? Why not for his own country?

Before many years passed, while in exile, he would use this very argument as self-defense. "I shall prove that after serving the cause of liberty in America, I have, without personal ambi-tion, served the true interests of France with all my powers. I shall prove that I am still serving her—even though I am the butt of a persecution as stupid from a political point of view as it is nefarious. I shall prove that it is absurd to believe that a man who dedicated himself to the reestablishment of the Rights of Man in America, in the hope of thus presenting France with a great model to follow, would have become lukewarm when it came to putting these principles into practice."

Alas, poor Beaumarchais, he had as little luck with the French Revolution as with the American! He had labored hard to be of service, he had spent a fortune, he had risked his life and liberty. As reward, his home was sacked, he was jailed, ridiculed, hounded, and exiled. His wife, his daughter and his sister, Julie, were imprisoned and escaped the guillotine by a mere fluke. It was not until the Terror was over, in April, 1796, that Beaumarchais was finally authorized to return to France.

Somehow, in the ancient manner of the French peasant, Beaumarchais managed to hide a mattress filled with gold coins and promptly again invested profitably. Once more he could live in comfort in his great mansion at Faubourg Saint-Antoine and give generously to the poor and to some of the returned emigrés, formerly his foes. But the pleasantest of his surprises was the marriage of his daughter, Eugénie, to André Delarue, who had fallen in love with her when her father was considered one of the wealthiest men of France and would not reject her when she was imprisoned and in danger of losing her head, and her father, in exile, claimed to be a pauper.

Beaumarchais' many loves were always lined with ulterior purposes—wealth, éclat, vanity. But love—unalloyed, pristine, utterly devoted—he had never before witnessed and he was enraptured. Figaro no longer needed to laugh in order not to weep; he wept now for sheer joy. And honest and honorable Monsieur André Delarue was duly rewarded, for two years later, when his father-in-law died, he left his daughter an estate valued at seven hundred thousand *francs* and an annual income of twenty thousand *francs,* thus assuring the new little family, already blessed with a daughter, permanent security.

The years between the two great Revolutions were not totally devoid of literary productions. As always, Beaumarchais returned to his first love, the stage. He had gone awhoring among the strange gods of politics and business, but he never stopped worshiping at the altar of the pen. In 1784, after years of intermittent labors, he completed the libretto for his philosophical opera, *Tarare*. Tarare is a man of low birth, but full of genius and of virtue. He fights the cruel and tyrannical King Atar of Ormuz, whose mighty weapons are superstition, ignorance, and preposterous traditions. Tarare is ultimately triumphant, frees his nation from slavery, and becomes its immortal hero.

Beaumarchais tried to interest Gluck in writing the music for *Tarare,* but the great composer begged to be excused. He was too old, he claimed, to undertake a work of such dimension and importance. However, he recommended Antonio Salieri (1750–1825), his best pupil, who was suspected of having poisoned Mozart.

Beaumarchais invited Salieri, then living in Vienna, to come to Paris and be his guest for the period he required to compose the music. The collaboration was very cordial and the music fitted the play—both artificial, maudlin, theatrical, and optimistic. Yet, these were precisely the attributes appreciated by the Parisian public only two years before the Revolution. So blinded is man by hope, the glowing lacquer which hides reality. On June 8, 1787, the Paris Opéra offered *Tarare* and had a hit on its hands, although it did not take its place in the permanent repertoire.

Beaumarchais always regarded Figaro and Count Almaviva as two phases of his own personality—the shrewd plebeian and the proud nobleman. The two plays, *Le Barbier de Séville* and *Le Mariage de Figaro* had not exhausted his "autobiography." "I thought with the actors, to tell the public—after having laughed at the *Barbier* and witnessed the turbulent youth of Almaviva—after considering gaily in the *Mariage* the faults of virility—come and be convinced like us by the picture of old age. . . ."

Therefore, he composed *La Mère Coupable*—"The Guilty Mother." The scene now is laid in Paris, in the mansion occupied by the family of Count Almaviva, and the time is toward the end of 1790, that is after the fall of Bastille. All the characters now have taken on the pallor of maturity. Figaro is no longer a delightful scoundrel. He is faithful, but his fidelity is heavy-handed. Rosine is crushed by her sin and is a mournful lachrimose shadow. Suzanne, attached as always to her mistress, has retained a bit of her youth, but no Count would sacrifice wife

and reputation for her. And Almaviva? He is a gentleman (not
a nobleman, for he has relinquished his title) portly, pompous,
without a sense of humor, yet liberal, as was natural for a man
who preferred to live in the new world. He should have been
deaf also, as poor Beaumarchais had become—"deaf as a funeral urn"—carrying his ear-trumpet around. For the stage it
would have been unpractical, however, and he would have been
a ludicrous character instead of a dignified one. This, then, was
the self-portrait of Pierre-Augustin Caron de Beaumarchais at
the age of sixty—this Figaro and this Almaviva merged into one
—a good, solid, honorable citizen.

And the villain? He is Bégearss, an Irishman, former major
in the Spanish infantry, who having opened the closet in the
Almaviva household, has discovered a dangling skeleton and is
ready now to despoil the former count and marry his daughter,
the sweet Florestine who is in love with Chevalier Léon, son of
Almaviva and Rosine. In the household, Florestine is considered
only as a ward of the former count.

Bégearss is a complete rascal—*L'Autre Tartufe*—"The
Other Tartufe"—according to the sub-title of the play. Tartufe, the character in Molière's play, whose name in the French
language signifies treachery and hypocrisy.

What is the skeleton? Rosine is Léon's mother, but Almaviva
is not his father. His father is Chérubin, the delicious imp of a
page of other days, who, in contrition for his mortal sin, had
himself killed in battle. And Florestine? Florestine is Almaviva's daughter, but not Rosine's. Being strangers, they could
marry, but the Irish villain tries to make the case appear as in-
cestuous, and the misery of the young people is beyond measure.

Between Figaro and Bégearss there is a constant duel of wits
and traps. Bégearss is more skillful, but Figaro having justice on
his side, ultimately wins. Almaviva's fortune is rescued and
truth saves Florestine and Léon. Their marriage, presumably,
will be as happy as that of Eugénie and André.

And now comes the best moment of all when Almaviva forgives his wife. "O my children!" he exclaims, "there comes an

age when decent people forgive one another's wrongs and their former weaknesses. . . . Our quarrels will be buried forever!" The former count, so pleased with the loyalty of Figaro, offers him the large sum of money which had just been recovered from "Tartufe." Figaro refuses. "No, if you please! Spoil by a vile salary the good services I have done! My reward is to die in your employ. As a young man, if I have failed often, let this day acquit my life! O, my old age, forgive my youth; it will honor you!"

The play is a paen to old age, to its wisdom, to its charity. Only from this angle does it have merit. Beaumarchais himself was uncertain of *La Mère Coupable* and in his *Introduction* to the printed form, he says: "Perhaps I have waited too long to finish this terrifying work which consumed my heart and should have been written in the heydey of my powers. It has tormented me for too long! My two Spanish comedies were made only as a preparation for this one. Growing old, I feared to tackle it; I feared I would lack the strength; and perhaps I did not have enough at the time I have attempted to write it; but, anyhow, I composed it with an intention both honest and just; with the cool head of a man and a burning heart of a woman. . . . I tried to paint the human heart; but my pallet is dried by age and contradictions. . . . *La Mère* must have shown it. O my compatriots, you to whom I offer this essay; if the play appears weak or it has miscarried, criticize it, but without insulting me. . . . Criticize the play—very well. . . . Insults profit no one and they are not even in good taste. . . ."

The old man has spoken. The grace of old age is the ability to suffer patiently. Time weaves about us a protective armor against the shafts of public opinion. Its thickness is one of the few advantages of old age over youth.

La Mère Coupable was first produced in the Théâtre du Marias on June 26, 1792, when it was greeted with boos, except the Fourth Act which is profound in its sincerity and simplicity and Rosine emerges as a martyr to purity and devotion. Because of this, the play lasted until the 5th of August. Five years later, it was revived by former actors of the Théâtre-Français, now established at the Théâtre de la Rue Feydau. Played on the 16th Floréal in the Year Five of the Revolution—5th of May, 1797 —it had a huge success. Now people were ready to weep. "The tears which one weeps at the theater are very sweet," Beaumarchais said, delighted. "One becomes better when one weeps. One feels good after compassion!" But it is impossible to ascertain whether by making men happy, we make them good, or by making them good, we make them happy. Man has never any choice save between the lesser of evils and happiness is a truce between one sorrow and another.

Beaumarchais, still anxious to add a few stitches in the embroidery of politics, contrived through his son-in-law to get an audience with the new idol of France, General Bonaparte. "I shall be glad," the General said, "to meet the author of *La Mère Coupable*." The meeting was brief and unsatisfactory. The young officer, certain of his rising star, was impatient with a deaf old writer, whose ambition was to become ambassador to America. It seemed preposterous to him, as it would seem to other high officials whom he tried to interest.

Always Beaumarchais had his ten fingers in as many pies, two of which now had particularly literary interest. Playwrights were absolutely at the mercy of the actors, who kept nine-tenths of the receipts, and if the receipts fell below a certain specified sum (which they juggled as they pleased) the play could be withdrawn without the author's permission, and if revived, the actors were entitled to all the money. The author, if he complained noisily, often found himself, repenting, in jail, for at the court, the mummers had powerful friends.

To remedy this injustice, plus others, Beaumarchais founded the "Société des Auteurs Dramatiques de France," not without the bitter opposition of many of the established men of letters, fiercely jealous, as usual, of the "outsider" who made good. To-day authors protected by copyright in all nations owe a debt of

gratitude to Beaumarchais, one of the first to do successful battle
for their rights and privileges.

Jean François-Marie Arouet, better known as Voltaire, came
to Paris after an absence of thirty-three years in a trail of glory
that was his undoing. The strain of listening to the perpetual
applause led to his death on May 30, 1778, at the age of eighty-
four. Between the months of February and May, Beaumarchais
had one or more long interviews with Europe's most celebrated
man. Voltaire was aware of the fact that his days were numbered
and he was anxious about the fate of his writings—more voluminous, perhaps, than those of any author preceding or following him. But the books were scattered in all directions and some
were printed anonymously, while others had fictitious names,
and there were thousands of letters in the drawers of countless
recipients, among whom were princes and kings and empresses.

Shortly before his death, Voltaire said: "All my hopes are
centered on Beaumarchais." And he had judged correctly.
Beaumarchais decided to undertake the publication of his complete works. It was an enterprise strewn with roadblocks of
jealousy, chicanery, theft, intrigue. Undaunted and unswerved,
as always, Beaumarchais devoted himself from 1783 to 1790 to
what he considered a holy duty to mankind, which cost him one
million *livres*. He had counted on thirty thousand subscribers,
but found hardly two thousand, despite all his ingenious adver-
tisements (he was considered a past master in the art) even including a drawing of lottery. Nevertheless, Beaumarchais had
the prideful pleasure of a monumental achievement—two editions, one in seventy volumes octavo; the other, a cheaper one,
in ninety-two volumes duodecimo.

Thwarted in his efforts to reenter the political arena, Beaumarchais finally accepted the narrowed circle of his home.
"Happy in my household, happy because of my charming daughter, happy because of my old friends, I ask nothing more of mankind, having done my austere duty as son, husband, brother,
friend—in a word of a man, of a Frenchman, and a good citizen." To complete the picture, he would have wished to mention

that he was happy with his young sweetheart, Amélie, who knew her way around with the Procurator of the Commune, and had saved Beaumarchais from the prison of L'Abbaye and the gallows during the Terror.

As a careful merchant, Beaumarchais took a detailed inventory of his career. "I was the most hated and the most adored of the men of the eighteenth century. I have had countless enemies, and yet I did not cross anyone. Since my mad youth I played all instruments, but I did not belong to any association of musicians—the musicians detested me. I have invented a few good machines, but I did not belong to the Mechanics' Guild, and they spoke ill of me. I wrote verses and composed songs, but who would recognize me as a poet—I was the son of a watchmaker! I composed plays, but they said: What is he meddling for? He isn't an author, because he is doing immense business. Not finding one who wished to defend me, I printed *Mémoires* in order to win the trial against me. The lawyers shouted: Can a man like that be allowed to prove without us that he is right? I have treated with ministers about important points of improvement in our system of finances, which were necessary, but they said: What is he meddling about? He is not a financier. I raised the art of publishing by the superb edition of Voltaire's works, but I was not a printer and the Guild of Booksellers inveighed against me. I was in high commerce in all parts of the world, but I did not call myself a merchant, and the merchants scorned me. I had forty boats on the high seas, but not being a shopowner they abused me in all ports. A battleship of mine with fifty-two cannon had the honor of fighting among the other battleships of His Majesty, but regarded as an intruder, I lost my flotilla. Of all Frenchmen, whoever they may be, I was the one who did most for the freedom of America, but I was not classed among the negotiators and was completely ignored.

"I was nothing but myself and myself. I remained free amidst chains, serene during the gravest dangers, braving all storms, lazy as an ass, yet working always, the butt of a thousand calumnies, but happy inside of me, never joining any coterie, neither literary nor political, fawning upon no one, and left, rejected by all, and yet, how often have I overheard men say about me: What the devil sort of a man is he, and how provoking! He speaks well of everybody!"

Before he definitely closed his books, he wrote another *Mémoire—Mes Six Epoques*—an excellent accomplishment, detailing his sufferings during the Republic. Yet here, too, his cheerful disposition never deserted him. He knew that happiness found at one's doorstep should be rejected, for happiness must be the ultimate victory after long and hazardous battles. Few had fought as many and fewer still had learned the lesson as well.

On the morning of the 18th day of May, 1779, sixty-seven years and three months after his birth, Pierre-Augustin Caron de Beaumarchais was found dead in bed from cerebral hemorrhage. Death relieved him of man's two implacable enemies—time and man. And life offered him the gift she offers only her most cherished favorites—a swift and painless death.

He was buried in a grove in his park. Some months later, his ever loyal friend, Paul Philippe Gudin de la Brenellerie, composed the much quoted quatrain destined for the bust:

> *Bon père, bon époux, bon maître, ami sincère,*
> *Simple dans le procès, fier dans l'adversité,*
> *Auteur original, homme à grand caractère;*
> *Il sut dans tous les temps garder sa liberté.*

> Good father, good husband, good master, sincere friend,
> Simple in trial, proud in adversity,
> Original author, man of noble character;
> He knew at all times how to retain his liberty.

ARTHUR SCHOPENHAUER

The Bomb Is Planted

"My book is a new system of philosophy, but when I say new I mean new in every sense of the word; it is not a restatement of what has already been said, but it is in the highest degree a continuous flow of thought such as has never before entered the mind of mortal man. It is a book, which in my opinion, is destined to rank with those which form the source and incentive to hundreds of others."

Herr Brockhaus, the Leipzig publisher, laughed ironically. He had read countless letters from authors accompanying their manuscripts for consideration, and all spoke of their wares as unique in quality and certain to bring riches and fame, but never had he read one as colossally vain as this by—what was his name?—Doctor in Philosophy Arthur Schopenhauer.

Once upon a time a philosopher was expected to be modest, even humble. Was he not a man of wisdom, and how could a wise man be vain, since watching fools, he saw how much he had in common with them? But this was a generation of pompous egoists, as if no one walked any more, but all rode on horseback and often their haunches did not touch the saddle, but they stood stiff, their toes in their stirrups.

It was all the fault of that peacock, Napoleon Buonaparte. He showed the world how an undersized second-lieutenant could, by luck and pluck and by the corruption of man, become emperor of nations. But could not those who would imitate him and strut upon the earth, see what awaited them? Was he not rotting in that hell hole of St. Helena? Was not that a sufficient moral lesson and admonition?

Alas, what did it avail man that history repeats itself? Did he profit even by his own experiences? So let those who would ride high and gallop wild, for they were sure to tumble into the dust. And if fortunately they were mere philosophers, the dust would only stifle themselves.

The World as Will and Idea, Brockhaus read the title. He
himself had studied philosophy in his youth and was not frightened. He turned the page. "The world is my idea," so the book
started. He smiled. One more who would stuff the universe into
the gullet of an aphorism! The universe, however, always managed to break its way out and the Road to Philosophy was
strewn with the debris of aphorisms as the road of a carnival
with collapsed balloons.

Herr Brockhaus read on. He had to admit that whatever
the merit as an original work the manuscript might have, it was
clear, concise, and even beautiful, as the author immodestly
claimed. It had nothing of the pompous, empty, meaningless
vomit of words so characteristic of the current books of philosophy, even (perhaps in particular) by the most celebrated of
authors. It was, indeed, a new German, a language fluent and
comprehensible. Yes, it was a pleasure to read, but was that an
advantage? Would people buy a book of philosophy which was
not smothered in erudite, recondite, tortuous verbiage? If accessible to all, where was the pride of culture? One must show
the mud and manure on one's boots, proof of having trudged
through the swamps of futile loquacity, before one was admitted
into the temple of the aristocrats. A publisher had to be careful.
He must not offend the public taste.

Nevertheless, he would take a chance. He would publish the
book, particularly since the name of Schopenhauer was becoming famous—Johanna Schopenhauer, popular novelist and
mother of the philosophic author. People would doubtless
think that he had inherited talent and would be curious to read
him, or at least to buy his book, and was not that all that
mattered?

And what were the conditions this daring author was asking?
A ducat for each printed sheet; the publisher must promise on
his word of honor not to betray the contents of the book, or
even the title, before publication; the book must be printed on
good paper with handsome characters, broad margins with no

more than thirty lines to the page, etc. etc. Plus a contract—everything must be put down black on white.

Brockhaus accepted, but long before the book appeared, he had his qualms. Schopenhauer pestered him with letters, became fearful that he would not get his money on time, the book would be published in two volumes instead of one, the publisher would not act honorably, until Brockhaus, unable to endure it all, answered insult with greater insult, and demanded that he appoint one with whom he could deal, for with such a windbag it was impossible. "I only hope," he added, "that my fears regarding your work, of printing mere trash, will not be justified."

It was not mere trash, but his fears, alas, were more than justified. A whole generation had to pass away, before *The World as Will and Idea* would be resurrected from its coffin of dust upon the shelf of the Leipzig publisher.

Schopenhauer had planted the bomb, as he said, and now he would await its detonation, which should rock the world in warmer and more congenial climes. And yet: "I confess that I do not believe my teaching could ever have arisen before the Upanishads, Plato, and Kant could throw their light combined into men's minds. But truly many columns have stood and the sun shone on them, yet only Memnon's sang." And only *The World as Will and Idea,* published as promised, on Michaelmas Day, 1818, was pure and unadulterated truth. All the rest, even the very best of them, were "interwoven with absurdities, in the most grotesque shapes." All the rest were stepping-stones to newer truths; his alone was an eternal monument. Yet truth approaches immortality only as it becomes a platitude, while the acid of time corrodes it, but adds a protective layer of reverence to falsehood. *His* truth was immune and perpetually fresh. He would need this vast, immodest assurance which, like a hidden source, would feed his embittered heart shrunken with neglect.

But now Schopenhauer was thirty and confident, and he looked his part. He was not handsome, to be sure, but his brow was luminous, his blue eyes shone with the flame of genius and his head was massive. He was rather short, certainly not above medium height, his figure square, muscular, and slight. He carried himself with dignity, almost haughtiness. He was scrupulously neat and meticulously well dressed, as a philosopher should not be. But he was so many things a philosopher should not be—human, inconsistent, querulous.

È dolce far niente—"how pleasant it is to do nothing!" And where in all the world should one find this pleasure as exquisite and as soothing as in that pearl of a city, which in youth had been the Mistress of the Seas and as Dowager Mistress of the Palace of Love—Venice? Venice! Sky, sea, and the arms of women—all without compare!

But what had the Pontiff of Pessimism to do with all this? Is not life evil? And is not woman its perpetual propagator? Ah, if only woman would say: "*Basta!* Enough of this! Henceforth my womb shall remain barren and the cycle of birth and of death shall freeze in its futile pulse and the mighty Will shall be defeated and be manifest only in fires and vast spaces, in things which cannot know the meaning of pain and of sorrow!" But woman is perverse and in travail creates those who in travail must live and die.

There was no one nobler than a saint, Schopenhauer said, one who like the Hindu "enters into the trance in which he becomes a living corpse." But, "I am not a saint," he sighed in disillusion and relief. His eye rejoiced in beauty, animate and inanimate, in things created by nature and by the hand of man. He himself was a great artist and he loved the flow and the rhythm of his prose. What shall a man do? If it is a sin to live and enjoy, is it not a more grievous sin to betray one's nature and claim a virtue one did not possess? Is not hypocrisy the sin of sins?

At any rate, in Venice not to sin was the only sin. And in Venice to be thirty, presentable, well-to-do, author of a masterpiece without peer in the annals of thought—oh, let the Will have its will!

Venice was hostess to another mighty pessimist in the year 1818—George Gordon Lord Byron. He, too, was thirty, full of scorn, misanthropy, fury, and despair—and withal the lover extraordinary. His harem, constantly refreshed, boasted ladies of the highest degree and ladies of the lowest, and the poetry they inspired was the finest in Europe. Flowers bloom most luxuriantly and waft the sweetest scents when their roots plunge into the earth and draw the dark milk from its depths.

Byron, however, was already world famous while Schopenhauer was still but a German Doctor of Philosophy, a species as common as mushrooms and as pesky as gnats. He alone was certain that he was Minerva's favorite son, but the Goddess of Wisdom was unconscionably reluctant in acknowledging his legitimacy, and the world did not even confer upon him a state of bastardy. Yet he bore no ill-will, born of envy, toward Byron, and he considered him a supreme artist, second only to Goethe, God of Poetry. After all, poetry was more readily understood and appreciated and therefore poets were more speedily glorified. Philosophers frightened people, unless they were the expounders of futile platitudes such as those who were presently professors in the German universities, or spinners of meaningless tapestries such as crowded the salons in France. Rheumatic spiders all, weaving in dark labyrinths where the dew of Truth never studded their threads with glittering gems.

Goethe, his old and revered friend, gave Schopenhauer a letter of introduction to Lord Byron, and Schopenhauer had long rehearsed both the praises he would offer and the analysis of the deep philosophical implications in the poet's masterpieces. Their meeting was to be memorable, historical, substance for many a beautiful legend, for what event survived the storm of time save anchored by legend?

Yet, Fate would not allow their meeting to take place. And Fate often takes the shape of woman, as in the ancient days when they were three, the sister goddesses who controlled the destiny of man—Clotho, who spun the thread of his life; Lachesis, who determined its length; Atropos, who cut it.

"With my sweetheart, Teresa," Schopenhauer narrates, "I went for a walk on the Lido, when suddenly my Dulcinea cried

out in great excitement: *'Ecco il poeta inglese!'* Byron swept
by me on horseback and the *donna* could not escape from this
impression the whole day. Then I decided not to deliver
Goethe's letter. I was afraid of the horns of cuckoldry. How
much I have regretted that since !"

Thus Byron never heard the name of Schopenhauer, for he
left for Greece, to snatch her, as a knight snatches a beautiful
maiden, from the old and ugly talons of Turkey, the villainous
captor and died in the attempt, at the age of thirty-six.

But Fate often weaves back and forth and unties even as she
ties, and while she cut the thread which might have united Byron
to Schopenhauer, she also cut the rope which would have united
Teresa to Arthur. Schopenhauer, in fact, had been contemplating marriage, or rather, like a meticulous apothecary weighing
poison, he weighed all the arguments philosopher and peasant
had ever placed on the scale of matrimony. And he wrote to his
sister, Adele, nine years younger, that he was tempted. She was
enthusiastic. "Domestic happiness is certainly the most beautiful
life affords." Yet now the feather of jealousy outweighed all
the gold of domesticity, and Schopenhauer was saved.

The loves of the Philosopher of the North had not the glamor
of the loves of the Poet from across the Channel. Or rather, he
would not render them glamorous. Indeed, with the exception
of his mistress, Teresa, beautiful, rich, and distinguished, he
names no one, and his escapades become anonymous philosophical maxims. Only the variety of these maxims and the multitudinous professional descriptions reveal how copiously he had
grazed in the pastures of Holy Venus.

From Venice Schopenhauer went to Florence, from Florence
to Rome, mingling his amorous adventures with studies of the
arts and the poetry of Italy. Meanwhile, he heard bad news
from Germany. The Dantzig firm in which he had invested a
goodly portion of his patrimony, was bankrupt and would give
only thirty percent to all its creditors. To all, but not to him ! He
would accept nothing less than full payment or woe to the House
of Muhl ! "I want what is merely mine," he wrote to his debtor,

"and on which my whole happiness, my freedom, my cultivated leisure depends; a good fortune, that in this world is so seldom the lot of my kind that it would be almost as unconscionable as weak not to defend it to the last drop and hold it fast with the utmost power. . . ." And defend it he did, and so adroitly, that he received every pfennig back. Triumphantly he proclaimed to the world that "a man can be a philosopher without being a fool—" a most startling notion.

Meanwhile, too, his ears were cocked northward. Silence. Utter silence. The mighty bomb which he had planted proved a dud. It lay heavily upon the publisher's shelf—the heavy weight of the dead. And the copies distributed to reviewers? They had filled their baskets, unnoticed, unsung, aye, even uncursed.

And Schopenhauer went in search of consolation, for what is wisdom if not the ability to discover adequate consolation? He was wise and he found it in great abundance. The more one wrote for posterity, the less one pleased his contemporaries, as witness the honor roll of the world's mighty figures, "and I should like to see the man who can boast of a more miserable set than mine." And therefore, who shall achieve greater glory in the future than Arthur Schopenhauer?

"The coldness and neglect with which I was received might have made me doubt of myself. . . . But fortunately at the same time I heard the trumpet of fame proclaiming the entirely worthless, the palpably bad, as excellent, as the very acme of human wisdom. Would a musician be flattered by the loud applause of an audience if he knew that they were nearly all deaf, and that to conceal their infirmity, he saw one or two persons applauding? And what would he say if he discovered that those one or two persons had often taken bribes to secure the loudest applause for the poorest player?"

The grapes of success became sourer and sourer, until it seemed that there was no honor equal to that of being scorned and no pleasure equal to crucifixion.

Yet Schopenhauer was certain that he had "lifted the veil of truth higher than any mortal" before him, and he was equally certain that the world would eventually admit it. Still, "life passes quickly and comprehension is slow: therefore I shall not live to see fame." He was wrong. He did see fame, but many, many years had to pass, and the footsteps of Death were already heard on the staircase leading to his door.

The Seed Achieves Fruition

On the 14th of July, 1789, Bastille was destroyed. Henceforth the world would never again be ruled by rapacious lords, wily priests, illiterate mobs. There would be liberty, equality, fraternity. Ah, the poor heart of man! How it yearns for peace and love! How often and how sorely it is deceived!

In Paris Bastille fell and all the Bastilles everywhere, in every country, began to totter, and all men who loved freedom rejoiced. No one rejoiced more than Heinrich Floris Schopenhauer, rich merchant of the Free City of Dantzig. He rushed to his estate in Oliva to convey the glad tidings to his wife, Johanna, and his son, Arthur, a year and a half old.

That so wealthy a man as Heinrich should welcome a revolution which might even endanger his position only indicated his profound convictions and his deep honesty as well as his fearlessness. But he had already given high proof of these qualities, when once watching a parade in Berlin, Frederick the Great spotted him out in the crowd and bade him come to his castle. Undismayed and frank, he discussed political and business conditions and refused special prerogatives and courtesies which the Emperor offered him if he would establish himself in Prussia. Prussia was under the heel of the military and the elite, and Heinrich preferred his Dantzig, which for centuries had fought to remain an independent entity inhabited by courageous merchants. It never succeeded entirely, but precisely because of this, its spirit remained tense and alert.

Heinrich's ancestors had come to Dantzig from Holland three or four centuries previously, became rich and consequential. For the last three generations, however, the Schopenhauer family showed traces of insanity, and one was born an idiot. The brothers of Heinrich squandered a goodly portion of their patrimony, but they all died, and he was left alone to carry on the business. Not only did he carry on, but he expanded it so that it became one of the leading firms of the city.

Heinrich is depicted as something of a monstrosity—heavily built, round face, big mouth, short nose, protruding eyes—a man of tremendous energy, pride, and intelligence. Whether he had been too busy to indulge in romance in his youth, or too indifferent, it is not recorded, but at the age of thirty-eight, he fell in love.

Johanna Henriette Troisiener was eighteen, blue-eyed, brown-haired, mignonne, gay, affable, and talkative as a magpie. Was it Heinrich's instinct, guided by the Will which will brook no contradiction, the Will which demands that the race continue and be balanced, that he proposed to this girl? And did she, too, despite her youth, unconsciously consider this man, so different in temperament, the one most suitable to father her children?

Many years later, their son said in one of the keenest studies on love and sex in the history of philosophy: "Through a thousand physical accidents and moral aberrations there arises a great variety of deteriorations of the human form; yet, its true type in all its parts is always again established; and this takes place under the guidance of the sense of beauty which always directs the sexual impulse . . . each one will specially regard as beautiful in another individual those perfections which he lacks, nay, even the imperfections which are the opposite of his own . . . the *sense of the species* which desires to maintain the type of the species, chooses, while the individual imagines that he only seeks the heightening of his own pleasure."

At any rate, Heinrich proposed and Johanna accepted without the customary three-day wait for the "consultation of one's heart." She was proud, she said, to belong to this man, who was an important citizen and most open-minded. She spoke neither of passion nor of love. Nor did he indulge in extravagant protestations. It was in the best sense of the word a marriage *de convenance,* which, according to the son, was the most suitable for the race. "Love marriages," he wrote, "as a rule, turn out unhappy, for what the couple thought would be private pleasure turned out to be a public interest. Deluded, they resent the imposture and turn upon each other. . . . *Quien se casa por amores, ha de vivir con dolores"*—"who marries for love must live in sorrow," warns the Spanish proverb.

Like a muezzin Logic calls to all lovers: "Beware the trap! Beware the trap!" When they hear him, they are no longer lovers and do not need his warning. They are now fathers and mothers and the race is saved for one more generation.

But there was something quite tempting for Johanna, who doubtless was well trained by her mother. There was wealth, security, luxury in her marriage, and whether she thought of the future of the race or not, she certainly thought of the present of Johanna Troisinier.

Heinrich's estate in Oliva had a stretch of forest and the sea was always in sight. Surrounding the tall white house was an English garden, flowers and fruit trees, a fountain and a fish pond. And there was a stable of horses and a kennel of dogs, and there were sheep and lambs. And within the house, elegantly furnished, its walls hung with fine engravings and paintings, all the conveniences of the period were installed. And there was, besides, an excellent library—books on history and biography and satire, which Heinrich particularly liked, as well as the latest French novels, which was the style to own. Voltaire and Rousseau and Diderot and d'Alembert and Montesquieu—the great encyclopedists—had penetrated into the very texture of the minds of the Teutons and they who could speak French considered themselves the aristocrats of the intellect and the salon, and would so consider themselves for more than a century after the downfall of the Little Corporal who had marched in triumph over their lands. Then they switched to English, for it is *chic* and profitable to speak the tongue of the rich and the strong.

No beauty awakening in the arms of the beast could feel unhappy in such surroundings, or more than vaguely regret that the arms were not those of a handsome young prince, passionate and radiant with joy. Somber and moody though Heinrich was, he did not lack social graces and was kind and considerate. Moreover, Johanna had her respite, for Heinrich remained in Dantzig five days a week to conduct his business properly and came to Oliva only for week-ends.

But while friends and guests were welcome on these two days and the entertainment was often lavish, they must all depart when the host departed. *La donna è mobile* is not only an excellent refrain for an operatic tenor, but also an uncomfortable prosaic truth known to all husbands, and in particular to those who marry pretty women twenty years younger than themselves. But that ugliness in woman means virtue has been the undoing of many a man, for there is nothing more distressing than to be made a cuckold by one whose sole offering was security.

For the time being, however, Heinrich was without suspicion and Johanna was gay, dancing about her manifold possessions, and reading endlessly the French novels. Two decades later, she herself would begin to write and became the author of two dozen novels, setting a vogue in which the heroine marries for duty rather than for love and remains pure although she loves other men than her husband. Plato, whose good name has so often been taken in vain, becomes the true hero and Platonic titillation is exalted as the noblest of emotions. Goethe himself praised her work and became her friend and frequent guest, but Goethe, after all, was both poet and courtier, two professions always associated with flattery and falsehood. Indeed, Plato excluded both from his Utopia.

Hemmed in by a half-dozen countries, Dantzig suffered from perennial pressure, now on one side, now the other. At various periods of her history, this city of beautiful buildings and great

warehouses, fell into the hands of Poland, Denmark, Branden-
burg, and now seemed within the grasp of Prussia, the worst of
all, according to Heinrich Schopenhauer. He was determined
not to remain in his beloved city when that misfortune finally
befell her. In the interim, he would take a trip with his wife
who was pregnant.

They visited Belgium, France, and reached England, "the
land of freedom," where Heinrich contemplated moving his
business, and where his child (without doubt a son) would be
born and thus achieve English citizenship. But Johanna was
homesick, and despite the vicious waters of the Channel, which
like furious hounds have for centuries torn to bits all those who
would crash the gates of the Tight Little Island, the couple set
sail for home. They nearly met with disaster, but finally succeeded in reaching the Continent, and on February 22, 1788, at
117 Heilingengeist Strasse—the "Street of the Holy Ghost"—
a male child was born to Herr and Frau Schopenhauer, a male
destined to challenge all the holy ghosts, religious and philosophical, and slash them with his mighty sword. That their
wounds were healed and that once again they stalk upon the
Earth, is due to the fact that truth must be judged in terms of
time and space; superstition in terms of eternity and infinity.

His name had been decided upon the moment he rapped
against his mother's belly informing her that he was no longer
to be taken for mere seed. It was, so the father decreed, Arthur.
Arthur, he explained, retained its form in most languages, and
that gives the person a sense of stability and permanence, the
main requisites to a merchant, who one day would head a great
and famous house. And merchant Arthur would be, but of such
goods as the father never dreamed of and never lived to see.

And so Arthur was begotten and born, and "every time a man
is begotten and born, the clock of human life is wound up anew,
to repeat the same old piece it has played innumerable times
before, passage after passage, measure after measure, with
insignificant variations." So Arthur would say, when the clock
reached a certain measure of time. Meanwhile, to make certain

that he would not have to spend eternity in hell, should any untoward thing happen to the baby, Arthur was baptized with
due solemnity in the great and beautiful Marienkirche.

The holy water, however, saved him only for the time being,
but nothing in the vast arsenal of ignorance and bigotry could
frighten him in maturity, and as he died unrepentant, his destiny
is well known, for a man who understood the meaning of things,
"could not be terrified by an endless past or an endless future in
which he would not be, for this he would regard as the empty
delusion of the web of Maya. Thus he would not fear death
any more than the sun fears the night." And he would become
part of the all-powerful Will, shapeless, therefore without
pain. "*This* is immortality."

There was much merriment in the Schopenhauer household
at Oliva and Johanna's delight knew no bounds. "Like all young
mothers," she related, "I was convinced that not in all God's
earth was such a beautiful, pure, and intelligent child to be
found." Had she guessed how bitter their relationship would
become when he grew up, how he would torment her with his
relentless criticism of her way of life, how he would plague her
with his sarcasm, so that she had to drive him out of the house,
and for a quarter of a century would not see him again, until she
died, old and lonesome, would she have pressed his little nostrils
until his lungs collapsed or mixed his milk with a few drops of
poison?

For the first five years of his life Arthur was utterly happy, or
so it seemed to him as he looked back in his old age. At any rate,
it was not his happy childhood which determined his philosophy
of life and the sorrow and pain which he saw everywhere in the
world were not viewed with the tear-stained eyes of the boy.

Now the drums of the conquering Prussian army were heard
on the outskirts of Dantzig, and Heinrich Schopenhauer, republican, liquidated his business in great haste and at a great
loss and established himself in the sister-city of Hamburg, capital of the State of Hamburg. Hamburg had a long and glorious

history, which means, among other things, much bloodshed and much misery.

Hamburg was founded as fortress and church by Charlemagne in the ninth century, became the chief city of the Hanseatic League in the thirteenth, a free imperial city in the sixteenth. In 1871 it was incorporated in the German Empire and in 1944 it was virtually leveled during the Second World War.

There can be no polite revolution, since the primary cause of revolution is politeness itself—the satin cloak hiding society's leprous sores. And since a revolution is the parturation of an idea, like the parturation of the flesh, it is accompanied by travail and agony, and history records no effective anesthesia. The French Revolution was in full swing—terrors, wars, liberations, and the Corsican, his left hand in his tunic, began his triumphant marches.

And Arthur Schopenhauer passed from the chiaroscuro of childhood into the daylight of boyhood and adolescence.

The Whelp Becomes a Lion

Heinrich appreciated books, but the book of experience he valued more highly. "My son shall read in the book of the world," he said, and for that purpose he took him on extensive trips through the main countries of Europe. In those days, despite wars and revolutions, man was allowed to circulate, for it was known that as long as people met people, there was transfusion of blood and the veins emptied by madness were refilled by companionship. The time would come, however, when the earth would shrink to the size of a courtyard and the oceans to ponds, and one could breakfast in one continent and sup in another between sunrise and sunset, but nations raised enormous barbed fences and lowered curtains of iron, and people shouted to one another: "Let not your feet cross our thresholds nor your eyes peer through the cracks of our gates nor your mouths utter the thoughts of your minds! We are neighbors, therefore mortal enemies! Far better to rot apart than flourish together!"

Arthur was put in *pensions* in France and England in order that he might learn the languages, and he learned them with astonishing rapidity, idiom and accent and dialect. Later he learned Italian and Spanish with equal alacrity, not to mention Latin and Greek whose mastery was the *sine qua non* of culture.

With a passion unbecoming a philosopher in search of nirvana, Schopenhauer began and continued throughout his lifetime, to hate different peoples for different reasons—the Germans because of their heaviness and affection. . . . "Wherefore, in provision of my death, I acknowledge that on account of its infinite stupidity I loathe the German nation and I blush to belong thereto. . . ."

The French—"Other parts of the world have monkeys, Europe has Frenchmen, *ça balance.*" The Americans—"They are the *plebs* of the world, partly, I suppose, on account of their republican government, and partly because they descend from those who left Europe for Europe's good." The Jews—his hatred for them was boundless. "The Jews are God's chosen people, are they? Very good, tastes differ, they certainly are not mine." He only regretted that Nebuchadnezzar had not destroyed them totally. A century and a quarter later, one of his compatriots almost succeeded. Would Schopenhauer have applauded? He accepted only one set of ethics and one morality —compassion for all, including animals. Would the Jews have been the exception?

Philosophically he despised the children of Israel because their religion was one of love for the earth and the earth's good things. They remained confirmed optimists throughout the ages, despite their miserable fate. Even Spinoza, whom he greatly admired, was always cheerful. "The Jews are a joyous nation, full of love for life," he growled.

But the anti-Semitism of Schopenhauer and that of Kant, his master, and that of Wagner, his disciple, as well as that of Goethe, half genius, half stuffed-shirt, had besides a local habitation. Among the civilized nations, the Germans treated the Jews most ignominiously, and although Napoleon tore down the walls of the ghettoes, at his defeat, they were promptly raised again.

The collective injustice, which these representative men were keenly aware of, and yet were unwilling to fight against, required powerful reasons—philosophical, esthetical, historical—of extenuation. Guilty, they hated their victims and sought—and found—just causes for their injustice. Their consciences stilled, they could write books on universal compassion and dithyrambs to the Universal God and compose music to thrill the universal heart of mankind.

But Schopenhauer did exclude one people from his hate and disdain—the English, the noblemen of the earth, and their language he preferred above all others. And often in his essays, he would write paragraphs in English.

Arthur's eyes were wide open and his memory excellent. On his trips he saw magnificent scenery and gay capitals, but he also saw "the miserable huts and poverty-stricken people." And already the silt which was to form the river-bed of his philosophy, was gathering and turning into rock, and whatever the waters that would cover it and however violent the storms, there would be no turning, no fissure, no cracking.

While Arthur was growing into manhood and learned the prerequisites of one who would be a prosperous and important citizen—riding, fencing, dancing, flute-playing—his father showed definite and progressive symptoms of disintegration. He lost his hearing (an affliction which would later befall his son); he had lapses of memory; fits of violence and melancholy; and his wife's liveliness and social activities only irritated him and generated dark suspicions.

Arthur was apprenticed to one of the large mercantile houses for training in a career which he despised, but pursued to please his father. From a dreary labor, he would return in the evening to witness a *ménage* of friction and subdued but deep hatred. To his despair was added misogyny, for in his mother he saw all women, and in his father he saw all men, tortured by women.

The dénouement finally took place—Heinrich Schopenhauer jumped to his death into one of the canals which catacomb Hamburg. Arthur had always loved and admired his father. "Noble and beneficent!" he wrote in a contemplated dedication to his book. "I value you, my noble father. And everyone who finds anything of joy, or consolation, or instruction from my work shall learn of your name and know that if Heinrich Floris Schopenhauer had not been the man that he was, Arthur Schopenhauer would have gone to the bottom a hundred times. . . ."

"The character or will," Schopenhauer said, "is inherited from the father; the intellect from the mother." And the character is immutable. Never during one's entire life, may it be altered. Whatever changes may seem to occur to character are fictitious, used to conceal or to deceive. Since character is the Will itself, the life force, it is the repository of passion, of desire, of suffering, of power, of intuition, and therefore the fountainhead of genius. The intellect, on the other hand, is something that may be developed, and is essential to man's continuation in society. It is the source of the graces, the color, the brilliance. It is knowledge, or the eye, which gazes upon the Will and understands it and explains it.

Schopenhauer possessed character in an extraordinary degree and thus drank deeply from the very source of existence and thereby became a genius, and geniuses are "scarcely one in a hundred million people." His intellect, which he developed with time and study and application, lent his work subtlety and charm and distinction.

He should have been grateful, then, to both his parents in equal measurement, but he was not. His father's gift—the ability to feel the vast misery of life, the agonies and the futilities, he considered far superior to his mother's gift—the capacity for pleasure and artistry, for these were in a sense, merely the valueless glass which glitters in the sun. Even more, his mother's gifts, this desire for sensual satisfaction and applause, were the very cause for his inability to achieve sainthood and the anni-hilation of self, which he considered his tragedy.

But for the moment he was only vaguely aware of these con-tradictions in his nature. His father was dead. He was seven-teen years old and an apprentice for a life occupation which he despised, but which he would pursue, in memory of his good progenitor.

Freed from the burden of matrimony, Johanna Schopenhauer disposed of her late husband's business, and less than a year after his death, left with her nine-year-old daughter, Adele, for Weimar, then the cultural center of Germany, in search of lit-erary fame and social glamor.

Arthur had gone to work as usual, and when he returned he found a letter addressed to him:

We have spent the evening together very happily; let that be the leave-taking. Farewell, my dear, good Arthur! When you receive these lines, I shall presumably not be here; but in any case do not come! I cannot bear the leave-taking. . . . I hope that it will not grieve you that I have deceived you. I did it for my own sake; for I know how weak I am in such moments, and how every violent commotion affects me. Farewell! God bless you!

                         Your mother,
                         J. Schopenhauer.

Arthur would find many such notes from his Mütterchen, for she feared his anger and his scrutiny and preferred to write him rather than confront him, even when, for a time, he lived in her house. It was these brutal and selfish messages, coated with the honey of sentimentalism, which gave him an insight into her nature, and which made him despise her. She reminded him of the whole period in which he lived—vacuous, self-centered, cal-lous to the poverty and the sufferings of the great masses of people, and all sprinkled with the sickening perfume of roman-ticism—leprous sores studded with precious jewels.

Despite his best intentions to follow in his father's footsteps, Arthur soon reached his tether of endurance. He would not be a merchant, however rich and respected one might become. He would be a scholar, a philosopher, however unremunerative, however obscure one's position. His mother, who held the purse strings, finally consented, and at the age of eighteen, when the average German student entered the university, Arthur began his studies at the *gymnasium,* or high school, at Gotha, near Weimar.

He made astonishing progress, but already got into trouble with the professors. It was to be a war to the death and until his death. No devil who tormented the souls of the pious was as black as the professor who darkened the minds of his students, and no devil ever had such unholy water splashed over his head or ever heard such cataracts of vituperation.

Arthur was forced to quit school, and his mother allowed him to come to Weimar to complete his preparation, but on condition that he did not live with her. Hofrätin Schopenhauer had already become a social star and her salon was frequented by the elite, the glory of German letters and arts. There was Goethe and Wieland and Grimm and Zacharias Werner, the poet, and the two brothers Schlegel, poets and critics, and even the Grand Duke and the Duke von Sachsen.

Ah, if only Arthur willed it, he could become a social lion, but to become a social lion one must allow one's teeth to be pulled out, and Arthur preferred to keep his sharp and glittering, and to use them mercilessly on imposture and hypocrisy and their votaries, however medalled their chests and laureled their heads.

At twenty-one, Arthur forced his mother to give him his share of the inheritance, which despite her foolish investments and her lavish household, was still considerable. With it, if prudently invested and prudently spent, he could lead a life of leisure and cultural pursuits. And Schopenhauer was prudent. He had inherited caution and sagacity from a long line of ancestors who knew the value of money. Nor had his own experience of several years in the mercantile world been without profit. And although his life lasted beyond the three score years and ten allotted man, and despite his almost complete literary failure, he succeeded in leading the life of a free man and philosopher. Nor had he ever been obliged to relinquish the pleasure of travel or the comfort of a good home or good kitchen, and his clothes though forever unvaried in style, were often renewed.

He knew how to manage his affairs, but he also had the good fortune of living in a period, which, though unpleasantly shaken by revolutions and wars, still was sufficiently well anchored to allow permanence to investments and constancy to money. A century later, the gold coins he would have hidden from the hands of thieves, would have been as theft in his own hands, and the shares and bonds would have disappeared in the maws of the rats of taxes and depreciation.

Gladly he left his mother stew in her social *ragout,* and set out for the University of Göttingen, the citadel of science and free inquiry. Since he did not have to major in any particular branch for the ulterior purpose of teaching, he could indulge in the pleasure of drinking from all the casks of knowledge. And his thirst was not then, nor ever would be assuaged. He matriculated for Natural History, Mineralogy, Anatomy, Mathematics, Physics, Chemistry, Botany, Logic, Metaphysics, History, Psychology, and the Classical languages. He took voluminous notes to which he added marginal notes of criticism, becoming more and more virulent. Many of the things learned here would later be used as examples to reenforce his great thesis and give it not only verbal, but scientific validity, despite its purely philosophic approach.

Those were the days of duelling and drinking in the German universities, which afterwards became the romantic themes for operettas. *Gaudeamus igitur!* Therefore, let us enjoy! It was the song of youth and its echoes mingled with the echoes of the dull clinking of the giant *Steins* foaming with beer and the sharp clinking of the swords dripping with blood. And what spirited young lady would bother with a man who had not a saber's cut across his face, symbol of virility?

Arthur Schopenhauer, however, despised vulgar pleasures

and condemned vitriolically the use of swords to "redeem honor," or show bravura. He was never young, in the accepted meaning of the term. His pessimism is not the romantic "pining for what is not," the sigh of love, the amulet to protect one's happiness from the evil eye, from the jealousy of the gods.

Schopenhauer's pessimism is the pessimism of age, of maturity. Oak though he was, he did not need the long years generally required for its growth. The sapling, overbrimming with the sap of intuition, shot upward and spread its vast branches in all directions.

Long before he had played a significant part in it, he already realized that the world was a stage and everything about it amateurish—miscast characters, poor direction, tawdry scenery, vulgar *claqueurs,* absent-minded prompters—and the play a hotchpotch of tragedy and farce, bombastic verse and gutter prose, without beginning, without end, without point. No wonder the Author was in hiding.

He spent two years at Göttingen, then left for the University of Berlin, where he continued his scientific work and attended the lectures of Jean Gottlieb Fichte, disciple of Kant, whose philosophy finally developed into a sort of pantheism, which he called transcendental idealism, and which by circuitous ways influenced profoundly the American school of transcendentalism headed by Ralph Waldo Emerson.

From Fichte Schopenhauer learned something about the Will, which became the foundation of his own philosophy. But Fichte, in his opinion, mixed so much falsehood with truth, that he ended by hating him. Moreover, he could not stomach a style involved and impenetrable, which appealed to those who believed that light was too frivolous for depth.

At Berlin he spent two more years and left precipitously, for it was 1813 and Napoleon, although shaken by the Russian fiasco, was taking threatening gestures in the direction of Germany. Now was the time for all patriotic Germans, once and for all, to break off her chains from the victorious chariot of the

Little Corporal who called himself the Big Man of Destiny. And even philosophers like Hegel orated and waved the flag and the students bared their swords.

Schopenhauer was not patriotic. For him the state had no reality. It was the acme of irrational power, the sum-total of all individual irrationalities, and its malignity had no end. No wonder that nations chose as their symbols murderous birds and beasts of prey. He fled, therefore, to the little town of Rudolf- stadt, where the drums and the trumpets were not heard, to write his thesis for the doctorate. In those days there were still oases in the vast desert of human folly. Man did not have to bury himself miles underneath the earth to escape the fumes and the fires which his genius stole from the invisible atom.

By the end of the year he completed his manuscript which he entitled: "The Fourfold Root of the Principle of Sufficient Rea- son." He presented it to the Jena Faculty, and in the fall of 1813 he received his doctor's diploma. Promptly he inscribed his name and title upon his window-pane—with a diamond! If van- ity did not sustain us, what could?

The fourfold root is the law of cause and effect in four forms:

1. Logical, or the determination of conclusion by premises.

2. Physical, or the determination of effect and cause.

3. Mathematical, or the determination of structure by the laws of mathematics.

4. Moral, or the determination of conduct by character.

He elucidated Kant, which, perhaps, was its chief merit, but it was a doctor's thesis and only adumbrated his *opus maximum* which needed a further gestation of five years.

Still, Schopenhauer, who considered everything he wrote communicated to him by the Spirit of Truth, as Mohammed's words were communicated to him by the Angel Gabriel (al- though Schopenhauer was generally right and Mohammed a liar), published the thesis as a small book at his own expense and sent copies around. The world, however, had other things to do than read the young thinker's theories, and his rage against it, which was to rise in a steady crescendo during the many years of neglect, hurt it not at all.

One copy he took with him to his mother at Weimar. She, surely, would take pride in her offspring's offspring. Unfortunately it was ill-timed, for Johanna had recently delivered her own baby, *Gabrielle,* dripping with the treacle of romance, and which was catapulted to fame by the applause of Goethe's gloved hands. A momentary fame, to be sure, but what does one live by save by moments?

Johanna's hands, still wet from vari-colored paints, for she also indulged in the use of palet and brush, touched the little book her son offered her with that timid daintiness one touches a thing suspected of uncleanliness, and read the title: "The Fourfold Root of the Principle of Sufficient Reason," and asked with fictitious naïveté: "Is this an apothecary's treatise, Arthur?"

It is not recorded, but Arthur, who often was Rabelaisian, might well have replied, and with a tone infinitely more venomous: "It's a clyster for your dear, stinking, constipated *Gabrielle, Mütterchen!*" What *is* recorded is that Arthur retorted: "This book will be read when there does not remain one single copy of your writings on any shelf." To which she spilled her own maternal venom: "Of yours the whole edition will still be available."

Johanna was the luckier, for while she lived she continued to be read and her son's books still slumbered on the shelves of the melancholy publisher. But when he became famous and her works were tumbling into the abyss of eternal oblivion, his success lost half its savor because she was not there to suffer humiliation. Is it to please our friends or spite our enemies that we labor to succeed?

There was one other little matter which annoyed Arthur—Herr Müller von Gerstenberg, a man of thirty or so, who lived in his mother's place and assumed the air of lord and master. Despite Johanna's protestations of unadulterated friendship toward the man, Arthur carried on violent scenes, both with his mother and Herr Müller, who, indeed, had been but the latest in a long line of "spiritual lovers."

Arthur's grievances against his mother were manifold: She was squandering his father's wealth, presumably meaning that at her death he would inherit nothing. And in this he was right, for Johanna died penniless. She was disgracing his father's memory by her love affairs which started promptly after her husband's death and seemingly never terminated. In vain did she claim that they were all "spiritual." He understood, as few others, or according to himself, as no other, the basic urge of creation, which calls itself love and must achieve its aim, always the same aim. Of course, he could not actually prove that his mother had shared her bed, since even in the days of Solomon it was already known that the way of a woman with a man was one of three mysteries forever unverifiable. His mother led a social life in which, with one or two exceptions, rattling empty heads listened to other rattling empty heads, because they could not endure their own rattling, and worse still, their hearts were equally empty. His mother poisoned the mind of his sister, Adele, whom he loved, against him, by making him appear as an unreasonable monster. But worst of all (and this in his pride he probably never openly confessed) his mother's heart was stone toward him, her son, her first-born. He had suffered anguish and disillusion in the world, but her ears were stuffed and she would not hear him and her hand was limp and would not soothe his burning brow. She had spawned him and she went her way—a forgetful bitch.

And now, he would put her to a final test. "Choose between von Gerstenberg and me!" he shouted. It was the eternal struggle between pleasure and duty—the pleasure of a handsome young admirer, who danced attendance upon her and the duty toward a son, difficult, unsociable, exigent, and in her opinion, only mildly talented, but who considered himself a genius without compare and demanded appropriate honors. And the woman whose novels created a literature of self-sacrifice as the noblest aim for maiden, wife, and mother, chose pleasure and chased the son.

More than a quarter of a century passed, and he was old and she a cripple, fat, lonesome, and poor and they had never met again. And she died. Nor did he ever meet his sister again and she died four years after their mother.

"You and I are two!" he exclaimed when she had made her choice. And thus angrily he tore the umbilical cord. But he could not spill the blood which coursed through his veins. Each man's neck is a scaffold from which hang his ancestors.

The World as Will and Idea

"The world is my idea—this is the truth which holds good for everything that lives and knows, though man alone can bring it into reflective and abstract consciousness. If he really does this, he has attained to philosophical wisdom. It then becomes clear and certain to him that what he knows is not a sun and an earth, but only an eye that sees a sun, a hand that feels an earth; that the world which surrounds him is there only as an idea, i.e., only in relation to something else, the consciousness, which is himself."

Man's perennial struggle is to rationalize an irrational universe. The relation between man and the universe may be compared to a melodramatic actor declaiming a pompous monologue to a deaf and dumb audience.

Our very bodies, how do we become aware of them? We are not immediately conscious of them. They are objects, perceived in space. Mere feeling is not sufficient. The child speaks of itself in the third person. "Only in the brain does our own body first come to appear as extended, articulate, organic"—therefore individualized. We are, then, subjects and objects, conscious of our existence, as conscious of all existence. Yet, this is not achieved by mere rationalization, by the process of cause and effect, but by intuition or understanding, and the world and ourselves are valid because of this understanding, and in proportion to its depth and development.

The world, however, does exist. It is not merely an illusion, or rather, illusion is also real, and "idea," in the Schopenhauerian sense, is not merely the residue of an object, but it is the object as it impinges itself upon the consciousness of the beholder. As a matter of fact, Schopenhauer does not use the word "Idee" or "Begriff," which would be the German equivalent for the English "idea." He uses the word "Vorstellung," which from the verb "vorstellen" means "to set in front" or "to place before" or "to present" or "introduce." It may also mean a theatrical performance or an expostulation. In short, it is that which confronts us, is examined, scrutinized, enters our consciousness, and finally is understood.

Even the higher animals are capable of a limited comprehension of this "Vorstellung," and a man's intelligence is graded according to his capacity to grasp all its functions and correlate them. And if, besides, he is able to universalize, to grasp the idea which is the sum-total of all ideas, the vast, the limitless idea, the tapestry which has no frame of space or time, then he is a philosopher.

"To repeat the whole nature of the world abstractly, universally, and distinctly in concepts, and thus to store up, as it were, a reflected image of it in permanent concepts always at the command of reason; this, and nothing else is philosophy."

But as we contemplate the immensity of the universe and meditate upon the long ages which have preceded us and which will follow us, "we feel ourselves dwindle to nothing . . . we feel ourselves pass away and vanish into nothing like drops in the ocean. But at once there rises against this ghost of our nothingness . . . the immediate consciousness that the universe exists only as our idea. . . . The vastness of the world which disquieted us before, rests now in us; our dependence upon it is annulled by its dependence upon us . . . we are one with the world and therefore, not oppressed, but exalted by its immensity."

As long as we deal with perception, we are within the boundaries of truth, and "no truth is more certain, more independent of all others, the less in need of proof, than this—that all exists for knowledge, and therefore this whole world is only object in relation to subject, perception of a perceiver, in a word, idea. . . . But in the sphere of abstract thought, error may reign for a thousand years, impose its yoke upon whole nations . . . and by the help of its slaves and dupes, may chain and fetter those whom it cannot deceive. . . . If it is mind, if it is knowledge that makes man the lord of creation, there can be no such thing as harmless error, still less venerable and holy error."

And Schopenhauer with unbecoming optimism, perorates: "This is the power of truth; its conquest is slow and laborious, but if once victory be gained it can never be wrested again." The greatest danger to truth, however, is this belief that it must necessarily triumph over error. Truth, in fact, is always at the mercy of error and may be rescued from its wily clutches only by supreme efforts. Nor is its survival assured. Its robustness is only apparent and it can draw breath only in an appropriate climate.

But Arthur Schopenhauer had written down his thoughts for years and at thirty his system had opened before his eyes "like a beautiful landscape through the morning mists," and to think that such a truth could ever perish and the landscape turn into a Fata Morgana's vanishing garden, gripped his heart in a vice of misery. Therefore, "though this our world, which is so real, with all its suns and milky-ways . . . is nothing," *his* truth about this "nothing," not only is something, but must remain something for all time. For this, he is willing to grant all other truths unequivocal permanence.

Thus, Schopenhauer was shuttlecocked between colossal pride and limitless humility. "The vast world with all its colors and sounds is but *my* idea and would cease to exist if I closed my eyes," and "I am an unmentionable small worm in the endless

empyrean of space, a speck of misery, caught for a moment on
the warm edge of a racing planet amid the nightmare vastness
of stars and clashing matter, and so fragile and insignificant,
that let there be the slightest change in my environment I would
no longer exist." On this loom of grandeur and wretchedness, he
wove his great thoughts and his deep intuitions into the magnificent pattern of his philosophy.

Nor was this hypocrisy on Schopenhauer's part, for every
man must lead a double life, that of his words and that of his
deeds, and only thus can he achieve even a precarious balance.
Even a wolf has in his wardrobe a sheep's coat and is bilingual—
he howls and he bleats.

But is this all there is to the universe—these phantoms, these
images, the idea reflected in the myriad minds of the myriad
generations? Is it "an empty dream or a baseless vision, not
worth our notice?" If it has any meaning, any validity, it cannot
be grasped "from without," by logic, by mathematical mechanics. In this way we achieve nothing save more images and a
nomenclature. "We are like a man who goes round a castle seeking in vain for an entrance, and sometimes sketching the fa-
çades."

Schopenhauer claimed that this futile method of walking
around had always been followed by philosophers before him,
and consequently they never discovered the truth. With him
commences a new dispensation. In fact, however, many philosophers sought the hidden wheels which turn the perpetual merry-
go-round. There were those who identified it with music, with
numbers, with evil powers, with gods, with God, but they could
not reconcile infinite compassion, infinite wisdom, infinite love
with a world of infinite pain, infinite ignorance, infinite hate, and
their involved, pompous, rhetorical arguments and declamations enraged Schopenhauer and he spewed his bile upon them.

Even as Schopenhauer said: "The world is my idea," he now
added: "The world is my will." This is the thing-in-itself, the
essence, the great, limitless power which moves the wheels of the
merry-go-round, and also supplies its musical accompaniment.

And the musical accompaniment is a threnody without variations from eon to eon, a futile *Miserere*.

How does man become aware of this Will, this mighty, endless stream of energy? By his body. A man is aware of movements, of actions, of pains and fears, of desires and needs, of appetites and satisfactions. If he were only a *knowing* subject, however, as, for instance "a winged cherub without body," he would follow these manifestations, cause and effect, yet he would have no insight into his own personality. But man is rooted in this world of Will and partakes of it, and his intuition tells him that he lives by the grace of it and dies when discarded by it. He, too, in his microscopic entity, *wills,* as the cosmos *wills* in its entity without bourne.

Thus, the universe is explicable only as the result of forces immanent within itself, as man is explicable as a result of the forces within him, and man and all things in the universe can be comprehended only as modifications of one single existence, the Universal Unity. "After the teaching of Bruno, Spinoza, and Schelling, my age had understood perfectly that all things are One; but the nature of this Unity, and the rationale of its appearance as plurality, were reserved for me to explain."

While previous thinkers regarded Intelligence or Freedom as attributes of the Will, called by various names, Schopenhauer grants it nothing save omnipotence. It is a blind, mindless power, purposeless save that of perpetuating itself. And it perpetuates itself by what Schopenhauer calls "Vorstellung" or "idea." And "idea" means all that exists in time and space, the external world, the world of phenomena. And this purpose of the Will to perpetuate itself is identical with our will to live. But the Great Will is not concerned with the individual, but with the species, and even the species may disappear, and the Will is unconcerned, provided it finds other means of expressing itself.

The Will is everywhere, immutable, in what we call animate or inanimate things. There is the tendency of water to flow; the longing of iron to attach itself to the loadstone; the violence with which contrary currents of electricity *endeavor* to unite;

the *choice,* one might almost say the *passion,* of certain fluids to join or to reject other fluids. In sum, the Will-to-Live!

"When we think of the future and of the coming generations, the millions of human beings, and we try in imagination to fancy them with us, we wonder from where they will spring, where they are now. . . . And where can it all be save there, where every reality has been and will be. . . . And you, foolish questioner, who do not recognize your own essence, you are like the leaf on the tree, which withering in autumn . . . cries—'I am no more!' Foolish leaf, whither do you go? Whence do the fresh leaves come? Where is this chaos whose gulf you fear? See, your own self is in that force, interior and hidden, acting on the tree which, through all generations of leaves, knows neither birth nor death. And now tell me, tell me, is man unlike the leaf?"

Like the leaf we are, and like the leaf we wither and pass away, and though we know that others will replace us and the tree of life will continue to blossom, we mourn and bewail the loss of ourselves. And there are those who, to escape death, proclaim life an illusion, yet how they cling to it! And there are those who deny the existence of death, but, they, too, are buried. And none of those who rent mansions in heaven willingly surrender their huts upon earth. Indeed, only our afflictions reconcile us to death, and this is the sole conciliatory gesture of Nature to Man.

And this Will, reflected in every living being, from ameba to man, this passion which cannot be gainsaid, what does it offer to all who partake of it, save suffering? "Unless suffering is the direct and immediate object of life, our existence must entirely fail of its aim. It is absurd to look upon the enormous amount of pain that abounds everywhere in the world, and originates in needs and necessities inseparable from life itself, as serving no purpose at all and the result of mere chance. Each separate misfortune as it comes seems, no doubt, to be something exceptional; but misfortune in general is the rule. . . . I know of no greater absurdity than that propounded by most systems of philosophy in declaring evil to be negative in its character. Evil is just what is positive; it makes its own existence felt. . . . It is the good which is negative; in other words, happiness and satisfaction always imply some desire fulfilled, some state of pain brought to an end."

But is the Will a wicked Ogre who delights in torturing all things capable of response to pain, and in proportion to their capacity—starting at the base of the Pyramid of Misery with the lowest type of animal life and reaching the apex with man, the creature of countless agonies? No, the Will is not an Ogre. It is not even conscious of the endless varieties of torture which it stirs in the boiling cauldron, called the world. It wills only to be, and therefore it calls to all things: "Live!" And all things obey.

But to live is to transform, which is another word for murder, for mutual destruction. That one may live another must die—this is the law inexorable. The worm kills the fruit, the bird kills the worm, the man kills the bird, the man kills the man—and that is the grimmest war of all. In a general cataclysm man finds consolation for his personal tribulations. This is the reason wars have appeared to him in the nature of a relief.

The Earth has no teeth, but it devours all; has no stomach, but it digests all; has no womb, but it recreates all. In the salt of the sea lies buried the sweet of all the rivers. We come naked and leave naked—that is all the bookkeeping. "Certain it is that work, worry, labor, and trouble form the lot of almost all men their whole life long. . . . In every individual the measure of pain essential to him was determined once and for all by his nature; a measure which could neither remain empty nor be more than filled. . . . If a great and pressing care is lifted from our breast, another immediately replaces it . . . and occupies the throne."

Many are the swords which hang over man's head, but the two whose points always graze his neck are labor and boredom. When one lifts the other presses deeper. Boredom, ennui, is by no means the blunter of the two, and could drive man "to the greatest excesses, as does famine, its opposite extreme. Public precautions are taken against it as against other calamities, hence the historical *panem et circenses*—bread and circuses."

And thus between the two shores of desire and attainment, man's life flows on, a river murky with dead hopes, dead ideals, dead pleasures, dead loves, dead ambitions, dead honors. "If you try to imagine, as nearly as you can, what an amount of misery, pain, and suffering of every kind the sun shines upon its course, you will admit that it would be much better if, on earth as little as on the moon, the sun were able to call forth the phenomena of life; and if, here, as there, the surface were still in crystalline state."

And what is the secret of all this misery without end? Why is man such an insatiable creature? Why is it that "every satisfaction he attains lays the seeds of some new desire, so that there is no end to the wishes of each individual man? The real reason is simply that, taken in itself, Will is the lord of all worlds; everything belongs to it, and therefore no one single thing can ever give it satisfaction, but only the whole, which is endless. For all that, it must arouse our sympathy to think how very little the Will, this lord of the world, really gets when it takes the form of an individual; usually just enough to keep the body together. This is why man is so very miserable. Human life must be some kind of mistake. . . . In fact, the conviction that the world and man is something that had better not have been, is of a kind to fill us with indulgence toward one another. Nay, from this point of view, we might well consider the proper form of address to be not Monsieur, Sir, Mein Herr, but Fellow-Sufferer, Soci Malorum, Compagnon de Misères !"

There are those who attribute Arthur Schopenhauer's philosophy of pessimism to the quarrels he had with his mother, as if the war between generations had ever obtained an armistice; there are those who attribute it to the romantic period, in which he lived, as if all periods have not their romanticism, even if concealed in brazen vulgarism; there are those who attribute it to the fiasco of the French Revolution, but does not every gen-

eration, breathless, await the birth-cry of the millennium? And
there are those who attribute it to the fact that his age was an
age of transition, but is not man always on the bridge between
despair and hope—the past and the future?

The disdain, the contempt, the anger with which people dismiss pessimism, gives rise to the profound suspicion that we are
dealing with reality. There is no gesture more typically human
than that of concocting invectives and presenting them in full
payment for truth. Cornered, animals snort, spit, discharge evil
smells. Man insults. Truth, however, is patient and enduring,
and as on a gigantic primordial tree, each cycle of falsehood
carves a hoop to indicate its age, but leaves it flourishing.

The fact is that Arthur Schopenhauer envisaged the world
with his own eyes and with his own mind and with his own guts
and with all the impressions and experiences he had gathered in
his fugitive career in time and space, but how else is it possible?
He saw what *he* saw, and he presented to the world his conclusions in a style unique in philosophy and worthy of the laurels of
art and poetry.

Those who would contradict him and prove his philosophy
false, must first remove from the cosmos pain and cruelty and
murder and war and disease and old age and death, and discover
the magic fluid which would hold together creations of beauty
and genius and not allow Time to surrender them to the maws
of worms and the claws of spiders. Indeed, they would have to
capture the Will and make it alter its ways.

Yet, the philosophy of pessimism has brought consolation to
countless sensitive people, and few philosophers have been read
as avidly, as pleasurably, as Arthur Schopenhauer. For those
who could not accept the shallow preachments of optimism and
the infantile promises of worlds of beatitudes without end,
found solace for their personal misfortunes and disillusions in
the universality of misfortune and the eternity of vanity. Only
as we realize that we are not singled out for sorrow, that we are
not life's stepchildren, that the very scheme of Nature makes

all living beings legitimate members of the Family of Pain and Grief, we are solaced and placated, and we can pursue pleasures and draw blueprints for immortal fame.

Hope Deferred Maketh the Heart Sick

Two years had passed since Arthur Schopenhauer had delivered his manuscript to his publisher and left for Venice. He traveled about Italy, loafing, studying, and always hoping that some day, in some place, the *cameriere* would rap at the door to inform the *illustrissimo signor* that the mayor, his officials, and the dignitaries of learning had come to pay their respects and offer him the key to the city, in honor of his great, epoch-making masterpiece.

But sixteen times two years he would have to wait until the miracle of recognition would take place, for by then it seemed indeed a miracle. And in the meantime he would return home. He had a brush with possible disaster when he recovered his money only by a shrewd and daring strategy, but supposing the next time he were not as fortunate, or as clever? He would go home and seek a professorship, a dreary and almost indecent occupation, he had always claimed, still affording a stable income. Moreover, as a professor he would have the opportunity of expounding his own theories and exposing the charlatanism of his competitors, and in particular, that of George Wilhelm Friedrich Hegel with his dialectical method, his intricate, cumbersome style, and his disgraceful cosmic optimism. He was a doctor of philosophy and an author and he would seek a chair at the University of Berlin.

He bade *addio* to his *inamorata* Teresa, for the sake of whom he had never met Byron and which might have altered drastically his career. For, had the great poet been impressed with Schopenhauer, which was quite likely, since Schopenhauer had (when he so wished) seigniorial ways and spoke English almost without an accent, he would surely have recommended him to the world of letters and thus spared him the long anguish of waiting at the locked gate to the hall of recognition. He bade *addio* to the beautiful, but always miserably poor Italia, where the crows of bigotry devoured the fields of progress. He bade *addio* to Eros and Venus, whom he never again pursued with equal ardor or with equal success. He bade *addio* to whatever of youth still pulsed in his veins, and left for the cold, morose, mystical North to do battle for immortality.

But what price immortality in a world of Maya and her web of illusion which offers nothing as delectable as utter annihilation; and what merit the applause of humanity, composed as Schopenhauer claimed, of ninety percent immedicable idiots? Schopenhauer never explained, could not explain. Nor should he be required to explain. Sufficient unto each man his measure of vanity and his peck of foolishness. Every unlit candle is certain that if lighted, it would outshine the sun, and every author, if only properly hearkened to, would be enshrined in the memory of man into all eternity.

Arthur Schopenhauer applied to the Faculty of the Berlin University for permission to lecture. It was a petition in Latin and bold, verging on arrogance. Nevertheless, the dean wrote: "Aside from the extreme presumption and extraordinary vanity of Herr Schopenhauer, which proceeds from every circumstance, I hold that in view of his qualifications, nothing can be objected to his installation."

And so Doctor Schopenhauer was installed as *Privatdozent* at the University, with the approval of Hegel, the most prominent of the professors, indeed, the most prominent of European philosophers, whom Schopenhauer heckled at his lectures and vituperated orally and in print. From one insult to another, beginning with "sophist," he ended by calling him "fool" and "charlatan" and "mountebank" and "windbag." "He should be shut out from the ranks of philosophers as of yore the moneychangers were cast out of the Temple." And even when Hegel, "the intellectual Caliban," died of the cholera ten years later, Schopenhauer did not follow the courtesy of the ancient Latins, whom he admired—*de mortuis nil nisi bonum*—of the dead say nothing but good. Indeed, after his death, his venom thickened, since he no longer feared, as during his life-time, retaliation and libel. But Hegel always returned insult with silence, and silence is the most ominous of answers—except the silence of the grave.

Hegel deserved only a portion of Schopenhauer's abuse and certainly both heels of Schopenhauer and his works were vulnerable to attack, if anyone had a mind to aim arrows. The tongue undresses us and the pen flays us, and Schopenhauer revealed himself priggish, envious, irascible, and inordinately anxious to succeed even if need be by the ancient trick of stepping on another's neck to appear taller.

Although Hegel eventually suffered by Schopenhauer's attacks, he himself did not escape unscathed, for many pages of his works are marred by irrelevant and unnecessary offensive remarks about Hegel and other contemporaries, and arguments that could have achieved universal truths were pygmied into personal opinions, banal and irritating.

Schopenhauer's lectures at the University proved a complete and utter fiasco, and his stay in Berlin, "physically and morally a damnable nest," was aggravated by a tragic-comic incident, known as the "Case of Marquet."

Schopenhauer had rented lodgings in a *pension* across the University, but certain women, for one reason or another, occupied one day his ante-chamber, sewed and chattered. The sight of them sent his blood hammering against his head, for added to their misfortune that they belonged to the feminine gender of humanity, which the philosopher despised, they were also old and homely.

He ordered them out, but one, Caroline Marquet, who had a little back-room in the same house, refused point-blank and assured him that it was not a bit her intention to obey his unmannerly command.

In the Court of Justice, Schopenhauer deposed and swore that "since she offered me resistance. . . . I seized her as my purpose required, around the whole body and so dragged her outside, although she resisted with all her strength . . . but she had the audacity to return the entrance-way once more, and once more I threw her out, although she resisted with still greater violence and screamed with all her might, in order, if possible, to alarm the whole house. When I evicted her the second time, she fell down, I believe, intentionally. . . . But now I declare the assertion that I tore off the complainant's cap, that she fell in a faint, and that I trampled her under foot, and struck her with my fists, is entirely false and fabricated. Not a word is true, and whoever knows me in the least, will understand *a priori* that such brutal roughness is quite inconceivable in one of my character, position, and education."

Caroline Marquet, however, swore that lameness, paralysis, internal injuries, as well as nameless ills had resulted, for she was a lady of modesty and could not reveal in public that which is permissible only in private.

Alas, for poor Schopenhauer! The case dragged from one court to another for five years, and finally Caroline was granted the sum of three hundred dollars and an annuity of sixty dollars for the rest of her mortal life, which, multiplied at least five-fold to equate it with modern values, was a tidy bit torn out of the modest income of the philosopher. And in the female tradition, Caroline Marquet continued to mulct him for twenty long years. Not only was the poor man's purse flattened, but his good name and reputation were defiled for the remainder of his days, and even beyond his grave.

"Every act rewards itself," says Emerson, and while this is an optimist's wish-fulfillment, the great pessimist drew some victory out of his defeat, and in his essay "Of Women," which made him both famous and infamous, the magic formula for success, he distilled the essence of his experience. "Hence, it will be found that the fundamental fault of the female character is that it has *no sense of justice*. . . . They are dependent, not upon strength, but upon craft; and hence their instinctive capacity for cunning and their ineradicable tendency to say what is not true. . . . Hence dissimulation is innate in woman, and almost as much the quality of the stupid as of the clever. . . . But this fundamental defect which I have stated, with all that it entails, gives rise to falsity, faithlessness, treachery, ingratitude, and so on. Perjury in a court of justice is more often committed by women than by men. It may, indeed, be generally questioned whether women ought to be sworn in at all."

While the case was dragged from court to court, Schopenhauer sought refuge from Berlin that city "where one lives as on a ship; everything is rare, expensive, hard to get, the food stuffs dried up and hard," and once again he went to Italy. This time to Florence. He let the Will enjoy itself to the full in him, made friends, dined luxuriously, played his flute, laughed, curtsied to the ladies in Italian, made love in French, discussed philosophy in English, and when the company was suitable quoted from the Latin and the Greek. For eight months he forgot that nasty seamstress, who would not forget him; forgot Hegel; forgot his own lectures which had been attended by as many as seven and as few as three; when suddenly the awful truth of his philosophy, that a man's life is misery, and happiness but a truce between one misfortune and another, came to roost in his own nest.

He paid the price of promiscuity, and stricken with that disease to whose horrors the hawkers of sin have added shame, he rushed back to Munich, where for months he lay riveted to bed —paralysis, spells of faintness, endless pain, and fear of loss of his great treasure—his mind.

Gradually, however, he recovered, and as he convalesced, he meditated further upon love and its ramifications, and was, in a sense, the founder of the new science of sex, which has since become so elaborate and so all-pervading. He conceived the theory of *Tetragamy,* or a quadrille without the music. "Inasmuch as Nature makes the number of women nearly identical with that of men, whilst women retain only about half as long as men their

capacity for procreation and their suitability for masculine gratification, the human sexual relationship is disordered at the very
outset. . . . A man has one wife for the satisfaction of his
procreative capacity only for half the time for which that capacity endures; he must then, take a second wife when the first
begins to wither. . . . On the other hand, a woman is capable
of satisfying two or three vigorous men simultaneously. . . .
In monogamy woman employs only half her sexual capacity and
satisfies only half of her desires." In order to bring sense and
justice in marital relationship, then "let two men always have
one wife in common; let them take her when they are both
young. After she has become faded, let them take another young
woman, who will then suffice their needs until they are old."

This highly reasonable quadrille without music had never
been thought of or adopted, "for half their life men are whore-
mongers and for the other half cuckolds; and women must be
correspondingly classified as betrayed and betrayers." And the
poor prostitutes—"What are they but human sacrifices on the
altar of monogamy?" Moreover, "concerning polygamy, there
can be no dispute, for it must be looked upon as a fact universally
present, and the only question is in regard to its proper regula-
tion."

Now that he was well again, except for the loss of hearing in
one ear, Schopenhauer continued his search for an occupation to
recoup his expenses in his long illness. He tried the universities
of Wurzburg and Heidelberg. What Heidelberg answered, we
do not know, presumably nothing, but in the archives of Bavaria,
there is a letter from the Count of Luxburg, who evidently was
an important trustee of the Wurzburg University or an alumnus
of much influence. He writes from Berlin: "The independent
scholar, Dr. Schopenhauer, whose father was a burgomaster and
erstwhile a very rich banker of Dantzig, and whose mother is the
well-known writer of this name in Weimar, has no reputation
of any kind, either as a writer or as a teacher. He is said to have
been involved here in a disagreeable lawsuit with the seamstress
Marquet, which is, no doubt, the basis of his desire to transplant

himself. I will content myself in general with the humble remark, that the said Schopenhauer, who formerly went about a few years in Dresden and whose unattractive exterior is well known to me, could be no great gain for the University of Wurzburg."

Schopenhauer was now forty years old and his masterpiece had been in a deep coma in the dark stockroom, so like a morgue, of his disgruntled publisher. He had written to Brockhaus: "If now, in return for this great work, you are willing to do me a very little favor, and one that is easily performed, I will beg you each Easter to let me know how many copies have been sold." He doubtless chose Easter, for that is the period of resurrection in Nature, and why not of the beloved and wonderful child of his brain? Brockhaus answered: "In reply to your inquiry concerning the sales of your book, I can only tell you that, to my sorrow, I have made a very poor business out of it. Further particulars I cannot enter into." But later, he did enter into particulars, for he informed him that the greater part of the edition had been sold as waste paper.

Since the halls of learning were closed to him, Schopenhauer would try his hand at translations, master as he was of several languages. He had grandiose plans. He would translate Hume, Giordano Bruno, Calderon, Don Quixote. Meanwhile, as a sample, he translated a book by Balthazar Gracian, a Spanish philosopher of the seventeenth century. Brockhaus rejected it. He sent it to another publisher in Frankfurt. He waited and waiter for a reply, patiently, but not without fulminating maledictions.

Seven years passed, and as the period of leanness had elapsed, he expected the fat, but the publisher returned the manuscript. Schopenhauer hid it away in one of the boxes in which he kept his possessions, ready to carry out in case of fire. It was published posthumously, "truly and carefully translated by Arthur Schopenhauer," and despite the "heaviness" of the subject, it had three editions. Poor Arthur, how comforting *one* edition would have been to you before you relinquished your shape and merged with the measureless amorphism of the Will!

Translation, even as teaching, would have none of the philosopher, who could invoke no redress, since he himself had proven beyond any peradventure that Folly reigned and Falsehood was her Chancellor.

From the Land of the navel-gazers, those philosophers who plunge their individual emptiness into the cosmic emptiness, there came to Berlin their emissary, the vomiting cholera. Whomsoever it touched perished in agony within twenty-four hours. Schopenhauer, India's great admirer, let Hegel, the man of historic faith, represent the courage and dignity of the West, and die of it, while he, whose motto was—"it is safer to trust to fear than to faith," engaged the first vehicle he could find.

He urged the postilion to urge his horses to a constant gallop. He did not mind this time even if the man cracked his whip, which, however, in his essay on "Noise," he considered the most inexcusable and disgraceful of all noises . . . a truly infernal thing. . . . I denounce it as making peaceful life impossible. . . ."

He traveled about seeking safety from the epidemic and finally decided to establish himself in Frankfurt-on-the-Main. Here Goethe was born and had his early romances. He was dead now, but his house remained, and one could walk through his rooms and imbibe the spirit of the World Spirit.

Frankfurt had been the ancient capital of the Eastern Franks in the ninth century, became a Free City a thousand years later, was incorporated into Prussia in 1866 and into the German Empire in 1871. Now, in 1833, it was a great commerical center, a city of shopkeepers and stock-jobbers, of wine-cellars and *pensions* for traveling salesmen. Schopenhauer, raised in a mercantile milieu, found the spirit of the place preferable to that of a university town, for the parvenus of learning exhibited the same vulgarities as those of money, and in the final count what were professors but scavengers of futile knowledge?

Schopenhauer's house faced the Main River, along the shores of which he took long, vigorous daily walks, followed and preceded by his beloved white poodle, whose name was Atma or the Soul of the World. He would also plunge into its waters, for he was an excellent swimmer and he believed in the virtue of exercise.

Daily he dined at the most fashionable of Frankfurt's hotels, *Hôtel d'Angleterre,* for the philosopher liked good food, good wine, good cigars, good service, and if procurable, good table companions on whom he could whet the knife of satire and wit. However, he became more and more solitary as he grew older, but was never a hermit. Simply he would not spend his time and brilliance on those who were not worthy of them, and the worthy ones became rarer and rarer, as the years passed by. Thus each withering generation clatters its contempt of the freshly burgeoning one.

And now started his peculiar ways and phobias, which were the gossip of neighbors and later the *leitmotif* of the more formidable gossipers, the biographers. He was afraid of thieves, and at the least noise at night, he would seize the loaded guns which lay ready at hand. He would never trust himself to a barber's razor. He would carry a little leathern drinking-cup to avoid contagion if he drank from public fountains (which was not without merit). He hid bonds among all letters and gold coins under his inkstand or in out-of-the-way boxes and cabinets. To baffle thieves he wrote his account book in English and his business notes in Greek and Latin and labeled his valuable papers *Arcana Medica.* To make certain that he would not be buried alive, since a trance might be mistaken for death, he ordered that his body be laid out for a longer period than customary and should not be hurried to its resting-place.

And so it happened that he was nicknamed the "Whimsical Fool of Frankfurt," the "Modern Ascetic," the "Misanthrope of Frankfurt." But the time would come when he would be known as "The Sage."

Why did not his philosophy bring him comfort and security, as a similar view of the oneness of all things brought comfort and security to Spinoza who was harassed by disease and persecution? What had he to fear since he could not avoid his fate; what could he do, since freedom of the will was an illusion; what had he to lose, in the final count, save misery clamoring for relief, which fools and charlatans call happiness?

He was torn between the knowledge that life was utterly worthless and a deep passion for life. Life was a whore that betrayed and mocked, but he loved her. He loved her and he despised her. He loved her and knew that it was undignified and stupid and unbecoming to clamor for her embraces. Yet he could not overcome his passion for her. He was a saint in the desert tormented by the vision of lascivious women who would rob him of heaven and hurl him into hell.

Other people, indeed the vast majority of mankind, also love life. They, too, battle for her smile. They, too, grovel at her feet for her favors, for her crumbs. True, but the others do not proclaim that she is a whore, an illusion, and that she is an ugly and miserable hag. They say she is beautiful and real and good and desirable under all circumstances, even the most harrowing kind. The others, therefore, are secure and confident, or, at least, sufficiently so, to be called normal. Schopenhauer, however was divided, mind and heart in perpetual war. He lacked the power or the cunning to solder them together. It was as if his mother and father were forever at each other's throats. For this reason, he was irritable, a man of peculiar habits, an eccentric.

Nevertheless, he was a good man and not unkind, despite his porcupine way of shooting arrows at things and people who in any way offended him, or against whom, he thought he must defend himself, for the world was a jungle and one's teeth must always be bared. He was charitable, and no hand which stretched toward him remained empty, even if he was careful not to fill it. He was absolutely honest and even his mother acknowledged that he had never told a lie. He did not, to be sure, like Voltaire (who was both dishonest and a liar), take up cudgels in defense of the unjustly accused, but his entire philosophy is fundamentally one which seeks universal justice, for what hurts one hurts all, since we are all children of the Will. And, while Schopenhauer considers monarchy the best form of society, he is essentially a democrat, for to the Will, which is Life, there can be neither favorites nor outcasts, nor in a deep sense, aristocrats.

Planting in the Desert

Eighteen years had passed since Schopenhauer published his book, *The World as Will and Idea,* and much water, mostly bitter, had flowed under the bridges, and now he considered himself, and was so adjudged by his contemporaries, old. "His blue, vivacious eyes," wrote Foucher de Careil, the French statesman, "his thin lips curling in a sarcastic smile (he had lost his teeth early), his wide forehead framed in two white locks of hair, impressed upon his physiognomy, so sparkling with intelligence and spitefulness, the stamp of nobility and high distinction. His clothes, his jabot, and white cravatte reminded one of an old man at the end of the age of Louis XV; his manners were those of a man of good society. . . . He avoided discussions and combats in words, but he did so that he might the better enjoy the charm of familiar conversation. . . ." But when he did speak, "happy are they who heard this last survivor of the conversationalists of the eighteenth century! . . . his hatred of excess of every kind; his love of order; and his horror of obscurantism . . . make for him a physiognomy entirely different from any other of the century. . . ."

During these eighteen years, he wrote nothing save copious notes on all things, and he published nothing. How could he allow the golden years of a man's maturity to lie fallow? Had he been so terribly hurt by the neglect of his contemporaries? Was he, indeed, so certain that he had said all that had to be said, and that even his own words would be superfluous? Or, had his masterpiece, composed so early in life, sapped his creative vitality?

But now, when he was nearly fifty, there was a second blossoming. In 1836, he published a new book—*On the Will in Nature,* an exposition of his findings in astronomy, physics, biology, and "spiritistic phenomena," which confirmed once again the truth of the Will as the cosmic power. In 1839 he contended successfully with a prize essay in answer to the question propounded by the Royal Norwegian Society of Science at Drontheim—"Can the Freedom of the Human Will Be Proved from the Evidence of Self-consciousness?"

A brilliant essay, which he never mentions without stating the fact that it received the prize. And why not, since it was the first gracious gesture of the world which he so hated and so loved? Another essay on the "Source and Foundation of Morality," presented to the Royal Danish Society at Copenhagen, was not crowned, and he never mentions this essay without adding that it was rejected, assured that his sarcastic laughter would annihilate the members of that exalted institution, for the time was at hand when to have offered him the laurel would have sufficed as an excuse for their existence.

In 1844 he offered fifty new chapters of supplementary material to *The World as Will and Idea,* to his old publisher, Brockhaus, for a new edition of his book, without cost to the author, but also without any profit. It was, he wrote, "the fruit of a whole lifetime devoted to perpetual study and reflection," and the finest thing he had ever written. Brockhaus at first declined the offer. "Well, then, my work shall be left to appear as posthumous, when the generation has come that will welcome every line of my writings. It will not fail to come. . . . If you were here, I would show you the chapter 'On the Metaphysics of Sexual Love,' which traces this passion to its primal source. I will take my wager you would hesitate no longer."

That did it. Brockhaus was convinced, published the second edition, and again tore his hair, for the book sold even less than the previous one, and the cabal of silence among critics persisted. Nevertheless, Schopenhauer continued to plant in the desert, and in 1851 he had a manuscript ready, which he entitled *Parerga et Paralipomena.* The translation of the title is approxi-

478   SEVEN AGAINST THE NIGHT

mately "Odds and Ends," but in the English editions, the book appeared under the simple appellation of *Essays*.

Now Brockhaus refused categorically. He would have nothing more to do with that braggart. He wrote for the future generations? Let the future generations print him. This time, however, Herr Brockhaus guessed wrong, and it was not long before he tore his hair again (if he still had any left), for now he threw away a fortune. But he was not the only one who refused to publish the book. Each publisher who was approached thought that if the manuscript had any value the previous one approached would have published it.

Finally, through the efforts of Doctor Frauenstadt, a disciple, (he had a band of them) succeeded in "inveigling" a publisher to undertake the publication in two volumes for which, Herr Arthur Schopenhauer, Doctor of Philosophy, author of several volumes, aged sixty-three, received as full payment ten copies.

Now the fruits in the orchard of Schopenhauer's mind were heavy with all the days of the season and he culled them and presented them to the world. And those who partook of them knew that there had never been such delicious food, sweet with the honey of wisdom, bitter with the bile of truth, sharp with the pepper of wit—precisely the recipe to delight the palate of maturity jaded by the countless concoctions offered by the purveyors of illusions and mystifications.

There were two things to marvel at in his *Essays*—the depth of the ideas and the style, and the style perhaps even more, for he wrote in German, which he says "is heavy. . . . In reading German memory is obliged to retain mechanically, as in a lesson, the words that are forced upon it. . . . When the Germans get a hold of a vague and unsuitable expression which will completely obscure their meaning, they pat themselves on the back . . . and if they can manage to be emphatic and affected at the same time, they are simply afloat in a sea of joy. . . ."

Schopenhauer took this cumbersome vehicle and tempered it in the flames of his genius and burnished it and made it glow and sparkle and dance. It was a great feat, greater than the conquest of a continent, for language is more recalcitrant to the pen than a mountain to the axe and words are fortresses which must be invested and taken by storm before they relinquish their treasures.

Art and intellect are the only two gates by which man can escape from the prison of Will, at least for short periods of time. The guards, Hunger, Sex, Envy always bayonet him back. And in the *Essays,* Schopenhauer unlocks the gates for us. Open the book anywhere, and on every one of the nearly thousand pages, you will find lines and paragraphs that will delight, instruct, console, and the pessimist will seem an optimist, only more robust, more vigorous, more cheerful, for he will not be timorous lest the soap bubbles of his desires fall as shapeless globs upon the streets. He does not seek needles in haystacks of hay, but takes delight in the scent the hay spreads. He cherishes all things of beauty with that exquisite tenderness mingled with sorrow which characterize a last kiss, a dying dawn, the overtones of a melody.

He does not, as the routine optimist, indulge in excessive wailing, for he has not a magnified conception of the importance of things and of himself in relation to them. He knows that man is conscious of his happiness only as he measures it against the misfortunes of others, and that misery need not seek company, for the sorry procession is without beginning and without end. And the cognizance of this universal frustration makes for the peace of mind of the individual.

The pessimist, emerging as optimist, from the pages of the *Essays,* realizes that life is not a Goliath which a little David can slay with a pebble, however well aimed. He knows that defeat is inevitable for all. Meanwhile, however, the blows may be tempered by expecting them and warding them off. Thus prepared he often turns the blows into caresses, and so it happens that the Worst is the Best and the Best is the Worst. Such is the meaning that hovers over the words of Schopenhauer whatever might be the subject he treats.

By the very conception of the unity of all things, which is the basis of Schopenhauer's philosophy, he could say, even more truthfully than Terence, the Latin comic poet: "I am a man; nothing human is foreign to me." Nothing human and nothing unhuman was foreign to Schopenhauer. And in his *Essays* he writes of the entire gamut of man's relation to man and to the universe.

Schopenhauer was a philosopher of the world, who drew his inspiration and achieved his conclusions from events related directly to himself or those that he saw with his own eyes, and his eyes were sharp. Everything that came within their field, they registered while his mind rushed to weigh, to analyze, to integrate. And when the time came, they would, as in his essays, serve as examples, as guiding-posts leading to his main thesis.

He also quoted copiously, for his memory was excellent, from many languages, but books played a secondary part in his essays. As for books, one should read only in moderation. "When we read, another person thinks for us; we merely repeat his mental process. . . ." Reading too much, "a man gradually loses the capacity for thinking; just as the man who always rides, at last forgets how to walk. This is the case with many learned persons —they have read themselves stupid."

One should be careful to limit the time of reading and to devote it "to the works of those great minds of all times and countries, who overtop the rest of humanity. . . ." If one wrote the "tragical history of literature. . . . It would tell the martyrdom of almost all those who truly enlightened humanity, of almost all the great masters of every kind of art; it would show us how, with few exceptions, they were tormented to death, without recognition, without sympathy, without followers; how they lived in poverty and misery, whilst fame, honor, and riches were the lot of the unworthy . . . how in spite of all they were kept up by the love of their work, until at last the bitter fight of the teacher of humanity is over, until the immortal laurel is held out to him, and the hour strikes when it can be said:

Der schwere Panzer wird zum Flügelkleide,
Kurz ist der Schmerz, unendlich ist die Freude.

"The heavy armor turns to wings—short is the pain, unending
the joy."

The Hour Strikes and the Knell
Sounds

Parerga et Paralipomena or the *Essays* appeared late in 1851
and Schopenhauer wrote: "I am right glad to witness the birth
of my last child, which completes my mission in this world." And
while the first review was laudatory, Schopenhauer expected the
usual silence to follow. He was reconciled to the idea that fame
would come after his death, for "not fame, but that which deserves to be famous, is what a man should hold in esteem."

But the hour struck and soon he could say that "unending is
the joy." Wistfully, to be sure, for although time had brought
the roses at last, he pointed to his silvered hair—"it is white.
. . . After one has spent a long life of insignificance and disregard, they come at the end with drums and trumpets and think
that is something."

And it was all so casual. In 1853 the *Westminster Review* of
England published a long article, quite laudatory and compre-
hensive on Arthur Schopenhauer. The article was reprinted in
Germany in the *Vossische Zeitung,* and other articles appeared,
now in one city, now in another. Presently the little tongues of
flame joined and became a conflagration.

Arthur Schopenhauer became a best-seller. Newspapers began to write anecdotes about him; photographers pestered him;
artists begged to let them draw his magnificent head; translators
battled for the rights to carry his words to far-flung places;
decorations were offered. The University of Berlin, where

Hegel once ruled supreme and Schopenhauer was sneered at, invited him to become a member of its faculty. He promptly declined. "They have turned their back on me all my life and after my death they want my name on their catalogue." But other universities began to teach his philosophy and he had become a classic—who was read!

The adulation had no limits. People came to kiss his hand and bring him flowers. Poetasters composed sonnets. Women, despite, or rather because of his scathing essay on their sex, did their usual swooning, for the invectives of man against woman serve as a phosphorescent background for her to glow more seductively. From woman we expect the impossible and get the incredible.

It was all so jolly, yet also annoying. It interfered with his cherished habit of solitude and his reverberating roaring against life and mankind. His roaring now lacked resonance and the fangs of the lion which once tore the flesh, now merely grazed it. The tongue even licked it. Yet, who shall begrudge a poor man who has been chilled by all the evil winds for so long, the warmth of the sun—the winter sun? Let him bask in it. He had roared for so long, let him purr now.

Now he was afraid. He was well, and if he did not pay attention to the little inconveniences common to the aging male, he might even say that he was robust. He took his long walks, did he not, and even tired out his youthful companions; he ate double portions of things, for as he said, a thinking brain needs much feeding; he slept soundly with windows wide open; he swam. He did not boast. He knew that when an old man begins to boast of his prowesses, his inheritors begin to rejoice.

He was afraid. "It would be miserable if I should have to die now." He read in the Old Testament that man's life is threescore and ten and "if by reason of strength they be fourscore years, yet is their strength labour and sorrow; for it is soon cut off, and we fly away."

According to Schopenhauer, however, the Old Testament was the book of the lowest and most miserable of people. The

Hindus, the wisest of the inhabitants of this merry planet, on the other hand, held that man's span of life was one hundred years and decrepitude only the punishment for evil and stupid living.

Schopenhauer accepted the judgment of the Hindus and as he lived most intelligently and without evil, he would become a centenarian. Besides, it was no more than right, no more than fair. Fate had been cruel to him for many years, would she be so mean now as to tease him by showing him paradise and promptly drive him out of it? He would forget that Nature has no special design for man. He would forget that Nature is neither kind nor cruel, neither just nor unjust, and is unaware of man's presence except as one of her particles in her vast totality, to be perpetuated or obliterated by the pressure and reshaping of space.

And so in his seventy-first year he rented a new home on *Schoene Aussicht*—"Beautiful Outlook"—on the Main River. From the windows he could see the spires of the majestic churches and the ancient buildings of the once great capital of the Eastern Franks and the taverns which Goethe frequented in his youth.

And within, he furnished it with comfortable things as befitted a man of means and of taste. His walls had some valuable paintings and many photographs of his beloved Atma, the dog, or more truly the several Atmas that succeeded one another, the incarnations of the Spirit.

The housekeeper was faithful; the visitors, not only reverential, but circumspect. They would wait for hours until the master was ready to grant them audience. He read his favorite books, played his flute, saw his name in countless magazines and newspapers of all the languages he could understand. He took his siestas, smoked his pipe, five feet long. Ah, how good is life for a pessimist! Oh, if it could but last, long, long! If one could but capture and imprison Time! Alas, each day is a fragile blossom whose petals curl and drop and whose perfume is forever scattered. There is no hot-house ingenious enough to keep it from perishing.

The pessimist of the Bible was right and the Hindu fakirs were wrong. And on September 21, 1860, as Arthur Schopenhauer was eating his breakfast, blood gushed out of his mouth, and he sank back in his sofa, and was no more. He had reached the age of seventy-two.

At his burial, a Protestant clergyman, in the name of the Evangelical Church, performed the services and sent his spirit, cleared of the dross of atheism, on its way to the heavenly abode. Others delivered speeches and there was much manifestation of sorrow. What a pity, though, that just when people are so nice to us and say such nice lies about us and spend so much money to entertain us with flowers and music and recitations, we have to be so deeply asleep, hear nothing, see nothing, feel nothing—and even be unable to laugh!

In the cemetery of Frankfurt-on-the-Main there is a tombstone of black Belgian granite. Upon it is carved: ARTHUR SCHOPENHAUER. That was the will of the philosopher when he would merge with the Will of the Cosmos. Neither dates, nor epitaph, nor the pathetic good-night salutation: "Rest in Peace."

"They will find me," Schopenhauer said. "No matter where they will find me, and they will know me. And the time will come when anyone who does not know my doctrine will be accounted an ignoramus."

And the time came. . . .

Yet, how shall we honor the dead? The praises offered them for their earthly deeds are as pleasing to their ears as to the oysters are the exclamations of delight at the pearls found within their stony shells.

ANATOLE FRANCE

The End

October the 18th, 1924. Fog hung over the City of Light. Not the impenetrable fog that chokes the inhabitants of the Metropolis across the Channel, but a gentle mist which the sun, weakened by the season, could nevertheless penetrate in broken rays, as if through a partially clogged sieve.

October the 18th is not a secular holiday in France, celebrating one of its many triumphs or one of its many disasters, nor is it a church festival, despite the countless saints and martyrs, so welcome to the hearts of the youngsters who thus escape from the bondage of education. Indeed, one might even venture to say that these saints have no other raison d'être save giving children the opportunity to commit mischief and their teachers the chance to rest their arms from the wielding of their ferules.

Yet, this October the 18th, the youngsters did have a reprieve from school—a half-day only, to be sure, but even a half-day is not to be disdained. And there were also soldiers and officers in their gala uniforms, not for a full army review as on the 14th of July, certainly, but still some companies of infantry and squadrons of cavalry. And there were thousands of people, many thousands, lining the streets along the embankment of the Seine ranged with bookstalls and flower vendors. And the highest dignitaries of the state—the President of the Republic and the Prime Minister among them—were also away from their accustomed offices and duties. Not to mention celebrities of all the arts and the leaders of labor and trades. Only the church was not represented—neither the hierarchy nor the humbler members. No incense, no bells, no prayers. Imprecations, yes—violent ones, and promises of eternal punishment.

The source of this long, meandering river of people was No. 5, Villa Saïd—a tiny street with few houses. Here the body of a man, surrounded by hills of flowers and wreaths, lay exposed to the view of thousands of eyes. They were the eyes of mourners, of curiosity seekers, of admirers, of those who, in later years, wished to be able to boast that they had seen the Master, if not alive, at least as a corpse; the Master, whose name was the same as that of his country, and so representative of it that it seemed the most natural to possess. Even the chauvinistic found it not incongruous that this man should be so closely identified with the *patrie,* that when one said France, the mind conjured Anatole France.

But now, the body could only inspire pity for the fate of man. The face was old, sunken, bearded, evincing long tortures. Stranger still, it was a body without a brain. Since the brain had been the finest in Europe, the richest of the century, medical science wished to see what had made it so; as puerile a deed as that of a child breaking a clock to see what had made it say tick-tock-tick-tock and where the hours hid themselves.

Were not the doctors aware of the fact that a man thinks not only with his brain, but with his glands, with his bowels, with his nerves, with his skin? Did they expect to find genius tucked away in one of the convolutions? Well, they weighed it and measured it, and numbered its fissures, and comparisons were made between it and the brain of a criminal executed at Tours a month before. And it was found that the brain of the criminal weighed more heavily!

There was, as a matter of fact, in this extraction of the brain of Anatole France a precious symbolism. Europe—the world—had embraced the cult of Unreason. The very names of the schools of arts and letters had an idiotic infantilism about them. An American authoress repeated her words as madmen repeat theirs walking back and forth in their padded cells; an Irish novelist wrote his lines upside down and formed his vocabulary from bits of foreign words; music was inadmissable unless it discarded all melody and topped all city noises; painting and sculpture were decadent and worthless unless they imitated the primitives who had carved into cave walls thousands of years ago or painted monsters to frighten enemies and frightened themselves and thus created armies of gods. And there was no more evil label than that of "high-brow." The truly patriotic brow was low and the chin massive—ignorance and pugnacity. And in a great joust, a former Secretary of State and thrice candidate for the highest post in the mightiest nation, fought and died to prove that man was no relation to the ourang, and that the legend of a man making his home in a whale was a literal truth—all of which proving the eternal wisdom and goodness of God, the Creator.

Nor was the heavier weight of the criminal's brain without *its* symbolic value. For only a few years later, across the Rhine, a chief murderer with a gang of murderers and with the ecstatic approval and love of all the Land's citizens, established a government in which the more criminal a brain a man possessed the higher he climbed and the greater his rewards. The leaders of many other nations applauded and took them as models of conduct for their own people. What happened to all is a matter for history, and should prove, if mankind is capable of learning, that history with all its evils repeats itself because it is so often ignored, and that virtue must not be allowed to be solely its own reward.

The brain of Anatole France, placed in a receptacle and carefully sealed, was prepared to be buried with the body. Ah, if it had had but a few more moments of life and could once more be illumined with thought! Through its convolutions there would have passed two currents—irony for man's folly and pity for man himself—the two currents which had given France his magnificent balance.

"What is this?" one current would have revealed: "Have I not asked that I be buried, quickly, without the pretentious clamor of praise and the indignity of pressing flowers into stony nostrils? And the government—the government run by fools and knaves in the interest of fools and knaves—has made my departure a state affair at public expense! Hasn't anybody read my books? Have they all forgotten what I said about those whose hands wield power? Have they all forgotten what I said

about the masses that allow themselves to be stupid sheep
fleeced and devoured? Have I so quickly become a mere classic?
The folly of man, then, is even greater than I had believed. One
has to be stretched out, it seems, and emptied of brain and
bowels to understand fully how colossal it truly is."

This current darkened, the other would have revealed: "Oh,
a child has touched my coffin—a child, embodiment of all that
is good and beautiful! And whose tear is this that dropped upon
my hand? A man in a worker's blouse—a worker—he who
creates, who makes life possible, who, despite the centuries of
oppression and travail, still believes in ultimate justice and
truth and love of one's neighbor. And who has bent to kiss my
frozen forehead—a peasant woman, older than I was six days
ago when they pressed my chin into place. She loves me, she is
not afraid of the mocker. Since the simple and the miserable
ones have been allowed to come and pay their respects to their
friend, I do not mind the vain words of the vain and the pompous. People need illusion. Perhaps they wish to make me their
illusion. Pity I haven't been braver, more honest, juster, but
illusion lacquers things. They must pardon me even as I pardon
them—yes, that is it—pity and pardon for all. Adieu!"

The cavalcade of cars and pedestrians started at No. 5 Villa
Saïd and wended its way to the left bank of the Seine, to the
Quai Malaquis, where the catafalque had been raised at the
foot of the bronze statue of Voltaire. Like a guardian angel he
watched over the mortal remains of his beloved spiritual son,
and welcomed him to the exclusive heaven of precious dust.

Now began the speeches. All observed punctiliously the Latin
admonition: *De mortuis nil nisi bonum.* Anatole France would
have ridiculed the idea. Why should we speak only good of the
dead? Often they are more formidable enemies than when they
were alive. The truth, gentlemen, the truth! The dead do not
like liars, and the tongues of flatterers strike them like tongues
of snakes.

Léon Blum spoke for the Socialist party. Jouhaux spoke for
the Conféderation Générale du Travail. Basche spoke for the

League of the Rights of Man. For the government, François Albert and for the Chamber of Deputies, Paul Painlève. And there was the choir of children singing the *andante* of Beethoven's *Fifth Symphony* and there was the march from Gluck's *Alceste*. It was an excellent performance, but even as the honors were showered upon the Master, young writers who would have found his quill too heavy for both hands, and whose sentences stumbled and shuffled, meandered among the spectators, distributing a vulgar pamphlet entitled, *Un Cadavre*. In it they rejoiced that the *vieille carcasse* was at last to be consigned to the worms and to eternal oblivion.

As a matter of fact the pamphlet had been printed several days previously, even before Anatole France was dead, so impatient were the dealers in darkness and cacophony to rid the world of the one whose watchword was *clarté,* and who had always obeyed the dictum: *ce qui n'est pas clair, n'est pas français*—"what is not clear is not French." But evil days were in store both for France and for the French language, and for generations there would be neither clarity nor truth, and song would desert the language.

To keep the pamphleteers company, the Catholic papers added their condemnation, for had not the priests tried to tempt the dying man to repent and accept the last sacraments? Had they not warned him: "Anatole France, you are about to die. Get ready to meet your God. Remember the fires of hell, Anatole France!"

But Anatole France opened his right eye (the left had closed weeks before and the nerveless lid never rose again) and ancient and blood-shot though it was, it saw through the machinations of the black-robed men who would scare with childish hallucinations. His mouth, which had spoken some of the wisest and the most beautiful words, was twisted with pain and would not open, but his hand, still retaining something of its shapeliness, managed to wave a last and irrevocable—"No!"

The services were over and the *cortège* began its march. It was a long march, past the Louvre, past the Place de la Concorde, along the Champs-Elysées, through the Arc de Triomphe, and then straight to Neuilly. And all along those miles of travel, the road was lined deeply with people, and there were flags, the tri-colored and the red—the tri-colored which had introduced the revolutionary idea of *Egalité, Fraternité, Liberté,* and the red which represented the hope that it would at last be put into practice. Alas, that the womb of history should deliver stillborn Utopias! Alas, that the ideal should turn to rag even before the flag which waved its triumphant advent!

It was already night when the procession reached its destination—a small cemetery where François-Noël Thibault and Antoinette Thibault, parents of Anatole France, rested, doubtless, in peace. For in the whole of the language of man, there is not a more pitiful and ironic invocation than "Rest in Peace," uttered by the living for the dead—the living who toss about in the storm of their days.

This much Anatole France had won, that he should not be buried in the Panthéon, among the "gods," but be gathered to his ancestors, whose flesh and blood he had been and with whose dust he would mingle.

The Beginning

Napoleon Bonaparte had accomplished his destiny, and was no more. The good he had left behind was pounced upon by the wolves of reaction and torn to shreds; the evil remained. The evil—mountains of corpses, burnt cities, poverty, hate, rancor, and a vast disillusion in the hearts of men, the sickening feeling that a magnificent revolution which was to bring justice and freedom to all mankind only gave birth to a tyrant who ruled the world for a handful of years, and then was locked in a prison, to shame his country, defeated and torn.

The Revolution, however, was not as dead as it appeared, and although the reactionaries had their day, there were other days to come, which would show that they who bury ideas do but plant them. Meanwhile the vicious Bourbons mounted the throne again, first Louis XVIII, then Charles X, and with them returned the nobles and the Church, and there was no longer the cry—that cry torn out of the heart of mankind—*Egalité, Liberté, Fraternité,* but for "God and King," which meant for priest and despot.

To the peasants of Anjou on the River Loire, this was welcome news, for they had suffered by the wars of the Emperor and they loved the Church and the ancient ways of the monarchy. Perverse mankind, that loves its yoke and its chain! For, what had these people as reward for incessant labor but poverty and misery, and what for incessant prayers, but illiteracy and the threat of the fires of hell?

Throughout the ages man has developed a powerful neck and finds the yoke of slavery a light burden; his head, however, aches in the posture of pride, and freedom distresses him, and he believes that knees were made for kneeling before tyrants.

Anjou is a district of gentle hills and moderate climate and its inhabitants are, or at least appear to be, as gentle and as moderate. But it is folly to judge a nation by its geography, for then a country of great mountains eternally snowcapped should harbor people of lofty, unswerving ideals; the inhabitants of a city on the shores of the sea should be as profound as the waters that lave it; a province with mines of gold should give birth to generations of prophets rich in visions and incorruptible.

Doubtless, the fires which burn in all humans are not extinguished in the people of Anjou—hate and fear and jealousy, as well as love and hope. But the majority of them—the peasants —are not articulate, and moreover, full of toil, they prefer to go about their hard chores, uncomplaining, undramatizing.

Among them lived the Thibaults, generation after generation, perhaps, who knows, as far back as the Latin invasion and the counter-invasions of the barbarians. Like leaves of the same tree, they were born, they lived, they died, yet they always seemed the same. But the proverb: *plus ça change, plus c'est la même chose,* could more truthfully be: *plus c'est la même chose, plus ça change*—for precisely when we think that something is inalterable, the change has already begun to take place.

And so it happened that among the Thibaults, one François-Noël, born in 1805, peasant like the rest of them, made suddenly aware of his ignorance by his inability to sign his name and, ashamed, decided at the age of twenty-one to leave the tilling of the soil, and till the mysteries of the written word, and thereby become a man free and proud of his manhood.

Whether he really loved the army or not, he knew that outside of it he could not achieve what he desired, and so, he left for Angers, the capital of the Province, and enlisted in the forces of Charles X.

François—France, as he was called and which he was later in life to use more often than Thibault—was a serious young man and bent upon learning, for which he was often mocked by his comrades. There is no hatred as merciless as that which ignorance bears knowledge and fools bear the wise who have forgiven them their follies. But Ignorance has good reason to be proud, for many in the highest places are her most devout worshipers.

François-France was a good and faithful soldier, for he was a great hater of the Revolution and a profound admirer of the monarchy. His services were duly recognized and he became a corporal in the King's bodyguard. Alas, for poor François, the world would not sit still a while and give him the chance to read all the books against the Revolution and increase the number of his stripes in the service of His Majesty, Charles X. The rabble once again began to sing the *Marseillaise,* and on August 4, 1830, the King with a decent regard for his own neck, fled. His bodyguard was dissolved, and the saddened corporal, like the famed Petit Caporal, lost his uniform and his profession.

For several years, François worked at all sorts of jobs to

keep body and soul together, but he never forgot his main objective—to become a man of learning, and therefore, of merit.
The day was yet to come when learning had little merit and
less dignity, and those who owned it carried it like a hump upon
the back, ashamed and apologetic.

Already, François was so much a bookman that he became a
bookseller. Not a *bouquiniste* with a stand along the shore of the
Seine, but the owner of a shop, with books especially devoted to
works on the Revolution. Before long it became apparent that
this distinguished-looking gentleman, something between a
scholar and a soldier, was more than a mere seller of books. He
was also a great reader of them and loved to discourse about
them, and scholars found his store a pleasant rendezvous.

And now *France-Libraire* (he was definitely forgetting his
original name) bethought himself of a wife. He was not a man
of passion or escapades, but of severe rectitude, simple and
honest in his business, in his thoughts, and he would be likewise
in his choice of a helpmeet. He discovered her in the person of
Antoinette Gallas, twenty-nine years old, *fille naturelle*. Antoinette was reserved, pious, and past the age of romance, for in
France at that time, romance was for the extremely young. At
the age of thirty, as all novelists wrote, a woman was at most
suitable for adultery of a temperate kind. Better days awaited
her, for morals, like dresses, are a matter of fashion. And though
dress points to the trend of woman's social attitudes, yet it is
by no means so absolute as to allow us to predicate that when
she amplifies her bosom, for instance, she has become more
courageous, or when she lengthens her skirt, her fidelity has
been made more secure, or when she brushes her hair from her
forehead, she is about to widen her mental horizon.

Antoinette believed in the supremacy of the male, and that
a husband was the master of the house. Matriarchy had not yet
lifted its challenging head. In François she easily discovered the
master, for he was now a man of erudition and dignity, and
withal good and kindly. Their marriage was successful, a model
of the bourgeoisie and its solid qualities, not yet satirized by

the poets and novelists and dramatists, who, all out to destroy it, finally swept it off, name and all.

Paris had its troubles. Louis-Philippe succeeded Charles X, and became the "Citizen King," for no other reason than that the Parliament elected him. Like all the kings before him, he knew only suppression and reaction, and the time would come when he, too, would have to seek refuge across the Channel. François bemoaned the uncertainties of the day. But his troubles were not unalloyed, for on April 16, 1844, his wife gave birth to a boy who was named Jacques-Anatole-François-Thibault, and who was duly baptized on June 9th at Saint-Germain-des-Prés.

Burgeoning

The Muse did not place a halo around Anatole's little head, for all to see that it belonged to a genius, and therefore pay due reverence. It would, indeed, have been a dire misfortune, for Anatole required many years to fully develop, half of his long life. Anatole was not to be one of those exquisite flowers that are bud and bloom and withered stalk all in one spring—a Chatterton, a Keats, a Shelley.

Anatole was to be a poet, but that only incidentally, or as an apprenticeship; his true stature was to be achieved in the realm of wisdom and satire, and that means living long, suffering much, passing judgment on the ways of men; hardihood, boldness, tenacity.

Anatole was not a pretty child. His nose was too long, so was his face, and he was awkward in his movements. He was, besides, timid, and his timidity made him stutter frequently. Nor was the environment conducive to overcome his shortcomings, for *père* France demanded respect and attention, and hated noises. He was not merely a seller of books; he was a devourer of books, and that type of ogre needs silence to digest and attentive ears into which to pour the honey of his hive.

Anatole's mother had relinquished romance and would not indulge in adultery, and so she showered all her emotions upon her son. He was mama's boy and would so remain, in one way or another, to the end of his mortal days, for those who are tied to mama's apron-strings will always seek new mamas and new apron-strings.

It was not too difficult for a French boy of a century ago to be respectful to his father and obedient, for that was the national mores, particularly among the bourgeois. Fathers could, therefore, indulge in their tyrannies, secure in the knowledge that they would be appreciated as the fruits of paternal love and wisdom.

Perhaps, too, there was no better environment for the boy than the sea of books around him. Now he would plunge in, and swim far, far toward the horizon. Of course, he preferred the trips with his nurse or his *maman* to the Luxembourg gardens, paradise for youngsters or the Trocadéro, or Jardin des Plantes with its flowers and plants and more particularly the zoo. But more exciting than all was the *Guignol*—Punch and Judy—which still thrills the French children, despite movies, the radio, and television.

But while Anatole was becoming steady on his feet and his fingers followed the words in his primer, another revolution broke out. Would *père* France never be given a respite from those malicious manifestations of human stupidity? This one nearly wrecked his business, but added further to the enormous literature of revolutions in general and the deeper study of the Revolution, in particular. In time, *France-Libraire* would have the largest collection of books on the subject, and *père* France himself would be recognized as one of its great authorities.

Louis-Napoleon Bonaparte, son of Louis Bonaparte and nephew of Napoleon the First, had tried on two occasions to usurp power unsuccessfully, but this time he achieved his ambition. He promised everything to everyone, and became "President" of the new "Republic." Four years later, he no longer needed the ridiculous façade, and proclaimed himself Napoleon

III, Emperor of the French. Napoleon II, son of the great
Napoleon, died in 1832 at the age of twenty-one, without having
mounted the throne.

Anatole was four years old and much more interested in his
dog than in the history of his country, but what happened would,
as the years passed by, have deep significance in his life; for
the first quarter of his career in time and space were impreg-
nated with the spirit of the Second Empire.

Maman was a good teacher, but her reservoir of knowledge
was soon emptied, and as the child grew into boyhood, she engaged tutors to teach him the mystery of numbers and the
majesty of grammar. He was destined never to master either.
Père France was annoyed. His son was a dunce and something
more drastic must be done. Anatole was sent from school to
school, but to little avail.

He was a *flâneur*. The dictionary translates the word as
"loafer"—a travesty, pointing out the eternal truth of the
Italian proverb—*traduttore, traditore*—translator, traitor.
There is something sinful about "loafer" in the Anglo-Saxon
conception. One should go to the ant and learn her ways—her
ways of slavery. Even the man who has accumulated wealth
must continue the habit of his hungry days. He must remain the
ant, the Big Ant, if you will, but still the ant. The Lord help
him if he should take it into his head to follow the ways of the
butterfly and sip drops of honey here, there, wherever the wind
blows—sip honey and have no hive to deliver it to. Behold the
Big Ant—he has become a traitor to the Race of Hoarders—
what a disgrace! Let him be punished! Let no Ant, however
small or big, have intercourse with him! Anathema upon the
Vagabond!

But, then, how shall one truly loaf, anywhere, except in Paris?
Only Paris has been created for that delightful purpose, and
only in Paris has it full meaning and beauty. At least in Paris of
the grand days of Anatole France—Paris, when there was room
for a man to carry and twirl a cane or sit at the table on the
trottoir in front of the café unmolested by an impatient waiter,

or read half a book at the stand of the bearded *bouqiniste* who greeted you cordially and bade you adieu, whether you bought the book or not.

Anatole France was a born *flâneur* because he was Paris incarnate. Even as a boy, it was already evident by the way he gazed at things, by the way he would wander, his hands upon his back (a *flâneur's* natural manner, meaning that nothing that the foolish world calls useful will be done), by the indulgent smile. *Papa* France was irritated and scolded, but *maman* France said that her son was an *ange* direct from heaven.

At the age of twelve, Jacques-Anatole-François Thibault, who had begun to sign his name Anatole France, entered Collège Stanislas, an old and honorable institution—therefore, dreary, stuffy, and permeated with an insufferable stench of pedantry. The teachers were priests and their chief objective was to turn their charges into Latinists, subtle and devout.

Unprepossessing, in a home-made suit, timid, with a report card from the preparatory school so disgraceful that he dared not hold it to the light, Anatole made his entrance. Nor would his exit be any less ridiculous. He would, however, have his revenge in time. He would present the bigots who were his teachers, in an even more ridiculous attitude, and help rid the French schools from the grip of the clergy. In time. Just now he was miserable, and would seek ways of attenuating his misery. Man —even little man—is the chameleon to his interests.

One way now was to ferret out the ludicrous and grotesque in both teachers and fellow-pupils, and they were not difficult to discover. Later, this sense of the ludicrous would become satire, sometimes gentle, almost caressing; at other times, sharp, penetrating daggers. All his life he would be in need of armor, for he was sensitive to his own chagrins and sensitized to the griefs of all men, nay, the whole universe. The true poet is an Atlas carrying on his back the sufferings of all things, and in his heart compassion for them.

Another way was to write poetry—well, let us say, rhymes— and, of course, a diary into which only his own long nose could bury itself. "My soul has need of poetry," he wrote. And later, he would enlarge upon that, and introduce "imagination." "Imagination with all its falsehoods, sows all beauty and all virtue in the world." How strangely different "virtue" is from *virtù* of the Renaissance! So dazzling and so empty!

The teachers of Stanislas were meticulous men and they kept detailed records of their pupils and what they recorded about Jacques-Anatole-François Thibault should never be recorded about any mother's son. Not only was his work consistently poor, his efforts bad, his assignments never finished, but he was extremely listless, distracted even by a fly, careless, frivolous, and had the habit of throwing pellets around. He was, indeed, the twenty-second out of a class of twenty-two. Only his mother's tears kept the headmaster from kicking him out, and only because *père* France was such a fine man and fine scholar and his books on the Revolution and the revolutions upheld the sacredness of the Church and considered the priests as the rightful teachers of men, by law divine and eternal.

France-Libraire had now become *Librarie de France,* one of the great bookshops of Paris, rendezvous of poets, authors, scholars, the most famous in the roster of France—and its owner had to have a son of so little merit! Would he have the intelligence to supplant him when he was ready to retire? He was already past middle age, and, like every good Frenchman, he was dreaming to *cultiver son jardin*.

Not that Anatole did not read books—he read them all the time; nor that he did not have the appropriate tenderness and reverence toward a rare edition or an exquisite binding. His seigniorially-shaped hands had all the finesse required and his heart thrilled appropriately. But to run a shop one must also have stability, punctuality—and a sense of money. He himself— *père* France—was not a businessman, *proprement dit,* and never quite mastered the mystery of money, but his progeny—alas! He might as well live among those tribes who could not count beyond the five toes of their feet. As for punctuality, he lived as though clocks had not yet been invented, not even calendars, and he was no more reliable than a weathercock turning to all the passing winds.

Père France was to be further hurt, for, of all things, his son would become a Republican and a freethinker. Had one ever heard of such irony! But *père* France was spared still further consternation by dying before his son, world-famous and member of the French Academy, became first a socialist, and later a communist. Strange and unpredictable are the ways of one's children! It takes a wise son to know his father? Bah! The difficulty is to know one's son!

Each generation must uproot the noxious weeds which the preceding one planted and pompously proclaimed as flowers magnificent and perennial.

Somehow, Anatole managed to graduate from Stanislas, but that had no significance unless backed by the successful passing of the examinations at the Sorbonne, for it was only thus that one received the *baccalaureat* or the *bachot*, as the students call it, a degree similar to the bachelor of arts, but obtained after fewer years of school attendance. Those were tough examinations, most of which were oral and to which the public was admitted.

What did Anatole know? Little of what was required and much of what no professor would take it into his head to ask. And this being the case, any wonder that when his name was called, he was atop the Towers of Notre Dame looking, entranced, at his much-beloved—the City of Paris?

He came running, out of breath, just when the doors of the examination hall had been closed. All theater, perfectly timed, so that *maman* would not suffer too much. She could explain to *père* France that, after all, the poor boy *ran* all the way to the examination hall of the Sorbonne, but Paris is such a big place, and its streets so intricate—who doesn't lose his way, now and then? Moreover, the dear boy—*pauvre petit*—was so young— he had so much time—why push him? He might even get ill— *mon Dieu*—he was not too robust. And, of course, all this sprinkled with tears. And what good husband could look upon a weeping wife, his heart not melting?

Anatole did indeed present himself to the Sorbonne—four times, four years—until he finally "made it," but not without being publicly told by one of the most famous of the professors: *Monsieur, vous êtes un âne!*—"sir, you are an ass!"

This was not the first time that Anatole was so identified, and surely not the last. And doubtless, since he became one of the wisest of men, he had many occasions on which he acknowledged to himself his close kinship with that good creature, so basely maligned, for what is man but a hunter of scapegoats?

And now, what? The doors of the University were open to him, but what profession should he embrace, or rather, should he allow himself to be embraced and smothered by? Law? It could lead to high posts in the government. But he did not care for the government. He was barely aware of its existence. Moreover, one had to have a glib tongue and a shrewd mind. His tongue could declaim poetry, but was paralyzed in argumentation, and as for shrewdness—*c'était à rire,* "it was to laugh." No, not Law.

Medicine? That was, indeed, a noble profession. That he would have liked, for it meant the healing of men's wounds. But if it took him four years to pass the preliminary examinations, how many times four would it take him to pass those infinitely more difficult tests? Just to think of it gave him the vertigo. Engineering? He knew no mathematics, no physics, no chemistry— it seemed to him that he knew nothing at all every time he thought about a profession. The army? While he still thought well of the army, and had not yet become its foe, he was, to be blunt, a coward. The very thought of physical suffering, his own above all, made him shiver; nor could he endure the type of comradeship required in the barracks. Always when challenged to a fight, he would refuse with dignity, and if that was unacceptable, he would take to his heels.

In a period in which the duel, while officially banned, was constantly invoked to prove almost anything, and surely solved honorably the eternal quarrels between critic and author, Anatole France, both critic and author, never indulged in one. He was more than once challenged, but always ignored the challenge. He was ever readier to face an insult than a sword. It was easy for him to argue that spilling blood did not spill ignorance or injustice, and that they who pushed pens should draw ink. He would never reach the rank of corporal like his father.

The world was large, occupations were countless, but there seemed nothing for Anatole to do—nothing profitable, that is. He loafed better than ever, for now his mind was well-stored with the history and legends of Paris and his eye was sharpened for its peerless beauty, as well as for the beauty of woman, its delicious inhabitant. But loafing, delightful though it was, brought no money, that strange substance without which, it seemed, one was barely allowed to breathe. Yet, he knew better than all economists that poverty corroded and wealth corrupted. He knew that poverty was a crime, but the poor were not the criminals. No one wrote with greater tenderness about the poor and the homeless, the simple and untutored. And he warned that it was prudent for the rich to become philanthropists when the poor became misanthropists.

Critic, Poet, Soldier

The truth is that Anatole knew what he wanted and the rejection of all professions derived from this knowledge. He wanted to be a writer, a serious writer, a man who lives by and for his pen. But did he have the required qualifications? His father had often said no, and so did the chorus of all the teachers in Stanislas including Monsieur Paul Cheron and the Abbé Lallane, who had been kind to him and understanding. All, all except *maman* France. But she was, if not illiterate, certainly not a competent critic of letters, and blinded with love. She could not be relied upon, and yet time was to prove that, in this case, "mother knew best."

Timidly, tentatively, Anatole France began writing book reviews, dramatic reviews, and always, of course, poetry, and he managed to find little magazines, short-lived papers, which published them. The amount of money he received for them, when he received any, would not lead him into sinful pursuits; fortunate if they kept body and soul together, although as yet he still lived with his parents and he need not fear either hunger or patches on his pants or irate concierges rapping at his door.

There was, evidently, some merit in his work, for he made friends among the best of the younger poets and also called the attention of the older master, Leconte de Lisle, head of the Parnassians. It may have been due to the fact, though, that Anatole had written about his *Poèmes Antiques,* as being "one of the greatest works of modern poetry," and poets, young and old, are very susceptible to praise. On what else do most of them feed?

The Parnassians were making a lot of noise in the world of letters. They were demolishing the citadel of the Romantic School, and they were particularly desirous to hang Victor Hugo on its ramparts. Hugo was still a voluntary exile from Paris, and would be so until Napoleon the Third, daubed by him, the Little, finally fled and the Republic was re-established. Meanwhile, he wrote poetry, fiction, drama, which made their way throughout the civilized world. Was that in itself not reason enough to wish to destroy him and his disciples? They occupied so much room—fattened as they were by success—on the back of Pegasus, and how spacious was Olympus altogether? The old must die that the young may live! Would it not be prudent of the old to relinquish power graciously and willingly to the young, before they are unseated violently and unceremoniously? But is temporary fashion to dictate who should remain and who should be chased? Many a hobby horse snorts like Pegasus and many an ant-hill proclaims itself Olympus.

There was, to be sure, a valid literary angle to the war against the Romantic School. Its devotees had wept so long and so loudly one had the right to suspect that their tears were croco-dilian. Also, how long can one wear one's heart upon one's sleeve without its becoming nothing but a shapeless patch?

The Parnassians went back to the ancients, and proclaimed a reign of austere beauty and objectivity. Anatole France had been an ass in his school work, but that was precisely because he spent his time and energies upon the classics, and in time, he would know more about their prose and poetry than all his masters put together. Indeed, the day would come when he would be offered a professorship at the Collège de France, the highest in-stitution of learning in the land, which he would reject. He would never have arrived at the scheduled hour for his lecture, perhaps not even the scheduled day—sometimes due to absent-mindedness, sometimes to laziness. He established a most con-venient reputation, so that he could skip unpleasant visits and avoid boorish guests. No one could take it amiss: "You know how Anatole France is—so forgetful! Charming genius!"

His objectivity in poetry was surely a strange thing. Did he not say that no man could get out of his own skin, that he could escape all people, save himself? And were not his reviews of books and plays, largely speaking, reviews of his own attitudes and his own emotions, and only incidentally those of the authors involved? The truth is that Anatole France could never "be-long." He would always be Anatole France, different, unique, and endlessly inconsistent.

He was a solitary, and despite all his social triumphs in later days, he would always feel uncomfortable among people. "From my childhood onward, I have always been in love with solitude." And now, as a young man, as a tyro of literature, he was fortu-nate enough to mingle with the poets of the day, those who were on their way to fame and those whose words were destined to die as echoes in the wilderness of forgotten songs.

The doors opened more readily, to be sure, to the son of the bookseller and publisher, whose name and erudition and honesty were known to all and sundry, but he himself was beginning to evince merits, sufficient to make him acceptable, and yet not great enough to excite jealousy and envy. Mediocrity makes all mankind kin. He who abandons it forsakes the fold and is appropriately punished.

Some day, Anatole France would abandon it, and be justly punished, but now the gawky, silent guest served as a sounding-board to those who read their poems and to those who declaimed their opinions, and since he was a good listener and a nodder, he was welcome.

He continued to write, and *maman* France was always encouraging. "Be a writer, *mon fils*. You have brains and you will make the envious hold their tongues." *Père* France, on the other hand, remained unimpressed by his output, verse or prose. "Not having followed my advice, he has no job. He writes—I should say, he scribbles. What I feared most since his childhood, has, by a fatal destiny, come to pass. He has always been absorbed by the one idea that has ruined his career. I am through struggling with him and I shall leave him to his own resources, as I am afraid that otherwise he will leave the house. Has he enough talent for the business of Life? Alas! Alas!"

Père France became at last firmly convinced that his son would never take over his shop, or if he did, it would promptly go to ruin. As for himself, at sixty, he longed to be free, to *flâner* in his own manner. He was quite vigorous and he would live for many years yet, but he had had enough of business. And so, a quarter of a century of joys and sorrows and triumphs and troubles were written off and the *Librairie de France* was no more, and the family Thibault became *rentière*—lived on income.

But peace was to be short-lived. Always those *maudites révolutions* which had pursued *père* France since he lost his grade of corporal and Charles X his throne. Why could not at least one generation of men live quietly, pursuing their labors or their hobbies? And why must France, and in particular, Paris, always be in the center of the storm? Were the French better people, worse people, more irritable, or more anxious for justice than all the rest of the Earth's inhabitants?

From 1852 to 1860, Napoleon III was monarch absolute; from 1860 to 1867, he felt sufficiently secure to offer certain freedoms to the citizens; from 1867 to 1870, the freedoms increased to the point in which his regime was called *l'Empire libéral*. The socialistic ideas, which percolated through the various strata of society, were not ignored by Napoleon. He turned his attention to public works, encouraged agriculture, industry, commerce. There was talk of the rights of labor and destruction of poverty. A decade more and Napoleon would have made France prosperous and her people, if not content, certainly not rebellious.

Alas, that man must be valet to his name! He was NAPOLEON! As Napoleon, he must carry forward the grand tradition—*la gloire*—spill blood, squander fortune, cause tears to flow, hearts to break, turn cities into rubble and gardens into dust. What matters it, as long as Napoleon is the glorious emperor of France!

To achieve this, he began the usual maneuvers—meddling in other peoples' business. He took part in the Crimean War; went into China with the English and grabbed Cochin-China, part of Indo-China; helped Italy gain her independence from Austria; sent Maximilian to grab Mexico and, finally, as the culminating act of utter asininity, declared war on Prussia—a war which the shrewd and ruthless Bismarck had so carefully prepared. Never had a spider woven so subtle a web for a vain, buzzing fly to land in.

"I have been to the wars and you may believe me when I tell you that to strike an enemy and lay him low is, for nine men out of ten, an ecstasy of the senses compared to which the tenderest of love's embraces seems pale and insipid." So Monsieur Dubois, an old gentleman, scholar and soldier had told Anatole years ago, when he visited his father's shop to talk of poetry and the follies of man.

The boy shuddered but remembered, and now at the age of

twenty-six, his country was at war, and he was involved in it. Nine men out of ten might find their greatest thrill in murder, but he was the tenth for whom the sight of blood, nay, the very thought of it, turned his own to ice. He was by no means ready, at this juncture, to say that war was evil. Indeed, under the influence of the Darwinian theory of the survival of the fittest, as every one was, he believed that war was a necessity and nations which stopped fighting, stopped living, or, at least, stopped prospering artistically. Many have been the heroes who sat upon their haunches in their parlors, applauding, in prose and in rhyme, those who died to rid the earth of the unfit, while they became the fit, the divinely chosen to perpetuate the species.

And poor Darwin, who had become the Devil to the religious fanatics, now appeared in the guise of Mars, worshipped by the generals, those who were destined to die in bed. In vain did he say that war was the wrong means to achieve fitness upon Earth, that it was a reversal of the process of natural selection, that the fittest did not signify the best, that modern weapons did largely away with courage and ingenuity on the part of the individual, that the moral qualities were advanced much more through the effect of habit, the reasoning powers, instruction, and he even added, religion. In vain. Darwinism meant that man came from the monkey and that war was essential to progress and civilization. No one knows how much mud there is around until he has done a particularly important service to the community. There is nothing more difficult than to scrape the barnacles of lies which cling to every truth.

"*A Berlin! A Berlin!*" "To Berlin! To Berlin!" Rataplan! Rataplan! The drums began to beat. The trumpets began to blow. Epaulettes and swords began to glitter. It was so gay and so colorful. The world had become young again. Man was a child once more—a child that loves to tear, to break, to destroy —and then to weep.

Anatole might have become enthusiastic enough to write an ode to Mars, had he lived across the Channel or across the Ocean, but in the midst of battle, he felt thoroughly uncomfortable and sought for alibis. There were ways of buying one's freedom from the army, and *père* and *maman* France saw to it that it was done. The army doctor found their boy unsuitable for active duty. Instead, he was ushered into the National Guard, to watch the fortifications of Paris. That was safety with honor, for the enemy would be destroyed even before the Emperor's forces reached Berlin, and all would soon be over, and one could once again withdraw into the ivory tower full of wonderful books, add to their number oneself, and thus live forever among the immortals.

But the Emperor's men were decimated and it was essential to send to the front even the quasi-soldiers of the National Guard. Only in an *opéra-bouffe* could the counterpart of Anatole France, Soldier, be found. Anatole contrived some cock-and-bull story for turning away from the front, and gradually marched back toward the Capital. France was lost, but not Anatole France. Still, the very uniform weighed too heavily upon him and the gentle duties irked, and he was beginning to look sick in truth.

Maman France was up and about, and once again Anatole was examined by the medical examiner, who for a proper baksheesh, found him unfit because of *faiblesse de constitution*. Not since he had quit Stanislas did he feel as happy as now doffing his uniform.

Henceforth whatever might happen to the *patrie* was no business of his. The war was over, since it was over for him. The family moved out of Paris that it might not suffer deprivations. The Emperor was taken prisoner and Paris was besieged.

Did Anatole rush to the aid of his beloved? He was only annoyed by the noise of the firing. Much later, during another war, already old and world-famous, he would utter the words which were recorded: "I don't like the noise of the bombs, and I am no hero." What he said at this particular juncture, however, we do not know. His words were not yet so precious as to be rushed to print as soon as they gushed out of his mouth.

The siege of Paris was lifted by the Prussians after a cataract

of gold tumbled into their coffers, but now a new thing occurred
which might make as great history as the Revolution. The people—the workers—took control of the Capital and proclaimed
a new era. Would Anatole see the magnificence of this? A nation might be merely an anachronism, a glorified tribal institution; a city, even Paris, might be merely a conglomeration of
shops and offices and restaurants; but the people, the poor, the
miserable, the hungry, the ill-clad—the people, how shall we
dismiss them? Who would build the museums and the libraries;
who would print the poetry; who would clean streets, unstuff
sewers, bake bread, raise vegetables, sew dresses—in short, who
would make life not only beautiful, but even possible? And for
all these services, must they forever be the pariahs, the serfs,
the dwellers in stinking, dark alleys, the illiterates, the dupes of
lords and of dispensers of fear and preposterous promises of
justice and rewards in another world, reached via the grave?

Should not a poet join the people, fight with them, or if one
suffers from *faiblesse de constitution,* should he not, at least,
wield his pen in their mortal combat against the oppressors?
Anatole was already twenty-seven years old, and in Europe the
human male of thirteen or fourteen was considered a man.
Should he not understand what is going on? Should he not see
the historic significance? He pretended that he was unaware of
any grand hour in the annals of man. He spoke only of the folly
of bloodshed. He preached reason and moderation. He reinforced his shield of skepticism to protect him from his nagging
conscience.

He would not hear it for a long time—he needed such long
stretches of time—but the day would come when, spear in hand
he would fight for the people, and he would challenge to combat
all the forces of evil, of injustice, of ignorance. He feared no
one, however high he might be hoisted by fortune. He might appear to the world as another Don Quijote, and had he been
gaunter and taller, he would have looked like him. But, after all,
who was more sincere than the *hidalgo,* and his madness, is it
not a thing of glory still?

Not that Anatole France would ever feel at home with the masses. He was in his *tréfonds,* his foundation beneath foundation, a recluse, so that all the more credit to him, who could steel himself to face audiences and harangue them. Mademoiselle Leprevotte, his faithful servant who, a few years before his death, became his lawful wife (the last of the mamas to tie him to her apron strings) said: "Monsieur France hasn't quite as strong a horror for anything as for a popular audience. He is sick when he has to deliver an address at a popular university or in a working-class district. . . . Every effort on his part to go to the people is painful."

The Commune was overthrown. The workers, defeated, returned to their homes, disillusioned and disheartened. It was the last revolution in France. France had grown old. There were to follow two major wars out of which she managed to escape more or less whole, but no more revolutions. The workers of another country would take up where France left off and a mightier revolution than all those recorded stirred the whole Earth. Those living during the middle of the twentieth century were incapable of thoroughly evaluating it or foretelling its destiny—good or evil.

Husband and Librarian

Things were returning to normal. Politicians duelled for power, the bourgeoisie blossomed, the penurious workers sweated at their quotidian chores. And poets, too, returned to their lasts and their intrigues. How to obtain bed and board while gathering laurels and clearing a pathway to Olympus— that has been their herculean labor, always and everywhere. Any wonder, then, that most of them look starved, bewildered, and alas, freakish—and some die young? And often, instead of fighting the cynical world, they fight among themselves, for

when we say "schools" of poetry, we mean "battlefields." No
grave is so forsaken as a poet ignored, while a poet placed in a
high position of state improves his art as the gilding of a nightingale's tongue improves its singing.

The Parnassians splintered, and anyway, Anatole would
never, could never be a joiner. But he discovered another master, one whom he would admire and love and follow to the end
of his long days. This man was not a poet, but he wrote prose
with poetic delicacy, and had the mind of a scientist, not in the
narrow sense of the word, but in its original—a seeker of knowledge. This man was Ernest Renan, who took Jesus out of the
Pantheon and brought him alive among men. Many years later,
their mutual blood would course in a youngster—Renan's great-
grandson and France's grandson.

Although Anatole was only a vague Parnassian, he was still,
for the time being, a writer of verse, and poet he would be always, even when writing prose. His first volume of verse,
Poèmes Dorés—"Gilded Poems," appeared in 1873. Here, as
everywhere in his books, the word *volupté* would appear often.
The meaning of the word would change as France himself
changed, from mental pleasure to carnal to spiritual and frequently overlapping, his jewelled language glowing always.

Three years later, in 1876, his second volume of poetry appeared, *Les Noces Corinthiennes*—"Corinthian Wedding." In
the preface to the main poem, he wrote: "I bring a sincere respect to bear on matters sacred. So long as a man sucks milk of a
woman, so long will he be consecrated in the temple, and initiated, in some degree, in divine mystery. He will dream, and
what matter if the dream be false, so it may be beautiful? Is not
man's destiny to be steeped in perpetual illusion? Indeed, is not
such illusion the very condition of Life?"

How often the problem of illusion and truth will appear in
his novels and stories—the truth which he discovered in illusion,
the illusion which he found in truth! This time the basic tale of
the poem is derived from the Greek mythology, and France in-

terpreted it to prove the superiority of the ancient viewpoint to that of the Christian—joy against pain. Yet, not without deep sympathy for the latter, for he knew that a philosophy which dismisses the reality of pain dismisses all the virtues of society— tenderness, compassion, friendship, love, politeness, courage, laughter—indeed it dismisses society itself; for society is premised on the idea that united, people may attenuate one another's pains, the pain of birth, the pain of living, the pain of dying. Is joy an entity, or is it only a relief from pain—a mere negation? Man's tragedy lies in the fact that his pleasure is a magic bird soon vanished in flight, and his pain a weary draft-horse pulling a heavy load across an interminable bog.

The book was rather well received and sold poorly, and the question posed itself to Anatole France, as it had done so often —how convert ambrosia into bread and nectar into wine? He was over thirty, and still lived at his parents' home, bored with his father's ever increasing pomposity and his mother's ever increasing possessiveness. He would always pull at the strings that tied him to his various mamas, but he would never succeed in freeing himself. In reality, he never wished to, terrified that it might happen. Freedom from woman—why, that was tantamount to freedom from life—a euphemistic word for death. And when we free ourselves from others, we but become slaves of ourselves. We are captured and caged, but those who flutter their wings against the bars have the illusion of freedom.

It became quite evident to France that a poet was no longer the main jewel in the crown of literature, but more in the nature of an anachronism, and poetry, like virtue, had become its own reward. Skeptic and cynic, though he was, he longed for applause, noisy applause, and with it the clinking of gold. These were still the days when gold was money and money was counted in gold coins, beautiful pieces that had form and reality. And thus it was, that while praises came from George Sand, who said: "I thank you for the splendid book you sent me. It is as beautiful and fresh as antiquity, and made me weep," and from

Gustave Flaubert, who told him he was enchanted, and even though the verses were recited at various performances, public and private, Anatole France decided that he would never again be a poet, but a *prosateur.*

There was, however, something much deeper than mere desire for recompense that persuaded him to switch to prose. He was growing slowly, but surely, and he felt that poetry no longer fitted his personality. Poetry was a flower in a vase, even a magnificent flower in an exquisite vase, but he needed to press his roots into the fat of the earth and enrich it with the fertilizer of passion and laughter, and let it be beaten by rain and wind and grow both graceful and hardy, and bear fruit, heavy with sugar, even the sugar of corruption, which gourmets find particularly to their taste.

For some time, Anatole was in search of a sinecure, for the government of France, being civilized, wished to help its men of letters without, however, exciting the anger or the jealousy of the citizens who would have to foot the bill. The jobs offered the poor poets would have to *seem* essential as though they entailed labor, ingenuity, and talent. There were, naturally, always many more aspirants than jobs, for if all the ambitious scribblers were to be taken care of, France would have to become a vast bureaucracy without enough bureaux to go around. (Bureaucracy has always been an endemic plague of the Republic.)

Much manipulation was required, many letters had to be written, and years had to pass, but when he least expected it, Anatole France was appointed *commis-surveillant* of the Senate Library. The title might be translated inspector-clerk or assistant librarian, but what it really entailed as duty and labor was to fill out cards for all new books and arrange the catalogue accordingly. The slow and meticulous required two hours per week. And for this, he would receive 2,200 *francs* annually— gold *francs*—certainly the equivalent salary of any bank clerk at the time, who had to work ten hours daily. Moreover, Anatole was also given a nice little study in the building, supplied with everything—coal, wood, oil—where he could do his own work.

There was only one day a month in which Anatole France made his appearance—in his official capacity—the day when the emolument was distributed by the head librarian, who fumed and wrote letters of protest against the delinquent, and would continue to do so for many years until France had become world-famous and wealthy, and the salary had lost its value in the market, and he resigned.

Not that he would not come to the library and his studio at all. He would, but only whenever he desired to consult books for his own articles which he wrote now for several of the prominent newspapers of the country. He acted, one might say, as a guest who should be served with the greatest courtesy and attention by the host and his minions.

And now the time had come to change mamas and apron-strings. Anatole was looking, not for a mistress, but a wife. His ideal was one who had all the tenderness and love and fidelity his mother bore him, plus the understanding that a man must be free, must not have his pockets searched for perfumed letters, must not be nagged about the quantity of work he produced, or about punctuality. In short, the apron he accepted and the string, but the string should be long and elastic. And, of course, she must be young and pretty, and what is a bride without a *dot?*

Anatole discovered the miracle woman. She was young, she was pretty, and she had enough of a dowry to buy a home and furnish it, and she belonged—distantly, to be sure—to the no-bility. And so, *père* and *mère* France could have no objection.

Valérie was thirteen years younger than her husband, but mentally thirteen centuries separated them, and Anatole set out to telescope this vast difference. He would be a teacher, he who was the worst of pupils. And the ghosts of his teachers must have danced and clanked their chains in merriment to see that poetic justice would finally be administered.

Justice with a vengeance. Valérie listened to her husband's

recitations of the classics, to his marginal criticisms, to his explanations. She also listened, as he read to her, the articles he
was preparing for the newspapers and the magazines, witty,
wise, profound. She listened, and she was silent, always silent.
Her pretty face showed no sign of understanding, and her nerves
registered irritability, which would later on be translated into
the vilest of language.

For the time being, however, she was vastly bored both by the
subject matter and by the teacher. The teacher, who delved into
the mysteries of existence and brought to the surface the rarest
of trophies, could not even scratch below the surface of the skin
of this woman, or to understand her disdain for his mind and
her hate for him as person. To her, he would never be more than
a peasant and she his superior by birth. To her only birth
counted, for that had its origin in the will of God, while education, scholarship, authorship were but earthly accomplishments
of secondary value.

She had dreamt of a knight, handsome and dashing, who
would present her at courts. She was confronted by a man who
could never be handsome with his long nose and face, and who
had to add to it a beard to make it still longer, a beard that was
never combed properly; a man whose clothes hung about him
with the sartorial elegance of a scarecrow. Besides, he brought to
the house men as disagreeable and unprepossessing as himself,
and who, like himself, talked and talked about dead things of
times long dead, not of living things, of life, the life she longed
for. They were all mummies resurrected. And she had to keep
silent, always silent, and it made her look foolish, for silence has
merit only when it is a placid cover for tumultuous depths. It
could not have taken those men much time to realize that beneath her silence there was emptiness, and she was shrewd
enough to read in their bookish eyes what they read in hers, and
she hated them and their host.

There was, moreover, a practical matter, too—the small
amount of money Anatole earned. And if that were not enough,

he had the evil habit of *flâner,* but loafing with a purpose now, and the purpose was the buying of antiques—pieces of worm-eaten wood and crumbling stone, which began to encumber the house and would, before too long, turn it into a warehouse. And Valérie who despised everything that was old and decayed, loved everything that was new and *à la mode!*

And so, the clouds gathered and became darker and heavier, oppressive and ugly, until the lightning struck, and there was some sort of relief, for rubble is preferable to a house that shakes and is ever on the point of crushing you. But many things had to happen first.

Of Good and Evil

The wheel of Fate accelerated its tempo, and within the next half-dozen years, Anatole France would discover what she had in store for him. That his cup would be filled with both honey and wormwood, he knew, for he knew that there was always beauty, but that sorrow and pain were two of its ingredients. But he could not tell what the proportion of wormwood would be to that of honey, and *this,* after all, is the test whether you are Fate's favorite or her stepson.

Nor was it sufficient to be a great artist to achieve great fame and great rewards. France knew that genius and the rewards of genius were not necessarily parallel. The history of art attested glaringly to that. Nor was the recognition of genius to be taken for granted. The history of art was a long record of the crowning of mediocrity and the crucifixion of the unusual. Nor was it an easy task to distinguish between the great and the lesser. At odds as to what constitutes merit in art, critics promulgate the criterion of longevity, the most fortuitous of all the elements. Many a weed outlasts an exquisite flower. Some consider honesty the touchstone. But a work of art whose sole boast to recognition is honesty is like a body of which we see only the viscera. On the other hand, one which lacks honesty, is like a body emptied of its vital organs. There is, in truth, no absolute gauge, and as in all things else, timeliness and proper exploitation play the main part in the acceptance and honor of genius, particularly during a man's life. After his demise—ah, then, all praises are as fresh feathers for a stuffed bird.

Anatole France could not tell whether he was on time and he was certain he could never do the proper exploitation. He had neither the appearance nor the shrewdness nor the ability to strut or to crawl, as the occasions required.

Meanwhile his beloved *maman,* after much suffering, passed on. She was seventy-four. Almost as if the old woman's soul had sought an immediate reincarnation, Valérie, some months later, gave birth to a girl, whom they named Suzanne. The father was all raptures about his progeny. He forgot his skepticism, he forgot objectivity, he even forgot all the petty and more than petty annoyances his wife subjected him to, for she no longer was all silence, but had begun to hone her tongue on the whetstone of acrimony, and before long made it into a sharp and cunning weapon.

But Suzanne was pretty and smart, and as she grew old enough to understand, her father would tell her tales that had never before been heard, and which, later on, he would polish into exquisite jewels to stud and grace his books. Yet, this did not last long. Valérie was jealous of her daughter's affection for her papa, and the struggle that ensued between the parents for her possession wearied Anatole, and taking refuge as always behind the shield of skepticism, he relinquished his daughter to her mother. Gradually, he almost forgot her existence, until he was informed that she had become the mother of a boy, who was the great-grandson of Renan, Lucien Psichari. He adopted the boy shortly before his death, that he might inherit a portion of his wealth and future royalties.

The stories he had told Suzanne were much prettier than

those he told her son, for now he began to reminisce, rather than to create, and to boast of his boyish escapades. He told Lucien, for instance: "I was always playing tricks in school. I used to unscrew my schoolmaster's and my teacher's leaden inkwells and amusing catastrophes would happen as a result of this. I was also known for setting off firecrackers in class." And when Lucien seemed not at all amused, he added, in order at least, to save his morals: "But I was always caught, I was never able to escape." Nor did this expiation amuse the lad, and what he thought about it all is not recorded. However, it is not unlikely that he thought what the young always think of the old—regarding them with an indulgent wonderment as if confronted by a species of beings, part monkey, part parrot, imitating the gestures and speech of man, amusing, but without consequence. And then he laughed. And Anatole France kissed his forehead —his treacherous forehead—and said that he had a sense of humor and rewarded him with a gold coin.

Only once did he recall his daughter in later years, when she died in 1919. France was grief-stricken and took the midnight train to be present at the funeral. He wept bitterly in his white beard. "My daughter—my daughter—all I had—all that was left to me. I can still see her as a child, playing about the house with her dolls. . . ." A week later, he was in the highest spirits, recounting stories to all those who visited his place, and all wondered and whispered among themselves—had he been a hypocrite? Had he played the comedy of the afflicted father? Had he worn a mask for so long that he had forgotten his face? But are emotions ever so clear-cut that some may be called honest and others fictitious? Isn't there a certain amount of glycerine in every tear? And how shall a man of seventy-five endure a long siege of grief? The chill in his blood freezes joy as well as sorrow; fortunate for him if his mind can still laugh. "Old age is difficult," France said, "and my existence is disagreeable." Old age may be called the House of a Thousand Discomforts.

But this was all in the future, nearly four decades: *grande*

mortalis aevi spatium—"a great space in the life of man," replete with many things. Just now, however, we are in the year
1881, when Anatole France was only thirty-seven, and when he
published his first major prose piece, *The Crime of Sylvestre
Bonnard.*

Monsieur Bonnard, an old scholar, will henceforth be the
prototype of most of France's principal male characters in all
his novels. He will appear in the guise of doctor or monk or
professor. He will be immensely learned; he will be disillusioned; he will be cynical about man, and yet he will be kind and
compassionate toward him and his weaknesses; he will be, in
certain instances, sensuous, but his sensuality will be all-inclusive
—he will kiss not only the lips of woman, but the lips of the
Earth with all its fragrance and all its honey; he will, when
aroused to anger by injustices, barb his words with fine stilettos
and offer cups of hemlock to all those who sit in high places, their
feet upon the necks of the simple and the poor—the cups, naturally, being studded with precious stones. And he will talk, talk,
talk. But never before had one heard such language—great
knowledge carried lightly as balloons at a fair; wisdom simple
as ancient proverbs; small gossip, illumined with colors like the
illumined letters of ancient scrolls. A language so simple, that it
seemed one could scrawl it with no effort whatever. But let one
try it—and many tried, alas for them—and he will find it easier
to imitate the song of a nightingale, the purl of a stream, the
laughter of a child.

As for the particular crime of Sylvestre Bonnard—certainly
no Crime Book Club in America would consider it as a worthy
offering to its readers. No youngster would shudder, no crime-
laden soul would find it an adequate cathartic. In fact, in a generation in which horrors must be piled upon horrors to stir the
jaded taste of men and women, one is almost abashed to recount
what this old bookworm had done. Well, of course, he did
abduct a young girl. That would be something, and impatient
readers of best-sellers would urge: "Go on—go on—tell us all
—leave not the minutest detail out—go on—go on!"

Alas, it is precisely as one goes on that one is embarrassed. The old bookworm abducted the girl from cruel guardians, but not for his own delectation, nor for the purpose of describing maneuvers of the ancient play that brought sin to the tear-stained earth, but to deliver her into the loving hands of a fine young man for nuptial purposes. If this is crime, what is virtue?

Moreover, as dowry he gives the couple the treasure of his heart—his books. This, too, is hardly a crime, although to many, who spend the hours of their days and the days of their years watching the antics of mummers on a screen, it might appear as such, if they were forced to read them, or even to own them, in homes where a book, like the Son of Man, has no place to lie on.

The true crime committed was the purloining of one of the volumes he had promised as dowry, although naturally, the girl had known nothing about it. Yes, but he, the scholar knew, he the honest man knew, and that was shameful. He had said in his mind that *all* books should go to the couple, and he hid one! Which is a greater test of honor—to pay a debt when the creditor has a note and the lack of payment would mean punishment, or a debt without material evidence, in which only one's word—one's thought—was given? *Noblesse oblige!*

Anatole France was decorated with the Legion of Honor for the book and it was crowned by the French Academy. And he knew that he was on time. And he would be on time for the rest of his life. But not beyond that. The vulgar young writers who distributed their offensive manfesto, *Un Cadavre,* at his funeral, triumphed. *Their* time had come—their cacophany, their brutality, their perversion, their confusion, their ignorance, their muddiness, like wild-fire consumed all that was beautiful and wise and clear, and Anatole France would be silenced above earth as beneath it. For how long, who shall know? And any author writing in his vein, and even as well, would not only not be hailed, he would remain unpublished. "To everything there is a season, and a time for every purpose under the heaven. . . ."

Why was Anatole France on time ? Ten years had passed since the French had been defeated by the Prussians. People talked of *revanche,* but gradually that was relegated to the back of national consciousness. It would appear to the forefront, but much later. Meanwhile, there was a resurgence of the desire to live, to enjoy, to laugh. Yet, too much had happened, too many wounds had remained only partially healed, too many hopes had been shattered, and therefore, youth had vanished and man had matured. For maturity cannot be achieved save through pain and disillusion. The people yearned to live and enjoy and laugh, but in a mature manner, in which a bit of cynicism, a sigh, a tear, doubt, suspicion, universal frustration, illusion, sensuality, would be among the condiments, but the dish would be leisure, garrulousness, symmetry, logic, melody—all the characteristics of maturity, and the literature which reflected this would be *à la mode,* for style in dress and furniture and love and art is all of a piece with a certain moment in history.

And Anatole France was the *chef extraordinaire*—the cook without compare of that moment, and therefore his genius would be recognized and be lavishly rewarded.

But now what was needed was the proper exploitation, the trumpet to call the attention of the world. In all countries, but particularly in France, there is no trumpeter more listened to than woman. Valérie, Anatole's wife, did not possess the proper requirements. Moreover, she was not convinced of his talent and she constantly reminded him of her opinion. Perhaps, in her heart of hearts, the tiny cave where truth takes refuge, squatting in darkness, she knew that her husband was a genius, and for that very reason, she feared his too great success, which would only mean a still vaster discrepancy between them. Self-interest is the most impassioned of orators. It was much better that he continue as *commis-surveillant* in the Library of the Senate, and she did her utmost to press his long nose to the grindstone.

But Fate was definitely set to make Anatole France her favorite son, and not all the tears, the harangues, the mockery, the insults of a desperate and foolish wife, could alter her decision. And when the moment was ripe, she brought to the turret the trumpeter without peer.

The Lion Combs His Mane and Fortifies His Roar

When Anatole France made his appearance, under the sponsorship of Jules Lemaître, literary critic, in the salon of Madame Arman de Caillavet, his beard was scraggier than ever, his suit more crumpled, and as he tried to compliment the hostess, he tripped over his tongue. He who could write like an angel, stuttered like a bumpkin. It was not an adolescent in this predicament, but a man of forty, a writer lauded by his compeers and read, moderately, by the bourgeoisie.

Madame de Caillavet, who took delight in handsome men with witty tongues, asked Monsieur Jules Lemaître not to bring the boor to the salon again. But Lemaître would not so hurt his friend and colleague, and continued to bring him again and again, and Anatole protested, as eloquently as his tongue allowed, that he never felt as happy as in the presence of Madame Arman, née Léontine-Charlotte Lippmann.

Léontine was born in Paris in 1847 (three years Anatole's junior), daughter of a millionaire Jewish banker. Hers was a distinguished family, and enhanced by the marriage of her brother, Maurice, to the daughter of Alexandre Dumas, *fils*. Nevertheless, Léontine, who yearned for the most exclusive society, felt her Semitic origin a stumbling-block. She turned Christian, but the holy water added nothing to her piety and detracted nothing from her native brilliance.

At the age of nineteen, she married Arman de Caillavet, son of a shipbuilder, who once had been wealthy, and was still influential, for the wedding ceremony was performed in the Tuil-

leries Palace and Emperor Napoleon III and the Empress
Eugénie were present.

Whether from the first the marriage was meant as one of
convenience, in which the young ex-Jewess would gain a name
and be hoisted upward on the narrow, slippery ladder of grand
society, and the groom, lover of horses, gambler, and viticul-
turist, would obtain the money he needed and could no longer
squeeze out of the flattened purse of his *papa,* is not certain.
Certain it is, however, that it so became. But here were some
aspects of this *convenance* which proved more laudable than
usual. Arman de Caillavet soon discovered that not for nothing
was his wife the daughter of bankers, for she well knew the value
of money, and while she loved elegance and luxury, she was sober
and her little feet were firmly planted upon *terra firma.*

She allowed her husband a certain, adequate sum which, however, he could not exceed. Before long, he was constrained to
give up his gambling habit and turn to vine cultivation, which
was not only a wholesome form of labor, but to his aristocratic
amazement, even profitable. Soon, too, he found that he was not
suitable for the type of salon that his ambitious wife opened.
There a man had to have wit, fame, culture, and so he would steal
away, without fuss and without fury, but only after the required
presentations, for Léontine wished him always to be the titular
master of the house. And the marriage also produced a son, who
became one of the foremost dramatists of his day. Thus, all in
all, considering the mores of the period and of the class, it was a
successful enterprise.

When Anatole France made her acquaintance, Léontine was
no longer in her first youth, but she was still charming, her face
dominated by large, sharp eyes—a petite vivacious person. She
had traveled widely, knew several languages, read philosophy,
had studied painting and music, possessed wit and rectitude and
courage and the impeccable manners of a hostess whose salon
was quickly becoming the most famous and *recherché* in the
great Capital, where the salon had been the institution of institutions, and competition was razor keen and merciless. Léon-

tine, despite the holy baptismal water, was still considered a Jewess by her rivals, and to succeed, she had to do what Jews are constrained to do everywhere—get beyond the reach of all antagonists, surpass them all, be supremely and utterly successful. And she was.

Nevertheless, Léontine's sharp eyes needed a long time to pierce through the unprepossessing armor of Anatole France, and reach the heart, the brain, the soul of the man. At last she did, and thereafter she became the *maman parfaite,* whom he so desperately sought, since Valérie had already become the queen of tormentors of husbands and the string of her apron was wound around his neck. The cord Léontine was to use was of pure gold, exquisitely fashioned, sufficiently measured to afford neither too much freedom nor too much slavery, and she pulled it with marvelous adroitness.

Now began a comradeship of more than a quarter of a century to be destroyed only one year before Léontine's death by Anatole's stupid and cruel desertion, which he regretted most keenly for the rest of his own days.

Once Léontine had reached the man beneath the crumpled uniform of his appearance, she quickly discovered both his weak and strong points, and she set out straightway to obviate the weak points and cultivate to the maximum the strong ones. First of all the façade—his beard was combed; his clothing must fit properly and be of the best material; his habit of waving his hands—beautiful though they were—like a conductor's baton, up and down and sideways, as he talked, must cease; the nasality of his voice must be moderated; his nervousness in the presence of people must be curbed and finally vanquished. And more important than all, he must be taught to work daily, regularly, and never be allowed the subterfuges of dilatoriness, which made it possible for him to write nothing between *The Crime of Sylvestre Bonnard* and *My Friend's Book*—an interval of four years. However delightful this small book was, a jewelled performance, it surely did not need years of gestation. True enough that he had written many articles for *Le Temps,* the great newspaper, and for many other papers as well, but no book—and at his age, the flower of manhood! That must never happen again!

Léontine fixed up a work-room within her magnificent library on the upper floor of her mansion, and here the changing Anatole France had to come punctually every afternoon and "make literature." No more *école buissonière*—school among the bushes—the excellent French expression for truancy. She would stay with him, as he sat at his desk, his quill in his hand (he was not even modern enough for a pen, and the forced use of a typewriter would have meant the end of his illustrious career), and never allow him to fall asleep, his nose in his sheet of paper, a habit he had long ago formed to get rid of unpleasant duties, for writing was a painful process for him.

"Allons! Allons! Mon cher, allons!" she would urge, and he would again begin to move his hand, sometimes to write words, at other times to doodle—breasts and buttocks—his specialty. And she would take the sheets with endless corrections, and rewrite them; and he would again rewrite them; and she, with Job-like patience, rewrite them clean again, until perfection was reached. When he needed reference books, they would appear upon his desk instantly, as if brought by those marvelous little beings which he created and with whom he conversed as no human ever conversed with fairy, sprite, elf, gnome, or peri— those wonderful creatures infinitely more agile and more capable than all the machines invented to relieve man of labor—and of thought.

And if his articles to the papers could not be written on time, she would write them herself and sign them with his name, and they were so good that none suspected their authorship. Moreover, they did not pay him so much for his articles as for his name. In the annals of foolish things told by great men, there is none more foolish than that expressed by Shakespeare: "What's in a name?" Why, everything! No double-humped camel carries such a preposterous load as man under the weight of name and label.

At the banquet-table, in the drawing-room, the guests were

instructed to keep utter silence when Monsieur France, henceforth known as *Maître*—Master—spoke. He was upon a pedestal and he had to learn not to topple over. He learned. He spoke now, leisurely, stroked his beard philosophically, recounted stories and fables from the classics, since his memory was prodigious, and all in all, he began to act as *Maître*.

But always he had his tongue in readiness to press against his cheek, and always there was the longing to run away from it all and loaf incognito on the banks of the Seine, turning the leaves of some masterpiece, which lay forgotten and forlorn in the stand of an old vendor, forgotten and forlorn himself, and where in time, his books, too, would lie forgotten and forlorn. In time, genius becomes fertilizer to pedantic mediocrity. The future is the creation of our despair.

"I married," Anatole said. "After the Sacrament, I learned what Hell is." He spoke for effect and exaggerated, but Valérie, his wife, had grown intolerable, and could not be expected to graciously accept her husband's relations with Léontine. Even when love is gone, there is always vanity, and vanity can be more implacable even than self-love, and the primal cause of self-destruction. But we do not know that we are vain; we only know that we are hurt.

The time had come to sever the foul umbilical cord that united the two in unholy matrimony. The last scenes of this tragicomedy were ugly, preposterous, and futile. But the knife finally cut, and on August 3, 1893, divorce was granted to Valérie for "extreme cruelty"—on whose part, it would be hard to tell.

Since practically all find husbands or lovers, or both, it may be said that there are no ugly women or undesirable ones, and that there is only an infinite variety of beauty and allurements beyond count. And so it happened that Valérie, stout, middle-aged, termagant, married again on July 12, 1900—happily this time—Professor René Dussaud of the Collège de France and curator of antiquities of the Museum of Louvre. But Valérie would not have her new home encumbered by broken statues and shapeless junk. If she wanted to see them, and be properly instructed about their merit, she could visit her distinguished new husband at the Louvre. Perhaps now that she was aging herself, she no longer cared for the young and fashionable, and found surcease in the midst of ruins. What are the old but archeologists in search of their dead world and caretakers of cemeteries?

Three years before the severance of his marital life, Anatole France severed earthly relations with *père* France, who died on May 11, 1890, at the age of eighty-five. We do not fully forgive the vices and shortcomings of our parents until we are old ourselves, for only then do we realize how much like them we really are, and how similar our vices and shortcomings.

France *fils* was not yet old enough, and so he came to the funeral leisurely, mingled with the crowd like a stranger, and left casually. But this man, whose seed he was, was remarkable. He educated himself to the point of becoming an *érudit;* he studied Hebrew and Coptic at eighty; he even began to write poetry, which his son, as if *en revanche,* would not recommend for publication. And quite like his son, his nose was powdered with the dust of the tomes. But he had been a better husband, a better father, a more reliable citizen than his famous progeny. And as Anatole looked through the old man's papers, he found the sum of twenty thousand *francs,* which in 1890 was a little fortune, bequeathed to him. At any rate, when the time came for the son to die, he wished to be buried between his parents, and did not mind to have his own precious dust mingle with theirs. He had become old enough.

The Well Gushes and the Tower Tumbles

When *Thais* appeared in 1890, Anatole France had, in truth, become the Master, and would, before another six years passed, be so accepted by the French Academy, and swiftly thereafter by all the cultured people of the world, of whatever language. No writer anywhere equalled him in fame or received plaudits as resounding as his, or was paid as extravagantly as he. Now he was the true son of Voltaire and he wore his imperial robes with grace and dignity.

Thais, indeed, is one of the most beautiful books penned by human hand. It is sad, it is ironic, replete with disillusion, and Death is the conquering hero. But it is also permeated with gentleness, with love, with pity, with a wisdom as delicate as the dawn and resplendent as the blossomed day. And Jules Massenet, who composed the opera based upon the novel, only added music to music.

There were detractors, to be sure. Some said—it is a book, but is it a novel? This they would say about every one of his books which he called *roman*—novel. They would all have the hallmark of the incomparable goldsmith, but would not resemble the accepted and prevailing criteria of that type of literature. From that point of view his critics were right, or, at least, partially right. But in the House of Literature there are many mansions, provided only that those who desire to dwell within them can fashion the golden key of genius with which to open the gates.

Others would hurl epithets which, in time, would become more and more charged with bile, but the most prevalent one would be "skeptic." "Skeptic! Skeptic!" he finally hurled back. "Indeed they call me skeptic. And to them it is the greatest insult. But to me it is the finest of praise. Skeptic! All the masters of French thought have been skeptics. . . . Skepticism! The word issued as synonymous with negation and futility. But our great skeptics repudiate only negation. They attack all those who trammel intelligence and will. They fight against ignorance which debases, against error which oppresses, against intolerance which tyrannizes, against cruelty which tortures, against hate which kills. . . . The most skeptical of thinkers are filled with a profound compassion for their fellows. Only they are the idealists. Their habitual irony is only the expression of their discouragement. They laugh—so they may not weep. . . . But then, if a man think, he is thereby considered a strange creature, disquieting, suspected by all. . . ."

Now masterpiece followed masterpiece in as quick a succession as the meticulous and scrupulous pen of the Master could scrawl on innumerable bits of paper which he found at hand—bills, envelopes, letters he never read—and never answered. He constructed as birds construct their marvelous nests with disparate, but appropriate bits, soft to the touch and sensitive to the ear, and all held together with the glue of genius.

Now, too, he began to wear his famous headgear, a skull-cap of bright red. It became part of his body or of his mind. He was not bald or predisposed to head colds—why, then, the skull-cap? "Unconsciously he makes his cap reflect his thoughts," said Monsieur Gsell. "When he is joyful his cap has a provocative air. . . . When listening he pushes it back on his neck, as though to allow the ideas greater ease of penetration to his brain; whilst reflecting, he pulls it back again, almost onto his nose, as though to concentrate his thoughts under his visor. . . ."

It seemed now that he could go on thus, peacefully, to the end of his days, creating, talking, receiving honors and rewards without count. Now he could sit in his ivory tower studded with gems and gaze out upon the world through his magical telescope, and laugh and weep at the antics of man and the ways of Fate. Now, too, he could indulge in his first—and last—love, his love which neither deceived him nor annoyed him, nor asked too many embarrassing questions, requiring ever shrewder and shrewder lies (such as, for instance, Léontine would ask upon occasions, regarding some pretty women with whom he had spent an evening or even an hour or so, for he preferred quantity to quality), his love perennial—bibelots, antiques, illuminated tomes, and although he was a freethinker, rare madonnas, who looked like courtesans and handsome Christs who looked like boulevardiers. The Church discarded him and would place his books on "The Index," but he had a weak spot somewhere in his strange heart for those bits of wood and ivory which gave comfort and relief to the simple and afflicted—and by reflection to himself, perhaps, for who is without fear and without hope? As for the Church herself, he said he had the affection he might have for an old aunt, cantankerous, dressed in old-fashioned ridiculous dresses, garrulous, a wart upon her nose, forever scolding and threatening—yet lovable withal, who brought him spice bread and hazel-nuts, and winked at his peccadillos. Why could not the Church reciprocate? He was a nephew to be proud of. How silly to ban his work and thus advertise it! Does she not know yet that those who take "The Index" seriously are apt to be the illiterates, who buy no books?

But, no, Fate had no such easy days in store for her favorite son, Anatole France, nor such fattening glory. She had granted him a jewelled crown, but what are jewels but pebbles and coal? Now she would line it with thorns, for thorns are the symbol of the ultimate royalty, and the blood which they press out is the only blue blood.

A French captain was accused of treason to his country, having sold vital secret documents to the Teuton enemy beyond the Rhine, for which he was degraded and condemned to spend the rest of his miserable days upon an island most appropriately named the Devil's Island.

Treason is not something without precedent; it had been committed in France as well as in every other country. But treason must have a motive—money, ambition, vengeance, love of the enemy. Alfred Dreyfus was wealthy; he was only a young captain, an excellent mathematician, totally devoid of political ambition, and only hopeful that he would gradually, in the regular manner, achieve higher ranks. Vengeance—against whom? Against France, the one nation that allowed a Jew to be a member of the General Staff? Love of Germany, the land of the ghetto? No—there was no motive—and Dreyfus swore by the God of his ancestors that he was absolutely innocent.

But, indeed, there was a reason—a motive—but not for treason, but for injustice. Dreyfus was a Jew, and a Jew was badly needed now as scapegoat in France. He had served so well for more than a millennium—served them all and everywhere—all, the army, the monarchs, the politicians, and in particular, the Church. And now all of them—Church and army and politicians, including the pretender to the throne—all, all were united to destroy the Republic, to destroy liberty, to destroy the unions, socialism, science, which threatened bigotry and the cult of ancient magic that kept men in ignorance.

Now the masses of France were given the black wine of hate to drink. Now they were groomed for murder—murder of truth and progress and justice. But this was not yet Armageddon. This was not yet the day when six million would be thrown into burning ovens and men all over the world would shrug their shoulders and go about their business, unconcerned. This was not yet the day when statesmen and scientists would speak of the instantaneous death of sixty million and six hundred million and the earth becoming a shambles, with mathematical detachment. This was not yet the day, when doctors would describe the monsters, the new sons of men, to be born to mothers, and the mothers did not march in vast phalanxes to demand the destruction of the fiendish weapons.

There were still men now who shuddered at the thought that even one single individual suffered for a crime he had not committed. There were still writers and artists who understood that one man was all humanity; that one injustice, deliberately inflicted, was a mortal thrust against the heart of justice. And these men were willing to take the risk of life and limb and reputation to do battle that one insignificant captain might prove his innocence.

The trumpets of Joshua may not have crashed the walls of Jericho, but the trumpets of justice that were blowing against the ivory tower of the Master began to shake it, and before long its famous inhabitant, cap on head and slippers on feet, found himself upon a heap of rubbish. But he did not try to hide behind it. Quite the contrary, he rushed into the marketplace, where the vile tongues shouted and the iron fists threatened. He was not intimidated. He did not flee in terror, as so many had expected him to do. This was not 1870. He would not offer the alibi of *faiblesse de constitution*. He would fight—unto the death—with quill and tongue, the mightiest weapons in the arsenal of man.

He wrote a series of novels entitled *Histoire Contemporaine,* in which he not only exposed the leprous blotches of civilization, but cut into them, cauterized them, and was even ready to destroy the evil patient, if he did not mend his ways. He wrote articles and pamphlets. He would do no less than his great friend, Jean Juarès (who some years later would be assassinated for thundering against war), than his colleague, Emil Zola, than that wonderful young writer who was destined to die so soon, Bernard Lazare, than the modest, upright, incorruptible Colonel Picquart.

The powers of good won. Dreyfus was freed. The clergy retired. The army began to reorganize. The Pretender resumed his gambling and the chase of fox and woman. And people spoke once more of progress and eternal peace.

Anatole France never rebuilt his ivory tower. He would hide now and then behind one of the pillars which still stood to write the delightful memories of his childhood, but he would return into the sun and the rain and the gathering storm. Henceforth, he would be with the poor and the dispossessed, even though they might not understand fully the rhythms of his thoughts or the periods of his chiselled language. They loved him and that was sufficient reward. He had weighed capitalism and found it wanting. He saw that "the law, in its majestic equality, forbids the rich as well as the poor to sleep under bridges, to beg in the streets, and to steal bread." And he was fully aware of the cynical fact that "the rich give a little that they may keep much."

He became a socialist, then a communist, then again a socialist. He was not an economist; he was not a dialectitian; he did not know the circuitous reasonings of the political parties.

On the other hand, he was not a typical dilettante, as his enemies sneered. He was profoundly honest and profoundly sincere. He feared compromise of ideals and warned against the pitfalls of opportunism. It sufficed to take one short step at a tangent to find one's self before long going in an entirely different direction.

To this compromising and opportunistic maneuverings, he attributed the outbreak of the First World War, which the workers of Europe could have averted, had they remained faithful to their international ideals rather than returning to their parochial allegiance. They were betrayed by their leaders, who themselves were betrayed by the inevitable results.

And the peace which followed, Anatole France warned, was not a peace at all, but would lead inevitably to another war, because once again those in power were not interested in justice and fidelity to ideals, but in expediency and temporary advantage—in the foolish belief that what is temporary leads to permanence, if cleverly manipulated.

Anatole France possessed wisdom; the others shrewdness. He possessed love and compassion for the poor and the underprivileged; the others possessed the professional subtleties of their factions. He wanted justice; they wanted power.

Fortunately for him, he did not live long enough to witness the truth of his bitter prophecy. "Let there be peace! Let there be peace!" he wrote and spoke ceaselessly during the last remaining years of his life. He might have been the Hebrew Prophet, whom now in his old age he resembled, crying out: *Shalom, shalom, v'ein shalom!* "Peace! Peace! But there is no peace!"

Meanwhile he continued to spin his marvelous tales, while the Fates continued to spin the threads of his days. Good and evil days were inextricably entwined. Our days are caught in the net of time as inexorably as the waves are caught in the net of tides. We are constantly at war with time. In joy, we battle to stretch it; in pain, we fight to shrink it; and how we struggle to enchain it at the approach of old age and death! Yet, who has ever scratched one second of time's tablet or altered the rhythm of one single step?

Hopeful of one more adventure before the curtain fell, Anatole France was misled into accepting a lecture tour to South America—and whatever romance that might bring. Therefore, he left Léontine home—Léontine, whose string had led him so safely for so long—not as a puppet, but as a man whose eyes gazed in all directions except at his feet, and who might easily stub his toe against the rocks, or be caught in the traps which the envious and the hypocrites placed in his path.

The trip was a scandal and a catastrophe, and the Master was made to appear as the lowest of scoundrels and the vilest of roués by his jealous and faithless secretary, Jean-Jacques Brousson. Léontine tried to commit suicide, was saved, but died soon after of chagrin and shame, and the Master grieved bitterly over the loss of his faithful companion, and he had good reason to do so, for now he was old and alone.

His home at Villa Saïd was becoming more and more a museum wrecked by a bomb, and though the litter might be precious, living was impossible there. He moved to his new home, La Bechellerie, where, gradually, order was established, and there was heat in the winter and ventilation in the summer, and a garden in which one could walk or sit and be surrounded by visitors from all over the earth, who would listen entranced to the Master's tales or opinions.

Marie-Héloise Laprevotte, more commonly known as Emma, had been a pretty country-girl whom Léontine engaged as her maid years before. At Léontine's death she became France's housekeeper. He was fortunate again, for Emma was a kindly soul and faithful to him, with the fidelity of a worshiper for his divinity. She could read, barely write, but had the good sense, the wisdom and understanding of the people whose roots are long nurtured in the earth.

Emma was destined to be the last of Anatole's *mamas,* but not until she had become middle-aged herself and lost a breast due to a cancer operation, and France was seventy-six years old. He knew that his life was now only a matter of months or at best a few years, and what would happen to this poor woman when he was gone? She would be brushed aside as so much dust; no matter what he wrote in his will and testament, it would be contested and she would be penniless, miserable, and lonesome. Yet, she had served him so well for so long, and her love was of the same rich texture as that of *maman* France and of Léontine, and nothing mattered in the final count save love. All good, all knowledge, all wisdom, all truth were but paths leading to love. What, indeed, were all his books, if not paens to love, even when he bantered about it, even when he pointed to its ludicrous or cruel phases? All commentaries were mere mental acrobatics, and served the artist with his threads to weave his stories, but explained nothing, could explain nothing, for love was life and life had no definition.

On October 11, 1920, Marie-Héolise Laprevotte became Madame Anatole France. While she tried to be worthy of her new station in life, to lend dignity by imitating the ways of the spouses of other luminaries, and often appeared ridiculous, she never for one moment altered her worshipful ways toward her master, her god. And the Master knew that he had done well.

The Summing-Up

In the year 1922, Anatole France received the Nobel Prize, not for one particular book, but for his entire literary creation. Rarely, before or after, did a writer merit the honor more, both for quality and for quantity.

There were besides the early volumes of poetry, four volumes of literary criticism and the four novels of the *Histoire Contemporaine,* for France was profoundly interested in the world about him, though steeped in the classical spirit:

L'Orme du Mail (The Elm Tree on the Mall)
Le Mannequin d'Osier (The Wicker-Work Woman)
L'Anneau d'Améthyste (The Amethyst Ring)
Monsieur Bergeret à Paris (Monsieur Bergeret in Paris)

Monsieur Bergeret, a timeless creation, is the *alter ego* of Anatole France, disillusioned, yet smiling, and always the possessor of a tongue, unequalled in modern letters.

There were the novels with revolutionary tendencies:

Sur la Pierre Blanche (On the White Stone)
L'Ile des Pingouins (Penguin Island)
La Révolte des Anges (The Revolt of the Angels)
Les Dieux Ont Soif (The Gods Are Athirst)

L'Ile des Pingouins is a sweeping criticism and condemnation of French society. All are included—friends and foes—for all are guilty. Lovers, however, are excluded, for what is more asocial than love? In lovers' embraces the universe is crushed.

This generic condemnation is even more evident in *La Révolte des Anges,* and in *Sur la Pierre Blanche,* the author predicts a dreadful cataclysm which destroys man and all his work —the evil and the good. His prophecy seems nearer its fulfillment now than it was when he announced it in 1903.

In *Les Dieux Ont Soif,* reverting to his father's contempt for the Revolution, France points out its failures and its follies.

There were volumes of stories and novels, pungent and graceful, wherein he wove his magic carpets of the philosophy of disillusion—the root of wisdom, of wit, of compassion:

La Rôtisserie de la Reine Pédauque (At the Sign of Reine Pédauque)
Le Lys Rouge (The Red Lily)
L'Etui de Nacre (Mother of Pearl)
Balthazar
Le Jardin d'Epicure (The Garden of Epicurus)
Le Livre de Mon Ami (My Friend's Book)

Les Opinions de Jérôme Coignard
Le Petit Pierre (Little Pierre)

And there was *Crainquibille*—Crainquibille, the simple *marchand de quatre saisons*—the little peddler, pulling his cart and calling out his wares, who comes in contact with the majesty of the law—the law which prosecutes the rich and the poor alike, for stealing bread and sleeping under the bridges of the Seine. For Anatole France's irony and cynicism are never directed against the poor and the dispossessed.

There were also:

La Vie de Jeanne d'Arc (The Life of Joan of Arc)
Les Sept Femmes de la Barbe-Bleu (The Seven Wives of Bluebeard)
L'Histoire Comique (A Mummer's Tale)

And his last work

La Vie en Fleur (The Bloom of Life)

Always and everywhere—whether a particular book achieved perfection or fell short of it—there was beauty of phrase, lucidity of thought, charm.

While Anatole France was crowned in Stockholm, he was hanged in Rome. *All* his books—*opera omnia*—were placed on the *Index Librorum Prohibitorum*. Thus the Ancient World of Intolerance ordered its vast multitudes of followers not to read the works of the Parisian under the penalty of losing paradise, where only those go who hate joy and laughter and thought.

"There is no life after death," the Master expostulated his ideas to his friends and listeners. "There cannot be. Death ends everything. It is all over then. All we can do is to resign ourselves to it. . . . We don't know how to resign ourselves to what really awaits us: repose, nothingness. And yet, it is quite simple and fundamentally desirable. . . ."

And when his hour came, he who had, despite his castigation, so loved Life, bade her adieu, simply and without tears. And the Earth embraced him, as she embraces all—the good and the bad, the wise and the foolish, the famed and the unknown—lovingly as a Mother.